A JEAN MONNET
CHRONOLOGY

Clifford P. Hackett

A JEAN MONNET
CHRONOLOGY

Origins of the European Union in the Life of a Founder, 1888 to 1950

Jean Monnet Council

Washington D.C.

The American Council for Jean Monnet Studies, also known as The Jean Monnet Council, is a non-profit educational organization dedicated to understanding and applying the lessons of Monnet's life to contemporary issues. For more information, write:

The Jean Monnet Council,
505 Constitution Ave NE
Washington DC 20002 USA
e-mail: jeanmonnetcouncil@yahoo.com

Library of Congress Cataloging-in-Publication Data

Hackett, Clifford P.

A Jean Monnet Chronology: Origins of the European Union in the Life

Of a Founder, 1888-1950/ Clifford P. Hackett

p. cm.

Includes bibliographical references and index.

ISBN 978-0-9642541-2-1 (hardcover: alk. paper)

ISBN 978-0-9642541-3-8 (paperback: alk. paper)

1. Monnet, Jean, 1888-1979. 2. Statesmen—Europe—Biography. 3. European

Union—History. I. Title

D413.M56H33 2007

940.5092—dc22

(B)

2007035576

Table of Contents

Preface

The historian's dilemma---to tell the story of events through great men mastering their ages or of men made great through the events in their lives - is nowhere clearer than in the interplay of Jean Monnet and his times.

Did a high school dropout from a modest bourgeois family in rural France really conceive and construct the first stage of the European Union? Or did the turmoil of a third war in 70 years between France and Germany produce just the right moment where that self-educated man---now over sixty years of age---was thrown up by these decisive events to a brief prominence?

This book will not answer these interesting questions. It attempts rather to start at the tip of the long line of people and events ---the taproot of his life---that constitute Monnet's first 62 years and trace his moves, his network of friends and the slow growth of his influence. The reader, whether historian, student or simply a lover of human history, must weigh the evidence and face the dilemma once again.

The simplest outline of a life often falters at the very start when parents, siblings and the immediate environs exert enormous influence on personality and character. When a child leaves school at age 16, as Monnet did, who made that young man? His parents might say they did, his brother and two sisters, all younger than Jean, might take some credit. And his teachers might point out their work. We have no eye witness accounts of these people in his earliest years.

His own memoirs give scant details of these early years and are perhaps dimmed by the years between the events in Cognac long before the First World War and their description when Monnet, in his eighties, worked with a collaborator on his life story.

We must, therefore, quickly pass over his early years and instead slowly fit together the written record as found in his long ascent through the cognac trade; through international ties, both in private and public affairs; during two world wars; in a checkered business career, and finally in the five years after the Second World War when his life focused on France and its new role in Europe.

In this chronology, laid out piece by available piece, with important gaps, we have a companion: Jean Monnet himself, in several senses. Almost every item listed is about Monnet or at least reflects or affects him.

Although he would have been impatient, I believe, with excessive attention to the personal ephemera of his life, some are included. In his own memoirs, he carefully and tersely covered his family, his wife and his children. He was deeply committed to them but thought these were private matters, not aspects of what he saw as his public enterprise in human cooperation.

Monnet was no saint so this chronology does not, I hope, represent hagiography. He could irritate people (and be irritated by them) but these largely unrecorded episodes now appear small in relation to both his goals and his deeds. He was no raconteur and seldom showed a sense of humor. He appeared to some co-workers (and to some staff under him) so single-minded in whatever he undertook that he lacked human perspective and empathy. According to Francois Fontaine, his collaborator on the Memoirs, he sometimes even quieted his beloved wife Silvia when she seemed to him sometimes to persist too long in an explanation.

The chronology tries, in sum, to anticipate what appears to me, after following Monnet's life for thirty years, he would have wanted known or at least accepted as relevant in understanding his work.

Not every item found has been included; repetitive, insignificant or questionable matter has been excluded. There are certainly important gaps in the chronology; the author would be grateful to know of facts to be added as well as of any errors.

JEAN MONNET: THE FORMATIVE YEARS
An Introductory Essay

(Years in parentheses indicate where the incident is found in the Chronology)

When Jean Monnet was born (1888), France seemed on a tranquil and secure path. The war with Germany nearly two decades earlier still rankled the country, especially Alsace and Lorraine, its occupied southeastern provinces. But the important news these days was the rapid industrialization of the whole country. This dynamic process dominated all western European countries, but principally Britain, France and Germany. Real incomes rose, public and private health improved, housing and education quality slowly ascended.

In southwestern France and especially in the Charente where Monnet was born, these changes came slowly. Tradition was the great teacher in the wine and cognac country which surrounded Jean's birthplace in the small city of Cognac. Part of that tradition was the overseas perspective of the region: cognac was (and is still) largely a drink of the world outside of France. So also with the best wines from nearby Bordeaux. A consequence was an interest in what happened in London and in North America and relatively less concern for the world of Paris.

Because little detail is known of Monnet's earliest years, the emphasis lies on his life and work during two world wars and the years between them. Those years ---from his mid-twenties to his mid-fifties--- seem decisive for the man, for France and for Europe.

Monnet was 50 years old when World War II started (1939) and he was over 60 when he conceived and then helped achieve the idea of a European coal and steel community (1950), the first stage of a united Europe. These actions brought him acclaim but his life before this public renown was quiet, methodical, even prosaic although broken by dramatic episodes like his early travels abroad (1904, 1906), his wartime roles (1914, 1938), his uneven business career and his runaway marriage (1934).

These middle years ---from the start of World War I until 1945---were truly his formative period, coming after a quarter century of preparation within a close family and amidst the family's cognac business. Central were these years of Monnet's life as they prepared him for a ten year trajectory which saw his influence and prominence rise in the 1950s and gently decline thereafter, settling into a role he played, not always happily, as an eminence grise during the final quarter century until his death (1979).

These thirty plus years produced Jean Monnet, the careful, confident, disciplined and productive man who helped redirect the fortunes of Europe in the twentieth century. They deserve examination.

Both his Memoirs(1) and his biographers concentrate on the post World

War II period when the creation of a united Europe took shape. Monnet's own account devotes only 79 pages out of 524 to his life before that war began. Francois Duchene's biographic homage (2) spends only 63 of 400 pages on his life before 1939. Eric Roussel's longer biography (3) commits only 200 out of nearly 1000 pages to the pre-WWII period.

The reasons for this meager attention to the years before 1939 are simple but involve some details of Monnet's life and lifestyle. The documented record of Jean Monnet's first twenty five years is scant because of a truncated education which ended without the university training and the network of friends that usually brings. He wrote few letters. And the years from WWI until the end of WWII, while better documented, were later seen by both Monnet and his biographers, as incidental steps to his real importance in uniting Europe. (Monnet's own papers from this interwar period were largely destroyed during WWII).

His memoirs give a general account in a few words written by his collaborator in the memoirs, and longtime friend, Francois Fontaine. The memoir was written over seventy years after the events of Monnet's childhood and youth when neither memory nor documents could be reliably consulted. The details of the Monnet-Fontaine relationship are not fully recorded but Fontaine gives some hints of the problem in his essay "Forward with Jean Monnet." He wrote:

> I helped, to the utmost of my powers, its author [Monnet] to write the story of his achievement and to draw its lesson from it. It would have been wise to stop there. Jean Monnet said all he wanted to say.
>
> But reticence stopped him short of fully revealing himself and for that reasons his Memoirs, written in the first person, are too discreet about the richness of his nature and the deep sources of his creative genius. (4)

In the same essay, the collaborator, himself a professional writer, describes Monnet's reluctance to talk of the personal details of his life. Fontaine asked Monnet's friends and colleagues to supply other details. But it is unlikely that the full story of his years before age fifty can ever be satisfactorily known or reconstructed. (Monnet, for example, largely limited his correspondence to business matters. He seldom confided personal details by letters.)

In these introductory lines, we try to put the reader in the footsteps of Jean Monnet in the years from his birth until his dramatic entrance on the public stag five years after the end of the Second World War (1950). We start with the first sketchy accounts of Monnet's home atmosphere and then his introduction to life outside of Cognac, as he traveled first to London, then to Canada to carry out his assigned family responsibilities.

I THE EARLY YEARS

The "richness of his nature and the deep sources of his creative genius" which Fontaine cites are tied deeply to the Monnet family and to his roots in southwestern France where Jean starts life. There he grew up under the close watch and the constant influence of his parents in a way possible only when all are intimate participants in a family business.

The family's cognac cooperative dominates Jean's early life as it did his father's career. Founded in the early 19th century, the cooperatives' members asked Jean Gabriel Monnet to take over its management when Jean, his first born, was nine years old. (1897) The parents and the three children move from the new house Jean Gabriel had just built for his family into the Vinegrowers Society's mansion, a social as well as a physical transformation. The Monnet children play in the large warehouses of the cooperative and listen at dinner as visitors tell of far off places where they live and work.

Jean goes to the local schools in Cognac but is an indifferent student. His father had no great faith in books and did not press his elder son to go off to a boarding school for his baccalaureat to qualify for the university. (In his long life, Monnet had little use for books which are never mentioned in his memoirs or his letters as inspirations or sources of ideas. "Tell me what it says," was his typical response to a suggestion by a friend or aide to read a certain book.)

Soon after Jean was born, a brother follows. (1890). His mother is only 19 when Jean is born and barely 21 when Gaston arrives. In 1894 Henriette came along and in 1901, Marie Louise. Each takes a different life course.

After Jean is sent to London (1904) to master English and the ways of his family firm's best customers, Gaston goes to Germany to learn another language and another approach to the cognac trade under the direction of the ambitious father. The daughters stay at home. Together they form a close, disciplined and traditional Charente family: the boys go into the cognac trade with the father; the girls stay with the mother to help in the solid homestead which often hosts the firm's customers for lunch, dinner and even overnight visits. But eventually each Monnet child drifts from the family circle.

Jean serves an informal apprenticeship in the Monnet cellars and offices but he learns mostly from discussions at the family table. Then, at age 16 (1904) he leaves to learn the wholesale trade in a London firm which sells Monnet cognac. Jean also learns the ways of the City, that heart of London's financial and business life, as well as the language. In two years he is ready for his first venture alone for the firm in distant North America. (1906)

To travel from rural France to Winnipeg, Canada at the start of the 20th century was an adventure comparable today to traveling to Tibet or Mongolia: it could be done by anyone with determination and resources but the distance and the hardships involved discouraged most people. But for JG Monnet et Cie, central Canada was the promised land for new business and young Jean set off at age 18 with his father's highest hopes but little else.

Jean probably sailed from an English port, since his two years in London facilitated arranging passage from Southampton or Liverpool. To travel on a British ship also seems natural since the British dominated Atlantic shipping throughout the 19th century. Ships of the Cunard and P&O lines sail regularly from British ports to Saint John, Brunswick, to Halifax, Nova Scotia and to Saint John's, Newfoundland, all Atlantic ports for the Canada's booming inland cities. Winnipeg, Jean's destination, lay 1800 miles or 3000 kilometers to the west, reachable best by Canadian Pacific trains.

Here is a picture of Winnipeg from a newspaper during the time Jean Monnet was in the Canadian city:

> All roads lead to Winnipeg. It is the focal point of the three transcontinental lines of Canada, and nobody, neither manufacturer, capitalist, farmer, mechanic, lawyer, doctor, merchant, priest nor laborer, can pass from one part of Canada to another without going through Winnipeg. It is a gateway through which all the commerce of the east and the west and the north and the south must flow. No city in America, at least, has such absolute and complete command over the wholesale trade of so vast an area. It is destined to become one of the greatest distributing commercial centers of the continent as well as a manufacturing center of great importance. (5)

Today this enthusiasm seems overblown. But Winnipeg in 1906, when Jean arrived, sees itself as a rival to Chicago although only a tenth the size of the American city. Capital of the province of Manitoba, Winnipeg had grown from about 40,000 to 150,000 between 1900 and 1915 when it became the third city of Canada after Montreal and Toronto. Incessantly activity, especially noisy construction, night and day, greets a visitor like young Jean Monnet. Stores are opening, urban and even suburban housing projects are underway, and much of western Canada's commerce, especially wheat, funnels through the city. Here Jean's father, JG Monnet, hopes to make a deal with trading firms, especially the ubiquitous Hudson's Bay Company (HBC) to sell his cognac. Jean is to be the instrument of this venture.

From his room at the new Royal Alexandria Hotel across from the railway station, Jean Monnet marveled at the expansion and the energy of the New World:"...I saw trainloads of Scandinavian immigrants pulling in. They were not refugees; they were not starving. They had come to hard, rewarding work---the conquest of new lands....[F]or the first time I met a people whose job was not to manage what already existed but to develop it without stint. No one thought about limits; no one knew where the frontier was." (6)

Jean and his father also see growth without limits for their cognac in the thriving North American world. Here where the cognac giants have as yet no monopoly, JG Monnet Co. could compete for price and quality for the new trade. Furs were coming into Winnipeg, for example, by the trainload. Traders wanted well-priced but quality goods like cognac for themselves and for their customers, including the native Canadian Indians.

Monnet soon met the Canadian chairman of Hudson's Bay Company who then wrote his London headquarters about the meeting. (1907) The young Frenchman worked hard to gain a privileged place among the HBC suppliers. In his first recorded letter,(1911),now in the HBC files, Monnet writes a top office of HBC in Winnipeg confirming their conversation that day: HBC would have exclusive rights to sell Monnet cognac "from Fort Williams to the Pacific Coast." It is a triumph for the young salesman.

Other successes in Canada and, eventually other countries, follow. Monnet travels back and forth across the Atlantic, stopping at the HBC headquarters in London where he makes valuable friendships and a wider perspective on international trade. His first business venture is a grand success for the 24 year old. It is also a useful prelude to what follows.

II. THE FIRST WORLD WAR

A striking feature of Monnet's life showed each phase built on previous friendships. He became a master craftsman of personal networks before that concept was identified and exalted. When tensions between Germany and its European neighbors grew early in the second decade of the century, Monnet probably consults his new friends at Hudson's Bay Company who include the company chairman, Lord Kindersley and his senior assistants, the men who actually ran HBC from London. From them Monnet no doubt heard that war was possible but he still concentrates on his work as cognac salesman.(1914)When conflict becomes imminent, he then considers the consequences for France and for himself at age 26.

His conclusions bring the young cognac salesman into the world of public service and well-placed friendships he could probably not have imagined in Winnipeg, Moscow, Cairo or Athens although he had visited these exotic cities in the pre-war years trying to make JG Monnet cognac as widely known as Hennessy or Martel. His perspective by the start of the war was thus quite sophisticated; few European men his age had traveled as much and as far as had young Monnet. He absorbed and digested each experience.

Putting this experience to work in the war effort was a challenge to his pragmatism. At this stage of his life, Monnet never seems to reflect on the bigger issues of war and peace, of rivalries between Germany and its neighbors, or of how to prevent a catastrophic war. He is not physically fit to serve in uniform but with considerable self-confidence thinks he can provide France, and its allies, with some insights into how the war should be organized and especially how Britain and France should coordinate and pool their resources. With remarkable, even brash, initiative, he pushes a lawyer and family friend from the Charante to arrange a meeting in nearby Bordeaux with the French prime minister. Jean has two assets to offer Rene Viviani whose government had just fled Paris before the advancing German armies: first, an insight into how poorly France and Britain were prepared to fight a common war against Germany and, second, his London friendships at HBC, a major world trading firm. Viviani listens, undoubtedly impressed by this young man who was about the same age as his two sons who, by terrible coincidence as the prime minister had just learned, were both reported killed in the Battle of the Marne still underway.

Monnet's audacity worked. He helps HBC obtain an immense contract with the French government as agent for commodity purchases and for ship charters (1914). He is sent by the French government to London, then back to Paris as an assistant to the Minister of Commerce (1916). Just two years into the war the young man, whom his family had discouraged for being "big-headed" for wanting to go to the top of the government with his advice, is now indispensable to a senior cabinet minister.

He was also an occasional irritant to other ministers. As he wrote many years later "it was not in my nature to respect established authority for its own sake." (7)   Monnet's audacity comes at a price. His boss's rival, the Minister for War, tries several times to move Monnet out of London and into uniform. Finally the war minister appeals to the prime minister. An angry Georges Clemenceau summons Monnet to Paris, prepared to dismiss a pushy and youthful subordinate. Instead, after a wise delay to hear Monnet's own account of his work, the prime minister tells the cabinet to approve a commission for "Lieutenant Monnet" to return to his London duties. Monnet's willingness to challenge authority must have grown with this episode.

Later in the war, when the United States enters the conflict (1917) a new dimension to Monnet's network of friends develops. His move to London as a French representative on Allied commodity commissions brings him useful American friendships in New York financial circles. After the war, his pragmatic, active and fruitful work style in these war efforts would bring him tangible benefits.

III. THE WORK OF PEACE

The quest in Paris and London for Allied war supplies ignited an interest in public service for Monnet. He is not anxious to return to selling the family cognac (even though, as the oldest child, he must keep his eye on the enterprise wherever he finds himself). Having been observed by many leading officials of the wartime governments, it is not surprising that he is soon considered for an important position in the structures of peace. What is unusual is that he first seems to think himself unprepared or suitable for such work. When he is proposed for an important post in the League of Nations (1919) he suggests someone else. Finally he is named a deputy to Eric Drummond, the British secretary general of the League. Monnet soon becomes the senior of four deputy secretaries general struggling to get the League of Nations started. He also becomes the deputy Drummond most relies on to take on new tasks but not always to stick to the boring details of the job.

The same year one can observe the conceptual thinking already growing in the 30 year old Frenchman. Although his writing is never polished, he outlines clearly how he sees the League organized. He offers unusual, even "radical" advice to some American friends on the future of Europe. (1919) Yet, more practically, he also outlines a plan to take over confiscated assets of a German champagne company in France to expand the family's cognac business (1919-1920). He is a whirlwind who impresses his boss, Drummond, but already Monnet shows signs of boredom with the routines of League bureaucracy.

With the League seat transferred from London to Geneva (1920) (against the advice of Monnet and the French government) he settles into work on the major political problems of the League: Austria, Upper Silesia and the Saar (1921). He is distracted from his work with problems at home as the cognac business falters. He borrows a large sum from the Hudson's Bay Company (1922) while his brother, Gaston, tries to borrow funds from Ivar Kreuger, the Swedish match "king." By the end of the year, Jean resigns from the League, forced to return to Cognac to manage the family firm.

Whether working for the fledgling world government or for his father's business at home, Monnet keeps in touch with his American and British friends from the war years. (At this stage in his life, he seems to have few close French friends). He is forced to seek more funds from HBC in London, this time without success (1923). He also travels to Paris, London and Stockholm helping to stabilize the family firm (1924). Monnet sells shares in brandy "futures" to his British and American friends to keep the firm above bankruptcy (1925).

Monnet seems anxious to get away from the tedious concerns of the cognac trade but his great respect for his family and its values keeps him working at home. Finally, with the business' stability finally in sight but with his personal finances under stress he goes to New York and Canada both to restore cognac sales with the help of his cousin, Georges, who is joining the family business, and to secure a new job for himself (1926).

He succeeds by taking a position in Paris representing an American investment firm. He can now end his immediate financial dependence on American friends, as he tells one of them (1926).

IV. AN AMERICAN BUSINESS CAREER

The boom on the American stock market, starting just after the end of the war, meant the country had enormous sums to invest. Some of these funds went looking for investment opportunities in Europe. Monnet's employer, Blair and Company, headed by Elisha Walker, is a new firm, aggressive and opportunistic. Poland, Rumania and Bulgaria are some of the new locales the young French banker must master. It is an exhilarating life for Monnet, now freed from the day-to-day duties of the older son which had kept him in Cognac for over three years.

But the family business could never recede from Monnet's mind. He keeps close watch over the firm as his younger brother, Gaston, and his cousin, Georges, slowly took over management. His father, now over seventy, gave only general direction and encouragement. But tragedy came only one year after Monnet joined Blair and Company. His brother, Gaston, only 37 years old, dies suddenly of acute appendicitis, leaving a young wife and two daughters, ages seven and ten (1927). Uncle Jean now has to assume also some of the duties of father. (8)

Poland (1926-28) was the first challenge in investment banking for Monnet, eager to apply his knowledge of international finance gained from his League of Nations days to new targets. He used his Geneva, Paris and New York contacts, especially Ludwik Rajchman from the League, Emile Moreau from the Banque de Paris and Benjamin Strong of the New York Federal Reserve Bank to reach the top levels of the Warsaw government. Against these assets Monnet faced entrenched banking competitors from New York and condescending oversight from London's bankers. His success in Poland leads to opportunities in Bulgaria (1926,1928) which were not always successful but which Monnet pursues with energy and imagination. These activities confirm to Monnet's boss in New York, Elisha Walker, that the forty year old Frenchman, bilingual in English, is ready for an exciting American opportunity (1929).

V. THE GIANNINI ADVENTURES

Walker has been approached by a wealthy banker, Amadeo Giannini, as the man who might project his prospering Bank of America nationwide (1929). Walker sees Monnet as his principal aide in the transcontinental venture. Jean moves to New York (1929) as vice chairman, under Walker, of the bank's holding company, Transamerica Corporation. The dramatic rise of the U.S. stock market would eventually find its retribution in a catastrophic crash just as Walker and Monnet got their new venture underway.

The same year another exciting adventure began for Jean Monnet with another, unrelated, Giannini. Nineteen year old Silvia de Bondini Giannini was the Italian bride of only four months when she met Jean Monnet at a Paris dinner he gave for business friends in his bachelor flat on the Left Bank (1929). It was an immediate and total infatuation, at least for Monnet. "She was very beautiful. We forgot the other guests." (9) By a striking coincidence, Silvia had just married a man with the same family name as Monnet's new business partner, the California banker, Amadeo Giannini. But the two families were apparently unrelated. By another odd turn, Silvia's husband, Francesco, was an Italian business friend of Monnet who also worked for Blair and Co in Milan. The dinner meeting would transform Monnet's life.

VI. FIVE DIFFICULT YEARS

The August 1929 meeting of Jean and Silvia comes at a tempestuous time for Jean and his career. He had just agreed to go to California as vice president of Blair-Bancamerica, the new affiliate of the Bank of America, at the moment when he must have wanted to pursue Silvia in his single-minded style. The American stock market was booming and Amadeo's dream was to use the profits of the shares of Transamerica, his bank holding company, to finance a coast-to-coast expansion of the retail banking business. Monnet, and his immediate boss, Elisha Walker, were to manage this expansion for Giannini, now anxious to retire to a less hectic life. But his retirement trip to Europe coincided with the dramatic stock market crash and a consequent collapse in Transamerica's stock (1929).

Amadeo Giannini, a West Coast adventurer who was always skeptical of his Wall Street counterparts even while dependent on them, now identifies Walker and Monnet as the cause of Transamerica's collapsed value. He turns against them (1931) and leads a proxy fight to resume control of his bank. Monnet and his boss suffer an embarrassing defeat (1932) in the company's annual meeting and are out of their jobs.

Walker easily finds a new position in a leading Wall Street firm but Monnet needs work in Europe nearer Silvia who is still with her husband and a baby daughter. He calls upon a friend, John Foster Dulles, whom he had known both in Paris in 1919 and later in the Warsaw banking successes. Dulles was now a leading New York lawyer whose work included protecting the interests of Americans who had invested millions with the Swedish match king, Ivar Kreuger. By another striking coincidence Monnet, who had dealings with Kreuger in business, was now asked by Dulles to travel to Stockholm to protect the interests of his clients. The Kreuger firm collapsed when the Swede was discovered at the center of massive frauds and mismanagement which led to his suicide in the same month that Monnet lost his Transamerica role.

Monnet had worked briefly with Kreuger (1929-1932) who had once offered the young Frenchman a key job in Paris (1928). Fortunately, Jean said no but he did meet occasionally with Kreuger on several complicated business deals. Jean's brother, Gaston, married to a Swede who knew the Kreuger family well, had sought a loan from Ivar Kreuger when the Monnet cognac firm, and its managers, were in serious financial troubles.(1925)

Jean Monnet now spends much of one year (1933) in Stockholm representing Dulles' clients, with side trips to Cognac and Paris to pursue Silvia. For while losing in finance in America and still, over 40 years of age, without steady work or a career, he realizes that he has found a wonderful woman in his life when he badly needs love and stability.

VII. THE PURSUIT OF SILVIA

Jean is in desperate love with a married woman, half his age, who has just had a child. He cannot afford to delay either his career or his mission to win Silvia. He labors nearly three years to convince her to leave her husband and to flee with her daughter, Anna, to Switzerland (1932-33). The infatuated bachelor pursues Silvia with a determination only hinted at in his business or public service career. He faces legal, moral and familial obstacles to his pursuit. Silvia is Catholic, as is Jean, so divorce is a problem. Further, Silvia was married in Italy which did not even recognize divorce. Finally, his family initially opposes this breakup of a new marriage by an impetuous son obsessed with an improbable romance. Against these obstacles, Monnet apparently senses that Silvia is his best chance for happiness in this life; he is not to be denied.

In the years between meeting and marrying Silvia, Jean Monnet works in America, Sweden, France and China. He endures a well publicized business failure in America, followed by several temporary positions. Between 1929 and 1934, Silvia is at the center of his attention even while he moves from job to job, country to country. He arranges to meet her in Cognac with Francesco and in Switzerland after she separates from her husband. Monnet cables her from China where he goes on business in 1933. He conspires with old friends and makes new ones to achieve his goal: getting Silvia divorced so he can marry her. He finally succeeds in an unlikely venue, the Moscow Hall of Marriage in November,1934 with the immediate help of a Soviet ambassador and the advice of American lawyers. (9)

His memoirs cover this dramatic story in two brief paragraphs as devoid of passion and as carefully constructed as possible. These sentences are the only part of his autobiography he wrote himself (he actually negotiated their composition with Silvia according to his collaborator, Francois Fontaine) but the story is not as simple as Monnet's account suggests. The five years between the first meeting and the divorce and remarriage suggest Silvia needed time or persuasion for the decision to end her marriage. In 1931, two years after meeting Jean, she gave birth to a daughter. She then leaves her husband but still does not divorce and remarry for three more years.

Decades later, Francois Fontaine judged that finding Silvia was the decisive moment in Monnet's life. The marriage was the "great dividing point [for Monnet]; before he was a worldly bachelor, not well fixed in time or space; after, he was a settled man, ready to challenge and succeed in whatever life brought him." (10) (The marriage in 1934 also divides his long life into two almost equal parts. He was just 46 when he married, nearly 91 when he died).

VIII CHINA AND THE ROOSEVELT ADMINISTRATION

Even after the wedding in Moscow, life is uncertain for the Monnets. The business climate in China, where Jean is living and where he brings his new family, (1935) is uncertain. Monnet himself is part of the turmoil brought about by Japan's insistence that it monitor and approve any foreign trade or capital transactions in China. Finally, the economic climate in China is poor, partly because the American stock market crash and subsequent depression had global consequences and partly because Japan finally threatens China with invasion.

The most tumultuous years of Monnet's life ---1932-33---include losing his California job, finding temporary work in Sweden and China and the successful presidential campaign of Franklin Delano Roosevelt. At the time, Monnet did not know it but the last-named became the most important of these three events for the next 15 years of his life. For while he soon forgot the California bank episode and his brief work for the disgruntled Kreuger creditors, the Roosevelt presidency helped bring him both to China in 1933 and to wartime prominence in Washington a few years later.

When Roosevelt is sworn into office in March 1933, Monnet may have already known that Elisha Walker, his former boss at Blair and Co and at Transamerica, was a friend of the new president. He probably did not know that Roosevelt had a long family relationship with China and took a personal interest in that country. Finally Monnet would not have known that the Chinese Finance Minister, T V Soong, who approached him with work (1932) just after Roosevelt's election, was also a fellow Harvard alumnus and close friend of the new president. Soong had learned, through a League of Nations friend, that Monnet's American and European banking connections were a good fit with his own need for western banking expertise. Soong's access to the president, whom he would soon visit on his way to Europe (1933) and his hiring of Monnet, brought the Frenchman to Washington just as the new Administration got underway.

T V Soong, who initiated Monnet into Chinese matters, was a prominent and influential son in the famed Soong family which dominated China in the years between the world wars and into the postwar collapse of the country into civil war and communist rule. His sister was the wife of Chiang Kai Shek; a brother, T L Soong, was prominent in Chinese banking; and a brother in law, H H Kung, would became finance minister when Chiang precipitously fired T V Soong only months after Soong offered Monnet a job in Shanghai.

Monnet thus arrives in China (1933) in great uncertainty about his work. He persists, partly at least, because he badly needs a job and because his affair with Silvia demands a haven for both of them some distance from Europe. Soong and Monnet agree, in the months after they meet, that the principal task in China was harnessing foreign capital to Chinese industry. The goal is to develop the railroads and other infrastructure for a role in the 20th century's global economy. That they never fully succeeded was not due to lack of skill or determination on their part but rather to the internal chaos and to Japanese attempts to dominate the country. In the midst of this confused work environment, Jean marries Silvia in Moscow and brings his new wife and her daughter to his home in Shanghai, ready to start a new life (1935).

IX. THE FAMILY AND THE PARTNERSHIP

Actual war between China and Japan started (1936) just as Monnet apparently realizes that his future in business and his new role as father and husband require more stability that China could offer. Without abandoning entirely his Shanghai enterprise, he leaves China for America to start a business partnership with George Murnane, also an acquaintance of John Foster Dulles who brings the two men together. Dulles believes, he tells his law partner, that Monnet and Murnane are a good bet to find success while working out their respective mid-life crises. (By a coincidence, Murnane had lost his last position with an American investment firm closely tied to the collapsed Kreuger empire). Dulles was only partly correct; the Monnet-Murnane partnership which lasted to 1944 kept both men working but was never a great success either in China, where it continued the work Monnet had started there, or in Europe where he now turned his attention. (11) With new responsibilities, Monnet does not seem greatly interested in making (or losing) another fortune but is more concerned with a stable job and a secure family situation.

Monnet's worries about his new family center on Francesco Giannini's determination to gain custody of his daughter, Anna. Italian law favored the father in custody cases and while China was more remote from the European legal system, America also seems safe. It was not. The Monnets move their home to New York City (1936) where George Murnane will handle the U.S. side of the partnership while Jean travels to oversee European matters. Silvia and Anna remain in the rented New York apartment overlooking Central Park, then, as now, an expensive venue for a beginning businessman and his family. Soon after their arrival, a lawsuit is filed in the New York courts (1936) by Anna's father to regain her custody. The suit ultimately fails but it made the first years of the marriage difficult.

X. THE COMING CRISIS IN EUROPE

Adolf Hitler and Franklin Roosevelt come to power in the same year (1933) but Monnet's initial focus is on the American changeover and its implications for China. Only when he comes back to the United States does he begin to recognize the nature of the new German regime. The violence against German Jews appalls Monnet; he recalled having dinner in New York in September 1935 when Hitler's first decrees against the Jews were reported by Foster Dulles. Monnet says to his friends: "A man who is capable of that will start a war." (12)

The next year, Monnet meets in New York with Heinrich Bruening, the former German chancellor, just as the Germans reoccupied the Rhineland. Bruening also predicted war unless the Allies acted immediately. Instead Europe drifted into a sullen pre-war spirit of challenge and counter-challenge. Monnet's partnership with George Murnane continues to undertake small commissions but Jean's life is gradually redirected toward preparing France to defend itself. When

Kristallnacht hits the German Jews (1938) (by coincidence on Monnet's 50th birthday although he never mentions either event in his memoirs) he must have sensed the imminence of another European disaster.

XI. REARMING THE ALLIES

There is a temptation to draw parallels between's Monnet's work in the first and the second World Wars but it is an incomplete comparison. Admittedly, for the second time in his life, Monnet witnesses an impending conflict between his native country and its neighbor, Germany. And in both cases, he is involved in finding the supplies the Allies need to win the war. But at the start of the first World War, he was only 25 years old and inexperienced except as a well-traveled seller of cognac. He pushed himself forward because he saw, in 1914, the obvious needs for Allied cooperation which others overlooked.

Now, in 1938, he is 50 years old with a quarter century of work experience in public in private life and on three continents. Armed with a network of well-placed friends and with the assurance that comes with maturity, he is as ready as he even would be for the coming crises. When war comes, he is thrust into new roles of great responsibility which, in turn, lay a foundation for the final and dramatic chapters of his life.

His immediate involvement comes with the rearmament crisis which France faced in 1938. After the China interlude, Monnet is back in Europe regularly with his new partnership. One happy coincidence is the arrival in Paris (1936) of Bill Bullitt, former US ambassador in Moscow when Jean married there, who is the new ambassador to France. Bullitt and Monnet had first met in Paris after World War I, renewed their friendship in Moscow, and are now together in the French capital; both worry about the rise of Nazi Germany and France's apparent inability to face this threat. Bullitt suggests to the French government that Monnet has the right American connections to buy US war planes for France (1938). Jean readily suspends his partnership role, telling Murnane that he has been recalled to public service.

Soon Monnet is meeting President Roosevelt and treasury secretary Morgenthau as France's agent. When war comes in late summer 1939, it was 25 years since Monnet pushed himself into Prime Minister Viviani's office in Bordeaux; he is now invited by another French prime minister (and his British counterpart) to take charge of Allied military procurement in London (1939).

As in 1914, Monnet will not go along with superiors simply for the sake of amiability. He questions procedures, assumptions and values. Throughout his life he leaves a trail of devoted friends but also a wake of co-workers, bosses and bureaucrats who often cannot understand or accept Monnet's single mindedness or his motives. In the eight months of the Allied job, he must work against these suspicions held by some Americans, British and even French observers. (1939-40).

When France falls to the Germans (1940), his role as supply chief ends abruptly. Monnet again experiences that personal void that comes from suddenly losing one's job. It had happened before in 1918 and in 1932. Each time, including 1940, he rebounds, usually into a larger challenge and apparently without either remorse or self-pity. These occasions of self-redefinition were sometimes smooth, as at the end of World War I when he found a place easily in the new League of Nations. But in 1932 when he is fired from Transamerica, it took over two years before he could restart his life and then it required a move to China, a Moscow marriage and trying without success, he says, to understand the oriental mind. The move to Washington (1940) to help the British reorganize their supply organization lacks the drama of the Far East but it has a military urgency and a personal challenge to a middle-aged Frenchman in the midst of a major wartime British outpost.

Monnet is more at home in Washington than most of his British colleagues in their rented Willard Hotel headquarters, near the White House.(1941). He had never had an office in the city before but had visited there many times in the first and second Roosevelt administrations. Now with the president reelected in an unprecedented third term campaign which Monnet witnesses, the Frenchman quickly finds and uses his well-placed American network: Supreme Court Justice Felix Frankfurter; lawyers John Foster Dulles, Donald Swatland and John McCloy; journalists Walter Lippmann, James Reston and many more. The network expands when he meets key war officials Dean Acheson, Robert Nathan and Harry Hopkins.

Even skeptical Monnet watchers like treasury secretary Henry Morgenthau and some of his British colleagues on the supply council have to admit that Monnet gets things done. By determined and sometimes blunt prodding of his friends, colleagues and Allied officials, he contributes importantly to the Victory Program that Roosevelt announces just as the United States enters the war (1941). He masters the wartime Washington world as the Frenchman who is both insider and outsider in the growing American war arsenal. (1942)

Algiers, capital of French Algeria, where Roosevelt and his adviser, Harry Hopkins, send him in 1943, was one more place in the mid-war years where things needed changing. Monnet, for the first time, immerses himself in French politics marked with prickly personalities and tender sensitivities. This work for France resumes back in Washington (1944). What he learns from these encounters certainly helps greatly when, once again, at the end of the war, he is without either a job or a direction.

While Monnet never kept any job long, he manages better than most men to take vital strengths from each endeavor into the next. He uses timing, location and the key friendships to find useful leverage and precise direction. A style edging toward obsession marks his work methods yet a complete lack of self-interest often disarms those suspicious of his unsmiling determination.

XII. PLANNING PEACE FOR FRANCE

Both job and direction come from Charles de Gaulle whose political and psychological dominance had eventually prevailed in Algiers and in the entire wartime French resistance. But de Gaulle, as Monnet puts it, wants to restore France's prewar grandeur before understanding how weak the country really is. The first task is to explain to the *grand homme* the enormous economic problems France faces. When de Gaulle accepts Monnet analysis, (even while retaining suspicions about Monnet the man) he asks him to plan the rebuilding of the country's economy. (1945) Monnet becomes head of the nation's planning office directly under de Gaulle. (1946)

Midst this planning effort, Monnet seethes during the next four years at political developments. He sees France repeating itself 25 years after the Versailles Treaty. A spirit of fear and vengeance burdens his native country in a way he, as a longtime self-exile, can see more clearly than many of his compatriots. Across the Rhine, a renewal of German energy and a determination to rebuild a fractured country feeds the French fears. The lust for national domination, though restrained by the immediate concern in both countries for reconstruction, is never far away.

Monnet mused in 1943 and 1944 about the future of Europe but not in a comprehensive or organized manner. In fact, this predominantly practical man never indulges in abstract thought for long. He is devoted to solving the immediate problem; he is, a friend says, a man for beginnings. But now the immediate problem---30 years after one world war, five years after another--- is how to find a permanent peace between France and Germany. His solution is neither dramatic nor sudden, neither grand nor grandiose. Rather it is like its author: plodding and determined, with more substance than glamour, yet more subtlety than is first evident.

XIII. THE MONNET IDEA

The European Coal and Steel Community---set up according to the Schuman Plan, named for the French foreign minister who proposed it with Monnet's outline---seemed at first a technocrat's dream and a politician's nightmare. The main underground resources of France and Germany were to be managed in common. The goal was an unprecedented self-denial for these two countries of the means and desire---fulfilled three times in the last 80 years---to war against each other.

But was this plan merely a clever trick of some kind? Would not Germans and Frenchmen still own the coal and iron ore mines? Could not war still be made despite a treaty since broken treaties often lined the roads to war? Could a clever plan extract hatred and suspicion from the ancient European hearts?

Monnet's plan, which he presented to Robert Schuman one weekend in April, 1950, was both more subtle and more naive than it appeared; subtle in assuming that trust was a habit, like the Aristotelian virtue, to be perfected. If you did the right thing regularly, that habit replaced others like anger, jealously, revenge. The coal and steel plan seemed naive, however, in suggesting that war could not be made without physically controlling mines and smelters or that national feelings could be so simply harnessed.

Behind the subtlety and gentle idealism of the community was Monnet's hard practicality: you could not stop with binding together only the coal and steel industries of France and Germany. The integration must then continue with other sectors, each adding in turn a political dimension. Even when other countries joined and progress slowed, a blending of nations goes forward. Coal and steel were to be the gritty nucleus around which Europe forms like a man-made pearl. Success was not certain; if the attempt fails, the ideal vanishes, the pearl dissolves.

XIV. THE CRUCIAL TIMING OF THE SCHUMAN PLAN

The coal and steel community idea needed both an opportunity and a strong thrust forward if it was to succeed. The opportunity came in May 1950 when Schuman has to provide a plan for dealing with Germany when he meets with his US and UK counterparts in London. He had been assigned the task the previous September by Dean Acheson, the US secretary of state after many failed attempts at earlier foreign ministerial meetings. Germany was slowly rebuilding after years of devastating economic and political turmoil. Its currency was reformed in 1948 and the Berlin blockade crisis between the wartime allies had made Germany a center of western worries. The Soviets would do much to capture or neutralize the entire country and the West was prepared even for war to prevent this.

But France is a hindrance to the plans of Britain and America to allow the full rebirth of political and economic Germany, now indefinitely divided with its eastern third under Soviet control, the rest allied to the West. France needs German coal for its steel industry but Germany's own growth would soon limit coal exports to France. Politicians in France in 1950 cannot tolerate the idea of full German sovereignty and especially German rearmament which London and Washington are already weighing. Schuman's delicate task is to move toward German equality and reintegration in western Europe without appearing weak to his compatriots or to be acting under outside pressures.

As Monnet and his small circle of advisers design the coal and steel plan, he understands there is not only a German problem but a French problem as well. His own country must make proposals when it prefers simply to delay any change in the Germany it helps to occupy. If France does not act, it would be exceedingly difficult for Britain and the United States to force action in the spring of 1950. But eventually a split would come among the western allies and France would be blamed; Monnet and Schuman see this but will other Frenchmen agree?

Schuman's dramatic reversal of French policy, under Monnet's plan, is the vital thrust forward. No longer will France be a drag on the western powers. Instead it will offer equality to Germany if that neighbor will accept international control over its coal and steel resources. The heart of the plan could end French intransigence if Germany (and France) accept limits to their sovereignty over war-making industries. This requires no idle gesture for the Germans; Chancellor Konrad Adenauer has insisted for years on the goal of a fully sovereign but peaceful Germany regaining a place in western Europe.

The Monnet plan, embraced now by Schuman and Adenauer, is, as the French foreign minister announces, a bold and constructive act.

No doubt the Monnet goal is political, not merely economic and certainly not limited to the coal and steel industries of which he knows naught. In one draft of the Schuman declaration Monnet wrote: "This proposal has an essential political objective: to make a breach in the ramparts of national sovereignty which will be narrow enough to secure consent but deep enough to open the way toward the unity that is essential to peace." Perhaps prudence makes this practical man drop this sentence from the final version for it would have needlessly inflamed the nationalists, then and now. (13) But the goal persists.

The low-key announcement by Schuman at a cabinet meeting on May 9 1950 and at a crowded press conference later that day proposing the coal and steel pool is not novel either in its elements nor in its themes supporting European unity. Neither in its focus on coal and steel, nor in its aspiration to integrate western Europe (beyond the French-German problem) is the Schuman Plan unique. There were, in fact, many radical ideas stirring in Europe in the postwar years on both integration and on what to do with Germany. Thus Monnet's ultimate design, as presented to Schuman and adopted by him and the perhaps naive French cabinet, is only one among these many. "The great thing about Schuman's statement was that these ideas were now French policy." (14) Only when Monnet and his small team of pragmatists began work in the weeks before Schuman's announcement do the specifics emerge and vision slowly focus.

Monnet, the eminently practical man, does not enter this crucial period just five years after the end of the greatest civil war in world history with any fixed plan nor with elaborated abstractions. His goal is to help solve the immediate Franco-German problem with a political solution clothed innocuously in a technical construction. But he had an additional spur. Beyond the western foreign ministers' engagement with Germany (and with France) and even without regard to wider integration, Monnet sees the pressure of the Cold War building. Out of the rivalry of the United States and the Soviet Union, western Europe has to find both its place and its voice. An integrated Europe which could incorporate Germany, the former enemy, under French leadership, in a new structure of neither American nor Soviet design could bring this new role.

XV. REACTIONS TO THE SCHUMAN PLAN

Reactions to the Schuman Declaration are predictable. Hesitation and confusion in France on the pool's significance; enthusiasm in Bonn for the expression of equality which slowly outweighs opposition by the Ruhr industrialists; cautious support by the United States; unhappiness in London which was not told of the Plan in advance and which refuses to participate in it; and more questions than immediate answers elsewhere in Europe where other countries are also eligible to join. As one American observer put it, questions "of motive, sincerity and feasibility" covered most of the reactions of both foreigners and Frenchmen. (15)

If Monnet inspires the Plan, Schuman is the hero of its execution. Robert Schuman was an austere and respected Catholic lawyer-statesman, born in Luxembourg where his Lorraine family had fled after the Franco-Prussian war of 1870-71. (16) Now, in 1950, a senior minister, he is among the least likely of cabinet members to upset the nation with dramatic gestures. But his religious faith and his life close to Germany (including university studies and civil duties there during the first World War) keep the French-German matrix before him as he enters the final years of long government service. His embrace of Monnet's idea made it properly the Schuman Plan but neither his encouragement of the plan nor its final acceptance is predictable.

Two visionaries---one a worldly pragmatist, the other a pious but remote bachelor---came together in the spring of 1950. They bring an odd but singularly well matched couple's skills to the task. Although different in background, experience and temperaments, they respect each other greatly, each recognizing the other's unique talents and potentials. (Books are an interesting measure of the differences of the two men: Schuman was a bibliophile, a reader and collector of ancient tomes; Monnet owned only the books others gave him, seldom consulting or referring to what others had written, rarely even asking friends to summarize for him a recommended book).

Together, they change Europe's direction; war between France and Germany becomes unthinkable; other countries join and still others await the chance. Two men divert the course of history which today flows peacefully around and through their huge construction and toward a European unity they could only imagine over a half century ago. They would not be surprised at the remaining difficulties; these could never equal those they faced and overcome in the spring of 1950.

ENDNOTES

(1)   Jean Monnet, Memoirs, Garden City, NY, 1978.
(2)   Francois Duchene, Jean Monnet: The First Statesman of Interdependence, New York, 1994.
(3)   Eric Roussel, Jean Monnet, Paris, 1995.

(4) Fontaine's essay, "Forward with Jean Monnet," in D Brinkley and C Hackett, eds, Jean Monnet: The Path to European Unity, New York, l991, 1-66.

(5) Quotation from a Chicago newspaper in Alan Arbitise, Winnipeg: An Illustrated History, Toronto, 1977, 23.

(6) Monnet, Memoirs, 45.

(7) Ibid 50.

(8) Interviews with Colette Autigeon, Monnet's niece, 1992-94.

(9) Interviews with Albert Connelly, Monnet's 1936 lawyer, in 1991-93.

(10) Interview with Francois Fontaine, 1992.

(11) Monnet's role in China, and indeed, in pre-WWII history, is clouded by the loss of his personal records during World War II.

(12) Monnet, Memoirs, 116.

(13) Ibid 296.

(14) William Diebold, The Schuman Plan, New York, 1959, 46.

(15) Ibid 11.

(16) For the Schuman background, see R. Poidevin, Robert Schuman, Homme d'Etat, Paris, 1986.

THE CHRONOLOGY: The Beginnings

The documented life of Jean Monnet in his early years is very sparse. His memoirs give a general account in few words of his years before World War II. Further, these were written over seventy years after the events of his childhood when neither memory nor documents could be reliably consulted. What is clear from Monnet's own account is his belief that his character and his personality had their sources in his family, its business and the distinctive French community in which he was raised. We start therefore with the facts of his childhood and the first meager accounts of Monnet's introduction to life outside of Cognac, as he traveled first to London, then to Canada to begin to carry out his family business responsibilities.

1888: 9 November: Jean Monnet born in Cognac, France (d.1979), son of Jean Gabriel Monnet (1855-1939) and Maria Demelle Monnet (1868-1956)

1890: JM's only brother, Gaston, born (m. 1916 Helmi Sundstrom; children Aline b. 1917, Colette b. 1920) d.1927. CA

1894: JM's sister, Henriette born (m. Marcel Chaumet; children Jacques b.1928; Pierre b. 1929; Therese b. 1931) d. 1991. TP

1897: JG Monnet, JM's father, is asked to manage the United Vintners Proprietors Company (UVPC), a cognac producers cooperative. The Monnet family moves into the UVPC property as it home even though JG Monnet had recently built his family a new home. JMM 39

1901: JM's sister, Marie Louise, born; d. 1988.

1904: Travels to London to begin two year apprenticeship at WH Chaplin & Co,10 Villiers St WC, wine and spirit dealers, an agent for the JG Monnet cognac firm. JMM 41 and London directories.

Monnet's first foreign travels, at age 16, constitute a decisive step in his life. Instead of following a university career or mastering the family business at home, he leaves his close family to learn the foreign markets and then to represent the family firm abroad where its destiny lay. A small firm like JG Monnet could not succeed in the cognac trade without building a distinctive customer base. It could not advertise or market cognac like the Hennessy, Martel and Hine firms with their worldwide reputations and extensive agent networks. Monnet went therefore, at his father's order, to live and work with a London agent. Here young Jean was to finish his education by learning the language and the ways of the English, a principal buyer of cognac.

Two years later, with that training, he left for Canada to capture a market where the large cognac firms were not so firmly established. "Don't take any books," his father said. "No one can do your thinking for you. Look out the window, talk with people." Into the harsh landscape with few cities and few customers, it was to be a trying and not entirely successful venture for the Monnet firm but for Jean it was, as his father wanted, the start of his real education. Eventually, his travels included Egypt, Greece, Russia and many other places but his experiences in England and North America became the basis of his life.(JMM 44-47)

1906: Travels for first time to Canada for family cognac firm. JMM 44-46

1907:

1 Oct: C C Chipman of Hudson's Bay Company, Winnipeg writes his London headquarters on recent visit by and proposal from a representative (JM) of United Vintner Proprietors (UVP), J G Monnet's firm. Subject of visit was expanding sales of Monnet cognac of exceptional qualities and prices. Letter refers to past dealings with Monnet firm. HBC Microfilm files D.13/28, FO.699

Germany's growing role in Europe threatened the continent's stability which Britain and France had tried to restore with their Entente Cordiale[of 1904]. But a well known economist, writing after World War I, describes the nature of the German challenge: The "economic interdependence of Germany and her neighbors [was] overwhelming....[B]y the system of `peaceful penetration' she gave these countries not only capital but organization. The whole of Europe east of the Rhine thus fell into the German industrial orbit." J.M.Keynes, The Economic Consequences of the Peace, (New York, 1920) 17-18,65-66.

1911

15 Sep: Letter from JM to H E Burbidge, Stores Commissioner of HBC in Winnipeg, confirms conversation they had the preceding day by which HBC will have exclusive rights for five years to sell Monnet brandy "from Fort William to the [Pacific] coast." This is earliest preserved Monnet letter. HBC I.

12 Dec: J G Monnet sends draft agreement to N H Bacon at Harrods based on talks in September by H E Burbidge and JM. Second JGM letter the same day confirms that a company agent, probably JM himself, will travel next spring with HBC travelers [salesmen] through western Canada. (Harrods was a major enterprise of Lord Kindersley who was also chairman of HBC). HBC I

1912

2 Feb: HBC confirms the 1911 agreement with the Monnet firm and indicates Jean Monnet will be in Canada this spring to help fulfill the contract. HBC I

1914

27 Jan: JM arrives in London; sees cousin Georges. GMD

With danger of war increasing, Monnet's life and its documentation draws into focus. Undoubtedly, his acquaintances in London at the HBC headquarters and in Canada at its operational center alerted Monnet to the impending crisis between France and England, joined in the 1904 agreement, and an increasingly restless Germany.

Lacking a formal understanding of the history of these powers and without the nationalism which marked most Frenchmen whose lives centered on Paris, Monnet sensed something else: how ill prepared Britain and France were to fight a major war together. He sought to use his HBC connections to help France improve its ability to work with Britain. At the same time he found a place for himself in the war effort.

11 Feb: JM departs London for France. GMD

AUGUST: JM travels from London to Cognac. JMM 48. En route he sees signs of war mobilization. When he arrives in Cognac war is declared. AW

10-17 Aug: Committee Internationale de Ravitaillement (CIR) established in London to coordinate Allied purchases following week-long conference. Expanded in the next month to include Belgium and Russia. KB 45

SEPTEMBER(2nd week): JM meets Prime Minister Rene Viviani in Bordeaux through intercession of family friend, Fernand Benon. They discuss Monnet's impression that Britain and France must coordinate their war effort beyond mere communication. "We need to set up joint bodies to estimate the combined resources of the Allies, share them out and share out the costs." Viviani, whose two sons had just died in the Battle of the Marne, sends JM to present his ideas to Alexander Millerand, the Minister of War. JMM 50-2

25 Sep: Through JM's intervention, HBC proposes general purchasing contract to French War Ministry. Negotiations begin to refine the contract's terms. HBC II

1 Oct: Frank Ingrams, HBC official, cables his headquarters that he is in Bordeaux (where French government has relocated) and expects "definite answer will be sent in few days after conclusion negotiations here." HBC II

9 Oct: Major contract concluded with French Government under which HBC undertakes to purchase "on the best possible terms and on the various world markets, the commodities which the French government would request them to obtain." HBC II

The relationship of HBC and the French Government developed early in the war with Monnet's help. He apparently facilitated the French loan from HBC which was contracted between Frank Ingram of HBC and Ministers Ribot and Millerand (finance and war, respectively). The relationship was then modified as the French government contracted for all US purchases with JP Morgan in New York and for HBC vessals for vital shipping. (GE, HBC II)

22 Oct: New York bankers interested in report French government negotiating 50m franc loan for war. Earlier J P Morgan company had arranged 16m credit for French government. NYT

26 Oct: JM writes Sale of HBC from Paris "on scheme our friends [French government] would favor" involving lease of steamers. HBC II

NOVEMBER: JM sent to London to work in Civil Supplies Service at Trafalgar House, Waterloo Place, London. JMM 53. This is first move in shuttle which brings him back and forth between the two capitals for the next two years until November 1916 when he settles in London until the end of the war.

As the Allies gradually realize that the war will not be over in weeks or even months, different strategies emerge for coordinating the efforts of Britain and France. American financing of the war's enormous costs becomes urgent. By the end of 1914, Monnet is regularly in London where he deals with Allied supply problems but he is also in Paris much of the time working out of several offices and actively managing the contract which HBC, with Monnet's considerable help, had obtained as France's purchasing agent.

26 Nov: JP Morgan executive Henry Davison sails for London with Basil Blackett and George Paish when Blackett suggests Britain might need a NY firm to coordinate its purchases. During visit, Davison discusses purchasing deal with many including Lord Kitchener, Sec State for War. Although French government was not covered in these talks "a plan covering roughly the same ground was eventually carried out [by which France also employed the JP Morgan company]." HD 220.

16 Dec: Davison of JP Morgan lunches with Lloyd George who asks if the US firm might, in a few months, help arrange financing for UK govt. Davison says they could act even sooner if needed. At later meeting with Prime Minister Asquith and others, Davison urged the European allies to get together in both finance and supply matters. HD, Ch XV.

1915

8 Jan: H Davison of JP Morgan Co, meeting in Paris with Ribot, of Ministry of Finance and de Margerie, permanent under secretary of foreign affairs, reviews discussions with French government that Morgan had "in the early weeks of the war." Davison suggests delay in decision on new financing until UK needs are clearer. HD 191

20 Feb: French government contract with HBC of previous October modified further in payment, credit terms; latter limited to 1 million pounds. HBC II

APRIL, MAY, JUNE, OCTOBER: Letters to and from JM indicate he is in Paris and receives mail there at three addresses: 43 rue Bellechasse; Ministry du Commerce and Bureau de Ravitaillement, and Ministry of War. His handwritten May letter covers accounts problem with Ministry of Commerce and shows anxiety of HBC and JM on their dealings with French Government. Correspondence also shows Lazard Freres, London as disbursing agent for HBC-

FG transactions. HBC II

APRIL: J P Morgan Co. agrees to bring out one year French Government loan of $30m. HD I92

1 Apr: JM writes from Paris long letter to Lord Kindersley(HBC chairman) about problems with information from and to the French government. HBC II

22 Apr: Credits arranged by HBC for French government purchases under the contract of October 1914 now total about 3.5m pounds. HBC II

25 Apr: JM writes HBC manager Sale from Paris. HBC II

3,4 May: R H Brand, who eventually becomes close JM friend, involved in HBC questions of avoiding competition between French and British governments for armament orders. BP

7 May: British liner Lusitania sunk without warning by German submarine off Irish coast with loss of 1198 lives including 124 Americans. US had previously warned Germany against consequences of its policy of attacking ships found around the British Isles. A series of warning notes now followed from Washington with Germany alternately retreating from and reasserting its rights to submarine warfare. EAH

By mid-1915, the financial crisis facing the Allies forces more drastic action than arranging credits from intermediaries like the Hudson's Bay Company. France is forced to alter its HBC contract to allow a role for JP Morgan, the great American banking firm. Later in the year a joint Anglo-French loan of a half billion dollars was arranged in New York. HD Ch. XV, KB 46,78

16 May: HBC proposals on changes in basic HBC contract accepted by French government under pressure from UK government under which JP Morgan has US purchasing rights; HBC purchasing would now be limited to Canada. (Written in code) HBC II

17 May: French government informs HBC that an American company [JP Morgan] has been entrusted to make all purchases for France in the United States but that all purchases made in Canada for the Ministry of War would continue to be made by HBC. HBC-II

7 Jun: October contract further specified in credit payments. HBC II

15 Jun: Sale(?) writes JM in Paris about shipping problems, adding that HBC has three addresses in Paris for JM and does not know when to use which address. HBC II

18 Jun: Charles Sale writes Mauclere (Director General of Ravitaillement, French War Ministry) that HBC has just been told [actually at least as far back as 16 May memo above] that its contract now excludes any purchases in UK or US but HBC will have exclusive purchasing rights in Canada: We have indicated the

problems we see with this arrangement. We cannot accept any further changes in our contract. Furthermore, we can no longer extend credit as originally foreseen and need to be paid as goods are ordered. [This letter marks a further retreat from the favorable terms JM helped negotiate between HBC and the French government at the start of the war]. HBC II

23 Jun: HBC contract with French government modified to allow credit of up to 3.5 m. pounds. HBC II

24, 26 Jun: JM writes HBC from Paris on purchasing and shipping details including goods to Archangel, Russia. HBC II

JUNE: H Davison back in London after J P Morgan new export department set up under Edward R Stettinius. French Government gets $40m Rothschild Freres loan through help of J P Morgan. HD 193

In the second half of 1915, Monnet gradually shifts his work from the details of managing the HBC contract in Paris to the wider issues of supply problems between the Allies. By the end of the year he is working often in London on these major problems.

6 Jul: HBC board authorizes new credit of 3.5m pounds under new agreement with French government. HBC II

7 Jul: Sale(?) writes JM in Paris on problems with the Archangel shipping route. HBC II

10 Sep: Lord Reading Commission arrives in NY and starts negotiation of $500m Anglo French loan which is issued 15 October; loan involves J P Morgan Co. which foreswore any fees for its work. HD 194

8 Oct: Letter from H H Burbidge, HBC stores commissioner in Vancouver to Governor and Committee, HBC London, advises that he just received order from Saskatchewan government for three carloads of Monnet brandies "whose agency we hold." NAUK (Hudson's Bay Company) BHl/2232

26 Oct: JM writes Kindersley of HBC detailed memo from Paris on steamer scheme by which HBC buys ships and French government charters them with example of how it would work. HBC II

NOVEMBER: First inter-Allied agreement coordinating wheat purchases made in London with JM participation which calls French Commerce Minister Clementel's attention to him. But the agreement does not solve the problem of speculation in wheat. JMM 54, 58.

29 Nov: Anglo-French conference on cereal program in London attended by M. Chapsal who represented Clementel. The meeting discussed and reaffirmed the HBC-French govt agreement from start of war with Lord Kindersley officially charged to establish liaison between the two governments for purchases on the Canadian market. EC 62-3.

The year 1916 marks an important transition for Monnet. By the end of the year he is stationed in London, on behalf of Minister of Commerce Clementel, but now charged with negotiating a series of "executives" to coordinate the Allied purchasing of most goods and services. Monnet is forming both vital friendships for his future and a world perspective. He sees, in the Wheat Executive, "the first step on the long road that led me gradually to discover the immense possibilities of collective action." JMM 58

5,7 Jan: Kindersley writes JM in Paris on the steamer plan, including proposing JM as French government member of board. HBC II

11 Jan: JM refuses management role in shipping firm in note (in French) to Kindersley for reasons he "will explain later". HBC II

4-5 Feb: Clementel meets Lord Runciman in London after briefings by JM on problem of French dependence on UK shipping controls. JBD I

13 Mar: JM writes Sale from Paris on problems with French Government in management of HBC contract. HBC II

18 Mar: JM writes Kindersley from Paris on problems of coordination of French and British officials. HBC II

20 Mar: JM writes Kindersley from Paris on problem with Lord Runciman, president of the Board of Trade. HBC IIAPRIL: JM becomes a delegate of the Minister of Commerce in London. EC 67

3,9 May: Sale and JM (Paris) exchange letters on JM need for press clippings on Archangel and other Russian shipping ventures. HBC II

17 May: HBC reviews contract changes made with French government one year ago and notes further changes in which French government has made purchases of wheat, flour, oats hay and timber outside the HBC contract. Letter to the French war ministry also renews HBC request it made on 1 Nov 1915 for the ministry to send a technical commission to Canada to improve use of Canadian resources. HBC II

29 May: Sale(HBC) in London writes JM in Paris on problem with call up for military service of HBC personnel. Asks JM to prepare to send draft letter by Ministry of Commerce to UK govt. HBC II

25 July: Kindersley writes JM in Paris on HBC gratitude for all JM work on French Government contract. "...without your kind and energetic support in France...we realize that this combination" [of France and HBC] would long ago have ceased to exist. HBC II

5 Sept: JM (Paris) writes R Brand (at Ministry of Munitions) thanking for A Commonwealth of Nations which he has partly read. I know you want to unite all parts of the British Empire but this is now only part of the job after the war. "The union of Allies or rather of some of the Allies must be made as complete as

possible..." BP

EARLY OCTOBER: Davison and J P Morgan meet in London with UK and French officials on huge new financial needs which Lloyd George suggests will be $300m a month for next 5 months). HD Ch XVI

24 Nov: J P Morgan Co announces it will issue short term revenue bonds on behalf of UK and French governments starting Dec 1. HD Ch XVI

27 Nov: Wheat Executive set up as first allied commodity organ to share supplies and limit hoarding and bottlenecks. JMM 58-9; JPD II, 60; AK I 152

29 Nov: US Federal Reserve Board warns members "it does not regard it in the interest of the country at this time that they invest in foreign treasury bills of this character [as JP Morgan had proposed]. UK immediately withdraws plan for issuance. Instead over the next months huge gold reserves of UK and allies enter US banks. HD Ch XVI

-----: Joint Wheat Executive Agreement signed by Clementel and Lord Runciman, chair of British Board of Trade. JMM 58;

3 Dec: Franco-British Shipping Agreement made which required the two countries to report monthly on how their ships were being used but the piecemeal procedure fell short of what was needed. RM 21

A Scandinavian sea captain, J A Mikkeborg, hired by HBC to supervise the French government contract, recalled meeting JM several times in 1916-17. In 1916 he went to France to look after chartered ships for HBC. At the Ministry of Commerce he gave his letter of introduction to "the well known Monsieur Jean Monet [sic]. He was in the prime of life, keen and alert. He read the letter, gave me a look, and I felt that he sized me up right there and then. `Well,' he said, `go down to Cherbourg, see what you can see and come back and tell me.'

"Having spent a couple of days at Cherbourg, I returned to Paris and I gave Monsieur Jean Monet an account of what I had seen." Later Mikkeborg summed up his dealings with JM: "Monsieur Jean Monet[sic] was an excellent boss and a hard driver." HBC II

1917

JANUARY: JM exchanges correspondence with R Brand who is a partner at Lazard Freres. BP.

------: A preliminary version of the Allied Shipping Executive is created. JBP-I; JM begins discussions with Clementel in Paris and Sir John Beale and Arthur Salter, British director of Ship Requisitioning, in London on improving coordination of shipping and of other commodities, based on the successful example of the Allied Wheat Executive, which Beale chaired. RM 20

18 Jan: Syndicate formed to issue Third UK Loan of $250m backed by US and Canadian securities. HD Ch XVI

29 Jan: JM goes to Paris but will be back in London soon, according to letter of his aide, Renauleaud, to R Brand. BP

31 Jan: Germany announces submarine blockade of England, followed by declaration of unrestricted submarine warfare. JMM 59-60

19 Mar: French Government issues, through J P Morgan Co, secured bonds of $100m in NY. Overall, through 1921, UK and France borrowed about $2b publicly in US. HD Ch XVI.

6 Apr: US Congress passes resolution declaring war on Germany in response to unrestricted submarine warfare.

The entrance of the United States in the war is important for both the Allied cause and for Monnet personally. The joint executives set up in London to manage war supplies will now include American representatives, usually drawn from the upper levels of New York businesses. Monnet works easily with men like Dwight Morrow, Gordon Auchincloss, Thomas Lamont and Benjamin Strong. Their friendships became the most valuable assets he gained in the war years.

APRIL: With US in war, J P Morgan Co withdraws from purchasing field and UK and French government agencies deal directly with US government agencies established for its own supply purposes. HD Ch XVII.

APRIL, MAY: JM in London. HBC II

13 Apr: UK withdraws 500,000 tons from Allied shipping pool as labor disputes and pacifism affects both UK and France. Mutual incriminations rise. JBD I

18 Apr: JM receives letter [from Paris ?] in office of Ministry of Ravitaillement, Trafalgar House, London on wheat shipping problem re France. HBC II

18,19 May JM (London) exchanges letters with Commission Internationale de Ravitaillement in India House, Kingsway, London on how latter should communicate with HBC. JM says directly. HBC II

23 Jun: Sale writes N H Bacon, HBC Montreal, on new policy of minimal commissions to be earned by HBC as part of war effort. "We are becoming more and more a purely transport organization on behalf of the French government..."HBC II

JULY: Clementel, at JM urging, proposes further Allied cooperation with new executives beyond wheat and shipping. JBD I

16-27 Aug: Franco-British negotiations on French shipping problems held in London between French Commerce Minister Clementel and several British ministers. JBD II 54

6 Sept: Sale writes JM at Ritz Hotel, London on raw materials and

blockade questions including views of President Wilson. Refers to Isaac F Marcosson book The War After the War which, he says, mentions JM's work on pp 27-39. HBC II . [This is final HBC reference to JM during war].

10 Sep: JM, from London, urges Clementel to take charge of both shipping and food supplies. Referring to recent negotiations, he said Clementel inspired such confidence that an Allied economic directorate could result "from which France would gain considerable advantage." JMM 63

OCTOBER: JM, Salter and John Beale, chair of the Wheat Executive meet privately on shipping problem. Salter memo is basis for his talk with Lord Reading who agrees to act as their advocate in November allied conference. AJS I 113

6 Oct: Clementel writes President Wilson asking for Allied statement that when Germany relinquishes territory it has captured, Allies will release wheat and other raw materials they command. The letter, which Clemenceau had approved, ended with plea that "A peace treaty involving economic sanctions against any state that violates the pact---that must be the very basis of the League of Nations. JMM 71-2

12 Oct: London conference on shipping opens with Clementel playing leading French role. JM suggests all shipping be pooled and directed by an allied body. JBD II 5; JMM 64-71

17 Oct: JM at Board of Trade meeting in London to discuss French-UK cooperation. JBD I

29 Oct: JM writes memo to UK government at Clementel's request that "maritime transport has the key role in the conduct of the war." He urges early action. JMM 65

3 Nov: At opening of London conference on shipping problems, Allies make major declaration on food cooperation. Clementel agrees that JM should continue work with British leading to establishing an Allied maritime transport committee and its executive body. JMM 67-8; JBD I; AK I 152-3

5 Nov: Sale writes Bruno Weyers of HBC NY on problems latter has had with the "opposition and jealousy" of HBC's work on behalf of French government which began, Sale notes, when military call up in August 1914 disrupted French economy and HBC was called upon to help with problem. HBC II

20 Nov: JM assures Vilgrain, French under secretary of state for food supplies, that 3 Nov agreement will assure Britain, France and Italy of food through September 1918 and lay foundation for more complete transport coordination. AN F 127779 quoted in AK 153. British resist full shipping pool and want US agreement but Clementel argues for presenting US with a united front of France, Italy and UK. JBD II 56 quoting EC 285

21 Nov: Salter writes long memo on talks with JM and others on need for major American role in providing shipping both by reallocations and by new construction. RM 23

29 Nov-3 Dec: Paris conference on allied cooperation creates commission on imports and shipping, chaired by Clementel, which agrees on Allied Maritime Transport Council (AMTC) and its executive (AMTE) [succeeding earlier shipping executive]. JM to represent France on latter. AJS II 113-122; JBD II 56

12-17 Dec: After Franco-British meetings in London, Commerce Minister Clementel designates JM to head mission of commerce and marine transport ministries in London for interallied cooperation. He is to work directly under the French embassy. JBD I; JMM 70

15 Dec: JM proposes "to assume direction of the mission team...assist as Delegate [from] the Ministries of Commerce and of Maritime Transport and to all Executives and have charge of following the division of tonnage among the Allies." JBD I

Monnet's increasing prominence as a young civilian in charge of coordination of military supplies and shipping provokes sharp criticism from the French Minister of War who begins a campaign to put Monnet in uniform and out of London.

16 Dec: French ambassador Paul Cambon protests to Paris on efforts of armaments minister Louis Loucheur to get JM transferred to military staff in London. JBD I; JMM 70

END OF YEAR: JM is officially appointed head of London Mission of the French Ministry of Commerce and France's representative on all Allied executives. But his small team demands considerable support from the ministries in Paris with consequent friction and, eventually, efforts to remove him from London role. Still leading the effort was Louis Loucheur, Minister of Armaments. JMM 70

1918

JANUARY: Armaments minister Loucheur continues effort to reduce or end JM London role, forcing Prime Minister Clemenceau to decide. JM offers resignation to Clementel who is unhappy but apparently unable to counter Loucheur. JM is called to Paris, sees Prime Minister Clemenceau twice and is reconfirmed in job by cabinet memo which, among others, Loucheur signs. JBD I; AK I 162; JMM 70-1

This curious case of a Minister of War trying to end the service of Monnet in London defies explanation outside the personalities of the two individuals involved. Monnet, in his memoirs, makes clear he had no use for the idea of following orders for their own sake. Loucheur saw himself as the center of France's war effort and resented apparently both Clementel's role as Minister of

Commerce and Monnet's role as his aide. Monnet used both Clementel and an American, George Rublee, to keep his job in London but he now had to convince a French Prime Minister, Georges Clemenceau, of the value of his work as he had to convince another, at the start of the war, of his idea of cooperation not competition between Britain and France. The episode testifies to the Monnet's powers of persistence and persuasion.

8 Jan: JM cables from London to advise Clementel on coming visit of Sir Joseph Maclay. Meetings, which JM attended, took place as Germany prepares vast offensive designed to seize victory before vital American aid could be absorbed into allied supply system. JPD l citing AN F 12 7779

15 Jan: JM turns over first section of mission to P du Halgonet but maintains overall direction of French interallied supply mission in London. JBD I

23 Feb: JM cables Clementel that US shipping remains completely outside Allied maritime shipping committee (AMTC). JBD I

11-14 Mar: First meeting of AMTC held, its Executive composed of Salter, Attolico, JM and George Rublee. AJS II 177; JMM 69

19 Mar: First meeting of AMTE with Salter in chair, JM heading French section and Attolico and G Rublee representing Italy and US, respectively. JBD I

23-25 Apr: Second meeting of AMTC in Paris. JBD I

27 May: JM sends note from London to his superiors in Paris on the information needed to justify tonnage from the Allied fleet for importing urgently needed cereals into France. JBD l citing AN F 12 7780

AUGUST: JM again called to reserve duty but again these efforts are blocked when Clementel gains delay until 15 Nov. JBD I; JMM 71

-------- Third meeting of AMTC. AJS 177; JBD l

1 Aug: JM helps prepare balance sheet for AMTC showing import needs and actual imports for year, including supplying countries. JBD l citing AN F 12 7809

2 Aug: Further order requires JM to report to 125th Infantry Division but apparently still under Clementel delay until 15 Nov. JBD l

17 Aug: JM writes Clementel on state of interallied cooperation and its considerable problems. Five days later Clementel agrees with JM plea for one committee to coordinate the work. JBD I

16 Sep: JM involved in delicate negotiations on allied shipping tonnage needed to transport American troops. AK 263 quoting AN FN 12 7802

18 Sep: JM tells Clementel that negotiations have succeeded and Newton Baker, the US Secretary of War, has accepted fully the AMTC mechanism. AN

FN 12 7800 quoted in AK I 264

Although victory seems certain by late summer, its timing and consequences are not. Monnet and his boss, Minister Clementel, start to think about postwar cooperation in economic planning which the war has slowly and painfully produced. They soon face a skeptical America.

19 Sep: Clementel writes Presidents Clemenceau and Wilson outlining ideas of future peaceful cooperation among nations. "It is urgently necessary that the Allied democracies establish an ...Economic Union of Free Peoples. Already, hints of the structure of this future alliance can be seen in the wartime inter-Allied economic Councils. " JMM 72,79

30 Sep-2 Oct: At fourth (final) AMTC session, US Sec War Newton Baker, accepts council discipline for interallied supplies. JBD I; AJS II 119

1 Oct: US formally joins all inter-Allied executives, set up to manage economic aspects of war. Clementel and JM believe this means US is committed to postwar cooperation for reconstruction. JMM 71

4 Oct: Germany submits first armistice proposal. Salter sees AMTC work contributing to Allied success in inducing German capitulation. JBD I

10 Oct: JM tells Clementel that negotiations last month confirm US role in allied supply and shipping cooperation and signify its full cooperation on same basis as other allies. AN FN 12 7802 quoted in AK I 265

24 Oct: Herbert Hoover warns Wilson that some allies are proposing that Allied Food Council continue after armistice and control world distribution of food. HH opposes this, saying US should maintain independence to enable it "to level up the deficiencies that will ultimately arise from the general grab for the balances of the world's food." Hoover-Wilson Wartime Correspondence, Francis O'Brien, ed.,(Iowa City, 1974) 276-7

31 Oct: French and British present recommendation to War Council that inter-Allied war executives control, under armistice, Central Powers merchant marine and supplies. Cable from Cotton to Hoover, FRUS, Supplement I 615

NOVEMBER: United States complete massive movement of 1.65 million troops to Europe from May to October bringing its total forces there to 2 million. This indicates effectiveness of the ATMC work and its vital role in the war. JMM 69

2 Nov: JM pleads with Clementel, and through him, to French government and its Allies, to maintain the spirit of inter-allied cooperation after coming armistice. Citing weakened economies of Belgium and France, he says "the social order depends on the economic order." This may seem in contrast to the Wilsonian principles of free trade, JM adds, but the economic coordination needed is both temporary and to be achieved in cooperation with our Allies. AK I 333, citing AN F12 7795-6; JMM 73; JBD 1

8 Nov: JM transmits to Clemental an agreement with British which guarantees France 500,000 tons of shipping under AMTC control as part of post war planning. AN FN 12 7796 and 12 7798 quoted in JBD 1

-----: Herbert Hoover tells his London representative "[T]his government will not agree to any programme that even looks like inter-Allied control of our economic resources after peace" whether food exports or raw materials. This policy conveyed because British and French representatives on AMTC and Food Council proposed that Central Powers shipping and food supplies after armistice be put under existing Allied organizations. Hoover also says he is leaving soon for Europe and that State Department fully backs his position. FRUS, Supplement l 615-617

11 Nov: Armistice Day. Clementel cables JM not to leave London post despite orders to report for military duty. JMM 71. American official George Rublee had also intervened via Stettinius to help keep JM from military service. Rublee interview, Columbia University Oral History Program

13 Nov: UK proposes continuing work of AMTC as General Economic Council for postwar Allied coordination. France and Italy agree; US refuses. RM 30

20 Nov: JM arrives in Paris to discuss postwar economic cooperation among Allies. He is instructed [presumably by his government} to discuss this matter with Herbert Hoover who remains unconvinced. Eventually, the inter-allied executives are dismantled at Hoover's insistence. JPD l; JMM 73-5.

The end of the war meant for Monnet, as for hundreds of thousands more, a sharp shift of location, function and prospects. But Monnet believed that the years of hard-learned cooperation among nations and men should somehow be preserved and enhanced for the uncertain peace which followed. This view conflicted with the same nationalism which precipitated the war and which was to continue in the peace which followed the Allied victory.

1 Dec: Colonel Edward House, speaking for President Wilson, and implementing the decision Hoover had announced to end the wartime economic cooperation among Allies, proposed a Directorate General of Supplies for the liberated, neutral and enemy territories to be headed by an American. This was a move to end London's central role in world raw materials and to prevent the enemy fleet in the AMTC shipping pool. JMM 73-74

3 Dec: David H Miller diary reports JM told Norman Davis, US Treasury delegate for financial affairs, that France needs US and UK guarantees for its security as part of League of Nations (LN) concept and that US exploiting its trade position before France has opportunity to compete will make US and LN unpopular. DHM

18 Dec: At Inter Allied Club in Paris, JM dines with large Franco-

American group. JM is "Clementel's right hand man and a very clever and attractive Frenchman... Cravath, David H Miller, Dwight Morrow, Rublee, Cotton of US delegation and Villegrain of French among others [present]....I sat between Cravath and Monnet and talked to him most of the time. He is an exceedingly intelligent fellow." GA

----After same dinner, Miller describes JM as "one of the French financial people on whom Clementel relies." DHM

23 Dec: Renauleaud (Paris) writes D W Morrow at American Shipping Board, London, noting JM asked him to invest 500 FF in French war loan on behalf of Morrow. Encloses certificate. DWM

Monnet's wartime experiences were remarkable for a young uneducated Frenchman who became, through audacity and diligence, quite indispensable to Minister Clementel and very central to the crucial Allied supply system.

His efforts in Paris and London gave him greater self-confidence (he already apparently had more than a normal share) and also positioned him for his next work in helping to keep the peace. Further, his HBC work earned him that company's gratitude and, eventually, a loan worth 40,000 pounds (or well over one million pounds in 2007 terms) most of which was forgiven and thus became an outright gift for wartime services rendered. This was, of course, not a charitable effort for the HBC which made of 1.25 m. pounds from the French Government business, "the most profitable single transaction in its long history...." (PN 268).

With the end of war and of his role with Clementel, the French Minister of Commerce, Monnet faces a search for new work in 1919, like many others. He is interested in how the victors can organize the postwar world and maintain the wartime cooperation even with though the Americans refuse to continue the inter-Allied executives. Back in Paris, he considers how peace can be organized and writes a long memorandum, his first on record, on how nations should organize for peace.

31 Dec: In sign of willingness to cooperate in postwar world economics, Lord Reading reports to French that the British Cabinet believes economic balance should be sought on raw materials by controls to guarantee their availability to all Allied countries. US seems willing to cooperate when, the next day, Col. House says President Wilson is coming around to European view. But opposition of American exporters gradually scuttles American cooperation. JMM 73-74

Age 31 to 40 (1919-1928)

25 Jan: The Supreme Allied Council, meeting in Paris to prepare the peace treaty, sets up a committee to draft the Covenant of the League of Nations. JMM 80

27 Jan: Supreme Allied Council starts move toward US position of full liberalization of trade and economic cooperation. JBD I

30 Jan: D Morrow (NY) to JM (Paris): I gave Thomas Lamont, my partner, a letter of introduction to you. Also sent you, Rublee and Salter Francis B Sayre's book Experiment in International Administration. DWM

18 Feb: JM receives telegram from Raymond Fillioux, Cognac school friend who was now in charge of Wheat Executive in London, announcing that US delegate had withdrawn declaring that the Executive was "contrary to the views of his government which intended that prewar methods of trade should be restored as soon as possible." JMM 74

3 Mar: JM is reassigned to Paris by a ministerial order for continuation of work on marine transport and interallied commodity matters as part of the Supreme Economic Council set up for the Peace Conference. JPD I

24 Mar: Supreme Allied Council dissolves Allied Maritime Trade Council. JPD 1

4 Apr: Final meeting of the Supreme Economic Council affirms breakdown of wartime economic cooperation in showdown between Clementel on one side and Bernard Baruch of US and Lord Cecil of UK on the other. Cecil insists that economic freedom would be a better guarantee of Germany's ability to pay reparations. Baruch says US could not accept peacetime control of raw materials. Clementel responds, in defeat: "The United States have made a grave mistake in immediately throwing off the harness of war as soon as the Armistice is signed. According to the principles advocated by President Wilson, should we not be seeking organized peace?"

Gradually the wartime executives were dismantled. JM noted: "There is no point in trying to apportion blame for this return to past habits; it was simply that Nature had returned to its normal course. It was to take many years, and much suffering, before Europeans began to realize that they must choose either unity or gradual decline." JMM 74-5

The experience of the Allied executives had a lasting effect on Monnet who reflected on the method developed during the war and which he later applied to many international enterprises. He cited (JMM 75-76) the description of this method by his friend and colleague at the executives, Arthur Salter, who wrote, in his book Allied Shipping Control:

> *...members of an international committee have a dual personal capacity, international in relation to their own country, national in relation to*

*other countries,[are in a position] of great personal delicacy. They
necessarily receive information from their departments...with regard to
policy while still in the process of formation. It is a problem of the utmost
difficulty to know how much of this can properly be communicated to the
Allied colleagues. So far as the Allies are regarded as competitors with
divergent interest any such communications weakens the bargaining
position of one's own country. But so far as they are regarded as
partners whose common interests are more important than any conflict
of claims, such communication may often be essential....If each one of
our separate countries considers a problem...from its own point of view,
develops a national policy, begins to give it expression in administrative
arrangements, fortifies it with Ministerial decisions and Cabinet authority,
adjustment will prove almost impossible. Four rigid and developed
policies will confront each other.... But if the national points of view can
be explained while they are still developing, if policies can be brought
into contact while they are still plastic and still unformed, agreement will
be easier and probably better. Given the proper personal relations, many
things can be explained which would never be put on paper....But the
delicacy of such work, and the difficulty of the questions of loyalty and
good faith involved, are obvious.*

11 Apr: Hoover writes Wilson advising against US participation in
various commissions set up under peace treaty which continued inter-Allied war
cooperation. Hoover states that US "is the one great moral reserve in the world
today and that we cannot maintain that independence of action ...if we allow
ourselves to be dragged into detailed European entanglements over a period of
years." Whether or not the Allies adopt your 14 point peace plan, we should retire
from Europe. "I know of nothing in letter or spirit of any statement of your own,
or in the 14 points, that directly or indirectly ties the United States to carry on
this war through the phase of enforcement or of the multitudinous demands and
intrigues of a great number of other governments and their officials." Papers of
Woodrow Wilson, vol. 57 (Princeton NJ, 1966) 271-4

*Monnet is greatly disappointed with the American insistence on
dismantling wartime economic cooperation. But his own search for a new start
in the postwar world leads to an interest in the League of Nations which the
Allies want established to preserve the peace. Initially he is asked for advice
on staffing the new organization. Monnet seems then to have been suggested
as a deputy secretary general of the League under Eric Drummond, the British
secretary-general designate but exactly who proposed him for this job is not
clear. When Monnet is discussed for essentially the second job in the League of
Nations, he hesitates, then suggests someone else take it with Monnet assuming a
lower position. This will be remembered as uncharacteristic modesty on his part.*

9 May: G Auchincloss, of US delegation at Peace Conference, meets with
Eric Drummond, LN secretary-general designate; Col House, President Wilson's

principal adviser, and JM on League of Nations organization. "Monet[sic]seems rather reluctant about taking the job of deputy secretary general unless he can have the support of the French foreign office through the instrumentality of Fleuriau, the French counselor of embassy in London. In fact Monet wanted to put this man in as deputy SG and take a subordinate position himself." Auchincloss and Drummond oppose this, not wanting any more French foreign office members in the SG office. No decision agreed and JM will see Drummond again tonight. GA

10 May: JM has given up on Fleuriau and wants [Paul] Mantoux instead. We will put Mantoux in as Director of Political Intelligence to satisfy Monnet but we won't let him "eat up the organization." GA

16 May: Stephen J. Pinchon [French foreign minister] asked me about placing Monnet as French representative in LN secretariat. He wished to know when the LN would sit in London and how often he would have to attend as French representative. House diary, EMH

--- Pinchon [of French delegation] asked me about placing JM as a French representative on the secretariat of LN. GA

20 May: Had lunch with JM and Gillet on LN organization. "The more I see of Monnet, the better I like him. He is going to be a very great addition to the secretariat of the LN." GA

-----Letter from Drummond [probably] to Robert Cecil discussing LN site, staff etc, mentions JM as adviser. William Wiseman papers, Yale University.

27 May: JM writes long memo on LN goals and institutions which states:
"a) Cooperation between nations will grow from their getting to know each other better....It is therefore important to make both Governments and peoples ...see the problems that face them not from the viewpoint of their own interests but in the light of the general interest.
"b) But if each interested party...is presented with the problem as a whole...all parties' points of view will be modified. Together they will reach a solution that is fair. They will do so all the more readily if they know that the debate is to take place under the eyes of other Governments or peoples who will pass judgment on what they do."
"c) To achieve this result, it is essential that the contact [among Governments and peoples] be constant and not just at the moment of conflict. It is thus necessary to have a permanent system permitting different governments and different peoples to follow continually matters and even to present them to the Council [of the League] without waiting for a crisis to develop.
"d) To achieve these ends, the League needs an assembly, composed of all its members; a Council, composed of France, Britain, the United States, Italy, Japan and the four smaller [Allied] powers; and a permanent international secretariat." DHM Vol IX, 447-53

------- JM aide Renauleaud writes GA (on Conseil Superior Economique letterhead) enclosing JM "draft he had made on the organization of the League of Nations." He encloses second copy for E Drummond. LN Geneva.

28 May: JM gives David Hunter Miller, co-author of Draft Covenant of League of Nations, copy of his LN memo. DHM

29 May: G Auchincloss discusses JM memo on League with Eric Drummond in London. GA

3 Jun: Drummond writes JM in Paris: Everything has been made easier by your definite acceptance of my invitation to work for the League of Nations. LN G

5 Jun: "Monnet does not want to have national representatives at the seat of the LN...but wishes to have each department of each government directly in touch with the international secretariat. This is a good plan if it can be accomplished." GA. [Drummond had the same goal of wanting to deal directly with the governments involved and wanted therefore to avoid permanent missions of members in Geneva. J.Barros, Office Without Power: Secretary General Drummond 1919-1933, (Oxford, 1979), 23-4]

9 Jun: Secret cable to [US Undersecretary of State Frank] Polk from GA: Present plan: Three Under SG: Frenchman is Monnet; Fosdick [US] and Italian, probably Attolico. Each to get 3000 pounds plus l000 more for representation; Drummond to get 4000 and larger representation allowance. GA

---JM gave "exceedingly interesting dinner" at Cafe Madrid [Neuilly, near Paris] with Drummond, GA, Comert, Mantoux, Salter. "I was very much impressed by the enthusiasm shown by the Frenchmen and their appreciation of the ideals surrounding the League and the possibility for their development....Drummond will have to look out or these Frenchmen will have the organization [run] away from him for they are a very able crowd." GA

10 Jun: Letter from Drummond to JM: "You are officially appointed today as one of the directors of the LN and designated as one of four Under Secretaries General." JM pay to be 3000 pounds plus l000 pounds representation plus l000 to the under secretary general I designate as my deputy in my absence. "Your emolument therefore is 5000 pounds per year". JM "Personal File" in LN G.

---Conference on LN organization with Drummond who is leaving for London tomorrow. Drummond, I fear, is scarcely equal to task and Cecil, who advises him, sometimes runs amok. House diary, EMH

A historian of the League of Nations described the important background of the team which Drummond assembled: "...the Secretary General's most important collaborators during this initial period were men who came to their task direct from the control of international administration as developed by the Allied governments as a war-time necessity. Men like Sir Arthur Salter,

Jean Monnet, and Bernardo Attolico, who had together played a leading role in building the Allied Maritime Transport Council and the various conjoint program committees, were not likely to serve as ordinary bureaucrats when they were called upon to organize the Secretariat....During the war they had been accustomed to executive authority and little or no interference from parliamentary organs in developing their essential work. In establishing the Secretariat their psychology was inevitably tinged by past experience and confirmed by the fact that here too they were free from any legislative control. Time was on the side of these early Secretariat builders, for it was a whole year after they began the work of organization in London before any account was rendered to the League Council, and another six months until the first session of the League Assembly was convened". The Society of Nations by Felix Morley, (Carnegie Endowment for World Peace, New York, 1932) 321

Monnet's lack of experience with parliamentary procedures may have influenced him later when, for example, in the construction of the European Coal and Steel institutions, he had to be reminded that an elected assembly would be needed.

12 Jun: "Monet[sic]came in to talk about getting [Dwight] Morrow to help in the organization of the League." GA

17 Jun: Lunch with Drummond and afterward talk with him and JM on LN plans. GA

20 Jun: Edward R Stettinius (senior JP Morgan officer in Paris) cables Dwight Morrow from Paris on talks with JM on a business proposition made by latter's family which might be affected by [alcohol] prohibition [laws] in US. Asks advice. Four days later Morrow cables that there is no chance of prohibition being modified. ERS.

23 Jun: "Drove to Cafe Madrid and picked up Monet [sic] to motor into town. Monet lives there and I consider it a perfectly good place to live---just near enough to Paris to be convenient and at the same time quiet and cool." [The Cafe de Madrid, actually called the Chateau de Madrid, was a resort hotel located in the Paris suburb, Neuilly sur Seine, near the Bois de Boulogne]. GA

26 Jun: Stettinius sends JM (both in Paris) copy of cable from Morrow (subject unknown) and asks JM for list of British, French and Italian food requirements during next 12 months, specifying only those goods to be procured in US. ERS

29 Jun: JM dines at Prof. Mantoux's home with Commert and Auchincloss. GA

Although there is no hint of Monnet's equivocation about finally taking a senior post with the League of Nations, he did become engaged in mid-summer in a plan to obtain a sequestered German champagne company for the JG Monnet Co. Perhaps he was only thinking of a means to help the family firm without his direct participation. Yet such an expansion would have been difficult for 65 year old Jean Gabriel Monnet without the assistance of his older son.

7 Jul: Stettinius, of Paris branch of JP Morgan, cables Morrow in New York on JM plan to buy sequestered wine stocks of unnamed company in wine/spirits business with JP Morgan Co. financing. Stettinius cautious and asks for NY office advice. ERS

10 Jul: [Gordon Auchincloss in London] "Met Fosdick. Told him he should concentrate [in LN] on labor, women's issues, with Drummond focusing on diplomatic and Monet[sic] on economic lines. Had a talk with Monet who asked me to get Col. House to write to Clemenceau to name Tardieu as France's representative at the League. Told him I would try." GA

11 Jul: From London where he has just resigned from US Peace Conference delegation, Gordon Auchincloss writes Sir William Wiseman in New York that Drummond "is working hard at the League and is now assisted by Monnet who ...will run away with everything that is not nailed down." Wiseman papers, Yale.

26 Jul: Morrow tells Stettinius that New York Federal Reserve Bank advice inclines him against JP Morgan [NY] involvement in Monnet plan for purchase of Mumm champagne company. Thinks idea has great merit, however and perhaps Morgan Harjes (the Paris branch) can become involved in plan with US bank branches in Paris. ERS.

31 Jul: Raymond Fosdick, the American LN deputy secretary general, writes that his boss, Eric Drummond, believes the League of Nations is inevitable with increasing economic interdependence of the world. "Monnet and I were inclined to qualify this point of view. We do not feel time is running on our side.... This generation is in a race with anarchy and Monnet and I stressed the point that the world has very little time in which to set up the framework of international government and establish the habit of teamwork." RBF 17-18

1 Aug: Dinner with JM at American Club [London]. "Monnet is rather tired out and seems to be worried about every little thing....His information is not as good as it used to be and he needs to get away for a rest." GA

Monnet carefully maintained many of his wartime contacts with British and American friends. He called upon them for help in his family cognac business which is not doing well. Helping run a new world organization while worrying about the family business may account for the frazzled Monnet whom Auchincloss met in London.

4 Aug: Gordon Auchincloss, leaving US Delegation, says goodbye to JM and Aubert "with great regret." GA

9 Sep: JM introduces Pierre Denis, former colleague in London during war, to Drummond. Denis later takes LN position in political section. LN G

11 Sep: Benjamin Strong, deputy head NY Federal Reserve Bank, has London dinner at Ritz Hotel with JM and Lord Kindersley, JM's friend from Hudson's Bay Co. days. JM "advanced the rather radical theory that the only thing that will cure Europe of its present distress is pain and suffering and the best way is to have it promptly and get through with it, letting down bars all around and forcing people to a realization that the war has entailed losses which can only be recovered by hard work and economy. It struck me that his ideas were a bit fatalistic." BS journal, FRBNY.

12, 19 Sep: Fosdick, JM and others of the League of Nations secretariat are regular visitors to Colonel Edward House, President Wilson's aide, in Paris. House diary, EMH

---Stettinius writes JM a humorous poem about a distressing physical reaction he had after a seafood dinner with Monnet. ERS.

25 Sep: GA writes JM from US: You haven't been a good correspondent. No doubt you follow the political fight here; "I can assure you that the Treaty and the League of Nations will be passed without amendment...." GA.

4 Oct: Drummond writes Raymond Fosdick, deputy SG in Washington, on LN site, proposing compromise, apparently suggested by JM, under which Brussels would be temporary seat of League which would eventually move to Geneva when buildings there are ready and after the LN has been able to keep in close contact with Western Powers. RBF 82

16 Oct: JM in League office in Paris (10 rue Paquet) writes D Morrow and E Stettinius, separately, on French delegates to the coming Washington Labour Conference. DWM; ERS

22 Oct: JM participates in LN Secretariat meeting of Directors just before Peace Treaty enters into force. In discussion of timing of entry, JM points out some problem of premature entry: Allied forces not yet in position to supervise plebescites nor has Supreme Council made all arrangements for these votes; also, the Armistice lapses with treaty entry yet Germany has not yet withdrawn from the Baltic states. This would make the League responsible for enforcing Germany's withdrawal, a difficult task. FJM LN File

6 Nov: Long, detailed outline [probably written by JM for study by JP Morgan Co] on how a champagne business would be formed and operate using sequestered wine from a French government sale. ERS

12 Nov: JM, at London meeting of secretary-general staff, warns that international labor conference underway in Washington is happening in isolation from Europe. He is worried that "this first experiment in cooperation, unless it works a conspicuous success, would weaken the system of cooperation in general." Drummond agrees and asks JM to draft something to Fosdick in Washington. JM warns that the labor conference "might be, in fact, the first

and last attempt at cooperation between labour, employers and governments, as opposed to the methods of the [Communist] Internationale."

JM also describes French government system of liaison with LN: L Bourgeois, the permanent LN Council member, will have a principal assistant at Geneva. Each foreign ministry department will have one officer responsible for LN affairs who communicates directly to corresponding secretariat office through a Central Office (under Bourgeois) which foreign ministry will establish. [This is JM's own plan which he has persuaded French government to adopt.] JM also expresses need for LN secretariat to make better explanations "to the world of the aims and spirit of the [LN] work. Mantoux Papers, LN G; FJM LN File

13 Nov: Stettinius gives JM long and pessimistic account of economic and political situation in US and concludes mood does not favor peace treaty ratification. ERS

1 Dec: In letter from Fosdick to Drummond, Col.House, with President Wilson behind him, rejects Monnet plan for temporary League headquarters in Brussels. RBF 81-2

2 Dec: Anonymous memo to Stettinius, probably by Dean Jay of Morgan's Paris office, on background of JG Monnet company and family. [Part of it is obviously wrong, e.g. describing three Monnet sons etc., but it apparently is requested by Stettinius or others in JP Morgan & Co who believe they need to know more of Monnet's background for future business dealings]. ERS

Monnet assembles an international staff for his League work. Renauleaud is his personal assistant at the temporary London headquarters of the League and Dr. Dixon is his private secretary. He also has Mlle Sylvestre as a private secretary in London with Mlle Chazulon as her assistant. In Paris he has Rene Cassin as a personal assistant where he also has Mlle Jauny as a stenographer. Over his three years with the League, this staff changes but Monnet usually keeps several nationalities engaged.

By October 1922, he has acquired Pierre Denis as his principal assistant in Geneva, Henri Bonnet as personal assistant, Mme Schlesser as his private secretary with Mlles Jauny, Mayres and Hakanauer as assistant secretaries.

His staff grew in size with his responsibilities. Although named as one of four assistant secretaries general in 1919, he soon became Drummond's principal aide, eventually with the title Deputy Secretary General. His pay was initially 3000 pounds sterling a year with a 1000 pound expenses allowance. Later another 1000 pounds was added to his salary with the additional duties. In a November 1921 League report, JM was listed with Drummond as the leadership for general policy matters and to supervise the staff directors, while the other assistant secretaries general handled the routine headquarters business.(From LN documents in New York and Geneva)

1920

1920-28: JG Monnet Co cognac firm has important contract with Wine and Spirit Corporation of Stockholm for exclusive export of cognac to Sweden. W&S

16 Jan: First meeting of Council of the League of Nations in Paris. Saarland is put under League control for 15 years with French ownership of its coal mines as compensation to French for German destruction of its own coal fields during the war. FPW 89-90. JM proposes a referendum on final disposition of territory but France refuses. JMM 91

21 Jan: JM dines with Dean Jay, recently arrived American member of Morgan, Harjes, Paris affiliate of J P Morgan. Jay has replaced E R Stettinius and will now deal with JM on Mumm proposal. ERS

22 Jan: Letter from League staff member Huntington Gilchrist to Fosdick, who has just resigned from LN secretariat, quotes Drummond saying he "is most enthusiastic about the way JM has organized the French Government for liaison with the League but Monnet does not enjoy looking over papers and giving the careful consideration to some of the memoranda and special problems which are presented...." RBF 111-12

31 Mar: LN Directors meeting discusses Siberian prisoners of war which Noel-Baker proposes for a coming special meeting of the LN Council. JM warns that the high cost of "no less than 8m pounds" would present the League with a great difficulty in raising such funds. We should raise the funds first, he says, to avoid a debacle for the League if it identifies the problem but cannot then solve it. FJM LN File

27 Apr: Cable from Morgan, Harjes to E Stettinius in NY that French government may sell assets of Mumm company in next few weeks. ERS

JUNE: Leon Bourgeois, French representative at the League Council, announces that E Drummond, the secretary general, has appointed JM to Drummond's place in organizing the International Financial Conference to open in Brussels in September. LN Official Journal, I:4:148, LN NY

19 Jun: Dean Jay (Paris) writes E Stettinius (NY) on status of Monnet wine business deal which he implies is dependent on how the French government will sell Mumm firm assets including foreign distribution rights. ERS

7 Jul: E Stettinius acknowledges Dean Jay 19 June letter and awaits further developments on Mumm deal in fall. Assumes Morgan Harjes can withdraw if advisable. ERS.

28 Jul: French government puts end to hopes of JM of acquiring sequestered champagne firm when it offers Mumm assets for sale; on 4 August they are sold to new corporation set up by former employees as Successors to G H Mumm & Co. F. Bonal, Champagne Mumm, Paris, n.d.,92-3

16 Sep: JM goes from London to Paris for League Council meeting. LN NY

24 Sep: International Financial Conference starts in Brussels with JM having major organizing responsibility. LN NY

OCTOBER: JM closely involved in League of Nation's economic conference in Brussels which is first LN conference. Attended by 75% of world population including Germany. JMM 95-96

20 Oct: JM to Brussels for League assembly meeting and then to Geneva where League will relocate. LN/NY. Move from London to Geneva made despite opposition of French government and of JM after President Wilson insists that he has authority to convene first Assembly session which he does in Geneva. Barros, Secretary Drummond, 81-84

1 Nov: League seat transfers from London to Geneva. LNR

15 Nov: First LN Assembly session opened in Geneva by President Wilson. LNR

------- Austria admitted to League of Nations. LNR

20 Nov: JM is secretary to Assembly Committee IIB. LN NY

31 Dec: Drummond advises secretariat that JM has been given responsibility for all technical organizations of the League under Drummond's authority. LN G

As he gains the trust of Drummond, Monnet expands his fields of responsibilities. As his months with the League grows into his second year he works on two major League problems: Austria and Upper Silesia, the first with some success, the second with only the effect of postponing an eventual collapse of confidence among the contending powers.

1921

5 Jan: League Secretariat Directors meeting discusses improving secretariat-Council-Member State relations. JM notes greater difficulties dealing with Member States in Geneva than secretariat experienced in London headquarters. He advocates each Member name a Council representative responsible for creating an organism in home capital to keep him informed of government departments interested in League matters. This Council member in turn should have a personal assistant who spends time in both Geneva and the home capital. JM warns that these assistants must not form their own sub-council in Geneva. He also advocates each Member state name an officer in charge of League affairs, probably someone in the Foreign Office. FJM LN File

28 Feb: (Mon) Paris: [Ritz Hotel] "...M. Monet[sic] has been here--- charming as ever. [The Morrows are on their first postwar visit to Europe and enjoy the companionship of JM who also helps in their travel plans]. ECM

MARCH: Financial Committee of LN Secretariat, under A Salter and aided by JM, starts work on reconstruction of Austria. "In March 1921, our task was to prevent an exhausted Austria becoming a prey to other countries....It was there that I realized the value of collective action, and the need to associate in a common enterprise, as equals, both victors and vanquished, both givers and receivers of aid...." JMM 91-92

-----: Voting takes place in Upper Silesia which has a mixed German-Polish population. Results favor Germany keeping control of territory but Poland threatens military occupation to protect its nationals. Allied forces intervene to prevent outright conflict and the League of Nations undertakes challenge of finding a fair solution between the neighboring countries. JM is deeply involved. JMM 87-88

6 Mar: (Sun) Paris: "M. Monet[sic] came for breakfast and stayed all morning talking about the League of Nations. I thought he talked very well. D[wight] is unconvinced. He feels he is trying to go too fast w. the League---not content w. things it can really accomplish. Monet goes to Barcelona tomorrow to a conference called by the League---delegates fr. all over the world to consider transit questions." ECM

12 Mar: (Sat) Paris: "tonight M. Monnet w. Mr Ribeanau or something like that and M. Carpentier took us to George V restaurant. M. Monnet very entertaining." ECM

4 Apr: League Financial Committee states main conditions for Austria reconstruction: Postponement of debts and drastic internal reforms. The Restoration of Austria, by Arthur Salter, Geneva, 1922. LN doc C.716M.428

20 Apr-10 May: First Conference on Communications and Transit, Barcelona, which JM helps organize. LNR; LN NY.

21 Apr: JM writes Kindersley at Hudson's Bay Co., London, after returning from Barcelona conference; advises HBC on how to transfer company ships (which France financed during war) to French ownership. HBC, French government business files

12 May: Soon after returning from the Barcelona conference, and at a Director's meeting of the LN Secretariat, JM speaks forcefully for the role of the Opium Commission and similar bodies as adjuncts to the League's work. He calls for the appearance at Assembly sessions of various commission chairmen and for corresponding efforts to identify these commissions as League functions, mutually strengthening the institutions. FJM LN-G File

24 May: Lamont writes Col. George B. Harvey, American Ambassador in London, suggesting he meet JM: "[Dwight] Morrow has always characterized Monnet as the wisest man in France...." While he works for the League of Nations, "his chief interest lies in the firm, broad settlement of European affairs."

LA

29 May: JM meets in London with M Norman, Bank of England; B Blackett, British Treasury, J Avenol, French Finance Ministry and others on Austria. As summer proceeds, opposition develops among private creditors to waiving their liens on Austria leaving the country in crisis. H.Clay, Lord Norman (London, 1957) 182-3; NP II 554-5

23 June: Lamont complains to JM that Drummond wrote him the "most despairing wail that I ever heard" on need for Lamont to do something [toward gaining Administration support for the League.] LA

Monnet's work at the League of Nations is sometimes distracted by problems in Cognac with the family firm. He tries to aid his father and his brother, Gaston, in running the cognac business: first, by supporting their efforts to guide and expand the firm but later, by spring, 1922, by directly seeking funds to keep the company alive.

4 Aug: Dean Jay of Morgan, Harjes, Paris writes letter of introduction for JM's brother, Gaston, to Stettinius and Morrow at request of JM. Gaston is traveling to Canada via USA for JG Monnet Co and wants information on possible changes in US prohibition legislation which might allow import of Monnet brandies. Jay indicates Stettinius probably knows Gaston already from earlier discussions in Paris on Mumm proposal. JM has warned Jay that Gaston tends to be naively optimistic and suggests that JP Morgan officials should therefore temper their remarks accordingly. ERS

11 Aug: United States invites major powers to disarmament conference in Washington. FPW 145

12 Aug: To great public skepticism, France and Britain, unable to agree on Upper Silesia solution, ask League Council to handle problem of compromising German and Polish interests. FPW 145. JM takes major role: "I resolved to devote myself utterly to making it a success." JMM 87-88

12 Oct: Using earlier referendum results, four rapporteurs, aided by secretariat staff and outside advisers, produces report on Upper Silesia which Council accepts and forwards to Supreme War Council. Plan would divide industrial heartland of area between German and Polish authorities with joint commission to resolve problems. FPW 153-4; JMM 88-91

24 Oct: HBC and JG Monnet & Co renew trading agreement. HBC III

28 Dec: JM reports at a Director's meeting of the LN Secretariat on his return from a visit to the Saar with two secretariat colleagues. They saw all Saar Commission members and studied its past actions and future policies. The Commission, under the Peace Treaty, does not in fact govern the Saar, JM said, because the earlier German administration was still largely in place and hostile to the League's commission. Strong social and political sentiments still tie the Saar

to Germany, especially in Saarbrueken, the capital. The area's economy is well placed to benefit from the different exchange rates in France and Germany. The commission's role is a difficult one: to prepare the territory to decide, in a vote in 15 years, on whether to adhere to France or Germany or for autonomy. FJM LN File

1922

5 Jan: JM leads discussion in LN Secretariat's meeting of directors on the proposed Cannes conference on commercial relations and assistance to Russia and other eastern European countries. A key question is reestablishment of relations with Russia, including de jure recognition, and that country's view of a business consortium of the kind to be considered at Cannes. The League must take an active role in such a conference; otherwise it would be considered irrelevant. As for the United States, JM said, it would come along once it saw real work was being done by the League. FJM LN File

FEBRUARY: JM agrees at Paris meeting with French, Czech and British representatives on Austrian reconstruction plan to coordinate efforts and refer problem to LN financial affairs committee. NP I citing 12 Feb 22 memo from J Avenol to French Minister of Finance.

24 Feb: JM discusses possible approaches to Austrian reconstruction with Basil Blackett, British treasury official: JM, in agreement with A Salter, head of the League's financial affairs section, says Austria must have an impartial fiscal controller who will not put the country under domination of either private capital or another country. LN G, cited in NP II 63

10 Mar: JM, at a Directors meeting of the LN Secretariat, says the coming Genoa meeting's prospects are entirely changed with the breakup of the Cannes meeting. An enhanced role of the League is one consequence of the recent meeting of the British and French prime ministers about Genoa. FJM LN File.

SPRING: American creditors reject League's Financial Committee's plan for Austria which proposes combining postponing debt repayments with Austrian governmental reform. FPW 46

28 Mar: Hudson's Bay Company board discusses JM need for funds for family business and in compensation for his WWI work for HBC. It agrees to loan him 40,000 pounds [about $2 million in 2007 values] under such favorable conditions that the sum and interest need not be repaid. Original loan was to repaid in 19 months but terms are later relaxed. HBC IV

13 May: JM-HBC loan agreement signed. HBC IV

15 May: German-Polish Convention on Upper Silesia signed after resistance of France, Germany and Poland is overcome. Regime to last for 15 years. FPW 156-7. Drummond and JM play vital role with their "intelligence, a sense of reality and of the international possibilities, working day and night and

with perfect loyalty" to the Council. L.Bourgeois, L'Oeuvre de la Societe des Nations 1920-23, Paris, l923, 267-8; JMM 90

28 Jun: JM reports at Directors meeting of LN Secretariat on his recent mission to Prague with five other secretariat officials. The goal was to establish ties with the new country with League officials. The trip was performed at a very discreet level without speeches or receptions and was very successful. It should be followed, he says, by a more public visit by the LN Council President and the Secretary General. FJM LN File

13 Jul: Paris "...tonight Mr. Monnet here (Ritz Hotel) for dinner and Judge Hand. Mary Hand came and dined with our girls and Mrs. G. downstairs.... Monnet, Judge Hand and D[wight] and I had a fine talk upstairs and after the judge had gone. Monnet stayed until almost l talking with us. He is as charming and fascinating as ever. ECM

14 Jul: (Bastille Day). "Tonight we took Elsie and McClure Day to Monnet's for dinner and their children and ours watched the fireworks and dancing in the streets". ECM

Jul 25: Gaston Monnet cables financier Ivar Kreuger at Swedish Match asking to meet tomorrow after Gaston arrives by boat in Stockholm. V

Monnet's deepening involvement with Austria's reconstruction coincides with increasing problems back in Cognac with the family business. The two unrelated events come to decisive stages by the end of the year. Over the next few years he must call again on old business friends from the war years for major financial assistance to preserve the family cognac firm.

AUGUST: Austria situation approaches crisis with its government proclaiming itself without resources to continue; Allies turn problem over to League. FPW 206-8

14 Aug: Allied powers refuse to guarantee loan to Austria, apparently rejecting any further responsibility for crisis. NP I 68

22 Aug: At Directors meeting of the LN Secretariat, Secretary General Drummond, JM and others discuss coming Assembly session and tendency of some delegations to avoid taking position by simply registering their "voeux" or wishes instead of passing resolution. JM and P Mantoux (of legal section) agree on this point but Drummond cautions that expressing "voeux" has some advantages. FJM LN File

31 Aug: League Council accepts active role in Austria. FPW 205-8

SEPTEMBER: League Council asks secretariat to work on Austria with Monsignor Seipel, head of Austrian government; Edouard Benes, Czech foreign minister and French and Italian delegates. JM, Salter, Basil Blackett of British treasury meet privately at a picnic on shores of Lake Geneva on Austria problem;

JM proposes a solution by involving major powers all of whom are anxious that no other power has predominant position. NP I 68; A Salter, Slave of the Lamp, London 1962, 98; JMM 94

4 Oct: Final and successful phase of League Austrian role starts with signing at Geneva of protocols on financial reconstruction. Confidence in country revives and Alfred Zimmerman of Netherlands proposed as LN Commissioner General for Austria. LNR; FPW 210; NP I 69

14-16 Nov: JM gets agreement from Zimmerman, currently lord mayor of Rotterdam, Netherlands to serve as Austrian controller. NP II 635

27 Nov: JM writes memo on his trip to Rotterdam where he tried to overcame Zimmerman's reluctance to take Austrian position. NP II 635

--------: Law of Reconstruction adopted by Austrian government. NP I 77

DECEMBER: Zimmerman, Austria's new Commissioner-General, arrives in Vienna after JM plays important role in recruiting him. NP II 636-7

18 Dec: JM sends letter of resignation to Drummond. LN G; Earlier, his sister Marie Louise had visited him in Geneva and explained that their father was having trouble with the cognac business. "I am not in the habit of quarrelling with necessity; I resigned from the League of Nations, although I enjoyed my work there and had the feeling that a great deal more could usefully be done. I certainly did not leave out of disenchantment with the League's weakness...If I had [realized how weak it was] I should have gone to great lengths to stay in a job where I could contribute to the maintenance of peace." JMM 99

With his departure from the League of Nations, Monnet returned to private life after over eight years in public service. In the coming years, he will maintain his interest in the League's work for peace and his many friendships from the years of the war and its aftermath. But now, at age 35, he must settle into a new life back in Cognac trying to preserve the family business. He has learned many management skills during his work for the French government during the war and for the League in Geneva. He needs these back home. He is also a creature of habit and discipline as seen in the management of his personal affairs.

He seeks separate living quarters outside of Cognac instead of living in the family home. And he buys his cherished office furniture from his League offices which, in turn, the League had earlier purchased in London, at Monnet's insistence, from the French government's Ministry of Commerce at the end of war. The incident shows the desire of Monnet for a comfortable and familiar office environment back home, his patience and persistence in pursuing that modest goal in a petty bureaucratic dispute, and, perhaps a bit of sentimentality for the furniture he has used in war and peace.

1923

JANUARY: JM buys his League of Nations office furniture which he had brought earlier from his WWI London job with the French Ministry of Commerce. The 1919 transaction engenders a prolonged dispute between the French government and the League over the value of an office desk and chair, several upholstered chairs and other equipment with a value of about eighty pounds sterling. Two years later the matter is still in dispute; JM intervenes to pay the French government what it asks (slightly over one hundred pounds) to settle the difference between the prices set by the two bureaucracies. With his departure from the League, JM pays to take the now heavily used furniture to his Cognac office. Jean Monnet dossier, document 888, LN G

11 Jan: France, under now Prime Minister Poincare, invades and occupies the Ruhr because Germany fails to deliver coal as part of its reparations payments. RM 37

2 Mar: JM writes to Deputy Governor General Charles Sale at HBC that he is traveling to Sweden [from London] in first half of March. HBC IV

10 Mar: In letter from C Sale to Lord Kindersley, former reports that during his recent visit in London JM has asked HBC for new 80,000 pound credit [about $4 million in 2007 values] against a French franc credit; also asks for revision of his 40,000 pound loan to allow franc repayment. JM told Sale that family firm's indebtedness is 9m French francs but assets are 2m francs more. Firm is trying to sell 4m franc of older brandies. HBC official Sale is doubtful about new loan, writing "As things are I did not think it either possible or wise to offer any encouragement...." Ltr Sale to Kindersley, HBC IV

23 May: JM asks to be relieved of 1922 obligation to furnish guarantees for his 40,000 pound loan. HBC IV

31 May: A Salter thanks Morrow for his work at J P Morgan on US share of Austrian loan under LN reconstruction, noting JM, Salter and Morrow are renewing their WWI work "in this most interesting of post-war jobs." HN 244.

19 Jun: JM writes C Sale of HBC from St Raphael where he is on brief vacation, thanking for help in modifying earlier loan terms. HBC IV

9 Nov: JM's 35th birthday coincides with Adolf Hitler's coup attempt in Munich for which the Nazi party founder is imprisoned. Every year hereafter the Nazi party marks this day with special demonstrations and worse, culminating in 1938 with Kristallnacht, the start of organized violence against German Jews. Ian Kershaw, Hitler, 1889-1936, (London, 1998) 206-11

27 Nov: HBC reports to JM on difficulties in selling JG Monnet cognac in Canada, as confirmed by Georges Monnet (JM's cousin) who recently went there on behalf of the family firm. HBC III

1924

Back home in Cognac, Monnet rents a small house, the Alsace, to maintain privacy as he engages in painful task of reorganizing the family

business which involves moving his elderly father aside. The family business is stabilized, avoiding bankruptcy, but Monnet himself is impatient to return to more demanding tasks in the world of international affairs he had grown to like. He finds one link to this outside world through his family's ties to the renown Swedish businessman, Ivar Kreuger.

21 Sept: JM meets in Paris with Sale and Georges Monnet on HBC business in Canada with Societe des Proprietaires Vinicoles de Cognac (SVP) which is new name for former Monnet business United Vineyard Proprietors of Cognac (UVP). In memo on the meeting JM expresses "great importance" the firm places on their "great and ancient relations." HBC III

1925

6 Mar: Helmi Monnet (Gaston's Swedish-born wife) cables Ivar Kreuger, the Swedish "match king" and international financier, asking for a meeting in Paris or Stockholm. V, vol 25 Corr STAB "M" (Helmi's family was apparently close to Kreuger since she and Gaston had lived in a Kreuger apartment in Stockholm in 1918 when Gaston was in military service in the Swedish capital. AR)

20 Mar: Kreuger writes Helmi (in French): Regret cannot come to Paris now but I'll tell you when I can. V, vol 25 Corr STAB "M"

9 Apr: Gaston Monnet writes Kreuger seeking a guarantee of a loan GM needs to make to cover obligations from fall of the French franc. Helmi Monnet cables Kreuger simultaneously saying she and Gaston must sell their house to obtain the 4500 pounds needed to "straighten out our situation." Kreuger refuses (April 17) citing similar position of many of his Swedish friends in financial crises who have asked for help and whom he has had to refuse. V

14 Jul(Paris): "...D[wight] invited the Leffingwells, Mr. Monnet, his sister Mme [Henriette] Chaumet and her husband etc to dinner. I sat next to Mr. Monnet who is so lovely." ECM

21 Jul: [After visiting Bidart] "...then drove to M. Monnet's sweet little house[in Cognac]---the Alsace. Dinner at 8. Mr. Filliout [sic] also there---very merry dinner--many wine glasses. Mr. M. wanted us to try everything. We left in the morning, sent on our way with flowers and wine. Lunch at Bordeaux. ECM

Monnet used several devices to ease the financial straits of the JG Monnet firm. After his failed attempt to expand the firm by buying the assets of the Mumm champagne company, Monnet borrowed a large sum from Hudson's Bay Co. But the family firm finances are still shaky; he proposed investment in brandy futures to several British and American friends to raise money for the firm. By the end of 1925, Monnet has apparently stabilized the family firm's finances and set it on a more modest business course. But he wants to make his own future beyond Cognac. With help from American friends, he gets a job with an New York investment bank.

8 Aug: JGM Co ltr to Wine & Spirit Corp, Stockholm on details of sales; refers to coming visit of JM. W&S

17 Aug: JM writes Morrow from Grand Hotel, Stockholm; regrets missing Morrows in Bidart, France but had to go to Sweden after seeing them in Cognac because family firm has sole right of importing wines and spirits into Sweden. Hopes to see them back in Paris. DWM.

29 Aug-6 Sep in Paris. No mention of JM but only of seeing [his friend] Louise Weiss. ECM

DECEMBER: Morrow writes that his son considers JM one of "small group which tries to get things done for which other people get credit." HN 286; JMM 519-20

10 Dec: D Morrow in NY writes JM in Paris: Much has happened since I saw you in the beautiful Cognac country. DWM.

12 Dec: JM (in Cognac) writes to Dean Jay, Morgan, Harjes, Paris, on brandy syndicate JM is trying to set up. DWM.

15 Dec: "Last Sat JM left for Sweden on important business." Ltr from JGMCo to Charles Sale, HBC IV

18 Dec: Dean Jay, Paris, writes D. Morrow, NY, [both of JP Morgan bank] on status of brandy syndicate, adding JM went to Sweden until end of month. DWM

19 Dec: JM (Stockholm) cables Morrow in NY: Arrive NYC about 12 Jan. DWM.

1926

5 Jan: JM letter from Paris (in French) to Morrow in NYC on brandy syndicate details. DWM.

14 Jan: Letter from Renauleaud, JM aide, to Dean Jay, Paris, on division of shares in brandy syndicate: Jay, Kindersley and Morrow, each to invest 5000 pounds; JM 3000; Robert Brand, 2000. Letter adds that as JM has already said, he has started the brandy purchases. DWM

------:Elizabeth Morrow leaves for Cleveland. JM arrives in Englewood NJ home of Morrows. ECM

19 Feb: JM writes Morrow as he leaves NYC: Regret missing you (Morrow is in Cuba). JM discusses Blair job offer which he has decided to take and which will end his need to rely on his friends. [JM was on business trip to Canada and US with his cousin, Georges, on behalf of the family cognac term]. DWM

20 Feb: JM sails from NYC to Southampton on SS Aquitania. HBC III; DWM

APRIL: JM tries without success to see journalist Walter Lippmann at latter's request in Paris after their messages cross. [They had apparently known each other at the Versailles Peace Conference]. Lippmann papers, Yale University

17 May: New York Federal Reserve Bank official B. Strong talks with JM and others in Paris on weak franc and lack of recovery plan at Banque de France. The next day Strong and JM talk again who had discussed matter with P Laval, Minister of Justice but government still without a plan. Strong memo to Harrison 23 May 1926, FRBNY

26 May: Strong reports from Rome on his Paris talks on French franc stabilization including several meetings with JM during 17-20 May. FRBNY

24 Jun: Briand government falls after six weeks in office; successor government is led by Edouard Herriot which immediately names Emile Moreau as head of Banque de France with goal of stabilizing franc. Moreau stays in post when Poincare government succeeds Herriot's on 25 July. EM GF, xvi-ii

26 Jun: B Strong reports from Europe to his deputy, G Harrison at FRBNY that Arthur Salter wrote Clarence Dillon in Paris that JM and Salter discussed a League of Nations loan plan for Poland and that JM, now with Blair and Co, was very impressed with idea. M Norman of Bank of England also wants a LN role for Poland but Poles strongly opposed idea both for political character of League but also because US banks, which Poland has approached, would back away from any LN connection. FRBNY

Monnet's new position with Blair & Co relied on his experience in WW I and with the League of Nations in rebuilding Austria and managing multinational problems. Now, as private banker, he must assess the interests of his company, its competitive status and raise private capital, all different from working for an intergovernmental agency. Monnet proved adaptable and inventive with these new problems as his successful experience in Poland showed.

30 Jun: Robert Warren of FRBNY reports to B Strong twice by detailed memos on talks in Paris on French franc stabilization: Banque de France has no confidence among "any important element;" it has no reform program and apparently no interest in one; Dean Jay [of JP Morgan, Paris] asked me to see JM but I will not do so, I said, without your permission. FRBNY

1 Jul: A Salter writes JM, now busy in his new job with Blair & Co, reflecting on Austrian reconstruction plan of the LN: There were few people who played a determining role and you were first among them. For my part, I do not think that in September 1922 the League of Nations would have taken a serious effort to solve the [Austrian] problem if you had not taken it in hand." LN G

17 Jul: Mob attacks Palais de Bourbon, where Chamber of Deputies is meeting,over inflation and sharp fall in value of franc. EM GF, xvi

24 Jul: JM meets E Moreau, head of Banque de France, for first time

through Charles Rist,[the bank's leading economist.]. JM is friend of B Strong, FRBNY and other eminent foreigners, Moreau notes. EM 43

2 Aug: JM sees Moreau as go-between for B Strong on franc stabilization. EM 58-9

Benjamin Strong of the New York Federal Reserve Bank, Dwight Morrow of JP Morgan Co. and Ludwig Rajchman of the League of Nation's Health Organization, are typical of the friends Monnet made during and just after World War I and who became business associates and personal friends. Morrow and Rajchman, in different ways, aided JM's career as he moved from public service to private investment banking.

SUMMER: JM establishes contact with Polish Ministry of Treasury through an intermediary [L Rajchman, a Polish medical doctor whom JM had known at the League of Nations] Pease 86

JULY-AUGUST: Undated letter from JM at League of Nations, Geneva, to Morrow discussing plans for latter to visit Geneva and lunch with E. Benes [Czech patriot and later president of his country]. DWM

AUGUST: Blair and Co of New York forms French subsidiary with JM as vice president. JMM 102

27 Aug. Paris: Tonight, M. Monnet took us all to Montmartre to dine with M. Benand (great friend of Berenger) and Mlle Louise Weiss. We ate outdoors under lovely acadia trees and a moon in a little square. Many tables, wandering artists, songs, flowers for sale etc. Later to Le Lapin Agile, a very small caberet where Pere Eddy---looking like Santa Claus---sang and played a guitar. ECM

1 Sep: B Strong and Governor Ivanoff of Banque National de Bulgaria meet in Paris at JM suggestion and discuss stabilization loan. FRBNY; This was apparently the start of an attempt by Blair & Co to arrange this loan. The American tranche failed to be achieved in autumn 1928 and further attempts were dropped after the stock market crash the next year. EB I 119; TCF 506

4 Sep: [Geneva] "...D[wight] dined with Sir Arthur Salter and Monnet. Benes---Czech Prime Minister was there and very interesting". ECM

6 Sep: "A wonderful day....Mr. Monnet got [train] tickets for us all ...."(ECM). JM sees Morrows off on train for Paris after helping them get sleeping accommodations. AML I 42

SEPTEMBER: Undated letter from JM (at Hyde Park Hotel, London) to Morrow giving latter addresses of Avenol, Hagenau and Quesnay and thanking for visit [to Geneva] DWM

23 Oct: Albert Thomas, head of International Labor Office, writes JM at 14 Rue de Conde on regrets on missing each other for lunch in Paris. FJM LN File

JM apparently acquired the small townhouse on Rue de Conde in 1926 as his base in Paris for his new position with Blair & Co. In fact, he spent relatively little time at his new home in the decade he owned it. But he later told Francois Fontaine that he regretted selling the building which was well located near the French National Assembly on the Left Bank. This central location was, in fact, an exception for Monnet who preferred to live outside of the city so he could walk in the country, a lifelong habit. FF I

11 Nov: A Thomas notifies E Drummond that JM has been appointed an ILO trustee, jointly with F Nansen, of the ILO Working Capital Fund. LN G

LATE DECEMBER: JM goes to Warsaw with Rajchman after getting invitation from Rajchman's friend, Minister of Foreign Affairs August Zaleski, while in London. JM, in Warsaw, is unaware of simultaneous presence there of Bankers Trust representatives, including Henri Fischer of Paris office, who have obtained agreement on tobacco monopoly loan which excludes other banks. Meanwhile, JM and Foreign Minister Zaleski agree to give Blair sole authority to organize stabilization loan and plan. JM and Rajchman are invited, with central bank head Mlynarski, to dine in Warsaw with Prime Minister Bartel. The next day, Mlynarski has to explain problem to JM and Rajchman. JM, first upset at confusion, agrees with Finance Ministry to solve problem. He returns to Paris where Bankers Trust agrees to a compromise. JMM 103; MLY 286-9; Pease 86

22 Dec: JM receives option from Polish Ministry of Treasury, valid to 22 Jan 1927, to proceed to NYC and negotiate Polish stabilization loan on behalf of Blair and Co and Bankers Trust. ZL 125

29 Dec: Cable from D Jay (Paris) to JP Morgan Co NYC: JM sailed today [arrives 6 Jan per note on cable] and staying at Madison and E. 58 St. DWM Before leaving Paris, JM had worked out conflict with Bankers Trust which agreed to join with Blair in seeking Poland's stabilization loan. MLY 289

30 Dec: Joseph Avenol, JM successor at LN, reports JM arranged Polish accord without Bank of England which pleases Moreau. EM 191

1927

3 Jan: JM is intermediary used by Bank of Poland to open talks with several large American banks toward stabilization of the zloty. EM 192

12 Jan: In New York, JM briefs G Harrison, vice chair FRBNY (in presence of Morrow who set up the meeting) on Blair's plans and actions in Poland on stabilization and development loans. FRBNY

19 Jan: JM sends Harrison documents on Poland from Blair's NYC office as promised at last week's meeting. FRBNY

------ Polish delegation leaves Warsaw for NYC (via Paris to see Banque de France officials) to confirm US stabilization loan which JM is preparing. They also meet Rene Pleven and Pierre Denis, JM's assistants, at Blair office. MLY 290-1

JANUARY: JM is highly respected "chief negotiator" for US banks in NYC discussions with Polish delegation. He is, a Polish principal reports, "not only superb banker but also a great politician, expert in European situation, someone with the great sense of compromise, something he had mastered during the League of Nations." MYL 293

Monnet's success in combining his wartime and League of Nations experience with private banking attracted attention and admiration. However, years later in writing his memoirs he said he could not recall the details of many of these bank transactions, perhaps because they did not fully engage his growing interest in how people and nations can solve problems of peaceful cooperation.

------ G Harrison memo on 12 Jan meeting with Morrow, Montagu Norman of Bank of England, and JP Morgan on Polish bank situation; Morrow also reports on separate talks with JM who had requested meeting with Harrison. FRBNY

21 Jan: Harrison acknowledges JM documents on former's return from North Carolina where he consulted with ailing B Strong. FRBNY

27 Jan: E Moreau reports to Prime Minister Poincare that, at Moreau's suggestion, Banque de Serbia went to B Strong at FRBNY after facing severe conditions proposed by M Norman of the Bank of England over the Serbian bank's external affairs. Monnet than concluded an agreement with M. Novakowitch of BS providing for a loan through Blair & Co to stabilize the dinar.

Moreau also reports on Monnet's work in Warsaw and NYC where he has succeeded in evading the efforts of M. Kraemer, an American representative of B Strong and M Norman to tie the Polish loan to pro-German conditions. Instead Blair will manage the loan, according to JM's reports from NYC who says the Polish representatives will now travel to NYC ostensibly to discuss Kraemer plan but actually to find agreement with his group. EM 213-14

BEFORE MID FEBRUARY: JM visits B Strong for first time in Biltmore, North Carolina; JM "combines wisdom and tact and...can do a great deal" for Poland as he did for France, according to Strong's note to Norman of the Bank of England. FRBNY

18 Feb: JM, Mlynarski (Vice president of the Bank of Poland) and G Harrison meet in NYC with FRBNY staff on Polish loan. FRBNY

24 Feb: Quesnay reports to Moreau that FRBNY is supporting JM plan on Poland and agreement is imminent. "Mr. Norman [of the Bank of England] has to be in a very bad mood because the success of the Monnet scheme means that his own imperialist designs on Poland have been defeated. EM-GF 224. JM has

prepared memo "Preliminary Observations on the Financial Situation in Poland." Loan talks in NYC start on difficult note when JM proposes eight percent interest and an international supervisory board. The Poles balk. Participants agree to refer problem to ailing FRBNY chair B Strong. Pease 89

28 Feb: JM visits Strong second time in North Carolina with Mlynarski and Harrison. FRBNY. Strong finally sides with JM but sweetens deal with assurances controls [on Poland] will be largely symbolic. Pease 89

------ M. Quesnay tells Moreau that JM has succeeded in getting the FRBNY into play with American banks which decided to bypass the Bank of England and use, among others, the Banque de France in helping European countries with financial problems. M Norman has reportedly said he is opposed to JM projects in Poland and Yugoslavia. EM 255 and EM GF 229

4 Mar: NYT reports on financial controls Poland faces in NYC negotiations (led by JM on side of US bankers). NYT 13 Mar. Monnet presses view that foreign financial control is needed not only for customs control (to insure repayment of loans with secured income) but also for entire stabilization plan. ZL 135

18 Mar: JM travels NYC to Paris on SS Aquitania.(Pease 90). G Harrison and Polish delegation also on board. Shipboard discussion concerned how to get the Polish government to accept the preliminary agreement which the two sides signed in New York. They decided to invite the foreign bankers to Warsaw which would make it harder for the Polish government to reject the agreement and also make it more difficult for the bankers to be too rigid. MLY 301-2

25 Mar: Strong writes Norman on Poland including visit by JM. FRBNY.

28 Mar: Before arrival in Warsaw, JM suggests compromise to break impasse over foreign control: B Strong to be an arbitrator. Both sides agree. In Paris, when Moreau hears of plan he comments that JM is cleverly hiding behind the FRBNY. EM 266-7. Landau suggests that JM and Strong had previously arranged for this compromise. ZL 136

------ In discussions with Rist and Quesnay on Poland, they report JM, working behind the FRBNY, has helped B Strong assemble a classic stabilization plan, with budgetary restraints, new taxes, supporting the national bank etc. The Poles also accept an American administrator in Warsaw. EM 267-8

29 Mar: Polish negotiators arrive in Warsaw; JM stops in Paris to brief Moreau. ZL 141, FRBNY. JM advises Moreau, who is to talk with G Harrison soon, that France should not emphasize desire of Banque de France to gain political advantage in Polish loan. EM 268-9

2 Apr: JM travels from Paris to Warsaw for final Polish agreement. Problem arises when Pilsudski demands removal of foreign supervision. Monnet declares this "indecent" and prepares to leave. Compromise removes other

foreigners but leaves American supervisor but other problems delay agreement.
Pease 91

3 Apr: Calais meeting of Harrison, Norman, Schacht (of German Bank),
Moreau and Rist (of French Treasury). EM 273

6 Apr: Harrison lunches with Moreau and agrees with latter's suggestion
that JM accompany Harrison to London. EM GF 250

9 Apr: JM back in Paris after Warsaw visit. DWM; FRBNY.

17 Apr: Norman reports to Strong on talks with JM and suggests League
of Nations role in Polish stabilization. (JM at this point, however, seems to
have abandoned any idea of a LN role in the Polish loan as Norman admits in
subsequent letter to Strong of 22 May.) FRBNY

3 May: JM, Norman, Morrow and Parker-Gilbert, US reparations agent,
meet in Paris on Polish loan without result. EM 298

4 May: Moreau meets JM and Morrow; latter will cable Harrison that
FRBNY must take more active role or Polish loan will fail. EM 298-301; EM GF
268-9

3 Jun: Agreement reached among central banks and FRBNY on Polish
stabilization plan which B Strong did not want to pursue alone (i.e only with
Banque de France). Other western European banks join by mid-June. ZL 151 The
second phase of negotiations between Poland and the banks now began in Paris.
Task is to revise New York accord and finish work soon in Warsaw. JM is chief
negotiator for the banks and John Foster Dulles his legal advisor. MLY 308

SUMMER: Negotiations continue over foreign control question for Polish
stabilization. Poles finally suggest electing the foreign adviser to the Polish
Bank's board to ease the appearance of foreign control and interference. Bankers
accept this and final problem of loan's interest rate is solved in Pilsudski's office
by shortening the amortization period to 20 years (from 30) and reducing the
interest rate to 7% after Pilsudski makes plea: Give me a half a point for Wanda
[his daughter]. JMM 104; MLY 301-7, 314; Pease 99; ZL 141-51.

8 Oct: Final negotiation on price of stabilization bonds. NY lenders agree
on 10 Oct. Pease 100

13 Oct: JM in Warsaw where final loan details agreed and signed: Loan of
$62m at 7 percent for 20 years of which $47m would originate in US. NP 100-1,
FRBNY; JM says "the cash boxes of the world are now opened to Poland and [she]
will be able to get as many loans as she wishes." ZL 245 quoted in Pease 202

*Gaston Monnet, JM's only brother, dies suddenly on October 16 of
appendicitis. JM takes over much responsibility for his widow, Helmi and two
young daughters, Aline and Colette. JM's twin cousins (Georges and Robert, sons
of JGM's brother, Abel) take over operation of family cognac firm which Gaston*

had managed. (CA)

22 Oct: JM in Paris cables G Harrison, FRBNY to arrange JM meeting with Charles Dewey (who is to be foreign adviser and member of Polish bank board) before he leaves NYC for Poland. JM sailing to New York on SS Majestic. FRBNY

------: JM, in Polish magazine interview, gives very optimistic assessment of Polish economy now that stabilization loan is approved: The main purpose of the loan has been achieved, to secure and strengthen the Polish zloty so that everyone will want to invest in Poland. "Tygodnika Ilustrowanego", 22 Oct 1927.

1 Nov: JM arrives in NYC on SS Majestic (cable to Harrison). FRBNY.

With his birthday on November 9, Monnet enters his 40th year with a growing reputation as a skilled international banker with a sensitive political touch. He is head of Blair's European operations and his work is followed closely and with growing admiration by Elisha Walker, head of Blair & Co, New York.

15, 28 Dec: General Antonescu represents Rumania in talks with E Moreau at Banque de France to consider a loan. JM is invited to Bucharest, with Gaston Jeze of the Paris law faculty, to study stabilization plans. Because of rivalries among French banks, Antonescu has decided for time being to negotiate loans only with American banks. RHM 104-5; EM 461; EM GF 400, 407-8

1928

JANUARY: JM aide Rene Pleven assesses Polish loan and concludes its significance was the role played for first time in such a plan by the FRBNY (aided by the Banque de France) and the consequent diminution of the role of the central banks of England and Germany. Revue d'Economique Politique (Paris), vol 1 (1928) 80-1.

17 Jan: JM and Denis leave Paris for Bucharest. FRBNY; JMM 105

21 Jan: Norman, of Bank of England, cables Strong, FRBNY, that JM is in Bucharest. RHM 105

10 Feb: C Sale writes JM on HBC plan to open a French affiliate to buy French goods for its Canadian stores. JM is asked to be one of the French "subscribers" of the new firm which was eventually established as Compagnie de la Baie. HBC V

21 Feb: Moreau tells Prime Minister Poincare that JM has received letter from Rumanian government asking for Blair's support in issuing a loan. EM 505. According to Paribas bank records, it was JM who initiated the Rumanian plan after the success he had in Poland. EB 331-2

LATE MARCH: JM, for Blair & Co, aided by P Denis and R Pleven, begins negotiations on Rumanian stabilization with Paribas. Very early on the talks stall on the division of roles between the two banks. Agreement come when Paribas and Blair divide the national markets in which each bank would work [to float loan]. EB 332

2 May: JM meets in Paris at the Blair office, rue Francois I, with representatives of Paribas and a Dutch bank. JM keeps parties talking after the Dutch official starts to leave in disagreement. EB 332

8 May: JM reports to Moreau that he has made great progress in Rumania on loan. EM 555

7 Jul: Start of arrangement between Blair and Co and Fairburn of Diamond Match with JM later in key role. Vol K 123, V ; KGH 147-52

4 Aug: Denis writes J. Chevalier of Paribas that he has just returned from London where the situation [concerning the Rumanian loan] is confused because of the English lawyers. He encloses for Paribas three documents concerning their views, adding that Denis and JM have not accepted these changes proposed by the lawyers and that JM is now in London discussing modifications of the proposals. Denis will advise Chevalier of the results of these meetings. Meanwhile, Denis adds, the Rumanian government seems to have settled on a loan of $20m with $5m from the French group, $5m from the British and the rest from the Americans and others. PB

6 Aug: JM writes P Quesnay of Banque de France, confirming conversation they had while JM was in London: Quesnay will write the Rumanian government making clear that the adviser to the French group will not be a Bank of Rumania official but he will be involved in the reorganization of the bank's statistical department as foreseen by the stabilization plan and that he will have the right to appeal where he thinks it necessary in the exercise of his functions. PB

11 Aug: JM writes J. Chevalier of Bank Paribas on results of London talks he and Denis just concluded concerning Rumanian loan and its guarantees in the form of dedicated revenues from specified monopolies. JM leaves same day on vacation. PB

25 Sep: Swedish businessman Ivar Kreuger writes JM, reminding him of meeting some years ago through his brother, Gaston Monnet, and offering JM position as his Paris representative in international finance. Kreuger suggests a Paris meeting next month. V

29 Sep: In Paris, representatives of Blair & Co and of Rumanian government, including Ion Antonescu, discuss means of insuring dedicated revenue from various monopolies, including tobacco and matches, for repaying proposed loan to Rumania. PB

1 Oct: JM politely refuses job offer from I Kreuger because, he says, he has just taken partnership in NY firm Blair & Co. He wants to meet Kreuger soon however to make suggestions on who might be the right person. V

----:Donald Swatland, of Paris office of Cravath law firm, writes Bank Paribas on text of Rumanian loan agreement. C. McLain of same firm also involved with JM on Rumanian loan. PB

8 Oct: Kreuger acknowledges with regret JM Oct 1 letter and hopes to meet him soon in Paris. V

22 Oct: JM confirms lunch with Kreuger at 14 rue de Conde [JM home]. V

9 Nov: JM's 40th birthday is spent on the Rumanian loan and other business matters but his life as a bachelor with a Paris townhouse and constant foreign travels is apparently beginning to pale.

Age 41 to 50 (1929-1938)

The year 1929 becomes a crucial one for Monnet's professional and personal life. In the financial euphoria which sweeps across America early in the year, Blair and Co is approached in New York to become part of the Bank of America, the leading instrument of A. Giannini, a phenomenally successful California banker. Monnet is asked by Elisha Walker, head of Blair & Co, to become a key member of the new enterprise. Later in the year, Monnet has a fateful meeting with Silvia Giannini, wife of his colleague Francisco Giannini [unrelated to the California family]. Monnet's life is transformed by these events.

1 Feb: Agreement signed with Rumania for $100 m loan after Kreuger's Swedish Match Co. agrees to take $30 m of the loan in return for 30 year contract to operate Rumanian match monopoly for minimum of $3 m annually. JMM 105;TCF 505-6; RHM 133. [This is apparently the first fruit of the Monnet-Kreuger relationship.]

5,16 Feb: Correspondence between JM (for Blair) and others for Chase Securities, Dillon Read, Paribas, Hambro & Lazard Freres, London with Swedish Match Co (SMC) including memo outlining complicated Rumanian bond deal in which SMC agrees to buy back at a premium a bond purchase option from others which SMC had first sold them. Repurchase price for SMC: $224,000 to Blair, $128,000 each to Paribas and Hambro plus $50,000 commission each to same three. V

19 Feb: JM (Paris) writes Kreuger (Stockholm): While you were in Paris we discussed international telephone situation which I have been studying some time and for which I would like to submit some possibilities to you. Can we meet in Paris or shall I come to Stockholm? V

25 Feb: Kreuger replies he will not be in Paris but can see JM in Stockholm 10-15 March. V

13, 22 Mar: Kreuger and JM finally agree to meet in Paris for lunch at JM's apartment. V

SPRING: JM attempts additional loan to Poland by European banks under Blair leadership but fails when President Moscicki kills deal with argument against American monopoly. Pease 119

MARCH: A. Giannini of Bank of America (BA) approaches E. Walker of Blair and Co. to manage expansion of BA across the country. Walker signs agreement with Transamerica Corp (BA parent company) to merge Blair & Co Inc and Blair and Co (the partnership) with Bancamerica, BA's securities affiliate, becoming Bancamerica-Blair, the Transamerica securities arm, with the deposit banking business of Blair going to BA. Walker becomes president of firm and chair of BA executive committee. Walker (and associates) get 363,637 shares of the new firm and of BA in exchange for assets with $50 m market value (BA assuming all

Blair liabilities.) JM among those Blair officials becoming associated with new firm. Tex Moore of Cravath represented Blair group. TCF 501, FB 148

22 Mar: NY Times reports that this was first ever merger of a private bank and a national bank. According to Walker this was not a sale or absorption but a consolidation. Officials of Blair & Co who will serve at Bancamerica-Blair include "George Benard, J. Grant Forbes, Jean Monnet and Lewis P. Sheldon in Europe." New corporation will have capitalization of $125 m., half from Blair & Co. Giannini used Transamerica Corp to control Bank of America which yesterday closed at $265 bid. NYT

25 Mar: JM writes Kreuger covering memo by "our lawyer" on procedure for Kreuger to get part of Rumanian bonds earlier than agreed. V

26 Mar: In consolidation with Bank of America, Blair & Co will receive $86m. in form of 363,637 shares of Bank of America. Out of total of 1 m. shares now outstanding, Transamerica owns 670,000; new total will be 1,363,637. NYT

SPRING: AP Giannini selects E Walker as president of Bancamerica Corp and chairman of Transamerica's executive committee, with JM as vice chair. FB 148, citing Bank of Italy News, Oct 1930; JM personnel files TA/BA

6 Apr: Francesco Giannini, a Blair representative in Milan, marries Silvia di Bondini. CA

17 Apr: JM note (in French) to Kreuger (both in Paris): Here is memo on London talks [on Swedish, French, English and US telephone companies. Memo gives details of ownership of various telephone companies and their concessions, facilities, manufacturing etc]. V

24 Apr: JM letter to Kreuger (both in Paris): I postponed NY trip pending outcome French telephone plan. I talked with Mr Adams before he sailed to NY where he will see E Walker; we can all talk when you get to NY. On Polish situation, Adams prepared to cooperate with Ericsson, you, and Blair on concession. Poland needs to take up some bonds which block new issues. Baranski of Polish Treasury agreed to telephone concession provided a fair amount of bonds be taken at same time. He will talk to his minister and advise me. V

6 May: Morrow writes to Claudi Mendoza introducing Georges Monnet [JM's cousin now helping run the family cognac business] as "my friend who will be visiting Cuba." DWM

MID-MAY: Blair Bancamerica agreement goes into effect under name Bancamerica-Blair Corp with Walker as president and also chairman of executive committee of Bank of America. JM is among those from the Blair Company now involved with new corporation. TCF 500-1

24 May: B Strong reports conversation with Dr. Stewart of Bank of

England in Cherbourg where, among other concerns, Stewart reports rumor that FRBNY got involved in Rumanian loan matter through JM. Strong denies this and gives Stewart details, including talk Strong had with E Walker of Blair & Co resulting in Walker cable to JM in Bucharest that FRBNY was not involved in loan question. FRBNY

5 Jun: JM in NY where he awaits Kreuger for lunch tomorrow with Walker. P Denis cables JM that Bank for International Settlements (BIS) to have 21 member board; Kreuger may be one member and Quesnay (France) likely to be offered governor job. V; JM greatly concerned about who will head BIS. FJM AMC 1/2

19 Jul: JM (Paris) writes Kreuger (Stockholm), agreeing to meet in London next week. V

AUGUST: JM meets Silvia di Bondini Giannini in Paris: "An Italian couple were among those having dinner with me. He was a businessman. That night, I saw his young wife for the first time. She was beautiful. We forgot the other guests." JMM 109 (The Gianninis had married four months earlier in Italy where he was a Blair and Co. representative. CA)

This was an audacious move as described by Monnet who was twice the age of Silvia, a recent bride of barely 20 years. Whether he (or Silvia) saw the situation as clearly as his memoirs indicate at the time of their first meeting is doubtful. Silvia stayed with Giannini for at least two more years and had his child in April 1931. It is possible that Monnet was immediately infatuated, as the memoirs suggest, but that it took some time to convince Silvia.

Francesco Giannini was a senior official of Blair and Co. in Italy and was possibly well known to Monnet from the time they both worked for the League of Nations. (DF 54 fn). Their relationship within Blair & Co is unknown but apparently close enough that Monnet invited him and his bride to that fateful dinner at Monnet's home in Paris.

13 Aug: JM from London writes Kreuger in Stockholm: With recent events in Hague we decided to postpone German railroad decision. Am leaving for two week vacation in Pyrenees and will see you in Paris in September. V

19 Aug: Identical cables from Swedish Match Co to Blair NY, Hambro London, Paribas Paris regretting that amounts specified in 16 Feb agreement this year have not been paid: "Have arranged cable remittance". V

23 Aug: Transamerica declares 150% stock dividend; its stock soars in roaring bull market to $165 in next month. NYT 24 Aug

4 Sep: P Denis writes Kreuger in Stockholm that JM will only return from vacation Sept 9. Kreuger replies he will not be in Paris before end of month. V

OCTOBER: JM accepts invitation to attend ceremony laying foundation stone at new LN headquarters in Geneva. LN G

29 Oct: Black Monday collapse of stock prices on Wall Street soon spreads world wide.

NOVEMBER 1929-JANUARY 1930: JM involved with Rene Pleven and Pierre Quesnay of the Banque de France on selecting new chair for the Bank for International Settlements in Basel. JM is living in NYC at Savoy Plaza [later the Plaza] Hotel and is considered a fallback candidate. JM office with Bancamerica-Blair is at 24 and 44 Broad Street. FJM AMC; ZL

26 Nov: Handwritten note from New York by JM precedes two telegrams, both to Rene Pleven in Paris about JM conversations with T Lamont of JP Morgan Co on chairmanship of Bank for International Settlements: D Morrow not available for job; Robert Olds of Sullivan and Cromwell may be available and good candidate; keep [Pierre] Quesnay [Banque de France] informed on all my cables and calls. FJM AMC

29 Nov: JM cables R Pleven twice on Bank for International Settlements: First is for P Quesnay at Banque de France stating that D Morrow will not accept head job at BIS and that finding right American who will accept is difficult. Second cable advances Robert Olds, Sullivan & Cromwell partner, as best candidate. Pleven replies that Banque de France governor agrees on Olds if Quesnay will be BIS manager. FJM AMC

26 Dec: JM cables Pleven that B Blackett of UK might be good choice for BIS job with Quesnay as manager. Asks for discreet inquiry at Banque de France on this if Americans cannot come up with candidate. FJM AM

1930

The consequences of the Wall Street stock market crash of October 1929 came slowly. The markets actually rebounded early in the new year. But the work of Monnet and Walker in managing and expanding the Bank of America was undermined by the sharp drop in the stock value of Transamerica Corporation, the holding company which owned Bank of America and which had hired the two men from Blair & Co. Meanwhile, Monnet continued his work with Ivar Kreuger, the Swedish financier, regarding international telephone companies. Kreuger's problems were not limited to the world stock market turmoil although they were complicated by it.

Two important Monnet connections---Transamerica and Ivar Kreuger---were to collapse almost simultaneously but for unrelated causes two years later. These disastrous experiences may have shaken Monnet's confidence in his business acumen at the same time his personal life---long-distance courtship of a married woman--- ran an uncertain course. Together these events and their consequences, coming just after the market crash and deepening economic depression, put great stresses on Monnet in the Nineteen Thirties, probably the most trying decade of his long life.

3 Jan: Cable JM to I Kreuger: [I] do not expect to be back in Paris for

some time. Will cable next week on plans. V

16 Jan: JM and Walker sign contract with AP Giannini committing them to coast to coast expansion of Bank of America. Contract in TA/BA cited by FB 152-3

4 Feb: E Walker and JM resign from Blair-Bancamerica to work full time for Transamerica Corp. Barrons [newspaper]

8 Feb: At annual meeting of Transamerica Corp, E Walker becomes TA board chairman at $100,000 annual salary with JM as vice chair at $50,000 salary. AP Giannini retires. These changes effective in January when contract of Walker and JM signed with Giannini. Bank of Ital News, Sept 1930, TA/BA; NYT 4 Sep 1931

10 Feb: London (Naval Conference) "D[wight] met the Princess Bibesco--Elisabeth Asquith--today at her request. Monnet had talked w. her about D[wight]. ECM

18 Feb: JM and Walker arrive in San Francisco, met by Mario Giannini who takes them to Bank of Italy headquarters at 1 Powell St. FB 153; San Francisco Chronicle, 19 Feb 1930

27 Feb: Transamerica board meeting addressed by E Walker; JM gives short speech. FB 153; JM personal file, TA/BA

7 Mar: D Morrow cables Joseph Cotton, under secretary of state, from London Naval Conference asking if JM was due in Europe within next few weeks since "he could be most helpful" at conference. NARA, Dept of State files, London Naval Conference, 1930

22 Mar: NY Times describes "consolidation" of Blair and Co and Bancamerica and names JM as participant. NYT

24 Mar: Letter from Count de la Ferriere asking Blair & Co to buy secretly for I Kreuger 350,000 shares of Diamond Match for $13.5 m which stock will be issued as part of Diamond's reorganization; $4m to be paid at the time offer is accepted and balance on 15 December (later changed to 31 Jan 1931). Blair & Co later in month confirms details. [File also covers 1920-30 arrangements between Diamond and Swedish Match as background for above purchase. JM presumably involved although his name is not mentioned]. Diamond Match file, V

26 Mar: NY Times reports Blair and Co to get $86 million in Bank of America shares in consolidation.

24 Apr: Blair-Bancamerica merged with Bank of America. Barrons

25 Apr: JM in NYC cables Morrow from SS Leviathan en route to Europe. DWM

3 May: AP Giannini leaves San Francisco for Karlsbad, Czechoslovakia;

en route hears of sharp fall in Transamerica stock confirming his doubts about Walker and JM. FB 161-2

6 May: Note from JM [in NY] (on 44 Wall Street stationary) to I Kreuger: Delighted to look forward to seeing you soon. Can we dine Fri May 9 at Savoy Plaza [where JM is staying?] V

8 May: ECM goes to Princeton, Trenton and Hightstown NJ campaigning [for husband's senate race] In Trenton she hears, at Republican headquarters, talkabout DWM "as a paragon of virtue.... Here at 12:30 and regaled it all to D[wight], Jean Monnet and George [Rublee] ECM

30 May: San Francisco Chronicle reports E Walker, Harry Bronner and Hunter Blair) yesterday elected Transamerica directors. Walker is chair of executive committee.

10 Jun: JM writes on Transamerica letterhead to I Kreuger at 791 Park Ave NYC long detailed account of problem with agreements made at Jan 1929 London conference on participation of various firms in international telephone work. He reminds Kreuger that General Electric and Franco-American Bank [which includes Blair] would have 50% share with Blair explicitly having 51% control [of its consortium].JM asks Kreuger to intervene with German partner, Siemens and Halske, to reverse their decision to leave the consortium because ITT [International Telephone and Telegraph] had decided to enter it. If they will not, we should go ahead without them and form French corporation to absorb Societe Industriele de Telephone. Keep me informed on Siemens through Pleven. Latest news from Bucharest indicates uncertainty on who will form government; until resolved no one can say if telephone concession will go to ITT or if we have a chance of having it reopened. V

JULY: Transamerica stock listed on NY exchange. FB 502

17-21 Jul: TW Lamont drafts memos on a Transamerica letterhead to stockholders, presumably at JM request. LA

17 Jul: Transamerica stock in deep decline; A P Giannini cables he is returning from Europe to settle matters with Walker. FB 164

24 Jul: Ernst and Ernst accounting firm writes JM on Transamerica's earnings statement which AP Giannini questioned. FB 367

8 Aug: Transamerica stock falls to 18, convincing AP Giannini that Walker and JM are causing the drop. APG to LM Giannini, from Transamerica cable files cited in FB 167

22 Aug: Walker and JM arrive in San Francisco for meetings with Transamerica executives over simplification of corporation amid AP Giannini's fears that the two are trying to take corporation from its roots. FB 168

4 Sep: JM, Walker and Giannini leave on ten day trip across state

(Sacramento, Fresno, San Jose, Bakersfield, Ventura, San Diego) ending in Biltmore Hotel ballroom in Los Angeles to reassure bank depositors. Transamerica press release 12 Sept cited in FB 169

23 Sep: HBC board hears that Renauleaud has repaid JM's 40,000 pound loan [in French francs at greatly reduced cost to him]. HBC IV

30 Sep: Diamond Match reorganized with 350,000 new shares sold to bankers at $37 a share or about $20 above market with indications that Transamerica was purchaser. "History of Transamerica" Barrons, 9 May 1932

9 Oct: Englewood. "...tonight Jean Monnet here and D[wight]. made me give him a Painted Pig [recent children's book by ECM] ECM

15 Oct: Englewood. "...we go home [from A&C Lindbergh's new home near Princeton] just in time to dress for...dinner. Also Mr. Monnet." ECM

4 Nov: DW Morrow elected to US Senate. NYT

21 Nov: JM is vice chair of Transamerica Corp on letterhead when he writes Morrow's office asking advice on situation in Mexico. DWM

22 Nov: JM leaves New York for extended trip ("for a fortnight or more") to California. DWM

DECEMBER: JM continues involvement with Kreuger on Diamond Match which is Kreuger's biggest US deal (Diamond Match file, V, which includes account of Blair & Co role in buying secretly 350,000 shares of Diamond.) KGH 147-52.

15 Dec: "Time" quotes Walker and JM as annoyed and "deeply embarrassed" at Giannini's accusations that Wall Street "diabolical conspiracy" was driving down TA's stock. FB 172-3

1931

In the midst of his financial struggles, Monnet encountered personal crises and tragedy. His beloved, Silvia, still married to Francesco Giannini, gave birth to a daughter in Italy immediately before the separation of the couple. Monnet was suspected by some of his relatives of being Anna's father but he was in the US at the time she was apparently conceived. Also he in New York when Anna was born which seems unlikely if he is the father.

Later in the year Monnet's close friend, Dwight Morrow, recently elected to the US Senate, died suddenly. A few months later, Morrow's grandchild, Charles A Lindbergh Jr, was kidnapped and murdered.

31 Mar: JM cables Lamont who is aboard SS Saturnia to Europe apologizing for an effort to get information from Lamont's office in latter's absence. Lamont acknowledges and dismisses problem in letter from ship four days later and notes he will be back in New York on 16 May. LA

1 Apr: JM cables AJ Mount, senior VP, Bank of Italy, that he has been busy in an interesting Europe trip [which just ended]. TA/BA

6 Apr: JM hosts financial reporters at Broad Street Luncheon Club to discuss recent Europe trip when he found moderately hopeful outlook. NYT 7 Apr

10 Apr: Anna Giannini born in Italy to Silvia. CA

23 Apr: E Walker, chair and JM, vice chair, of Transamerica elected directors of Diamond Match which recapitalized last December with 350,000 new shares rumored to have been bought by Kreuger & Toll. (NYT 24 Apr) "Following the [December] sale...Jean Monnet and E Walker are made directors of Diamond Match leading to the belief that Transamerica had acquired the stock. "History of Transamerica" Barrons, 9 May 1932

6 May: Long Kreuger letter to JM at Transamerica asking for $6m loan from Bank of America to Swedish Match giving complicated explanation of why company cannot use regular banking arrangements. V

28 May: JM in NY cables I Kreuger in Paris that Bank of America cannot make loan now. "I am leaving for San Francisco but will leave letter at your apartment [explaining refusal]". V

31 May: JM cable to Kreuger: Remaining in NYC; look forward to seeing you. V

17 Jun: Walker in San Francisco for Transamerica board meeting at which he announces details of reorganization, its secrecy etc. This news gets to AP Giannini in Bad Gastein, Austria who fumes, deciding to come back into action. Bank of America minutes 17 June cited in FB 176

17 Jun: Letter from Barclay's Bank, London to Kreuger's Paris agent, Count de la Ferriere, refers to agreement for which bank was depository for the Diamond Match Co. transaction involving JM. Barclay's writes that stock deposited does not cover indebtedness and asks for further security. V

SUMMER: Transamerica in trouble and E Walker trims its sails; Giannini reacts violently and begins proxy fight to regain control of company. "Fortune" magazine series, Jan, Feb, Mar, Apr 1931; FB 150-81

13 Sep: Giannini cables Transamerica president declaring war on Walker-JM leadership in preparation for 22 Sept corporation meeting. FB 176-80

22 Sep: JM presides over San Francisco Transamerica board meeting which announces Walkers reorganization plan. Giannini protests in person, leaves, and his resignation is announced by Transamerica vice president Bacigalulpi; FB 183-4; MBJ 325.

----------: Three Gianninis replaced at Transamerica meeting by three Lee, Higginson partners according to Walker's letter to stockholders which also notes huge drop in Transamerica assets from $1.1 b on 31 Dec 1930 to $302 m. on 30 Jun 1931. NYT 23 Sep

The Transamerica turmoil was similar to that of many other firms after the October 1929 market crash. Many firms were obviously overvalued in the run-up to the market tumble; investors and company officials (sometimes the same people) were distressed at their losses and sought refuge or relief. Control of the surviving firms, as with Transamerica, took on personal coloration when founders, like Giannini, saw "Wall Street" manipulators like Walker and Monnet exploiting a family heritage.

----------: JM tells reporters that Lee, Higginson and Co and other new interests will strengthen Transamerica. 23 Sep reports in Denver Post, SF Chronicle and Oakland Tribune, cited by FB 184; MBJ 325.

24 Sep: JM tells San Francisco press of new plan's advantages. FB 183

------Giannini will fight Transamerica restructuring plan which would restore Blair & Co when Bancamerica-Blair is separated from Bank America and Transamerica. NYT 25 Sep

28 Sep: John Foster Dulles cables JM at 485 California St San Francisco: Hearty congratulations on Transamerica program etc. JFD, Murnane file

------ "Transamerica Control Passes to Lee, Higgenson," headline of story on replacement of three TA board members by representatives of Lee, Higgenson banking firm, including George Murnane. JM, Walker and Paul Cravath, among others, remaining on board. Barrons

5 Oct: JM close friend and Republican Senator Dwight Morrow of New Jersey dies suddenly from cerebral hemorrhage after holding office less than one year. NYT

After Morrow's death, Monnet stayed close to his family, offering advice, support and simple friendship. Morrow's widow, Elisabeth, [perhaps at JM's suggestion] asked journalist Walter Lippmann to write a Morrow biography but he declines, lacking time and background in finance, he says. Eventually, British writer Harold Nicholson writes the biography. ECM, HN

5 Oct: "Transamerica" story details efforts of stockholder group opposed to Walker plan for reorganization to organize protective committee. Of 24m shares, directors only own or control about 750,000 including about half controlled by Walker and 13,390 owned by JM. Barrons

4 Nov, (Wed), Englewood. "Tonight Mr. Monnet has been here. We have had a lovely evening w. him. C[onstance, daughter] enjoyed him very much and talked well." ECM

CHRISTMAS: JM dines at E. Walker's seated next to Anna Case (opera star who recently married wealthy businessman Clarence Mackay), to whom he sends red roses next morning. (On 27 Dec 1954 she tells this story to Phil Graham who, in a letter, teases JM about possibly telling Silvia of this incident which occurs during JM's pursuit of his future wife. FJM AMH 5l/5.)

DECEMBER: JM has different approach from E Walker in Transamerica proxy fight and wants a low key campaign directed to large stockholders. W H McGinnis memo 10 Dec and TA/BA, cited by FB 187.

1932

8-11 Jan: John U Calkins of Federal Reserve Bank, San Francisco, calls meeting in his office of Walker-Monnet forces and AP Giannini allies to seek compromise before next month's corporation meeting. JM and Bacigalupi represent Transamerica. Giannini refuses any compromise that leaves Walker on board; Calkins says that attitude can destroy two banks. MBJ 339-41 and Federal Reserve Bank memorandum by Calkins cited by FB 191

26 Jan: League of Nations Secretary General Eric Drummond announces decision to resign to LN Council which will try to change his mind. JM among those mentioned as possible successor [but his French successor as LN deputy SG, J. Avenol, eventually succeeds Drummond.] NYT 11

13 Feb: JM assistant Mr. Howe removes many papers [presumably at JM's request] from JM file at Transamerica in San Francisco. 24 Feb 1933 memo to LM Giannini. TA/BA

15 Feb: JM and Walker lose Transamerica proxy fight in Wilmington DE. At 3 AM JM, Walker and others ride back to NYC in chauffeur driven limousine. FB 192

In his Memoirs, Monnet wrote without apparent emotion: "I made and then lost a great deal of money [with Transamerica]. Experience was all I added to my capital." The loss probably involved about 13,000 shares of Transamerica stock which was worth, in the first year he owned it, about $3.54m (nearly $80m in 2007 terms). With the defeat of the Walker-Monnet team, Monnet's salary of $50,000 ended---he received only $6250 in 1932---and his Transamerica stock had fallen in value to about $200,000 (or about $4.4m in 2007 terms).

1 Mar: Kidnapping of two year old Charles Lindbergh Jr from New Jersey home of Anna Morrow and Charles Lindbergh. One of JM's best friends, Dwight Morrow, is the victim's grandfather. NYT

12 Mar: Krueger kills self in Paris. Shortly before his death, he tries again through E. Walker to get loan from Bancamerica-Blair. (John Rovensky, senior VP of Bank of America, interview with Bessie James, 1949. TA/BA)

30 Apr: JM writes Lamont from Hotel Baeren near Interlaken, Switzerland where he finds "high altitude and long runs" do "my moral" (sic) a lot of good. I will not return to US "until I have got myself in good shape which I very much needed." LA

Morrow's death, the collapse of Monnet's job with Transamerica, Kreuger's suicide and the tragedy of the Lindbergh kidnapping, disrupted Monnet's life thoroughly. He fled to a peaceful corner of Europe to recover and consider his future. By early summer, Monnet talked about work with John Foster Dulles of the New York law firm of Sullivan and Cromwell. They had met first at the Versailles Peace Conference where Dulles was a lawyer on the American delegation. They had also worked together on the Polish loan of 1927. Dulles had followed Monnet's work at Transamerica and knew of the collapse of that venture. He offered Monnet an interim job coordinating the work of the American trustees of the Kreuger and Toll bankruptcy. (Dulles Oral History project which includes interviews with George Murnane, George Sharp and John D. Traphagen, JFD; Kreuger & Toll papers, RA.

14 Jul (Thurs) Paris: "...Louise Weiss also gave us advice [about Britanny trip] last night at Jean Monnet's lovely apartment back of the Chamber of Deputies. [rue de Conde] ...." ECM

Jul 15 (Fri):"We are just back from Montmartre where we had supper in a gay little cafe w. Dean and Anne Jay and Jean Monnet. We got here about 6 last night.... At 7:30 Jean Monnet was here taking us out to dinner and later we went to Boulevard Montparnasse and watched the dancing in the street [for Bastille Day].ECM

Jul 16 (Sat):"...Jean Monnet here [Ritz] for dinner with A[nne Morrow Lindbergh] and me. Told us a good deal about his family..." ECM

Jul 26 (Tues): [Back in Paris] "... Jean Monnet took us to La Peronne for luncheon. Marvelous. Bouillabaisse." "...tonight Jean Monnet and David Le Breton here for dinner and went to see "Peg de mon coeur" together . Very good." ECM

29 Jul (Fri):[ECM Departure for NY on] SS Europa "...Jean Monnet sent roses." ECM

SEPTEMBER: JM travels NY/Paris/Stockholm/London/NY. RA

Monnet's financial status at this time is insecure. By the time he first went to Stockholm for Dulles, his shares in Transamerica (if he still retained them) were probably worth less than he needed to support his expensive lifestyle and to prepare for his coming marriage. His temporary job helping Dulles and the American creditors of Kreuger and Toll was thus a welcome if uncertain (and irregular) support when he did not know, at mid-life, where his next work would be. Apparently even Monnet's small nest egg remaining from Transamerica and other investments was dissipated over the next few years since he was forced, by 1934, to borrow money from Dulles and his law firm's cofounder to found his small investment banking firm. (JFD)

24 Sep: JM writes Pierre Denis at League of Nations Geneva offering him job helping on the Kreuger bankruptcy. Denis accepts and arrives by 28 Sep in

Paris to work for JM who shuttles between New York, Paris and Stockholm. RA

Oct ll (Tues) Englewood: "...tonight Jean Monnet here. A very happy evening. We drank some of D[wight]'s brandy at dinner and E[lisabeth, daughter] told Jean Monnet of her engagement....JM suggested a place in southern France [for honeymoon]. ECM

12 Oct (Wed): "...Jean M. went to see E's school [where she teaches] and was really impressed by it." ECM

18 Oct: JM (New York) cables Denis (Stockholm): Auchincloss will file $200 m claim for American creditors against Kreuger & Toll assets regarding International Match Co transactions. RA

22 Oct: JF Dulles writes Mr. Fehr of Kreuger & Toll in Stockholm on Dulles' recent visit there. RA

------   JM(NY) writes Denis in Paris after discussion with Gordon Auchincloss on latter's proposal for procedure on liquidation of Kreuger & Toll. RA

2 Nov: JM resigns as Diamond Match director in cable to Kreuger & Toll liquidators, so he can be "entirely free to act in interests of liquidators and reorganization." RA

Monnet's interim job with the Kreuger and Toll trustees lasted until early 1933 but in November 1932 he was already looking for other options while still involved with the Stockholm negotiations. He was approached by the Chinese Finance Minister TV Soong, brother of Madame Chiang Kai-shek. Soong, who apparently thought Monnet was still in banking, was seeking a western financial expert. Soong, a Harvard graduate, had many connections in the West and knew well Ludwig Rajchman, a Monnet friend from the League of Nations, who probably brought the two together. Soong also knew the American President-elect, Franklin Roosevelt whose election may have precipitated Soong's approach to Monnet.

8 Nov: Franklin Roosevelt elected president of United States. NYT 9 Nov

10 Nov: TV Soong, China's finance minister, cables his brother-in-law, Kung, to "approach Jean Monnet's bank [Blair & Co] officially" [to see] if he could organize American European groups to finance economic developments in China. Monnet knows of my plans through Geneva friend [probably Rajchman] FJM AMD 1/1/1

--------- TV Soong cables Kung again:" Please give Jean Monnet my specific authority to open negotiations on my behalf. FJM AMD 1/1/1

These two cables by TV Soong inaugurate a strange chapter in Monnet's life: his China years. China's need for western economic advice (as perceived by American-educated TV Soong) coincided with Monnet's availability after

his dismissal from Transamerica. If Monnet and Walker had prevailed over Giannini in Wilmington, Delaware, Monnet's life would have taken a different course, probably with Silvia and her daughter Anna joining him in America and with Monnet ignoring the audacious idea of going to work in China of which he knew nothing and which was in both political and economic turmoil. TV Soong's move toward Monnet further coincided with the election of American President Franklin Roosevelt who was friendly with both Soong and E Walker, Monnet's former boss. These friendships gave Monnet instant access in Washington, aiding both his work for China and his ties to the Roosevelt administration which would become increasingly valuable to him.

11 Nov: Lamont cables JP Morgan in Europe giving account of developments at Kuhn, Loeb & Co, a friendly competitor of the Morgan firm. Kuhn, Loeb has hired Elisha Walker and hopes to hire JM. JP Morgan Papers, Pierpont Morgan Library, NY NY quoted in J.P. Morgan Jr by John D Forbes, Charlottesville VA, 1986, 173-4

17 Nov: JM meets with Gordon Auchincloss [probably in New York] on French and other WWI debts to US. GA writes long memo of record on meeting prefaced by: "I have known him intimately for a number of years and I know he is very close to the French government and always has been." JM wants opinion on effect of Roosevelt victory on debts for which next payment is due 15 Dec. GA replies first by comparing Roosevelt position with that of defeated Republican candidate H Hoover, implying that Roosevelt (whom he apparently supports) would be more understanding of foreign debtors than Hoover was during the campaign. JM asks if Congress can delay December payment but GA replies present Congress is not pro-Roosevelt and will be replaced only in January by new Congress. JM agrees with GA analysis and hopes new Administration will give some sign that it understands international economic problems, including foreign debts, and will seek a conference to resolve them. EMH, Gordon Auchincloss folder, 1932-33

21 Nov: Dulles cables Fehr: Gravely concerned that no satisfactory action taken on compensation for liquidators. "The creditors cannot and do not expect that Monnet and other liquidators will devote practically entire time to this difficult affair without receiving currently some substantial compensation and the possibility of additional compensation if the matter works out satisfactorily...." RA, v. 361: Sullivan and Cromwell file

22 Nov: JM to Kreuger & Toll liquidators refers to "...my secretary in Paris, Raymond Meynial..." RA

30 Nov: JM cables KT liquidators: Auchincloss has discovered 1250 shares of Bank of Manhattan he believes belong to Kreuger & Toll assets. RA

28 Dec: JM attends wedding of Elisabeth Morrow in New Jersey with JP Morgan, George Rublee and many others. AML II 269-70

-----: Jacques Rueff, French financial attache in London, gives account of JM's advice on France's WWI debt repayment given in telephone call from home of Parker-Gilbert, US reparations representative: a) Roosevelt seems to want to start diplomatic talks on problem. b) There is great public interest in US on debt repayment; a French default would make all collaboration impossible for 30 years. c) The British and French debt situations are not the same and France should not insist on equal treatment. DDF i,II, no 45.

31 Dec: JM has lunch with Lamont and Emmanuel Monick, financial attache of French embassy on French war debts. F Freidel, Launching the New Deal 108, citing Lamont papers

END OF YEAR: JM earned only 6250 from Transamerica Corp this year, explaining in part his need for the temporary job with the Kreuger & Toll liquidation. In 1931 the Transamerica Corp. paid him 50,000 and in 1930, his first full year with the Bank of America subsidiary, he earned 44,861. These were large sums in the first years after the October 1929 stock market crash. NYT, "Salaries and Bonuses Paid to Heads of Corporations," 3 Mar 1934

1933

3 Jan (Tues): "...Jean Monnet was there [at Englewood dinner given by the Zaidee's] ECM

27 Jan: Englewood "Jean Monnet here for dinner and the evening." ECM

30 Jan: JM cables Kreuger & Toll Liquidators that he is leaving New York on SS Europa for Stockholm via Paris. RA

8 Feb: JM (Paris) cables Kreuger & Toll liquidators: Will be in Stockholm next week. RA

21 Feb: Dulles cables JM at Grand Hotel, Stockholm. RA, KT cable file

4 Mar: Franklin D Roosevelt inaugurated as 32nd President of the United States with his first task to confront the dire economic situation

10 Mar: JM leaving soon for US per Swedish Match Co cable. RA, KT cable file

17 Mar: JM's secretary writes Kreuger & Toll creditors from NY on reimbursement of recent trip. RA

31 Mar: JM arrives in New York according to his cable to Kreuger & Toll, Stockholm. RA

3 Apr: JM wants to see FDR on his China work but State Dept thinks caution appropriate until JM indicates more precisely what he wants to discuss with the President. JM says he has seen Dept of Commerce and Reconstruction Finance Corporation officials. Memorandum of Stanley Hornbeck, State Department expert on China. SH

Monnet's sudden and puzzling appearance in Washington on China business immediately after his arrival in New York, his US headquarters, indicates a burst of energy and concentration on his next venture. His audacity in seeking an appointment with the new American President must have been based on his well placed friends, like Lamont and Walker, on his probable knowledge that Soong, linked via Harvard with Roosevelt, would see the President during his coming visit to Washington and on Soong's demand that Monnet come immediately to Nanking to begin work (See 29 April below).

10 Apr: JM phones S Hornbeck, head of Far Eastern Division, Dept of State, from NYC where he saw Department of Commerce representative; Will soon return to see Hornbeck again. SH

10 Apr: John Foster Dulles in New York cables his brother, Allen, in Europe:"...[A]fter months of efforts and principally due to Monnet's efforts on his latest trip abroad, Swedish match interests have at last consented to participation in setting up some organization to study whole problem [of Kreuger and Toll debts]...." JFD. Dulles proposes Norman Davis, banker and head of US delegation to Geneva disarmament talks, as chair of Kreuger & Toll bondholders committee and suggests P Denis, whom Davis knows from Geneva, as his assistant, noting that JM must leave Kreuger & Toll work now for other activities. [Denis had already been working on K&T matters for JM since late September 1932]. ND

14 Apr: JM writes Kreuger & Toll from NY on compensation for himself and Pierre Denis. RA

15 Apr: JM & P Denis send interim cable to Kreuger & Toll from NY. RA, KT cable file

18 Apr: Frank Lee meets with State Dept official Hamilton on JM's role on China. Lee heard that Henry Morgenthau of Farm Loan Bank Board told people that JM was representing China here and that State Dept had verified his credentials. Hamilton reassures Lee, who says he is representing TV Soong on Chinese purchase of US commodities, that State Dept has not "verified" or examined JM credentials, only that latter has visited several people in State Dept on his interest in China. SH

20 Apr: State Department official Hornbeck meets with Morgenthau to clarify JM position which Morgenthau had confused. SH 29 Apr: JM writes TV Soong, Chinese finance minister who is en route to US via ship which will soon land in Seattle: he has received Soong cable from ship; instead of leaving immediately for China [as Soong had asked] JM wants to meet Soong in Chicago and travel with him by train to Washington so they can talk before Soong has any other private US meetings; reviews his cable exchange with Soong via Rajchman who advised talking with Norman Davis, US representative in Europe, which JM did and who in turn discussed matter with State Department; finally JM reviews

his activities in US and London regarding China's finance plans. JM says he postponed immediate departure for Nanking and will instead await meeting with Soong. FJM AMD 1/1/4 [JMM,110, indicates JM first met Soong in Europe but apparently they first met in (or en route to) Washington. The JMM reference may refer inexactly to fact that he traveled to Europe with Soong. See May 31 below.]

Personal considerations beyond employment perhaps provoked Monnet's sudden interest in China. Silvia Giannini, now living in Switzerland, was separated from her husband who wanted custody of their two year old daughter. Monnet sought American legal advice on where Silvia might get a divorce and retain custody of Anna which seemed impossible under Italian law. A remote location like China, he may have concluded, might provide the needed protection.

But before Monnet could solve these personal problems, he had to immerse himself in Chinese affairs and insure his American connections. He began by using his American friendships with Thomas Lamont, a JP Morgan partner, and Elisha Walker, now a partner in Kuhn, Loeb, New York investment bankers. Both were also friends of Franklin Roosevelt, the new American president.

T V Soong was also a good friend of Roosevelt. They both went to Harvard but more pertinently, Roosevelt believed himself a China expert because of his family's 19th century history in Asian trading. Soong, as China's new finance minister, was making his first visit to the new Roosevelt presidency. It was during that visit that Soong first met Monnet.

3 May: TV Soong, accompanied by American adviser Arthur N. Young, arrives in Seattle on SS President Jefferson. NYT. First among their goals: to negotiate an Reconstruction Finance Corporation (RFC) loan for cotton and wheat purchases in the U.S. D.Borg, US and Far Eastern Crisis 1933-38,(Cambridge, MA, 1964) 63; ANY 382

8 May: TV Soong arrives in Washington by train and has lunch the next day at the White House with the President. NYT

13 May: JM, in DC, tells Hornbeck in State Department, that Elisha Walker says that the Chinese have asked Kuhn, Loeb, for whom Walker now works, to represent China in US; Walker saw FDR yesterday and President seemed to support Kuhn, Loeb plan, according to Walker's talk yesterday with JM. SH

19 May: : JM makes first agreement with TV Soong to work in China on economic reconstruction "envisaged by Dr. Sun Yat-Sen." JM will help form international corporation to this end. FJM AMD 1/1/6,14

------:TV Soong writes JM to supplement contract specifying US$150,000 payment (half now, half in 6 months). In addition to this pay, original agreement provided that China would pay for JM's offices in China, Paris, London and New York related to the reconstruction plan and for cable and travel costs he incurred. FJM AMD 1/1/10

------ JM writes KT liquidators he is resigning as member of their committee. RA

Monnet's resignation from his Stockholm work was apparently delayed until he could be certain that the China job would materialize. His meeting with Soong and then with Walker confirmed this. But he combined his old and new jobs by sailing to Europe with Soong and then going to Stockholm to finish his Kreuger & Toll work, and, hopefully, to be paid for it.

26 May: JM writes KT liquidators he sails next Tuesday [30 May] on SS Europa and hopes to visit Stockholm briefly. RA

30 May: P Denis also resigns from Kreuger & Toll work, saying he is going to work for Norman Davis [US representative to Geneva Disarmament Talks]. RA

31 May: JM and TV Soong finally sail from NYC on SS Europa after delay from heavy fog. NYT 31 May, 1 Jun

4 Jun: JM and TV Soong arrive by ship and train in London. NYT

-----: RFC loan of $50 m for Chinese cotton and wheat purchases announced in Washington after negotiations by TV Soong, Arthur Young and JM. NYT; MAE, East Asia, China, v. 845, 28 May cable of French Ambassador in Washington, cited by MY 32

14 Jun: JM meets at Lazard Freres London with British financier Charles Addis, TV Soong, R. Brand, R. Kindersley and F. Denis. Addis diary quoted in R. Dayer, Finance and Empire(NY, 1988), 285

Monnet's Memoirs are somewhat confusing on his first meeting with Soong and how their work together started. Soong, probably on Rajchman's advice, approached Monnet indirectly in November 1932, shortly after Roosevelt's election when Soong decided to see the new President, an old friend, on his way to the London economic conference.

Soong offered Monnet work without even meeting him. They met not in Europe, as the Memoirs indicate but in the United States when Soong arrived soon after Roosevelt's inauguration in March 1933. They then traveled together to Europe where the League of Nations rejected Soong request to send Monnet on an official mission. Instead he went privately in late 1933.

After giving credit in his Memoirs to Rajchman's role in introducing him to China [and to Soong], Monnet described his first reactions to the new country: "When I reached Shanghai, I quickly realized that I should never understand the Chinese---and that in any case this was not the problem. I found myself face to face with men who seemed far more subtle and intelligent than Westerners, and who were certainly very different. This difference made them wary, and to tell the truth their pride had been deeply wounded by the intrusion of powerful European firms. So it was much more important to win their confidence than to understand them....The secret was simple: act as you speak. So that there is never any contradiction between what you say and what you do.... " *(JMM 110-111)*

4 Jul: TV Soong (London) appoints Lazard Freres as his London agent according to despatch by Foreign Secretary Sir John Simon to UK Peking Mission. NAUK FO I:17136/4548

5 Jul: Sir J Pratt (Foreign Office) interview with Ludwig Rajchman includes latter's profile of JM: [After reviewing WWI, League of Nations and early business career]: "Six months ago T V Soong invited him to China [probably on Rajchman's suggestion] but he didn't accept right away. When TV Soong went to America, however, Monnet joined him and it was really Monnet who negotiated the $50 m loan [from US Export-Import Bank]. The International Corporation is also Monnet's idea and he will stay with Soong until it is firmly established. Both Monnet and Salter are going to China in the autumn." NAUK FO I: 17136/4548

7 Jul: Soong, JM and Kindersley call on Lamont in London "re scheme". LA diary

This first week of July illustrates Monnet's well-developed skill in blending diverse friendships into an efficient pattern to pursue his goals. He undoubtedly intervened, with success, on behalf of Soong, his new employer, with Avenol, Monnet's successor as deputy secretary general of the League of Nations and now its secretary general. Another League of Nations colleague, Ludwig Rajchman, gave the above account of Monnet to the British Foreign Office, based undoubtedly on Monnet's own account of the matters discussed.(For example, it is clear that Soong himself, perhaps with help, arranged the $50m loan on his Washington visit in May; it was not done principally or entirely by Monnet as Rajchman's account indicates.

The appointment of Lazard Freres as Soong's London agent also suggests Monnet's influence. He knew well a major Lazard partner, Lord Kindersley, from their prewar work together with Hudson's Bay Company in Canada, which Kindersley chaired from London. Monnet had also worked closely with Lazard in his years with Blair and Co. We have already seen how Kindersley arranged for a large payment by HBC to Monnet for his World War I. Now Monnet, through his work with Soong, had a chance to repay Kindersley's kind and desperately important financial help for the Monnet cognac firm in 1923.

11 Jul: Soong in Rome for meetings with Benito Mussolini, Italian Foreign Minister Count Ciano and others. JM also there. Soong will next visit Paris and Berlin, he tells US ambassador. NYT, 12 Jul; FRUS III 371-2; MAE East Asia, China finances, v. 848 cited by MY 35-36

12 Jul: Lamont calls on Japanese ambassador in London, leaving him a note on the meetings with JM and Addis and indicating Lamont and Addis have been invited to join the consultative committee on Chinese investments [which

JM is to chair]. NAUK FO I: 17136/4548

14 Jul: Chinese official in London gives US Secretary of State Hull memo from TV Soong stating JM has agreed to chair consultative committee on foreign finance on Chinese economic development. FRUS III 495-7

----- J. Avenol, the new LN secretary general, asks US Secretary of State Hull to send observer to first meeting of new committee created to coordinate aid to China. LN technical agent [who will be JM's friend, Ludwig Rajchman] to be named to non-political committee, he adds. FRUS III 498-9

----- KT liquidators state bankruptcy judge has asked government for only four liquidators, meaning that JM will not be replaced. RA

18 Jul: First meeting of LN technical committee names Rajchman as adviser to China despite objections of US minister to China [who apparently suspects Rajchman's past role in China will inflame China-Japan relations]. FRUS III 495-501; Soong himself attended the meeting. MAE SDN (League of Nations) China, vol. 2033 cited by MY 36, 39

----- JM makes second agreement with Chinese government [reflecting the changes in mission developed during the Soong-Monnet meetings in Europe] further specifying work, outlined in 19 May agreement, he will do: to develop and direct an international corporation including foreign participation for country economic reconstruction and assist Chinese government in reorganizing its foreign purchases through one central department. FJM AMD 1/1/14

China's economic situation in the three years(1933-36) of Monnet's work there was complicated by the incipient civil war in the country, by Japan's insistence that it had paramount interests in the country and by the American government's role in raising the price of silver of which China was the world's leading importer.

The immediate occasion of Monnet's mission in China was the National Economic Council, set up before his arrival with support from the League of Nations. As finance minister at the time, T V Soong believed that Monnet's international banking experience, explained to him by their mutual friend and LN official, Ludwik Rajchman, was exactly what China needed to carry out the work of the NEC. (ANY 194,344-5)

19 Jul: JM writes KT liquidators from Paris on his compensation claim. RA

20 Jul: TV Soong leaves England for China via US and Canada, according to Foreign Office note of 11 Aug. He had also visited France and Italy and will stop in Japan before returning home. NAUK FO I: 17136/5350; MY 35-39; NYT 26 Aug

------: Soong writes a French foreign office official Paul-Boncour about a meeting he (Soong) and JM had with Alexis Leger, the secretary-general of the French Foreign Affairs ministry. At the meeting Soong described the new committee he wanted JM to chair composed of American, Belgian, British, Chinese, French, German and Italian members. Japan, China's largest creditor, was not a proposed member. AN MAE East Asia/China finances, v. 848, cited by MY 47-49

The resistance of the members of the China Consortium to participate in the Soong-Monnet plan meant a reworking of the plan's scope and goals. Instead of a corporation, the plan proposed a non-governmental advisory committee, chaired by Monnet. Although Japan was not initially to be a participant, as Monnet had apparently proposed, Soong agreed that development of China-Japan ties could allow the latter's eventual participation. HU II, pp 15-16, citing AN MAE Serie Asie 1918-1940, sous serie China finance, v. 845, 848, correspondence of Jul 1933; NAUK FO 371 18078 David Drummond to Francis 27 Aug 1934

26 Jul: V. Wellesley of British Foreign Office tells Addis that Soong-Monnet plan may be useful but only if Japanese approve. NAUK FO I: 17136/4779,2717

27 Jul: Addis, governor of Hong Kong and Shanghai Bank, and British member of the China Consortium, refuses to participate in the Soong-Monnet committee. Ltr to Kindersley, AN MAE Serie Asie, v. 848 cited by HU II 17

28 Jul: Further agreement of JM with Chinese government on central purchasing procedures he will follow and his preparation of international corporation including forming an international consultative committee. FJM AMD 1/1/16

31 Jul: Nohara, Japanese member on China Consortium, complains to his UK counterpart, Charles Addis, of TV Soong's consultative committee [under JM's direction] prospectively competing with or disrupting the Consortium. FRUS III 505. Eventually Addis and Lamont from JP Morgan refuse to join the committee which ultimately fails to survive despite the efforts of Soong and JM. MY 49-50

The ambitious plans of Soong and Monnet to form a new international corporation fail when the members of the China Consortium refuse to join because Japan will not be included. The next stage, more modest, was an international committee but this too falters when seen by European and US proposed participants as a variation on the Chinese anti-Japanese approach. Eventually, Monnet goes to China without this western support and finds a different approach to gain capital for China's ambitious economic plans.

AUGUST: Another attempt at reconciliation between Silvia and Francesco Giannini fails at Swiss resort. ACCSM.

1 Aug: JM visits French foreign ministry official Cosme to describe how

he proposes to run the consultative committee Soong has proposed. AN, MAE East Asia, China finances, v. 848, cited by MY 51

5 Aug: At invitation of Nanking govt, A Salter & M. Mannet(sic), economic experts previously with League of Nations are shortly proceeding to China in private advisory role. CWR 434.

8 Aug: Before returning to China, TV Soong has lunch with President Roosevelt at Hyde Park. NYT and FRUS III 512.

------: Soong in New York cables JM to let the press know of their work to improve relations between China and of "all the foreign interests who want to cooperate with China." AN, MAE East Asia, China finances, v. 848, cited by MY 52

9 Aug: JM tells French foreign ministry official Cosme that US Secretary of State Hull has told Japanese Ambassador in Washington that the United States will not support any measures against Japan and that President Roosevelt will tell Soong that he favors the proposed committee JM would head. JM adds that he is very happy with this news which he will relay to the Japanese when he starts his negotiations with them. Note, 9 Aug, AN, MAE East Asia, China finances v. 848, cited by MY 53

10 Aug: Japanese ambassador complains to Secretary of State Hull about U.S. loan for cotton and wheat sales to China and League of Nations efforts to aid China [both of which events involve JM but his name is not mentioned]. FRUS III 508

22 Aug: JM meets Prince Ishii, Japanese representative at the recent London Economic Conference, in Paris for long talk on proposed consultative committee. Ishii tells JM the committee plan excluding Japan will fail. JM replies he does not want to end the China Consortium and that neither Soong nor JM himself want to use the proposed committee to isolate Japan. Ishii cable to Japanese Foreign Ministry, 22 Aug, cited by MY 56

25 Aug: Japanese embassy counselor complains to S Hornbeck in State Department meeting of TV Soong plan to form consultative committee on Chinese development and JM proposed role. FRUS III 512

7 Sep: JM in Paris gets letter from Stockholm on Swedish court decision reducing his compensation from 45,000 to 35,000 kroner. RA

20 Oct: Lamont writes Nelson Johnson, US Minister in China, recounting his meetings in London in summer with TV Soong who has invited JM to visit China to survey economic situation. JM had suggested to Soong formation of advisory committee on finance and investment of Europeans and Americans (including Lamont but not any Japanese). Europeans replied they would not participate in anything excluding Japanese. Lamont agreed. Soong then asked Roosevelt, whom he saw on way home from Europe, and President suggested

several businessmen who might participate. Monnet is now on his way to New York and China. LA

20 Oct: Charles and Anne Lindbergh meet JM and Silvia by chance at Berkeley Hotel, London where they briefly discuss political change in America with Roosevelt's election. According to Anne Lindbergh's diary, JM spoke of his fear that "Roosevelt is trying to bring about social reforms in a period of reconstruction and that is fatal."

Anne Lindbergh adds, in a letter to her mother, Elisabeth Morrow, about the same incident, that she did not immediately recognize JM who walked up to us "followed by a beautiful lady. He looked strangely familiar, like a dream. 'Is that---no!---yes!-it is M. Monnet! ...The lady was Italian who only spoke French... it was quite right to see M. Monnet there---it belonged to the old world....he gave me the address of his sister in Paris and I hope to see her." AML, diary, Yale University

22 Oct: Cable in code from Dean Jay, Paris to Lamont, NY: JM sails 22 Oct SS Europe [to NY]; Salter sails SS Empress of Britain for Canada. LA

25 Oct: TV Soong resigns as finance minister and is replaced by his brother-in-law H H Kung. FRUS 519-20

27 Oct: JM arrives NYC on SS Europa. LA

31 Oct: JM calls on S Hornbeck, head of Far Eastern Division in State Department, says that despite TV Soong resignation as finance minister, JM is on way to China and that while international consultative committee now in abeyance, JM will try to get Government of China to act finally toward managing its credit and debt problems. International consultative committee Soong had wanted to start has foundered, JM said, on British government opposition and refusal of T Lamont to serve on it. SH; FRUS III 520-1

1 Nov: S Hornbeck advises Secretary of State Hull that with Soong resignation as China's finance minister all US cooperation with him toward finding US representatives on his proposed international consultative committee should be discontinued and President so advised. SH

2 Nov: W Bullitt tries to reach JM at Carlton Hotel (Washington DC) but he has already departed [for China, via New York and Canada]. WCB

William C Bullitt is another Monnet acquaintance from WWI with whom he now renews their casual wartime relations. Bullitt had been on the American Peace Delegation during Monnet's time in Cognac and Paris in the mid 1920s when Bullitt was living in Paris. Their friendship later blossoms when Bullitt is the American ambassador in Moscow and Paris.

3 Nov: Lamont in New York writes Nelson Johnson, US Minister in China: JM "is a well-known and competent Frenchman....At the suggestion of Mr. Monnet, [TV Soong] planned...an advisory committee for the benefit of

China." Lamont reviews those, including himself, invited to join committee and gives their reasons for declining, essentially to avoid offending Japan. All suggested committee members associated with China Consortium which includes Japan which was not approached for new committee membership.

"...Monnet has just arrived here [in US] and after one day in New York has started for China, planning to meet Salter in Vancouver and go across thePacific together.... They are both very fine men but it will take more than two eminent economists to get China started again," Lamont concludes. NTJ

4 Nov: JM cables Bullitt before sailing for China for first time from Vancouver, Canada. SH; LA; WCB

MID-NOVEMBER: JM arrives in Shanghai in preceding week with A Salter and D. Drummond [JM's new assistant who incidentally is son of former LN Secretary General and JM's former boss in Geneva]. CWR Nov 25, SH, JMM 110; They stay with Henri Mazot, former director of the local branch of the Banque de l'Indochine, and a friend of TV Soong who had accompanied him on the recent trip to the United States and Europe. MY 60

19 Nov: Japanese charge d'affaires at Paris reports on talk with a director of the Banque d'Indochine on JM's mission in China. The resignation of Soong seems a favorable development for Japan but "intrigues" of JM and Mazot, who apparently will work with JM, demands continued concern and scrutiny. MY 61 citing Japanese embassy cable to its foreign ministry.

21 Nov: JM arrives in Shanghai with Drummond and Salter and immediately received by Soong in his private residence. Central Daily News, 22 Nov cited by HU II 17

22 Nov: W Bullitt named first US ambassador to Soviet Union. WCB

26 Nov: JM cables congratulations to Bullitt from China. WCB

12 Dec: JM invites Suma Yakichiro, Japan's consul general at Nanking, to Mazot's home for long conversation. JM describes his private role in China and his meetings with Soong, HH Kung, (Soong successor as Minister of Finance and also a brother-in-law of both Chiang Kai Shek and Soong himself) and others and his study of reports of the National Economic Council (which Soong still heads). From these sources, JM says, he is pessimistic about China future but also convinced the country can be developed only with some Japanese participation. Cable, 13 Dec to Japanese foreign ministry from Shanghai office, cited by MY 62

END OF YEAR: Salter recalls JM in China "courting Silvia by cable and phone to France." A. Salter, Slave of the Lamp, London, 1967, 26

1934

JANUARY: Silvia, her mother and Anna go to Valmont Clinic in Switzerland for a "cure". Her husband, Francesco Giannini, visits them but Silvia never returns to Italy, or to Giannini. ACCSM

A major uncertainty for Monnet came with TV Soong's sudden dismissal as Finance Minister just before the Frenchman left for China. Hemmed in by both personal and financial restraints, Monnet may have seen no alternative to pushing ahead even if Soong was out of the Chinese government. Once in China, Monnet showed a striking ability to land well in a strange and conflicted environment and to set out a plan of action.

3 Feb: French foreign ministry note describes "the activity of Dr. Rajchman and of M. Monnet" as having no concrete result to date due to the political situation of the country. AN, MAE, League of Nations, v. 2034 cited by MY 63

15 Feb: JM writes Lamont from China: "Things have been so uncertain and often contradictory that I have put off writing you....My stay is indefinite and may last another couple of months....LA

------: JM leaves for two week rest to find a solution to the impasse with Japan but returns empty handed. Together with Drummond they decide to meet again with Suma who reports that, according to JM, Soong and Kung have now recognized that Japanese participation is necessary in any Chinese development and, furthermore, that Rajchman is not useful. Suma responds positively by citing as example the cooperation of France and Germany after the Ruhr crisis. MAEJ B-9-7-0-8, Cable from Suma to Foreign Minister Hirota, 8 Mar, cited by MY 66

26 Feb: JM cables [Denis?] in Paris: Tell or write Bullitt following immediately: Telegraph agencies reporting US considering recognizing Manchuria. This would be so serious to cause turning of good friends here against your country and would strengthen Japan's control over China. WCB

27 Feb: JM has long conversation with EMB Ingram of UK Legation Shanghai: M. Monet [sic] reviewed his role with TV Soong and the failure of London talks to get the International Corporation started. "In view of this failure, he had been engaged by Soong (salary paid in advance) to visit China and study situation...he has now reached definite conclusions. He was convinced that it was necessary to form here some kind of financial corporation to be organized by a combination of the principal banks themselves. This was to be a body to deal with finance as opposed to banking---a body with which financial interests in London, Paris, New York, Tokyo etc could deal when it came to any question of large scale of operations in China...." [This is first recorded description of what becomes the Chinese Finance Development Corporation (CDFC).Ingram tells JM to talk with [Sir Louis] Beale, the commercial counselor. NAUK FO I 18078/1933

6 Mar: Beale describes meeting with JM which is continuation of 27 Feb talk with Ingram. JM says breach between Soong and Chiang Kai Shek is less now than one month ago and that Soong would soon resume a high government role. NAUK FO I 18078/2227

8 Mar: Suma reports to Foreign Minister Hirota that in a conversation with the British minister, Alexander Cadogan, the latter said JM and Drummond now realize that Japanese participation in any Chinese development is absolutely necessary. AN, MAE J B-9-7-0-8, 8 Mars cable to Hirota cited by MY 66

10 Mar: JM invites Suma to lunch in Shanghai. Before the meal, which Drummond joins, JM and Suma meet privately for an hour. JM states that stabilization of Chinese central government and defeat of the communists are country's major priorities. While Suma believes internal stabilization is far off, JM replies that fiscal reform can bind the country together and reduce the excessive military expenses. Suma is skeptical but JM insists that development can only come by Chinese initiative and not by outsiders acting like colonial powers. AN, MAE J B-9-7-0-8, Cables 12, 13 Mars, Suma to Hirota, cited by MY 67-69

20 Mar: Draft of agreement to establish China Development Finance Corporation, a purely Chinese institution designed to combine foreign and domestic investments, including the official Bank of China, in Chinese development projects. Such cooperation had existed earlier but without a specific institution to define and promote it. Immediate Japanese opposition to CDFC delays its start but JM continues to seek that country's acquiescence. FJM ADS 3/1/1, cited by MY 69-71

Many years later, Monnet cited the difficulties he had in understanding the Chinese as he tried to set up the CDFC. He tried without success to use the negotiating methods which had worked in Europe. He had to learn patience and persistence with the Chinese, he told George Ball, undersecretary of state in 1968. (Averell Harriman Papers, Library of Congress, box 488, cited by ER 152-153). But in his Memoirs, Monnet admits he never quite mastered the subtle Chinese ways.

1 Apr: Suma reports to his foreign minister that Monnet stresses need for CDFC to harness Chinese nationalism and to limit foreign investments tied to specific regions of the vast country to prevent spheres of influence. AN, MAE J East Asia, China finances, No. 289-1 to 3, cited by MY 72-73

13 Apr: Japanese Foreign Minister Hirota advises his staff in China that JM's initiatives have been effectively limited but lists further points needed toward that goal: The Japanese Empire must put its interests first in maintaining peace in Asia even against the views of other countries and the League of Nations; we must prevent anti-Japanese tendencies of other powers or attempts to pit one foreign power against another; China must not be divided by foreign

powers for their economic or political purposes nor may these powers use military or political aid to China to frustrate our goals. AN, MAE J A-1-1-0-10, No 109, cited by MY 73-75

Monnet is clearly caught between his own views (and those of Soong, Rajchman, and probably Salter) about China's needs and those of imperial Japan. He recognizes that Japan cannot be ignored in his work for, among other reasons, the US and the UK, continue to support a major Japanese role in China. But he must slowly recognize that the fierce Japanese reaction to his initiative on the CDFC is part of the larger political and military challenges Japan is more and more clearly prepared to make in China without regard to western opinion.

17 Apr: Declaration by Amau Eiji, head of Japan's foreign ministry information section, that "we oppose ... any attempt on the part of China to avail herself of the influence of any other country in order to resist Japan." This judged widely to be reaction to TV Soong recent trip to US and Europe seeking international support and to JM's attempt to form China Development Finance Corporation to raise Chinese capital in cooperation with western interests. James W Morley, China Quagmire, (New York, 1983) 79-81

22 Apr: JM writes long letter to Lamont on China situation, including Amau Declaration, for which Lamont later says JM is partly responsible. JM insists he saw immediately that excluding Japan from any international venture in China was a mistake. JM says declaration now seems to be a trial balloon which Japan wants to retract. JM also describes work in setting up a Chinese finance corporation. LA

Although Lamont is certainly correct in attributing the Amau Declaration to Monnet's work on the CFDC, it is also clear that the Japanese crudely attempt to deceive and isolate Monnet. For example, the Japanese Consul General, Suma, tells Monnet at one point that Japan cannot accept the CDFC but later also tells him than he regrets the Amau Declaration. But one hour earlier, Suma tells an Englishman that the Declaration was his (Suma's) idea and its purpose was to kill the CFDC.(Monnet's account of this duplicity is contained in his talk in Moscow in July with American Ambassador Bullitt. See 19 July below) Whatever Suma's view on the Amau Declaration, its substance represents Japan's views opposing all actual or perceived attempts to exclude Japan from a central role in China.

23 Apr: Amb Lindley (UK) in Tokyo reports on reactions to Amau Declaration: "French ambassador connects statement with negotiations of JM for international loan to China, one of the conditions of which (according to him) was a stipulation by China that Japan should not participate. NAUK FO I 18097/2255

27 Apr: UK Minister Cadogan, discussing Amau Declaration, says Suma, the Japanese consul general in Shanghai, indicated Japan would take strong

exception to JM plan for a China Finance Corporation unless Japan was first consulted and then asked to participate. NAUK FO I 18097/2378

-----JM's assistant, David Drummond, writes Sir Francis Lindley, UK ambassador in Tokyo on their work in China, adding "Monnet and I would like to go to Japan now to explain the whole situation..." perhaps on the way back to the US. NAUK FO I 18078/3082

-----JM in Shanghai cables Lamont in New York: In view of Japanese [Amau] declaration and last year's talks with you in London, you should know of my efforts to have all [assistance?] directed to Chinese self-help though a purely Chinese Finance Corporation to finance country's reconstruction itself or associate itself with any and all foreign interests. All powers must have equal opportunity...and Japanese have been advised constantly of our progress. Their representative here says [Amau] declaration has been misunderstood. LA

MAY: JM writes 14 page memo with this date and with tables and other details on "Chinese National Railways" over his name in preparation for announcement of Chinese Development Finance Corporation (CDFC). NAUK FO I 18097/ F5611

3 May: Drummond meets with US Minister Johnson and describes Japanese mistrust of JM being based partly at least on their suspicions about the League of Nations and Rajchman whom they dislike. Johnson memorandum, FRUS III 377-79

4 May: R. Brand, Lazard Freres partner, sends memo to John Simon, British foreign secretary, on 26 Apr cable which JM ("my friend") has sent to his London representative who gave it to me. JM says CDFC almost ready to launch and he has kept the Japanese "constantly" advised of his progress. Recent Japanese statement [Amau Declaration] was based on misunderstanding and will be rectified. NAUK FO I 18078/F2668

5 May: JM meets for first time with US Minister Nelson Johnson and describes "Chinese bankers syndicate" he hopes to organize and gives background of his mission with Arthur Salter and David Drummond which is entirely private and not associated with League of Nations. JM sees three problems for China: a) Getting Chinese money to show lead in investment before foreign capital would follow; b) Managing debts including the 1918 Nishihara debts to Japan; c) Reorganizing its railroads. JM is very impressed with Chiang Kai Shek. FRUS III 379-81

10 May: Japanese government announces it will not participate in a silver banking program proposed by JM as a preliminary to raising a loan for China. The Monnet plan reportedly was one reason for the Amau Declaration. Current History, July 1934 510-11

12 May: Conversation of D. Drummond and A. Cadagon, UK minister

in China, on JM's activities: He saw Chiang Kai Shek for "2 or 3 long talks" and said that Chiang was first skeptical but later more sympathetic to CDFC idea. Cadagon remains skeptical and believes Japanese opposition will cause abandonment of plan when JM and Drummond leave at the end of the month. NAUK FO I 18078/4418

23 May: Chiang Kai Shek decides to support CDFC but insists that Soong's younger brother, TL Soong, becomes its general manager. AH No 002010200114032, cited by HU II 19

26 May: US Minister Johnson reports one of his officers was told by US journalist that Japan views JM proposal [to induce foreign capital to invest in Chinese corporation] with disfavor because China should first repay Japan; because JM proposal would undermine International Consortium on China of 1920 and finally because all money invested in China would be used for political ends. FRUS III 386

31 May: Minister Johnson meets JM again in Kaling, China while on tour. NTJ

2 Jun: CDFC comes into existence with a shareholders meeting at the Shanghai Bankers Club, according to 6 Jun memo by Beale, UK commercial counselor. PRO FOI 18078/4418. (The CDFC regulations are in FJM AMD 2/1/1; its headquarters was at 111 Kiukiang Road, Shanghai. The Soong family---brothers TV, TL and TA, and their brother-in-law, HH Kung---are the real power of the CDFC among the 98 persons attending the first shareholder meeting. MY 80-l)

11 Jun: British legation official writes that CDFC more likely to get support of foreign legations in China as a purely Chinese financing group "which would tend to make the investment of foreign capital in China more secure". NAUK FO 371 18078, Cadogan to Alexander

8 Jun: US Minister Johnson reports letter from D Drummond, JM aide, saying that CDFC has been launched to help raise capital with Chinese banks. JM to return soon to US and Europe. FRUS III 387-8

The first advice Monnet had received from Chinese businessmen was "It is no use trying to invest foreign capital in China without Chinese participation." The CDFC was a response to this view since the new corporation was a Chinese institution designed to inject long-term Chinese and foreign capital into public and private commercial and industrial concerns. (JMM lll)

14 Jun: D Drummond writes "Dear Alec" letter to UK Minister [to China] Cadogan: I will leave China soon; JM's position indefinite; he will act as agent for US and Europe concerning CDFC but "railways position" is less clear. JM and I will go to New York, London and elsewhere to explain our work. NAUK FO I 18078//4418.

15 Jun: L Beale writes A. Cadogan on "final" talk yesterday with Drummond and JM. Drummond leaving Sunday via Japan, JM at end of month "by air from Saigon or via Siberia". Both will return in October with JM acting as liaison between CDFC and lending countries including Lazards [in London] "with whom he is himself connected. He is, however, deliberately vague as to his intentions....Speaking of Japanese intentions, Monnet did not try...to minimize the dangers.... His aim is obviously to steer it [CDFC] as clear as possible away from the political rocks and place it on sound economic foundations but that is no easy matter at the present moment." NAUK FO I 18078/4418

22 Jun: J. Pratt of Foreign Office describes London talk with Li Ming, leading Chinese banker, who told him that Dr. Rajchman had introduced M. Monnet to TV Soong and had tried to form an International Finance Corporation. Soong then made agreements with Kuhn Loeb in America and Lazards in London appointing them Chinese government purchasing agents in the event of large reconstruction projects in China. Monnet believed these arrangements will induce the financial groups now associated with China Consortium to come instead with this corporation. Consortium group refused, however, since they saw this as a device to exclude Japan. Monnet then went to China to form a Chinese finance corporation but local bankers saw this also as a political not a financial scheme. Li Ming is convinced nothing can happen without Japan. NAUK FO I 18078/3834

Monnet's push forward against Japanese opposition and, probably, against the advice of Chinese bankers like Li Ming, shows both stubbornness and perhaps misguided knowledge of Asian realities. He also was mistaken in believing that TV Soong would soon be restored to a high government post.

26 Jun: E Walker cables Lamont that JM cabled he will sail 2 July for US [but this changes when JM decides to come home by train through Siberia]. LA

28 Jun: Beale, UK commercial counselor in China, reports long talk with Suma, Japanese consul general, who says he does not trust JM because of his associations with Lamont, the American banker. NAUK FO I 18078/3858

JULY: Silvia Giannini and daughter Anna get USSR citizenship at embassy in Switzerland or France. ACCSM

3 Jul: Letter contract for three years [confirming and expanding previous 1933 agreement] signed by TL Soong [TV's brother and replacement as general manager of CDFC] and JM (both in China) specifies Monnet duties and income of C$50,000 per year and a percentage of CDFC net profits. JM to be "Exclusive Representative" of CDFC in Europe and the US and to deal in China only through CDFC. FJM ADS 3/1/4 cited by MY 86-7; FJM AMD 6/1/1; Central Daily News 5 Jul, cited by HU II 21

----- JM cables Bullitt: I arrive [in Moscow] 15 July and want to see you; Bullitt replies "delighted to see you." WCB

4 Jul: CDFC formally launched, JM supplies list of stockholders in confidence to Minister Johnson. FRUS III 405

5 Jul: JM again meets Minister Johnson in China; says he is en route to Moscow, Paris, London, NY before returning to Shanghai in autumn. FRUS III 403. In memo on conversation, Johnson quotes JM views on dire situation in Japan and its similarities with Germany. Thinks revolution may come there soon which will end either in monarchy or communism. JM's manner is very depressed; he considered Nazi killings little better than gangster assassinations. Also describes CDFC progress and coming visit with Bullitt. NTJ

The preceding and the following entries illustrate some of Monnet's still-developing thinking about crises in international affairs. He is appalled at the turmoil in Germany which has just led to Hitler's assumption of power but he is, in retrospect at least, naive about Japan's "progressive spirit" and surprisingly complacent about that country's attempts to capture control of part of the Asian mainland. His view on Japan in Manchuria in the Bullitt report below also contrasts with his earlier message to Bullitt(26 Feb, above) when he warns of recognizing the Japanese occupation of Manchuria. In the conversations recorded below with Bullitt he is now more realistic, he says, than he was a few months earlier. He now accepts reluctantly a Japanese presence on the Chinese mainland. Clearly his views on Japan are still developing in his first year living in Asia.

15 Jul: JM arrives in Moscow. WCB

19 Jul: W Bullitt sends long report to State Department on talk with JM in Moscow on situation in China: JM was in Shanghai, Nanking, Tientsin, Peking, Hong Kong and Tokyo. He came to Moscow for one day on way to Europe but arrived ill and spent a week here. JM commented that TV Soong did not resign but was dismissed as finance minister by Chiang Kai Shek in order to establish latter's dominance over the "Soong dynasty." JM established a strictly Chinese finance corporation and told how Chiang stayed firm against Japanese threats against the corporation which is now in business. JM described Japanese attempts to deceive him about the Amau Declaration. [See 22-27 April, above]. JM is the foreign agent of this corporation and on his way to London, Paris New York and Washington before returning to China in November. Monnet described his two day visit to Japan and his intense impression of the progressive spirit and managerial ability of its people. JM also thinks "it is in the interest of civilization that Japan's position in Manchuria be recognized and that Japan should perhaps be encouraged to press on into Mongolia. The acquiescence of England, the U.S., France and other great powers in Japan's expansion would remove, at least for many years, the danger of war in the Far East." NARA 893.50A

Monnet's late decision to leave Japan via Moscow instead of sailing home may have been based more on personal than business considerations. In Moscow he had long conversations with his old friend William Bullitt, now the

US Ambassador. He also apparently talked with the French ambassador there. From these and other conversations Monnet probably confirmed the possibility of divorce and remarriage in the Soviet capital for Soviet citizens. Shortly after this time, Silvia Giannini and her daughter, Anna, became Soviet citizens at a Soviet embassy in Europe. This seems to have solved the major problem preventing Silvia and Jean from marrying: the Italian legal prohibition against divorce and the danger of losing custody of Anna under the laws of any European country, like Italy or France, which recognized the Napoleonic Code's presumption of custody to the father. According to his 1971 interview with Alan Watson on BBC-TV, Monnet had help with the Moscow marriage arrangements from Rajchman and from Soviet Ambassador in China Bogomolov.

26 Jul: Bullitt writes JM in Paris: Just a line to tell you how greatly I enjoyed having you in my house. WCB

29 Jul: JM cables Bullitt [in French] thanking him for friendship and hospitality during recent visit in Moscow. WCB

31 Jul: In response to State Dept request for more information on JM work, US Minister in China Johnson reports little information beyond his 26 May report; Johnson concludes however that Japanese suspicions of JM and his CDFC work come from his association with TV Soong whom Japanese dislike for wanting to exclude Japan from certain investments in China and for favoring other countries which Japan sees as contrary to 1920 Consortium agreement. FRUS III 403-5

5 Aug: Bullitt describes visit in Moscow of JM ("one of my closest French friends") in letter to Roosevelt, summarizing his longer dispatch to the State Department (see 19 Jul above). OB 92-3

8 Aug: JM writes Bullitt from Paris on his recovery from illness [which had caused JM to stay longer in Moscow than he intended and] which was "evidently more serious than I thought." He is sending Bullitt two cases of cognac. I sail tomorrow for United States. I have not seen [Alexis] Leger or anyone else but will send more information after meeting people in Paris and London. WCB

22 Aug: JM and D Drummond meet in London with Charles Addis, British representative in China Consortium, to discuss "rehabilitating Chinese railroads." Addis described JM as "a clever debater but perhaps a bit too adroit." R. Dayer, Finance and Empire: Sir Charles Addis 1861-1945, NY, 1988, 290

28 Aug: N Johnson reports to State Dept from China that in conversation with his staff on CDFC a Japanese official noted its LN origins which made it suspicious to Japan even though JM is no longer with LN. FRUS III 407-8

------JM writes Bullitt again from Paris on his recovery from mysterious illness. "If I see common friends I will say you nearly saved my life. Indeed since I returned to Paris I have been unwell until the last day or two so I dread to think what would have happened to me should I not have met your kind and thoughtful friendship in Moscow ....My present plans which I mentioned to you gave been somewhat delayed on account of certain (sic) young lady who was not [as]well as was hoped and also some external complications. I hope on my return from the States that everything will progress and you may one day see some mysterious hiding (sic) visitors appear in Moscow." WCB

29 Aug: J Pratt, Foreign Office London, describes meeting yesterday with C Addis, UK representative on China Consortium, who has just met with JM. "Addis explains that he has no great confidence in Monnet. `He is very clever and a great talker but somewhat elusive and it was difficult to pin him down.'" Memo describes participation in the $16m loan for the Shanghai-Hangehow-Ningpo railroad as a major CDFC project. NAUK FO I 18079/5280

31 Aug: JF Dulles cables JM on SS Ile de France "delighted you have escaped from China and will be with us again." JFD box 13

Monnet had gone to China as a single man, infatuated with a married woman who he desperately hoped would soon be permanently separated from her husband. The affair matured while he was alone in China. When he returned the first time from the Far East, it was with a determination to marry Silvia and to relaunch his business career in a more orderly manner than as a single adviser to a foreign government. It was on this visit to the United States that he made plans for a business partnership with George Murnane, a respectable financier who had fallen into misfortune in his dealings with Ivar Kreuger. Thus Monnet and Murnane, two men with somewhat starred business histories, came together with the help of their wealthy friends.

4 Sept: JM arrives in NYC on SS Ile de France. LA

8 Sept: JM has dinner with Anne Morrow Lindbergh and her sister, Constance Morrow, at Waldorf rooftop restaurant, NYC. They talked about China and Russia. He talked about Communism. "There was ease because we three knew and trusted each other and there was surprise because Con and I did not know M. Monnet too well....And M. Monnet was gay, perhaps because he was giving us pleasure, perhaps because he knew we like to hear him talk, liked his mind and his wit." AML III 198-9.

19 Sept: JM is in NY according to Lamont conversation with State Department official Hornbeck which reviews China situation including JM background , his friendship with Rajchman, and his role in establishing CDFC. FRUS III 412-17

20 Sept: JM meets with Hornbeck at State Department and reports, as Lamont told Hornbeck yesterday, that CDFC will finance completion of Shanghai-Hangchow-Ningpo railway as first major project. JM give more details on CDFC and Chinese railroad questions. JM also indicates he may seek US Export-Import Bank funding of some China projects. FRUS III 417

23 Sept: "Summer is over. I shall leave it in North Haven [Maine] tomorrow....H N[icolson] hasn't been able to see beyond the spruce trees--but he has had a wonderful afternoon of talk w. George [Rublee?] and Jean Monnet who arrived at 12 and left at 5:30! He told me the astonishing news that he is to be married in a few weeks---an Italian girl---married but to be separated from her husband. He seemed properly happy and very gay and merry. He had a long talk w. D[wight] Jr [who] thinks he is in love with Nancy Hoyt". ECM

6-7 Oct: JM [in US] and Bullitt [in Moscow] exchange cables on their respective travel plans and desires to meet each other; Bullitt is leaving for China and Japan on 10 Oct while JM leaves NY for Paris where he arrives on 19 October en route to Moscow "with party to carry out my private plans, then return to United States at end of November before sailing for China at end of year. Please wire me your plans." This cable crosses Bullitt's who writes: Sorry will not be here when you reach Moscow but John Wiley will help....WCB

10 Oct: Bullitt leaves Moscow for Japan until 10 Nov and thereafter in China until 27 Nov. In Shanghai he stays in JM house [while latter is in U.S. on business and in Europe to meet Silvia and travel to Moscow for their wedding.] OB 97; WCB

12 Oct: JM and assistant Mr. Howe [probably AS Howe; see 12 Aug 1936] meet in State Department with its Far Eastern area officials, describing CDFC and its work including participating in $16m bond issue for Shanghai-Hangehow-Ningpo RR. JM sails for Europe same day [to meet Silvia and travel to Moscow wedding] and says he will be back in 6 weeks. FRUS III, 421-23; SH; This was the first loan to the Chinese railways with Chinese among its underwriters. RM 48

------:JM writes Lamont from SS Majestic: I appreciated your note to me on ship with advice on the "complicated Chinese situation." LA

16 Oct: J Dulles asks William Cromwell, his senior law partner, to join him in investing in a Monnet, Murnane corporation. Dulles gives detailed background of both Monnet and Murnane and justifies proposed investment in MM "which should produce a large amount of legal business for us." Dulles says new firm is seeking $250,000 of which Dulles will personally invest $25,000 "which for me is quite considerable" and asks Sullivan and Cromwell to invest $50,000. JFD, Murnane file.

This initiative by Dulles marks a new stage in his relations with Monnet. The two had met at the Versailles Peace Conference and renewed their acquaintance when Monnet became an investment banker with Blair & Co. Now Dulles supports George Murnane, a casualty of the collapse of the Kreuger empire, and Monnet, a business friend of Kreuger whom Dulles employed to help clean up the Swede's bankruptcy, to go into business together. Cromwell has doubts about the venture (and he turns out to be correct in his judgment for

Monnet, Murnane never makes much money) but he loyally supports his partner Dulles after advising steps to protect their investment. Dulles was a strong minded lawyer but a loyal and devoted friend, as Monnet was to learn.

4 Nov: Robert Haas of League of Nations arrives in Shanghai as replacement for L Rajchman. CWR

10 Nov: Bullitt receives mail at 262 Route Ferguson, Shanghai which is JM's address where Bullitt is apparently staying in JM's absence. WCB

13 Nov: JM and Silvia di Bondini Giannini marry in Moscow, (JMM l09) immediately after she gets divorce in same building. They had traveled separately from Paris (she with her mother). After ceremonies, she and daughter Anna take JM's French citizenship and after four months of travel in Europe and US, they go to China. ACCSM

JM's friend, Ludwik Rajchman, a Polish doctor with wide international friendships---he eventually founded the United Nation's children's fund, UNICEF--- was apparently involved in arranging the Moscow marriage of Monnet and Silvia. The Pole was friendly with Dimitri Bogomolov, the Russian ambassador to China, who facilitated the Moscow divorce of Silvia and her remarriage to Monnet.(BM 104)

24 Nov: WC Bullitt arrives in Nanking on 20 Nov and is now back in Shanghai where he is staying with old friend, Mr. Monnett [sic] at 262 Route Ferguson. CWR; OB; FDRL PSF .[Bullitt obviously was not `staying' with JM who was already on his way from Moscow to western Europe but Bullitt probably stayed in JM's house in Shanghai. Bullitt had been informed of JM's marriage plans but was not involved in the arrangements. AW]

28 Nov: Dulles cables congratulations to JM in Paris. JFD, Murnane file

------:D Drummond summarizes his recent work for CDFC including meetings with JM at Lazards and with Imperial Chemical, British American Tobacco and others as well as various phone calls. "...it would seem that Monnet will be able to go back to China with sufficient data collected from this side ...to push forward the scheme over there." FJM ADS 6/1/1

29 Nov: CDFC signs agreement with British and Chinese Corporation to complete the Shanghai-Hangchow-Ningpo railroad which had been underway since 1908. But the Chinese money market, which was to supply funds for the project, could not produce the needed funds. CSRD 98-9

2 Dec: D Drummond writes his father that JM's attempts to help China get a large loans from the UK end in failure. NAUK I 18079 cited by MY 94

6 Dec: FDR writes Morgenthau, his treasury secretary, of his own family's background "of a little over a century" in Chinese affairs. Refers to "money changers in temple" controlling China which may need "many years and possibly

several revolutions" to build a "new China" which must stand on own feet "without complete dependence on Japan and Europe."

Later this month, FDR receives note from Chinese ambassador that TV Soong is sending president 20 chests of tea and 20 boxes of lichee nuts with his compliments of the season. [Soong had visited the president in both Washington and Hyde Park in 1933]. FDRL Official File #150

Roosevelt's interest in China was reflected in his administration, especially the treasury and state departments. Unfortunately this interest did not always benefit China. An American expert on China, who was a close adviser to TV Soong whom he accompanied to the US in 1933, wrote about the importance of silver to the American economy and its disastrous effects on China: "In 1933-35, the American silver-buying policy, with callous disregard for its effect in disrupting the economic life of a friendly country and, over China's repeated protests, drained away huge amounts of China's silver resources...." This policy raised China's silver dollars to high, overvalued levels and brought severe deflation and a slump to the country. (Arthur N Young, China and the Helping Hand, Cambridge, MA, 1963)6. It was in this financial climate that Monnet was trying to help China's development often using the same American friends who were, like Lamont and Morgenthau, the treasury secretary, involved in the aggressive American silver policy.

8 Dec: JM cables Lamont he has married and arrives NY next week. LA

10 Dec: Pierre Denis, Paris, writes D Drummond, London: JM asked me to send enclosed letter from William Rollo of Withers and Co of London, whom JM met (together with Mr V A Cazalet, also of London) on SS Majestic on his way from NY [presumably Oct 12 sailing]. JM sent each 3 bottles of cognac because he thinks they may be useful, Denis says. FJM ADS

28 Dec: JM, understood to be acting on behalf of Chinese governments, meets Hornbeck and Herbert Feis in State Department on silver outflow from China and possibility of US Export Import Bank loan to China with pessimistic responses by the two officials. FRUS III 459-60

1935

5 Jan: JM meets with Japanese ambassador at Lamont home in NYC. LA

30 Jan: Cable from Wm Cromwell in Paris, senior partner of Sullivan and Cromwell, to partner John Foster Dulles in New York: Re proposed Monnet and Murnane [loan]: I will join you in taking 50,000 each in preferred stock. My motive is solely to help the firm and yourself and upon your opinion that this foreign corporation will not constitute a partnership with us. Adds "purely personal" note of concern that "both Monnet and Murnane have reached middle age and neither has been able to accumulate but meager personal assets." Their death, retirement or incapacity would inevitably result in loss of all our investment unless you somehow protect us by life insurance. JFD, Murnane file

31 Jan: Lamont sends note of thanks to Silvia at Lowell Hotel in NYC for gift of Chinese tea and nuts. LA

1 Feb: Bullitt sends FDR's secretary a cable which he says JM just delivered to him. [Bullitt is at State Dept on medical leave from Moscow post] "Monnet has also informed me that Dr. Sze [Chinese ambassador in Washington] has received definitive proposal of Chinese government and will presumably present it to the Dept of State today or tomorrow." FDRL, PSF, Box 26

16 Feb: JM writes R Brand and others on opening of Monnet, Murnane offices in NYC, with Pierre Denis in Paris, D Drummond in London and Henri Mazot in Shanghai. Other recipients: Albert, Westrick and Hauss (of Berlin law firm associated with Sullivan and Cromwell); Dean Jay (JP Morgan representative in Paris); Jacob Wallenberg (Enskilda Bank, Stockholm) and others. Offices of the partnership were at 30 Broad Street, NYC; 225 Boulevard St Germain, 37 Threadneedle St, London and 113 Kiuking Road, Shanghai. FJM ADS 4/1/1, -/2,-/5

The partnership of Monnet and George Murnane brought together two men who may have met as early as WWI when both were involved in the war effort. At that time Murnane was deputy commissioner of the American Red Cross for France. Their paths crossed again in the interwar years when Murnane was involved with Lee Higginson, a Boston investment bank, which worked with Ivar Kreuger, the Swedish "match king." As we have seen, Kreuger's downfall came just after Monnet's career with Transamerica was abruptly ended. Both Monnet and Murnane had awkward years of restarting in business (including Monnet's in Sweden and China) when, with Dulles' encouragement, they came together in partnership. Monnet had a high regard for Murnane's intelligence, a feeling Murnane reciprocated. (Monnet's memoirs only briefly mention Murnane; this account is partly based on conversations of the author with George Murnane Jr in 1990-91.)

Monnet, Murnane was to include Monnet's Chinese work but not be limited to it. In the partnership's predicted income for 1935-36, payments from CDFC amounted to only about 12 per cent but Monnet was initially devoting most of his time and energy to Chinese matters when he returned there later this year. (FJM ADS, 4/4//1,-9l ADS 6/1/4; ADS 10/1/36, cited by HU II 22)

3 Mar: D Drummond memo on visit today to Frederick Leith-Ross who has high regard for JM who, Drummond says, will be back in the fall. FJM ADS 6/1/2

15 Mar: JM writes Drummond and Denis "on point of leaving for China" with details on what MM will be doing in China and on Murnane's trip to Europe. He gives guidance for dealing with Bank of England and UK Treasury: "They must see us as silent workers, happy to be of service without wanting for ourselves any credit." They must understand that a Chinese loan or partnership is vital for any investment there. The Lunghai railroad bonds can be a major project

for us. FJM ADS 6/1/4

-----: In second letter written same date to same addressees, JM says MM has only a "liquid operating fund" without capital and must earn enough from Chinese and telephone deals to pay immediate expenses. Also notes possible role of firm in recasting of Kreuger and Toll, apparently an JF Dulles idea.

"Murphy [?] and Foster Dulles have told Murnane and me that it is their intention once the Krueger matter is settled as a part of the new Kreuger and Toll settlement that they will propose to set up a company which would take over all the bonds now in K&T and ···MM will take the practical management···on a basis of a yearly fee and a certain interest [in the bonds]···. I attach the greatest interest to special efforts being made to arrange real friendship between George [Murnane] and Pleven as this will be most helpful in working out our telephone problems. [Pleven is with Theodore Gary Co. of London. Tone of letter is of introducing George Murnane to Denis and Drummond.]

Budget of MM proposes salaries of $36,000 each for the two partners; 3500 for NYC office rent; 2500 for rent of Paris apartment where Denis lives and which serves as Paris office of MM. Income includes 25,000 each from Adams and Solvay corporations and 20,000 (minimum) from CDFC. FJM ADS 4/1/8,/9

Monnet and Murnane's salaries of $36,000 would be equivalent to about $400,000 in 2007 terms, ambitious sums for a new and unproven firm.

18 Mar: Lamont gives lunch for JM who leaves today for China, invites Leffingwell and Parker Gilbert. LA

LATE MARCH: JM, Silvia and Anna leave Seattle on SS Empress of China to Shanghai. ACCSM

EARLY APRIL: JM stops in Tokyo on way to China and talks with French ambassador. Arrives in China later in same month. NTJ. ACCSM

Monnet's political understanding of China, reflected 40 years later when he was writing his memoirs, was of a country undergoing revolutionary change since the Manchu dynasty fell, in 1911, to a republican upsurge led by Sun Yat-Sen. The successor governments led to Chiang Kai Shek whom Monnet met soon after his arrival. But since Chiang spoke only Chinese, Monnet communicated through Madame Chiang Kai-Shek, an American-educated daughter of a Chinese missionary whose brother was TV Soong. This peculiar arrangement gave Monnet early and direct access to China's rulers. JMM 110-114.

Even while still working in China, Monnet drew some lessons from his experience there. He reflects below [20 July] on how an outsider can draw principals together if they trust the facilitator, in this Chinese case, Monnet himself. It is a lesson which he would later apply both during the coming war and in the turmoil in Europe thereafter.

17 Apr: JM describes to British minister Cadogan his recent talks with Kung and TV Soong who have complete confidence in him and with whom he

has fully shared his international correspondence and plans. NAUK 19242, 23 Apr cited by MY 100

3 May: JM expresses concern that UK is sending Frederick Leith-Ross as economic adviser to assess situation in China. He tells Cadogan than Kung and TV Soong are also worried that the Japanese may take advantage of interim by moving Chinese bankers to their side. Cadogan himself is concerned that JM is acting as intermediary for Soong. NAUK 1924l, cable from Cadogan in Beijing cited by MY 100

4 May: JM and his projects still distrusted by the Japanese government even though he may have modified his anti-Japanese views, according to UK Ambassador Clive in Tokyo. NAUK 1924l, minutes from Clive cited by MY 100

6 May: CDFC and British and Chinese Corporation make new agreement on financing Shanghai-Hangchow-Ningpo railroad. CSRD 99

13 May: JM writes from China to George Murnane on silver and Chinese government. He is working on a discount system with Chinese banks through CDFC and to arrange some imports here with, among other resources, US Ex-Im bank credits. JM is not optimistic on external aid to China. FJM ADS 1/2/4

5 Jun: JM in Beijing where he talks with US Minister Nelson Johnson. NTJ.

18 Jun: In talk with British minister, JM is pessimistic about the banking situation in China; he sees similarities with the US situation just before the 1929 crash. NAUK 19242, from Cadogan, cited by MY 103

25 Jun: JM, with support of Kung, TV Soong and HSBC bank he says, asks Cadogan for a credit of 5-10 m pounds sterling to help maintain the reserves of the government's banks, with payment guaranteed by customs fees. Cadogan says he cannot support such a request to London which has already indicated reluctance to discuss bilateral aid to China and which comes without official Chinese sponsorship. NAUK 19242, cable from Cadogan, 6 Jul cited by MY 102

10 Jul: JM is reported by British foreign officer W C Wilcox in Shanghai as being "extremely clear and convincing" in promoting the CDFC. But later in the month a UK treasury official, S D Waley, said his ministry tried to do "anything possible...to sabotage Monnet" because his CDFC was resented by the Japanese as a political device to exclude them, an exclusion contrary to British foreign policy. SE 39 citing NAUK FO I 19307/F4445 and 19252/F7782, respectively.

20 Jul: MM incorporated in Prince Edward Island, Canada. This incorporation ends 31 Aug 1937. PEI

-----JM (in China) writes G Murnane (NYC): He describes what has happened since he last wrote at the end of April [actually dated 13 May] when he arrived: He saw UK Amb Cadogan seeking London credits for deteriorating Shanghai situation but without success. Japan is putting Shanghai exchange under financial pressure.

JM gives broad account of how he is bringing together different viewpoints in China and how personal relations function there. "Anyone with experience in China will appreciate the part which can be played in negotiations by a person with no official capacity but who has the confidence of both parties. He is able to express the viewpoint of one side and another and to clear up any misunderstandings; at times he can throw out ideas .... His most valuable service, perhaps, is to keep the parties in touch with each other. It is a simple fact to say that ...I have been able to fill this role...." FJM ADS. 1/2/12

26 Jul: Christopher Chancellor, head of Reuter's far eastern news service, writes Simon Harcourt-Smith of Foreign Office who had asked for "City opinion" of JM. "I have inquired at the highest level (JR Morgan [sic] in the person of Tom Lamont) and he gave confirmation of my own conclusion---namely Monnet is very narrowly removed from an adventurer pure and simple. He is like a man who has secured neither bridgehead---talks to the Chinese about his `backing' from Morgan etc then talks to the City about his structure in China to which money may be loaned; he becomes more dangerous as time goes on and his expenses mount because his sole motive is the `rake-off' to Monnet...." He has antagonized the Japanese by his behavior and I can imagine no worse agent for British interests.....It is important for Leith-Ross [special British economic representative to China] to keep away from Monnet." (Copy sent to Leith-Ross by Foreign Office) NAUK FO I: 19243/4955

Despite this negative assessment of Monnet by Chancellor, apparently backed by Thomas Lamont, a long-time Monnet acquaintance, the Frenchman's role in China was much more complicated than the journalist's dismissive view. Monnet was audacious in style, inventive in commercial deals, and skilled at managing relations with a variety of officials, both Western and Chinese. He describes in his Memoirs the subtle ways of the Chinese he worked with and the anomaly of living in the French Concession---"with the atmosphere of a French provincial town" ---while trying to understand a very different culture. "By January 1936...we left that fascinating world without ever having fathomed it." JMM 115

15 Aug: FRBNY Chairman G Harrison talks with US Treasury Secretary Morgenthau at latter's request: Morgenthau seeking "someone familiar with Chinese government's procedure...on financing and its relations with the central bank." Harrison suggests Prof. Rogers or Jean Monnet but Morgenthau objects to both, Monnet because "not being an American and that anyway the President had some `question' about him." FRBNY, confidential files

LATE SUMMER: JM and family travel to US from China. ACCSM

SEPTEMBER: JM has dinner on Long Island with Murnane when Dulles arrives with news of Hitler's decrees against Jews. "A man capable of that will start a war. There are no limits to such bigotry and aggression", JM recalls saying at the time. JMM 116

SEPTEMBER, NOVEMBER: Various letters from JM in Paris to Denis (Shanghai) on routine MM business matters. FJM ADS

3 Nov: Chinese government takes "drastic move of taking China's currency off a silver base and putting it on managed paper [currency.]" All holders of silver in the country were ordered to surrender it to the Central Bank and to take paper currency in its stead. "The move was designed to check the steady fall in prices that has accompanied the rise in the value of silver brought about largely by the American purchases [of silver under legislation to benefit US silver producers]. Current History, Dec 1935 329

21 Nov: Leith-Ross, special UK representative in China, writes D. Waley, UK Treasury, on JM plan to channel foreign default settlement of Chinese railroad bonds through CDFC. "I only wish British railroad interests were represented here by somebody as active and fertile in imagination as Monnet!" [Attaches copy of "Monnet's Scheme" which is Leith-Ross summary of a straightforward plan by JM for devoting railroad income to past railroad bond repayments with CDFC acting as receiving agent and trustee of funds for the Tinetsin-Pukow and Huhuang railroad]. NAUK FO I: 19252/7782

Leith-Ross, an influential Foreign Office official, obviously took a much more positive view of Monnet's work despite receiving the negative assessment of the Reuter's chief far east correspondent [See 26 July above] and despite the similar negative view of Monnet by the UK Treasury aide which follows.

10 Dec: D. Waley, UK Treasury, writes L. Browett of Board of Trade, enclosing letter from Leith-Ross on JM: "I need not say that I entirely share the views which Leith expresses...[I] will do anything possible from my end to sabotage Monnet but any constructive effort seems to be for you rather than for me." NAUK FO I: 19243/4955

1936

JANUARY: JM decides he must stay in New York after final visit to China. JMM 116

Monnet, Murnane's work continued in China for several more years through a local agent but the confused political and economic situation prevented the country from gaining stability and the firm from achieving the income which both partners and their investors, including Sullivan and Cromwell, anticipated. Monnet's own relations with the Chinese seemed to blend his native energy and optimism with a formidable respect for their intelligence and their distrust of foreigners. In his memoirs he writes "it was much more important to win their confidence than to understand them." In this Monnet relied on his own values:

" [to]...act as you speak so that there is never any contradiction between what you say and what you do."(JMM 111-115)

Back in the West, an old problem---Germany and the disunity of her neighbors---rose to capture Monnet's attention once more.

MARCH: JM meets former German chancellor Heinrich Bruening in NYC. They discuss German threats to the peace and the need for Britain and France to act together. JMM 116.

26 Mar: JM meets former Secretary of State HL Stimson in latter's NYC office, describes "three years" spent in China; he predicts there will be no war between China and Japan "unless there should be a world war." The main problem in China is that nothing is being done for the peasant. Chinese capitalism may succumb to this failure. JM and HLS agree that liberalization in Japan will come, if at all, through industrialization and that the British approach to China is outdated and based on interests of the "Old Timers" [i.e. foreigners] there and on the City of London, losing sight of the political problems. HLSD

9 May: New loan of 1.1m pounds signed between CDFC and British and Chinese Corporation for completion of a major section of the Shanghai-Hangchow-Ningpo railroad by August 1937. CSRD l00-101

13 May: JM writes (from SS Hansa en route to Europe?) David Drummond in London; "Glad you stay with us." JM mentions business matters he and Drummond can further discuss soon in Europe. "[Concerning] Krueger and Toll: I will have to develop an angle on that business during my trip." The matter is evolving here [in NY] and there is nothing for you to do in London. FJM ADS 6/1/6

23 May: JM (NY) writes Bullitt (in Moscow?): Sorry we did not meet here or in Europe but I was in London and Paris "for important family and business reasons." I want to see you and have you meet my partner, George Murnane. WCB

END OF MAY: JM meets again with H Bruening, former German chancellor, now in London, to discuss danger of war. JM gives copy of Bruening address to Salter who also talks with Bruening on war threat. H. Bruening, Briefe und Gesp.rache, 1934-1945 (Stuttgart, 1974), 117-18

12 Aug: Letter from FX Downing of Sullivan and Cromwell to AS Howe Jr of Monnet, Murnane, NYC on ending MM incorporation in Canada. FJM ADS

25 Aug: W C Bullitt, JM friend for many years, is named American ambassador to France by President Roosevelt. B&B, 189

27 Aug: JM cables TV and TL Soong: I am back in NY after busy European trip. FJM ADS 6 1/10ADS 6/1/9

30 Aug: Bullitt writes Henri Mazot, JM aide in China, that he will see

JM next week, presumably in Washington or New York. Bullitt, involved in the reelection campaign of Roosevelt, has just been named ambassador to France. WCB

FALL: Francesco Giannini files action in NY Supreme Court seeking to take custody of Anna Giannini from Silvia and JM. Judge eventually gives Silvia Monnet custody, asking respective lawyers to consider split custody. ACCSM

OCTOBER: JM begins three year lease of 11 room penthouse apartment at ll58 Fifth avenue. FBI 1-40.

20 Oct: JG Monnet, JM's father, begins exchange of letters with Bullitt at JM's instruction to be helpful to new ambassador. Exchange includes gifts from JG Monnet and Bullitt invitation to JM's parent to embassy lunch. WCB

24 Nov: Francesco Giannini, former husband of Silva Monnet, has closed hearing before a NY Supreme Court judge on his suit for custody of their daughter, Anna. Giannini challenges validity of Moscow divorce and remarriage of Silvia to JM. He says his problems with his wife began in spring 1933 when he left her with the Monnet family in Cognac while he went to London on business. When he returned and asked her to rejoin him in Paris, she refused, asking for a separation, he states. NYT 25 Nov, p 12 [Eventually the judge refuses Giannini's request and instead asks the respective lawyers to examine joint custody which never succeeded. ACCSM]

14 Dec: Memo by D Drummond on NYC lunch with JM, Drummond, A Adams and Hunter Gray. FJM ADS

21 Dec: Letter signed by JM, Murnane, Drummond each agreeing not to make any loan to any Monnet, Murnane stockholder. FJM ADS.

This agreement and the 13 May letter to Drummond above suggest the partnership was undergoing some tensions. Drummond had been hired for the China work by Monnet and then brought into the Monnet, Murnane partnership as an employee. He apparently considered leaving but was persuaded to stay on. Why the agreement not to lend money to any partnership stockholder was made is not clear but Drummond is conspicuous by his inclusion. In spring 1939 Drummond and Monnet apparently had a further disagreement marked by Monnet telling his subordinate that he should not let personal "dislikes interfere with his judgments," (See 28 Apr 1939.) Later in the year Drummond finally left to take a job more directly involved in the war effort.

Monnet's life, and the work of the partnership with Murnane during 1936-37, is not well-documented and is covered in Monnet's memoirs with the laconic comment: "In New York, George Murnane and I worked on a number of projects of which I have only dim recollections. In fact, I was growing bored with international finance which ten years earlier had seemed so vast and rewarding" He adds what may have been the real reason for his lack of interest to his personal business: " The whole of my attention was directed to the dangers that were piling up in Europe and threatening world peace....I was ready to make myself useful wherever I could." (JMM 115)

23 Dec: JM [NY] writes Bullitt [newly arrived American ambassador in Paris] that he is sailing on the SS Normandie and will be in Paris for a short time. WCB

26 Dec: JM leaves NY on SS Normandie with his lawyer in custody action, Albert Connelly of Cravath, Swaine, Moore, who talks with French, Italian and Swiss lawyers about joint custody plan with Anna joining Francesco Giannini for summers. AC advises JM that US custody decree could not be enforced in Europe. ACCSM

1937

31 Jan: [Sunday] JM meets US Ambassador Bullitt for brunch at US embassy in Paris. WCB

27 Feb: A Connelly, Cravath lawyer assigned to case of Silvia Monnet and Anna Giannini, returns home from European trip; JM remains in Europe. ACCSM

20 Feb: JM writes TV Soong that he has succeeded in establishing a "Groupe Financier" which brings CDFC together with a group of French banks already involved in China. He thinks this will benefit CDFC's acceptance in Europe and also bring financial support to projects. FJM AMD 2/2/11 cited by MY 110

7 Mar: Long JM memo on pending Chinese matters. FJM ADS 6/1/11

30 Mar: JM (in NYC) cables US Amb Bullitt who is sailing to France on SS President Harding: Sorry to have missed you. Tell my father we are well and looking forward to going to Cognac soon and having a reunion there with you. WCB

11 May: JM back in France according to Bullitt diary which shows visit by "Monnet and 2 ladies" [probably Silvia, and perhaps, her daughter Anna] for lunch at US embassy. WCB

30 May: Cable from Amb Bullitt (Paris) to State Department reports JM, foreign agent for Chinese Reconstruction Finance Corporation (sic), newly arrived from London; says HH Kung, Chinese finance minister, told him British government approved Kung negotiations for a government of China loan to finance railroads from Lanton-Fukien and Pukow-Sinyang. "Monnet said he could hardly believe in the results of these negotiations. They were too good to be true." Kung coming to Paris next week and will then go to U.S. to seek another loan for China's Central Bank. FRUS IV 599-601

1 Jun: JM has lunch with Bullitt at US embassy in Paris. WCB

JULY: The initial three year contract between JM and the CDFC expired this year and was renewed. On the Chinese side, TA Soong replaced his brother TL Soong as CDFC general manager. For JM, the renewal included the foundation this month of MM incorporated in Hong Kong with JM alone as president . Drummond and Mazot are vice presidents. FJM ADS 5/1/8,-10 cited by MY 115 and HU II

There is no documented account of why MM shifted its incorporation from Canada to Hong Kong but Monnet had written a note to Murnane in January suggesting taxation and freer regulations in Hong Kong were the reasons. (FJM AMD 9/12/6 cited by HU 23)

3 Jul: JM (in Paris) sends Fourth of July greetings to Bullitt with bottle of cognac. Bullitt replies 7 Jul that he will enjoy gift since JM's father prescribed a teaspoon of it in his morning coffee. WCB

16 Jul: Hugh Saterlee, assistant at MM, New York writes JM in Paris that US agents have checked his tax returns through 1936 and found no problems other than one Frank McFeeley, JM's aide, had already reported and which JM agreed not to contest. FJM AMD 10/2/12

31 Jul: Murnane writes JM in Paris advising that MM Prince Edward Island incorporation to be replaced by MM Hong Kong. FJM AMD 10 /2/17

------: French Ambassador Corbin in London reports to Foreign Ministry on conversation of an embassy staff member with JM on latter's recent work in China. Japan, JM says, is motivated by fear of its giant neighbor and suspicious of any attempts by foreign powers to aid the growth and unity of China. Japan itself, JM says, is divided between pacifist and militaristic elements. DDF 1932-39, Series 2, Vol VI 539

AUGUST: A series of incidents between China and Japan bring about commencement of hostilities. [For background, see Parks M. Coble, Facing Japan: Chinese Politics and Japanese Imperialism, 1931-1937, Council on East Asian Studies, Harvard UP, 1991].

9 Aug: JM writes Henri Mazot, the MM agent in Shanghai, and TV Soong about another financial grouping between CDFC and the Societe Belge des Chemins de Fer en Chine. FJM AMD 2/3/10 cited by MY 111

23 Aug: Bullitt diary indicates lunch with JM at US embassy in Paris. WCB

24 Aug: Ltr from JM in Paris to Murnane in NY on handling MM HK accounts. FJM AMD

31 Aug: Monnet, Murnane of Prince Edward Island ceases to exist. JFD, Murnane file.

The year 1937 marks another attempt by Monnet to restart his life in business. The successes of his Blair and Co days culminated in a disastrous

experience with the Bank of America and the loss of his job. The interim work with the Krueger liquidation and the peculiar tangent into China were diversions in the midlife drift of his career. The relaunching of Monnet, Murnane as an American-European venture might have succeeded except for the intervention of another European political crisis that gradually distracted Monnet.

7 Sep: TV Soong replies to JM's report on an accord between CDFC and Belgian interests. [The CDFC ventures concerning railroad construction were never fulfilled because of the Sino-Japanese war.] FJM AMD 2/3/12 cited by MY 111

9 Sep: Lamont diary records conversation with JM who is "cautiously optimistic" and believes that "the only possible chance for world escape was freer international trade." LA

22 Sep: McFeeley letter to Denis, Paris refers to MM buying Mrs. Murnane's furnishings at 4, Rue Fabert apartment which firm is taking over. FJM AMD 10/2/45

Oct 4: JM indicates in letters to Denis in Paris, and Forbes and Mazot in Hong Kong that MMHK should be entirely separate from MM elsewhere. Therefore you should have own letterhead with HK address. Don't write me directly but send me copies c/o chairman, New York. FJM AMD 5/2/5

4 Oct: JM at MM meeting NYC. FJM AMD 10/2/53

5 Oct: Lamont note to JM at 1158 5th Ave NYC thanks him for 2 bottles brandy. LA

6 Oct: JM (NYC) writes Bullitt in Washington: I hope you will not sail for Europe without our meeting. Dine with Silvia and me in NY or shall I come to Washington? WCB

14 Oct: McFeeley (MM NY staff) writes Denis in Paris noting dissolution of MM PEI. FJM ADS.

OCTOBER, NOVEMBER: JM letters to Denis from NY. FJM ADS

1938

13 Jan(Thurs) Englewood: "[To] Town [NYC] this morning...tonight dinner at Jean Monnet's [presumably 1138 Fifth Ave]. ECM

17 Jan: JF Dulles leaves for two month trip to Hong Kong for MM at cost of $5714 including $1900 one way air fare on clipper. FJM AMD 10/3/64-5

11 Feb: MM Hong Kong meeting in Paris with JM. FJM ADS.

24 Feb: JM letter from Paris to Henri Mazot and JG Forbes(lawyers) in HK noting that MM Hong Kong entirely separate from MM in Paris. FJM ADS 5/2/18

30 Mar: JM writes David Drummond from Paris (18 Pl de la Madeleine).

FJM ADS 5/2/19

12 Apr: JM and Frank McFeeley, president and secretary respectively of MM (PEI) notify Prince Edward Island government that company has ceased business. PEI

14 Apr: JM aboard SS Europa [to NY]. FJM ADS 5/2/20

20 Apr: Prince Edward Island provincial government acknowledges dissolution of MM. PEI

24 Apr: JM in New York from today to 14 June when he returned to Paris. FJM AMD 13/1/23

22 Jul: Drummond writes JM and Grant Forbes, who also works for MM HK, separate letters on problems relating to rivalry of British and French interests in constructing railroad in Yunnan province. To JM, Drummond advises bringing all parties together around a table to avoid such competition. To Forbes, Drummond says "Our anxiety is to have the initiative in the hands of MM&Co". FJM AMD 4/4//94,-95 cited by MY 121

24 Aug: JG Monnet writes Bullitt that JM is in Sweden [on business] and will soon return to France "to take a cure." WCB

30 Aug: Murnane secretary writes MM asking reimbursement to JM of $363 for his trip to Europe on 20 July and $358 for his return on 17 August on the Queen Mary. FJM AMD 13/1/5

28 Sep: U S Ambassador Bullitt writes FDR from Paris on dire aircraft situation: France has 600 war planes, Germany 6500 and Italy 2000; tells FDR that French air minister Guy La Chambre asked Bullitt for advice on who can help France find military aircraft; Bullitt suggested JM whom he describes to FDR as an "intimate friend for many years." FDRL PSF: Bullitt; OB 297

This suggestion by Ambassador Bullitt sets Monnet on a path of war work which would continue for seven years and redirect him life permanently from business into public service again. It was an impetuous but insightful move by Bullitt who had indeed known Monnet since World War I but for whom Monnet was hardly an "intimate friend." They had known each other only casually in Paris during and after the Versailles peace talks and then apparently renewed their acquaintance briefly when Bullitt was ambassador to Moscow in 1934. Bullitt, a former journalist and early supporter of Roosevelt, sensed that Monnet's enterprise and friendships in American business and government were exactly what France needed at this critical moment. Although sometimes erratic in his judgments, Bullitt proved correct in his choice of Monnet.

30 Sep: Just after Munich conference between Britain, France and Germany concludes, Anne and Charles A Lindbergh meet JM at American Embassy with US Ambassador Bullitt. They discuss Bullitt's idea that France build aircraft factories in Canada. At lunch they are joined by French Air Minister

La Chambre. CAL sees some merit in factory plan but sees bigger problem in weak French political leadership. Talks continue all afternoon at embassy and then at French ministry. CAL

----- JM and Bullitt both look haggard. In garden we talk with JM and Silvia Monnet who are depressed [by Munich agreement]. "Silvia is charming. We argue about Europe. The French... are very depressed. They think this is only a temporary reprieve. They do not trust Germany... and only want to arm like hell in preparation for her next move. I argue that they must come to an understanding as they have no time to arm." In evening dinner at the Monnet's; Ambassador Bullitt, Charles and I alone with them... we are all too tired to talk well.

"All is not easy somehow. M. Monnet and Charles never seem to agree....I keep longing to hear the old Monnet who used to talk with Daddy [Dwight Morrow].... It is worlds away....my heart warm[s] to the conversation of one and yet I have been converted to the practical, hard facts-of-life of the other. And yet...Charles is not only `practical, hard facts-of-life' either. He is idealism too. But it is a new idealism, of another age. M. Monnet, in spite of his youth, belongs to another, my father's." AML III 364-5

Monnet's meeting with the Lindberghs and his subsequent meetings with Bullitt and French officials confirm his return to public service. He spent 12 years, from his departure from Cognac in 1926, in international investment ventures with mixed results. But his shift in work in 1938 does not result from business failure as much as from a perceived urgency in the European political scene. Even if he had made an actual fortune as a banker, his interests never centered on making money. Now he saw a need to help the old Allies of World War I again prepare to confront Germany.

This conclusion by Monnet has painful personal consequences. His income is uncertain and the threat of war begins to separate friends, including his close relations with the Morrow family whose daughter Anne is herself torn between the world of her deceased father and that of her husband, Charles, a rigid and often disillusioned man. Monnet never doubts however that Dwight Morrow's world, and his, are on the right side of history.

1 Oct: JM arrives and we go to ministry for meeting with La Chambre and Roger Hoppenot, French government economist, on Canadian factory idea. CAL

3 Oct: French Prime Minister Daladier asks JM to see Roosevelt on "urgent talks" on buying US aircraft. JMM 118

----- JM waits at embassy for C Lindbergh with paper in French outlining "Canadian Plan" [to build aircraft for France with American technology but in a factory across the US border in Canada]. Bullitt and JM want CAL to go to US "almost immediately to start inquiries and negotiations." CAL replies he is leaving soon for Germany. Daladier arrives with account of Munich meetings. After lunch group continues Canadian plan talks with JM interpreting for CAL and Daladier. Bullitt says he had Canadian plan idea months ago. CAL explains to JM, after others leave, of personal problems in traveling to US with or without his family. The group also discusses France buying German aircraft engines, an idea Lindbergh agrees to take up with German officials when he goes to Berlin. CAL Ultimately, although both countries are interested in idea, the plan fails after German moves against Czechoslovakia the following spring.

4 Oct: C Lindbergh, JM and Bullitt continue talks on Canadian plan and JM and CAL agree to meet 9 Oct on idea. CAL

9 Oct: C Lindbergh lunches at JM apartment [rue Fabert]; He had already written JM that he cannot go to US. JM agrees to meeting and will leave soon himself to see Roosevelt (and WCB) in US. Dinner also with JM in his apartment with Hoppenot. CAL writes letter of introduction for JM to Guy Vaughn, head of Curtiss Wright aircraft.

-----"[Monnet] is such a rare person---a true balanced wisdom into life itself. And he has that wonderful French quickness and lightness that makes communicating with him such a joy. He thinks it is very much overrated that children need their mothers all the time. Yes, I say, it is true, neglected children always turn out well. While, says Jean, neglected husbands do not!

"To the Monnets again for dinner. Nice talk with Silvia Monnet about women's struggle between husband and children...."AML III 370

11 Oct: Lindbergh leaves for his third major visit to Germany as JM prepares for departure for New York by ship to meet the American President on acquiring aircraft for the French air force. WSC 59; JMM 118

13 Oct: Bullitt arrives in NY from Paris and departs immediately for Washington to brief Roosevelt on French plane needs and JM mission. He phones JM who is about to leave Paris to confirm plan for discreet visit to the President at Hyde Park, NY. B&B 224-5; JMM 118

16 Oct Bullitt goes to Hyde Park with FDR, Morgenthau and Harry Hopkins to continue talks on French air needs. B&B 227

18 Oct: HD White writes Morgenthau memo opposing on economic grounds Bullitt's proposal that France construct aircraft factories in Canada across from US. HMD 166

19 Oct: After arriving in New York City the previous day, JM travels to Hyde Park to meet with FDR first time. JMM 118; HMD 146

For an unofficial foreign envoy like Monnet to see the American president on an aircraft deal reflects both the informality of the prewar Roosevelt administration and the President's own desire to get involved in minutiae, especially in foreign affairs. Roosevelt considered himself expert in foreign matters and was especially pleased when he could use his ingenuity and local knowledge---in this case the geography of New York State and adjacent Canada-

--in a clandestine plan to circumvent American neutrality laws and help rearm those Europeans ready to resist Hitler.

20 Oct: JM goes to Washington to start ten days of talks with Treasury Secretary Morgenthau and WC Bullitt, US Ambassador in France. In discussion with his staff, Morgenthau criticizes plan for French aircraft plants in Canada, asking, among other questions, "How long do we know that Canada and England are going to be our allies?" HMD 146

22 Oct: Morgenthau invites JM and Bullitt to supper after latter two return from meeting with FDR at Hyde Park. FDR had called Morgenthau requesting he see the visitors from Paris. Conversation is centered on aircraft plant in Canada which idea excited the President but HM wants to talk about financing aircraft for the French. HM suggests a decree by Daladier to force the return of gold which has fled France in recent years, much of it into the U.S. JM and Bullitt are enthusiastic with idea. HMD 146; JMM 119

23 Oct: JM and Bullitt return to Morgenthau's house for further discussion on financial problems of France. JM has checked boat schedules and can arrive back in France 4 Nov, well in advance of 15 Nov deadline for decree authority of Daladier. HM will help arrange JM meeting with Treasury's procurement chief and give JM memo on how to locate French gold in U.S. HMD 146

26 Oct: HM asks Treasury aide Merle Cochran, American Embassy, Paris to help JM in any way possible. HMD 148

27 Oct: JM sees Herman Oliphant of Morgenthau staff on three successive days including today, per Oliphant memo to HM, all on return of French gold. HMD 146

30 Oct-4 Nov: JM on SS Bremen to Europe. JMM 120, B&B 226, HMD 29 Oct

4 Nov: JM returns to Paris, briefs Daladier on US meetings. JMM 120

9 Nov: JM's 50th birthday coincides with Kristallnacht, the first orchestrated violence against Germany's Jewish community.

9 Nov: Long telephone call between Morgenthau, his Paris aide Merle Cochran, and JM who is in Cochran apartment. HM insists France acts before 15 Nov deadline on returning French gold from overseas. JM agrees. HM: "I've the greatest confidence in Mr. Monnet because he is a realist." HMD 150

11 Nov: Morgenthau's secretary acknowledges JM's gift of three bottles of 100 year old cognac for the treasury secretary. HMD, Correspondence and Gifts to Secretary files

14 Nov: JM reports in Paris to Guy La Chambre, French Minister of Air, that his talks with Roosevelt and U S officials indicate France can order 700 bombers and 700 fighters for delivery by July. JM also discussed possibility

of setting up aircraft factories in Canada to avoid possible problems with US neutrality laws. Paul Reynaud, Finance Minister, opposes this purchase for budget reasons. JMH 37-8; JMH-II; DDF, 1932-39, 2nd ser.(1936-39) v. XII 290

16 Nov: CAL talks with JM on his recent [U.S.] trip which focused on France's financial problems, not aircraft production. "The reason you go somewhere develops into something else before you return." CAL

18 Nov: (Fri) Paris. "We arrived this morning [from Illiec, the Lindbergh's European home] and have had a happy day of shopping together. C[harles Lindbergh] came for breakfast w. us and tonight we dined w/ [Dean] Jays and Jean Monnet was there. I love seeing them." ECM

22 Nov: JM has lunch with C Lindbergh and Hoppenot at JM's apartment ending in "argument about French politics and democratic principles which overshadowed our discussion about aviation. Monnet made a speech about the value of individual freedom....Even Monnet admits something must be done about the present instability of government in France." CAL

24 Nov: Major Anglo-French conference in Paris with Daladier and Chamberlain, and staffs, discussing respective military preparations against expected Nazi aggression. Daladier cites JM report from recent US trip that one thousand American warplanes could be available by the spring. Daladier cites fiscal problems in commitment of this size. DDF, 1932-39, 2nd ser.(1936-39) v. XII 760

2 Dec: JM at MM meeting Paris. FJM ADS

7 Dec: To JM home with Anne for dinner. JM's father, who speaks English fairly well, invites the Lindberghs to Cognac. CAL

------"...to dinner with Monnet; his father and sister are there. A wonderful old man---gay, quick, full of love of life and humor. Much joking between him and Jean. Jean is very proud of him. I like him for it. He is always mysterious, though in a quite and completely orthodox way. Interrupted by telephone calls, having to leave for England or America on something frightfully important but no one having the slightest idea what he is doing. It was a nice evening. He was not the man of the world tonight but only a simple, devoted, charming, admiring son. AML III 406

9 Dec: Daladier asks JM to return to US with Col Jacquin to order 1000 aircraft for delivery by July 1939. JMM 121; B&B 226

10 Dec: JM sails for NY on Queen Mary.(CAL) Travels to Canada this month, according to Bullitt letter to Morgenthau. HMD

16 Dec: JM in Washington with French air technicians. B&B 227

20 Dec: JM back with aviation commission on secret purchasing mission but Morgenthau refuses to see him unless State Dep't approves. FDR

intervenes and Morgenthau sends JM to Captain Collins, new head of Treasury's procurement branch. HMD 172

21 Dec: The US Army Air Corps refuses to let the French mission members see the latest American military aircraft despite Morgenthau's efforts. Finally the treasury secretary tells the President: "If it's your theory that Britain and France are our first line of defence, let Monnet have what he needs. If not, tell him he might as well go home. Give Arnold [air corps chief of staff] formal orders to show him the planes for reasons of state." JMM 123

Morgenthau's relations with Monnet are complex and, on the side of the treasury secretary, informed by contradictory elements. He respects the Frenchman's experience, contacts and acute judgment but suspects there is a darker side which he tries to uncover by collecting gossip on Monnet from American business friends and his treasury agent at the American Embassy, Paris. Monnet's business partnership is also suspect because the other partner, George Murnane, has deep ties to a major German subsidiary in the U.S. Finally, Morgenthau an intensely political person, suspects Monnet's friendships with many Republicans in the business world.

27 Dec: Morgenthau complains to Bullitt by phone that JM "doesn't seem to realize there has been a New Deal over here" [referring to JM's use of Sullivan and Cromwell, a Republican law firm, for his legal work on a proposed Canadian aircraft plant; the law firm had represented Spain's Franco government in a dispute with the US Treasury]. Bullitt says JM has gone to Canada on aircraft project. HMD 158,172; JMH 81

--------JM meets with Morgenthau and staff at Treasury on financial aspects of Canadian aircraft factory plan. JM offers personally to put up part or all of $250,000 needed to capitalize proposed aircraft corporation which would be independent of French govt for legal reasons. Morgenthau is incredulous but insists that $65 million must be deposited in NY federal reserve bank before US aircraft parts could be bought. Later Morgenthau tells staff he doubts JM would invest $250,000 "for La Belle France." HMD 172; JMH II: 81-2

--------Merle Cochran, US Treasury official at American Embassy, Paris writes Morgenthau about a recent conversation aboard the SS Queen Mary: Mr. [Edmond] Hall-Patch, British financial counselor in China and Japan, reported that JM gets preferential treatment from Chinese Finance Minister Kung which benefits Monnet's CDFC.

Cochran also reports recent conversation with Banque de France official who reported JM was responsible, through influence over an official of the bank "L'Union des Mines", for a loss of 380 million francs from an unexplained deal. "He said details in regard to Monnet's financial operations could be had from almost any well-informed Paris banker and ventured the opinion that he would some day land in jail."

Cochran reports a third conversation about JM with "a Paris [JP] Morgan partner. He said that some years ago, while Monnet was still with the League of Nations, he talked Morgans and Lazards into investing 20 million francs in a bank in Cognac, Monnet's home town I believe, with the understanding that Monnet would look out for their interests. When they finally got anxious and looked into the matter, the two Paris firms found they had lost ten million francs....My friend said Monnet was a smooth negotiator but too smooth to have business dealings with." HMD 172

30 Dec: Morgenthau tells JM in memo that secrecy of his mission must end with press announcement of purpose right away. The next day, Morgenthau tells JM in person that Bullitt has put HM in impossible position with "whole U.S. Army opposed to what I am doing" [i.e. preparing to sell latest planes to France secretly]. JM says he has cabled Paris for advice. HMD 172

31 Dec: JM tells Morgenthau he is going to NYC to see his family, and will be back Monday. HMD 172

Age 51 to 57 (1939-1945)

2 Jan: After JM tells Treasury Secretary that Paris wants to delay any announcement of the French aircraft mission in the US until planes are ordered, Morgenthau gives JM "ultimatum:" No more visits to US aircraft plants by his mission without an official announcement by French government of mission's role in US. Later, before departing for a two week vacation, Morgenthau phones Gordon Rentschler, president, Nat'l City Bank, NYC seeking background information on JM. HMD 173

9 Jan: Bullitt tells FDR of JM's inability to see US aircraft because of US air corps opposition to displaying latest planes to prospective foreign buyers. The President then orders French access to the aircraft. JMH 88-9

16 Jan: Lindbergh returns to Berlin where he pursues his idea, already discussed with Bullitt and the French including JM, that Germany might sell aircraft to France both to ease relations between the two countries and to help rearm the French air force. Daladier seems interested but idea dropped after a non-committal response from Roosevelt. WC 59-61

16 Jan: FDR orders Gen. Arnold to show latest US aircraft to JM team. JMM 121, HMD 173

17 Jan: JM talks with Edward Foley and Oscar Cox at Treasury Department, HMD

18 Jan: Rentschler sends unsigned background memo on JM per Morgenthau request. [Much of information is generally correct but with many mistakes in dates and work record]. Summary: JM "is highly regarded by all who have had dealings and contacts with him in France. He is reputed to have an unusually wide acquaintance the world over. He is, in fact, a financial diplomat. He has the ability to straighten out racial prejudices and also is clever in adjusting differences of opinion between various personalities. He does not have a ready understanding of the details of a balance sheet .... If results are to be accomplished expense accounts are not a consideration. He has no idea of the value of money although he is not an extravagant individual but he will go to any length in spending money to accomplish the desired end. He is considered to be thoroughly honest and very able ....[He] inspires immediate confidence." FDRL: H Morgenthau, Confidential Reports about People, 1939

-------Morgenthau phones Bullitt (both in DC) on whether a corporation is needed by JM mission to buy facilities to build warplanes for France. They conclude no corporation necessary since French financial attache, M. Beaulieu,can handle payments. JM coming next day with Bullitt to see Morgenthau. HMD

20 Jan: JM reports on second US mission for aircraft in letter to Daladier, stressing importance of US-French cooperation to get best American bombers and important role of Ambassador Bullitt as conduit to Roosevelt. JMH-III; DDF 1932-39, series II,v.13, no.457

21 Jan: Two of JM's assistants involved in test flight of new Douglas bomber which crashes in Los Angeles. JMH-II 94-5; JMM 122

The crash of a test model of the new bomber puts both Monnet and Morgenthau (and their cooperation) under an unexpected strain. The treasury secretary has to face congressional ire over the French observer (a Monnet mission member) who was injured in the accident. Monnet's mission to buy American military aircraft comes under intense public scrutiny. Morgenthau seems vindicated in his resistance to the whole French aviation business.

26 Jan: France signs first contract for US aircraft with Glenn L Martin for 115 medium bombers. Two months later another order is placed for 700 more aircraft. By September total French orders reach 1600 aircraft. RM 51

31 Jan: JM sees Morgenthau. HMD

----- Senate Defense Committee visits Roosevelt about French aircraft orders. President mentions casually that 'The frontiers of the United States are on the Rhine,' a remark soon reported in the press. JMM 122-3

13 Feb: Bullitt reports to State Dept on long discussion with Daladier, Reynaud and Guy La Chambre on French needs for aircraft and whether France should attempt to repay its WWI debt to US to ease aircraft financing problems. NARA 851.248/39

14 Feb: JM reports by French embassy telegrams to Daladier and other ministers on second US aircraft mission. Contract signed for more than 500 bombers and various related equipment. DDF, 1932-39, series II, vol xv, no 1180

19 Feb: JM has final meeting at US Treasury on air mission. HMD

23 Feb, Englewood: "The Queen Mary did not dock until 2. A great crowd of people waiting. I stood waiting... for George Rublee--the man on the boat. B. Hand and Louis were there and Jean Monnet ...." ECM

10 Mar, Englewood: "The [dinner party] last night went beautifully---- such delightful people---so many old friends--that it was an easy atmosphere. I sat betw. George Rublee and Tommy Thacher. We got George to say a few words at the end ab[out] the refugee problem and his settlement in Germany. Frances Hand and Louis Dow came [and] the Monnets and Rublees ...." ECM

23 Mar: Bullitt cables Roosevelt on meeting today in Paris with Daladier and Reynaud and on Bullitt's 22 Feb letter on how France might pay defaulted debt, including ceding some French overseas territories to US. Daladier initiated idea, wants JM to pursue it and will ask him to return immediately from NY to Paris for details and then again to Washington. OB 326-7; WCB

----- Morgenthau sees JM who is about to leave for Paris. "I appreciate very much the confidence and support you gave me personally ...in the French plane affair," JM said, and the results have had "a great effect in France."

Morgenthau countered that the experience of being caught between the President who wanted planes for France and the Army Air Corps which resisted meant that "for a month I went through hell." HMD 174 cited in JMH 101-2

27 Mar: Lamont writes JM who is sailing on SS Bremen: I told George Catlin, British economist, to look you up on ship. His wife is [novelist] Vera Brittain. LA

Monnet's frequent transatlantic travels pose a physical and financial strain. His home is an expensive rented penthouse apartment on Fifth Avenue in New York where he lives with Silvia and Anna. But he is doing little work for Monnet, Murnane which is increasingly left to George Murnane, his partner. With unsettled conditions in Europe and Asia, income for the partnership declines. Monnet tries hard to get money from the Chinese for work he and his staff have already done for the Chinese Development Finance Corporation. They have little success because, the Chinese say, the CDFC has made no money.

By June Monnet must give up the New York apartment. He and his family spend the summer in Rhode Island; by the fall, with war imminent, he and Silvia move to Paris to occupy the partnership's apartment-office but leave Anna with friends in New Jersey. Monnet's life enters an intensive pre-war working mode centered, as it was 25 years earlier, on helping prepare Britain and France for military cooperation.

3 Apr: JM arrives in Paris from New York. DDF ii XVII no. 354; WCB

4 Apr: Bullitt lunches with JM, Daladier, Reynaud, then writes Roosevelt that French approved two proposals including repayment of 10-15% of its gold to US as gesture on defaulted debt. OB 334. JM is charged with returning to Washington for a meeting with Roosevelt on the French debt. WCB

JG Monnet, JM's Father, has stroke about this time. JM leaves for Cognac. [JGM dies later this month.] OB 335

18 Apr: JM leaves France for third official trip to Washington for France, this time to discuss financing French arms purchases and the French debt from WWI. He also carries letter from Daladier to Roosevelt on the President's recent letter to Hitler and Mussolini. FDRL, PSF, cited in JMH 114; DDF ii XV no 413 and ii XVI no 177

24 Apr: JM arrives in NYC on SS Europa. FBI 1-38

27 Apr: JM sends coded cable to Bullitt on troubles so far in getting contact with Roosevelt's office, partly because of "various Royalties" arriving this week. [Refers apparently to visit of British king and queen to Washington]. WCB

28 Apr: JM in NY writes MM aide David Drummond in London: "I wish you would not let your personal dislikes interfere with your judgment. FJM ADS 10/1/32

3 May: In Washington, JM meets, in what he calls a very long and private talk, with Roosevelt on France's WWI debts. It is JM's second meeting with the President. No easy solution is found to the problem because of existing U.S. legislation and diplomatic agreements on foreign debts to the U.S. Involving the Congress is probably necessary and therefore rapid action is impossible. WCB, OB 317-355

8 May: JM meets with Morgenthau at latter's home on WWI debts of France which total, with interest, about $6.8b. WCB, HMD 188 cited in JMH II, 114

9 May: JM writes Bullitt about his talks with Roosevelt who stressed need for careful analysis of German public opinion in run up to war and urgency of Daladier himself focusing on this question. Roosevelt also stressed need for a Anglo-French declaration at start of war indicating their desire for equitable peace. Such a declaration would affect public opinion in both Germany and, JM thinks, in US also. Leaves to Bullitt decision on whether JM should write Daladier himself or leave Bullitt to convey these urgent thoughts of Roosevelt. WCB

13 May: JM writes Daladier and Reynaud from New York on his conversation with Roosevelt. He will give full details when he gets back to Paris. He has also seen treasury secretary Morgenthau and encloses as an annex a memorandum on the French war debt matter. DDF ii XVI no. 177

16 May: Summary memo indicates JM meets again with Morgenthau and other treasury officials on war debts. Morgenthau reads note from Roosevelt written after latter's meeting with JM. This note also responds to a letter Morgenthau wrote Roosevelt on the French war debts proposing to modify the "Monnet formula" that JM had suggested to the President. That formula, Morgenthau said, included forgiving French debts incurred before the Armistice, paying without interest over some years those made after the war ended, and paying in kind for American stocks bought by France after the Armistice. Morgenthau then reads Roosevelt's note which said JM's ideas were "an interesting basis for future discussions to be kept in our safe ready to take [out]" at a more propitious time. The President added he did not want to take funds out of France at this time. Morgenthau then said he and the President really appreciated the initiative of Daladier and Reynaud to solve the debt problem but that this was not the right time because Congress and therefore public opinion would have to be involved which would not be useful. JM responded that France had proposed, as a goodwill gesture, to pay the United States 10-15% of the reserves of the Bank of France toward the war debts and that the President had discouraged that gesture. (This summary was written sometime after this meeting and sent to Ambassador Bullitt in February 1940 q.v.). WCB; HMD 188 cited in JMH II, 114

------: Roosevelt writes Bullitt that he had nice talk with JM who has also seen Morgenthau twice. OB 353. Discussion included ways of reaching German people to separate them from their leaders. OB 355.

23 May: JM writes MM aide Henri Mazot in Hong Kong from NY on work he is doing for French govt and asks him to see if CDFC will compensate us for our work in years 1937-38 and 1938-39. FJM AMD 6/1/39, -94 (Also FJM ADS 5/2/58)

24 May: JM sends coded "strictly personal" cable from NY to Denis for Prime Minister Daladier, Finance Minister Reynaud and Ambassador Bullitt: Further interview with "Harry" [Harry Hopkins or Henry Morgenthau Jr, Treasury Secretary?] relates Roosevelt response to his talks with JM on France's WWI debts. (See 16 May above). Roosevelt does not want money to be taken out of France at this time. Matter rests for moment as satisfactory as possible. Harry asks me to see him before I sail in June. I have mailed report on interview today on RMS Queen Mary. WCB

JUNE: This is final month JM [and family] occupy 1158 Fifth Ave apartment; they are offering it for sublet until lease ends in October. FBI 1-40,41. JM and family spend some time in Wakefield, RI. FBI 1-42; [Then] Silvia goes with JM to London, leaving daughter Anna Giannini with JM's close friend, Donald Swatland, at his New Jersey home. Interviews July 1998 with Judy Leonard, daughter of D Swatland.

1 Jun: JM meets C Lindbergh in JM's NYC office where they discuss French purchase of U.S. aircraft and European situation. CAL

7 Jun: JM at dinner with Anne Morrow Lindbergh in NYC. AML IV 13

18 Jun: Mazot replies to JM's 23 May letter that MM business with CDFC has been unsatisfactory for two years: I believe that CDFC converted all of its capital to US dollars 18 months ago, part in NY and part here in cash. They are using Chinese dollars from local loans for working capital. They have money but they have not compensated you or Denis for your work with Groupe Uni. FJM AMD 6/1/94

24 Jun: JM replies to letter from Dorsey Stephens, saying he will be in Paris 7-10 days before going to London. FJM ADS 9/1/39

JULY: JM borrows $7954 from MM to buy "some shares in Cognac." FJM AMD 13/3/6

4 Jul: JM in Paris writes Drummond on need to seek Chinese compensation for CDFC work. Perhaps Rajchman can intercede with Soong. Memo for Rajchman by JM indicates that 1934 agreement of MM and CDFC called for 7 1/2% of CDFC profits or, alternately, a fair share of profits from specific business deals. MM actually got $23,000 in 1935-6; $15,000 in 1937 on debt settlement work on Automatic Telephone Co. and none since. JM adds: I want to take off several weeks in Switzerland starting 20-21 July with 3-4 days in

London before that. FJM ADS 5/2/65

7 Jul: JM replies to Mazot letter of 18 Jun: I am not absolutely convinced by your arguments. The contract between CFDC and MM must be respected. I recognize we do not want to break the contract. TV[Soong] could pay us, for example, $10,000 a year for 1938 and 1939. He would know how to do this if he wanted. FJM AMD 6/1/45

11-18 Jul: According to weekly report of MM, JM is in Hyde Park Hotel, London. FJM ADS 6/11

13 Jul: Drummond writes to Murnane, mentions "Latona" [as does JM] as major MM deal. FJM ADS 6/1

19 Jul: JM in Paris writes Murnane in NY on new clients, including aviation possibilities and mentions Col Jacquin whom GM should entertain; "he doesn't know of Pratt Whitney plans." JM adds he cannot tell if war will come but French and British public opinion are determined to fight latest moves by Hitler. FJM ADS 10/1/64

------: JM writes TV Soong about payments due MM from CDFC: I recognize this is a difficult time to write about money when the world is becoming engulfed in war, especially in China. MM has been working hard for CDFC despite the international situation. We have been working, among other examples, on the railroad between Burma and Szechuan where we have worked to keep CDFC in the center of the talks. If the CDFC is in deficit for 1938 and 1939 there could be another mode of payment for MM like representing the Bank of China in Paris, for example. FJM AMD 6/1/51 cited by MY 133

The above note to Murnane is a rare example when Monnet mixes his arms deals for the French government with his private business. There is no evidence that this referral of Jacquin, a French air force officer, to Murnane ever resulted in any business for the partnership. Monnet, Murnane was suspected by the US Treasury Department of maintaining ties with German-controlled firms at this time but even Morgenthau never alleged a personal Monnet business involvement in war contracts. But his partner, George Murnane, is deeply involved in a German-controlled firm. (See 10 August below). Meanwhile, Monnet works hard to get funds from China for work performed in Europe on behalf of CDFC, probably because his partnership is not producing much income for either Murnane or Monnet.

26 Jul: JM replies to 25 Feb telegram from TV Soong asking for assessment of events in Europe [JM's reply delayed because he had been in US most of intervening months]: Britain seeks to avoid hostility of Japan without making any concessions to her; Chamberlain wants to concentrate on Europe and oppose with full force any German aggression. Britain is in full preparation for war and German threats will not produce same reaction as in 1938. If the democracies stand strong, internal pressures will cause breakdown first in Italy,

then in Germany without a general war. Meanwhile, the democracies share China's problems. FJM AMD 7/2/73, 7/3/22 cited by MY 147-8

28 Jul: JM writes long, confidential memo on his conversations in Washington in May on the French war debt: a) Only full payment of the $700m from overdue installments can end the present default. In order for a partial payment to be accepted, there would have to be a revised loan agreement approved by the Congress. b) A basis for reducing the total debt burden includes designation of the pre-Armistice debts as U S contributions to the war; the post-Armistice debts would be repaid as capital lent to France but without interest; The American stocks purchased by France would be repaid in kind. c) After discussions with Roosevelt, JM also saw Morgenthau at President's request. Morgenthau read a note from Roosevelt referring to the "Monnet" formula which he called "an interesting basis for future discussion." Roosevelt added however that he did not wish "to take money out of France at this time." The French government however wants to make a gesture by paying 10-15% of its reserve gold or about $300m to the U S. DDF ii XIVI no. 354

10 Aug: Sudden death of Fritz Mannheimer, head of Mendelssohn & Co, Amsterdam bank, produces crisis in bank which extends to international bond markets where Mendelssohn was major lender. Firm also owns over 692,000 shares or 79% of American Bosch Corp of which George Murnane, JM's partner, is voting trustee for foreign-owned shares. HMD 536, memo 3 Jun 42 to Morgenthau by Treasury general counsel Foley; NYT 11, 16 Aug 1939.

Treasury Secretary Morgenthau, who keeps his department watching JM closely, is concerned here because he suspects Germany still owns Bosch's American subsidiary and therefore that JM still has ties, through Murnane, to the country against which France is rearming with JM's help.

11 Aug: JM, on vacation, writes Ambassador Bullitt from Pontresina, Switzerland: I am sending letter for "Henry"[probably Henry Morgenthau Jr, US Treasury Secretary who is apparently traveling in Europe] which I hope he gets before he goes back. I hope also you can get the French to make a gesture of recognition, perhaps from Daladier, since "Henry" takes great pride in what he did for the plane purchases in the US. I will phone you early next week. WCB

17 Aug: Mazot writes JM from China: I talked with TA Soong, to whom TV Soong had sent JM's 19 Jul letter. TA Soong, who was evidently angry, described many reasons involving the war that caused CDFC deficits and attacked the MM-CDFC contract which has caused CDFC to lose money. It is best to cancel contract and pay only on basis of specific projects where we agree to cooperate. FJM AMD 6/1/57

18 Aug: JM reportedly is in Amsterdam to pursue Monnet, Murnane interest in American Bosch shares at a meeting with Dr Otto Fischer, who Morgenthau says, represents German Bosch interests in Mendelssohn firm. HMD

525, memo by Morgenthau to President Roosevelt, 7 May 1942

23 Aug: Nazi Germany signs non-aggression pact with Soviet Russia. The next day Rajchman writes TV Soong that he has cabled JM, E Drummond and W Bullitt to help protect China in the confusion over the Soviet about-face on Germany which Rajchman fears. Rajchman papers, cited in BM-II 136

29 Aug: French Air Minister La Chambre asks Daladier to authorize an immediate mission to US to buy additional aircraft. The Prime Minister agrees both on mission and JM to head it. But JM says mission's goals exceed entire US air production capacity which cannot be counted on unless US neutrality laws are ended. DDF ii XIX no. 188; JMH 136-7; JMM 124

1 Sep: War declared by France and Britain against Germany which invaded Poland one day earlier.

With the start of the war, Monnet begins a two-month shuttle between Paris and London which ends with his appointment, despite some British resistance, to a key coordinating post in London. The appointment finally, if temporarily, ends Monnet's personal financial strains by giving him a firm income for what sadly becomes only a short term job until France leaves the war.

3 Sep: JM replies separately to Daladier and La Chambre in rejecting idea of a third Monnet mission to US. To Daladier instead he recalled the WWI experiences of Allied defense procurement including the Inter-Allied Council. A similar plan was urgently needed now. To La Chambre JM proposed a Franco-British Aviation Council whose staff would monitor air strength with a "balance sheet" accounting. JMM 125

The "balance sheet" was, Monnet thought, "the elementary starting point for any action; it was to come up time and again." (JMM 125) In April 1940, and May and August 1941, he used this concept to prod first Anglo-French, then Anglo-American thinking on war supplies. Later a balance sheet tracked progress at the Schuman Plan conference.(JMM 133, 169, 171, 334)

13 Sep: Bullitt writes Roosevelt that Daladier today proposed to Chamberlain that France and Britain set up joint purchasing board. Chamberlain accepts. Daladier wants JM to head board; otherwise he is to be French ambassador in Washington. OB 371.

16 Sep: JM in London. JMM 126

20 Sep: Daladier proposes allied supply cooperation as JM suggested. JMM 125

21 Sep: JM writes TV Soong: Thanks for friendly letter; After war everything will be better. FJM AMD 6/1/58

22 Sep: JM attends meeting of Supreme War Council in Hove, England with Daladier, Chamberlain, political and military staffs. (Alexander Cadogan,

The Cadogan Diaries, New York, 1972, 218-19); At end of session, JM alone of French participants joins British delegation on train back to London to meet with Sir Edward Bridges, secretary of the War Cabinet, to begin agreed coordination of Anglo-French war supplies. JMM 126; RM 53

26 Sep: JM arrives in London with Rene Mayer, who represents French armaments ministry, to start effort to persuade British to create a joint Allied balance sheet on military needs and resources and to establish a joint purchasing agency in US. JMM 126-7

30 Sept: JM discusses coordinated UK French purchases with E Bridges, cabinet secretary, and need for balance sheet. "M. Monnet is an advocate of a single purchasing agency in each country on behalf of Great Britain and France." But no agencies or missions to US should be undertaken, he said, until neutrality laws are repealed. Then the first move should come through US Ambassador Bullitt in Paris who has the President's ear to a greater extent than Mr. Joseph Kennedy [the US Ambassador in London]. He [JM] also stressed that Britain must buy many US planes to obtain air supremacy, stressing great speed with which US industry could expand, Bridges reports. (NAUK CAB 104/161); JM confirms discussion when he gives Bridges memo on organization of purchases. OB 377

OCTOBER: France produces 319 planes in September and UK 450 while Germany makes l000 monthly, Bullitt reports. OB 377.

1 Oct: Friendly note from TV Soong to JM thanking for his work "for my country. Laura joins me in sending you and Sylvia [sic] our affectionate regards." [TV Soong evidently tries here to modify the harsh tone his brother TA Soong took with Mazot in August]. FJM AMD 6/1/56

4 Oct: Bullitt writes Roosevelt on French-British war cooperation; JM went with Daladier to London last week and will return this week to London where he will be appointed head of Anglo-French Coordinating Committee. OB 377,383

13 Oct: From London, JM writes Bullitt to ask Roosevelt to support a single Anglo-French purchasing mission in the US instead of either a private purchasing company or dual missions. WCB

15 Oct: Murnane drafts new partnership agreement with JM to take account of latter's full time government work. JM to receive 25% of MM income. He will draw $1000 monthly, annual $4000 life insurance cost and costs of US taxes. In later note, JM says he became US non-resident in October and is now London resident for tax purposes. FJM AMD 13/3/4

17 Oct: JM returns to London . JMM 127

18 Oct: Daladier and Chamberlain agree to set up five Executive Committees on major supplies. JMM 128

19 Oct: From Paris, JM writes Bridges, War Cabinet secretary, that Daladier has received from Ambassador Bullitt a message indicating that "President Roosevelt believes that a single joint Franco-British Mission would be the most efficient mechanism for purchases...in the United States. The President has assumed me that such a mission would receive in Washington the same sort of cooperation which was accorded to Monnet last winter." Please keep this confidential since such a mission must await elimination of US Neutrality Act embargo. WCB

26 Oct: Memo by Sir Frederick Phillips (UK Treasury official) on liaison with French government: JM has won confidence of Daladier "but a good many people distrust him ... and so do I." Phillips opposes JM plan for French chair of joint UK-French purchasing commission in US and attaches draft to Washington to see if US really wants that as JM has stated. PRO CAB 104

The hostility toward Monnet by some British officials parallels that of Henry Morgenthau but with different sources. In London suspicion flourishes partly because Monnet knows his way so well around the British business and government circles and partly from his unorthodox style. The same familiarity in Washington and New York and the same clever and quick style arouses the readily suspicious American treasury secretary who also suspects Monnet's business background.

27 Oct: Cabinet secretary Bridges note to SD Waley at treasury rejects Phillips memo of 26 Oct as inconsistent with earlier meeting and appearing to attempt to bypass both JM and Daladier. NAUK CAB 104

30 Oct: Letter from F.W. Leith Ross (Min of Economic Warfare) to A Robinson (Treasury) says information [from Washington visit] indicates "Monnet seems to be sadly misinformed as to the activities of his people in the United States....[T]he [U.S.] Administration was somewhat disturbed at the activities of the French....[F]or Monnet to give you the impression that the French...are working in full harmony [with U.S. government] is presenting a very inaccurate picture....[W]e should be very cautious about Monnet's activities.... NAUK CAB 104

NOVEMBER: JM writes Henri Mazot in Hong Kong that he is setting up "Franco-British organization...which meant an absolute departure from peacetime working methods and even more [that] I have very little freedom." JM adds that Paris MM office is closed and Mazot's pay to be cut from 300 to 200 HK dollars monthly. FJM AMD 10/5/1

1 Nov: Bullitt writes Roosevelt: JM leaves tomorrow for London job. OB 383.

2 Nov: At JM's suggestion, French government sets up comite des programmes et des achats allies, corresponding to British Inter-Departmental Committee.

-----: Simultaneously, US Congress agrees to amend Neutrality Act which becomes law two days later. RM 54;JMM 130

3 Nov: McFeeley (MM NYC) writes JM, indicates Silvia was getting $1800 monthly [presumably while she was living in US and JM in Europe] and that MM paid $1700 for JM final federal tax for 1938. FJM AMD 10/4/89

-------UK Ambassador Lothian in Washington cables UK treasury that US treasury secretary Morgenthau has no preference for or against joint UK-British purchasing mission as long as full cooperation exists between allies. "The President's aim is the elimination of unnecessary profits, to keep prices steady and to avoid competition between the British and French and the U.S. government." NAUK CAB 104

7 Nov: T N Wilson, Chamberlain's foreign policy advisor, writes JM at the Hyde Park Hotel, London, on his "overnight reflections" on their talk last night: Let's keep two separate UK and French purchasing missions in the US with possibility of changing this later. WCB

-----: JM replies to Wilson, Chamberlain's foreign policy adviser, that proposal for separate heads of UK and French purchasing missions in U.S. is contrary to early agreement and to what Roosevelt said he wanted through his communications with US ambassador in Paris [Bullitt]. Also notes that French concurred in UK head of joint mission in Canada. NAUK CAB 104

Monnet's push for a joint British-French purchasing agency reflected his WWI experiences when both countries initially insisted on their own purchasing plans with inevitable competition for supply and consequent shortages and rises in prices. He could not accept that those lessons of only 25 years earlier were already forgotten. His determination finally prevailed.

9 Nov: JM's 51st birthday coincides with first serious assassination attempt against Hitler in Munich beer hall where he was commemorating his 1923 coup attempt. Hitler escaped uninjured but eight others were killed in explosion. Ian Kershaw, Hitler 1936-1945, (London, 2000), 271-3

8-11 Nov: British government discussions on suitability of JM to head Anglo-French Coordinating Committee(AFCC). UK embassy in Paris asked for advice. British finally accept JM with Arthur Purvis to head joint UK-French purchasing mission in US. NAUK CAB 104

10 Nov: Roosevelt demands that Britain and France coordinate their arms purchases in cable sent by Secretary of State to Bullitt. NARA 841.24 cited in JMH II:142

17 Nov: Supreme War Council formally agrees on JM's appointment which is announced the following week. RM 55

23 Nov: JM sees Prime Minister Daladier who declares "We must have

absolute superiority in the air and to obtain it the Allies must buy 10,000 aircraft
in the United States. The first deliveries must be made at the beginning of 1940
and the rest continue into the spring of 1941. I know that American assembly
lines are already working to full capacity. But there ae automobile factories that
can be converted." JM later comments that Daladier "thought big, and he was
right---a few years too late, perhaps;....the future was to show that World War
II was partly won in the automobile factories of American, and that the initial
impetus came from these first Allied orders." JMM 130-1

------Bullitt cables FDR on meeting he just had with Daladier, La
Chambre, and JM on urgent Allied need for US aircraft and coming mission of
JM aide Rene Pleven on that goal. Daladier desperate for aircraft and is prepared
to sell any French possession (including Versailles) to finance them. He will
also leave government if he cannot gain Allied air domination. Daladier wants
Bullitt to accompany Pleven; La Chambre and JM agree.[Hull later replies, after
conferring with FDR, that Bullitt should stay in Paris]. FRUS II,520-22

25 Nov: Daladier sends FDR message through Bullitt on UK-French
coordinating war efforts. JM named chairman of London coordinating committee
and Arthur Purvis to head Anglo French Purchasing Board in NYC. NAUK CAB
104; JMH II:154

27 Nov: Dulles cables JM congratulating on AFCC appointment
recognizing and using "your unique ability." JFD, Murnane file

29 Nov: E Bridges welcomes JM by letter as chair of AFCC and says
Purvis and Bloch-Laine agree downtown New York City is best office location.
NAUK CAB 104

4 Dec: Dulles letter asks JM help on "very severe treatment in France
of...conscientious objectors." Dulles writing as participant in World Council of
Churches conference last year in Oxford. Asks JM to support letter Dulles sent
French ambassador on same issue. JFD, Murnane file

8 Dec: JM writes Purvis on coming secret mission of JM aide Rene
Pleven to Washington to determine US aircraft production capacity. NAUK CAB
85 file 59 cited by AS 112-13

11 Dec: Amb Bullitt writes H Morgenthau on R Pleven's coming trip to
US: "you can have as absolute confidence in his intelligence and discretion as
you were able to have in Jean Monnet's similar qualities." [Pleven traveling as
assistant to JM, head of the "French-British Committee of Coordination" (sic)].
WCB
------:Bullitt writes Roosevelt: Lunched today with [Prime Minister]
Daladier, JM, Rene Pleven and [Air Minister] La Chambre. Pleven is JM's
"right hand man and old and close friend of mine" who is leaving for US today.
Daladier thinks France can't win war without ten thousand US planes which
Pleven will seek. Daladier's attitude on war turns on success of Pleven mission.

Daladier also wants me to drop my job and go to US to carry out this goal. La Chambre said "thanks to Monnet" he is now getting exact figures on UK plane production. WCB

14 Dec: JM aide Pleven leaves for US on circuitous route for safety reasons, reaching New York on 21 Dec and sees Morgenthau right away. JMM 131

21 Dec: Draft JM letter to Finance Minister Paul Reynaud claiming reimbursement of 3400 FF (375 pounds) for travel and secretary for French government business. FJM AMD 10/4

28 Dec: E Bridges relates comment by JM that no matter what Bridges or anyone else said, JM would continue to use the trans-Atlantic telephone to conduct the AFCC business with Washington. [JM had been indirectly criticized in a UK ministry for expensive phone calls to Purvis in Washington]. NAUK CAB 104

29 Dec: Mazot writes JM, indicates things in China not good for MM. FJM AMD

--------: [London] Daily Telegraph reports Purvis "and his assistant,"[sic] Rene Pleven, [who is actually JM's aide] saw the President at the White House today. Morgenthau and Harry Collins of the U S Treasury also present."

30 Dec: McFeely (MM NYC) sends Dulles $750 which is the 6% interest due on loan of $12500 [probably from 1934 startup loan for MM]. JFD Murnane file

------: Mazot writes JM on conversation with TA Soong on future CFDC-MM cooperation: CDFC has a bright future but the present is difficult. CFDC has lost a lot of money making it impossible to pay MM the 7 1/2% foreseen in the contract. He repeats earlier proposal to annul the contract and make a new one based on actual work done by MM and not on profits of CFDC. FJM AMD 6//1/61 cited by MY 136

END OF DECEMBER: JM has sold his Rue de Conde apartment on left bank in Paris (FF I) and will take over MM apartment on 4, rue Fabert on 1 Jan [for use on AFCC business when he is not in London]. FJM AMD 10/5/18

1940

2 Jan: Purvis cables JM on meeting yesterday with Morgenthau and staff on key minerals in war effort. FJM AME 4/8/3

------: Mazot writes JM from Hong Kong that during dinner TV Soong indicated he understood contribution of JM and that he must intervene in quarrel between MM and CFDC But the conversation stopped when TA Soong suddenly appeared at the table. FJM AMD 6/1//63 cited by MY 137

5 Jan: At AFCC meeting the UK Foreign Office representative asks,

on behalf of Ambassador Lothian in Washington and the French ambassador there, that all communications between JM and Purvis [head of the US based Anglo-French Purchasing Board] be through the embassy in whose language the message is prepared. JM says that the committee should defer to the ambassadors but without delaying important communications. The British consul general in New York had also objected to messages directly to and from Purvis who operates from a New York office. JM fears such changes can cause delays. NAUK CAB 85

15 Jan: JM memo to Guy La Chambre, French minister for air, on need for a balance sheet of relative strengths of Allied and German air forces. JMH II:190

17 Jan: Anglo French Purchasing Board (AFPB) holds first meeting after long effort by JM and Purvis to attain unified British-French arms buying in US. NAUK CAB 85 cited in AS 126

18 Jan: JM drafts letter from Daladier to Chamberlain discussing balance sheet JM is preparing on relative weakness of Allied air forces compared to Germany. JMH II 190

22 Jan: JM writes Purvis on coordination problems and praises latter's presence in Washington which has improved cooperation between UK and US governments. JM says he has consulted French and British foreign offices and agrees that they should get copies of Purvis messages via both embassies since even some of their technical communications may have political significance. JM also says sometimes messages will have to go through embassies. FJM AME 4/1/2

23 Jan: AFPB announces its existence at 25 Broadway NYC with A Purvis as chair, F Bloch-Laine as vice chair. NAUK CAB 85 cited in AS 126; NYT, Wall Street Journal, 24 Jan

With the Monnet-Purvis team in place, Monnet can concentrate full-time in London on the war. Although he retained his partnership with Murnane until 1944, he no longer took either an interest or an active role in its work. He wrote an occasional letter for Monnet, Murnane, usually seeking payment for past work but his concentration---his most formidable characteristic---was now to be directed for the rest of his life to public service, one goal at a time. For 1940 and beyond, the goal was war production to defeat Hitler.

27 Jan: JM writes again to TV Soong reminding him of the successes of CFDC with the French aspects of the Suifu-Kunming railroad over past two years. FJM AMD 6/1/65 cited by MY 137

2 Feb: JM, in letter to MMHK, resigns as chairman of MM Ltd effective with coming board meeting, noting that he would no longer be able to devote his time to the company. FJM AMD 13/2/1

-----At AFCC meeting Rene Pleven, personal assistant to JM, gives account of his mission to US in December and January and need to notify US treasury of Anglo-French purchases in US. JM explains central role of US treasury department in arms contracts. [Rene Mayer named first in French delegation list after JM]. NAUK CAB; CB 63-4

JM also presents a balance sheet summarizing the aircraft of the Allies and of their German opponents; the figures show a 2 to 1 German advantage in bombers and fighters. It would take, he says, five months to make up the shortage of fighters and more than two years the gap in bombers, unless American help comes sooner. RM 58-9

3 Feb: JM sends Bullitt two copies of a memo dated July 1939 which recounts their efforts earlier that year to resolve the problem of France's WWI debts to the United States which was becoming a political problem for the Roosevelt administration. The 11 page document, written in French apparently by JM but in the third person, starts with a March 1939 meeting JM and Bullitt had with Prime Minister Daladier and Finance Minister Reynaud in which the United States might be offered certain non-monetary assets in lieu of or in addition to direct debt repayments which France found difficult to afford. JM was asked by the French government to undertake discussions with the American government which included a meeting he had with President Roosevelt on 3 May. The total French debt default of about $700m. was addressed at the meeting with several possible payment modes discussed for the entire outstanding debt of about $4 billion. These discussions continued with Secretary of the Treasury Morgenthau. Finally, the memo reports, the President decided on a large forgiveness of France's wartime debt and postponement of discussion of the remaining debt until France was in a better position to pay. WCB

Why this memo was written in July 1939 and why Monnet sent it to the US ambassador in Paris seven months later is not clear. It may have been written at the request of the French government shortly after meetings it describes since it is also found in a similar version in official French records. (See entry 28 Jul 1939, above). It may have been sent in 1940 simply to clear another item from Monnet's busy desk in London in anticipation of an end to his work there. Or perhaps it was requested by someone, even Bullitt himself, but Monnet's short cover letter (signed for him by someone on his staff) gives no hint. It may be conjectured that Monnet was trying, in the early months of what was already a most trying period for France, to perfect the historical record of French leadership in the prelude to the war.(His cover note says he already sent copies to Daladier and Reynaud and asks Bullitt to send a copy to Morgenthau). But Monnet generally displayed no great interest in the historical record; he was always focused on action for an immediate goal. Did someone ask for this account and was this request made in July 1939 when the memo was apparently written or in early 1940 when it was sent to various participants? The only hint of an answer is within the memo itself which displays both the sincerity of the French leaders in trying to solve the problem of France's outstanding debt and the magnanimity of Roosevelt in insisting that France keep the money for its own urgent needs in the months when another war was about to start.

5 Feb: Pleven trip report, accompanied by JM memo and his balance sheet, is presented by Daladier to Supreme War Council in Paris. It outlines need for drastic action to prevent enemy aircraft production overwhelming that of Allies. JM memo ends with words: "Where there is no vision, the people perish." JMM 132-33; JMH II:189-93

-----:JM urges Daladier to approach Chamberlain urgently to approve the American aid program despite the objections of the UK treasury. FJM AME 7/7/14 cited in ER 221

9 Feb: Daladier leads debate over French air power to Chamber of Deputies. He praises Roosevelt for his cooperation and says "I have brought to France the potential of American aviation". JMH II:94-5

16 Feb: AFCC meeting discusses sending British-French team on "secret mission" to US to assist Purvis in his meetings with Morgenthau on economic warfare and to help State Department keep some essential commodities from reaching "dangerous destinations." NAUK CAB

------: JM sends instructions to Purvis for massive Allied plane order. JMH II, 195 ff

------: Murnane writes Arthur Roseborough, MM lawyer in Paris: "China once showed great promise---events changed that. We concentrated enormously on it---Mazot, all of his time---David and Denis, most of their time---Jean, some of his time....My feeling is we should avoid becoming responsible for those matters in which we must initiate, arouse interest and spend many hours....We haven't the time for that and the general outlook is not such as to command it." FJM AMD 10/5/ll cited by MY 153

Monnet resignation from MM and Murnane's letter mark the end of Monnet's China venture even though he had ended his more active involvement after he became fully engaged in war preparations in 1938. Thereafter, he tried for a time to pursue some European efforts for the CFDC but without great success as the correspondence with Mazot indicates. The war in China and then the war in Europe closed effectively the strange China episode in his life which started in 1932 as an interlude in his private banking career when he believed it served his personal interests (and, eventually, Silvia's) to be away from Europe.

22 Feb: Purvis shows JM cable of 16 Feb to Morgenthau who says "It [the plane order] may be the deciding factor in having the Allies win the war." JMH II:196 citing HMD 242

------: Daladier orders Pleven and Colonel Jacquin to U.S. to join British mission under Sir Henry Self "to submit concrete proposal for execution of the order of February 16." Pleven arrives in Washington 4 Mar. JMH II:196; JMM 134CB 65

24 Feb: After MM board meeting in Paris, memo from Roseborough [a Sullivan and Cromwell lawyer in its Paris office] to Murnane notes that JM resigned as chair, stays as director and has taken over apartment at 4, Rue Fabert, near the Invalides, [which had been company office since 1937] as his apartment a/o Jan 1 40. Roseborough is taking over MM books for Hong Kong and Paris offices. FJM AMD 10/5/18,24

MARCH: In undated letter, JM writes Murnane that he receives 200 pounds monthly pay [in London job] and does not have to pay taxes as diplomatic resident. Refers also to $7954 he borrowed last July to "take up some shares in Cognac.... I still owe $5415 of this." FJM AMD 13/3/9

-----Undated JM letters to Murnane refers to latter's 15 Oct 1939 draft letter on adjusting the MM partnership income to 75/25% in favor of Murnane now that JM is in war work fulltime. JM mentions his need for $1000 monthly plus insurance and possible federal income tax. FJM AMD 13/3/4

[JM's draw of $1000 monthly from MM would be about $13,000 in 2007 terms, a sizeable annual income of about $150,000 if realized. His London salary in the preceding paragraph would be about the same amount.]

2 Mar: JM writes long memo to Alexis Leger, secretary general of French foreign ministry, warning that American isolationism is driving the fear which animates the American administration and public opinion. The Allies are seen as weak; aiding them will draw the U.S. into the war, it is feared. JM suggests instead an attitude of strength be shown to Undersecretary of State Sumner Welles on his coming trip to Europe by both French and British authorities. Memo, which JM also sent to French ambassador in London, also suggests that the British-French alliance after the war may become the basis of postwar reconstruction. FJM AME 3/4/3

13 Mar: Mazot meets again with a now-familiar stern and abrupt TA Soong: Why does JM write TV Soong and not me? Am I a baby? For months MM has done nothing for the Burma-Kunming railroad. The CFDC has done all the work. I never liked JM; I detest him. I have decided to annul the contract [between CFDC and MM].I will give MM at most 5% [of the profit from the Kunming-Suifu railroad].

The next day TV Soong asks Mazot to his office and tell him of a long and sad conversation he had with his brother, TA Soong: He is the only one in my family devoted to me and I cannot break relations with him. But I also do not want to break relations with JM. I could not sleep last night. I wrote a letter then to give 20% to JM from the Kunming-Suifu railroad profits. TA resisted but I made him sign it.

Mazot was then called to TA Soong office again: TA is still unhappy but accepts his brother's decision on JM. (Mazot adds that it was his work with TV

Soong which got the final result).   FJM AMD 6/1/79 cited by MY 138

14 Mar: Murnane writes JM on reducing costs with closing of Monnet apartment at 1158 5th Avenue and Murnane's willingness to help financially. "Your general cost of life has probably decreased with abandonment of residence here [in NYC]....We will help on any costs we can for you. We are out of debt and if several retainers come we may have more [income] next year than ever." FJM AMD 10/5/26

15 Mar: TA Soong signs letter to JM[dictated by TV Soong; see 13 Mar]: TV Soong sent your Aug 1 letter to China Development Finance Corporation (CDFC) board which offers to rewrite 1934 agreement with Monnet, Murnane. Even though [David] Drummond and [Pierre] Denis are on military duty, we hope you will work on Kunmiag Suifu railroad project in exchange for a 20% share in its profits. "I sincerely hope that when the war ends, cooperation between us which has been so pleasant and profitable before the war will be even closer to the enhanced benefit of both parties."

JM acknowledges the letter and reciprocates the same vague sentiments. FJM AMD 6/1/73, -95 cited by MY 139-40

18 Mar: Britain and France agree not to negotiate a separate armistice with Germany and to work together in postwar reconstruction. JMM 18-19

-------:Arthur Roseborough, lawyer in Paris handling Monnet, Murnane matters, writes Murnane on whole Chinese "mess" which he does not yet understand. FJM AMD 10/5/24

------: Pleven reports to JM on the problems of isolationism and Axis propaganda he is seeing during his US visit. FJM AME 6/6/9 cited in ER 221

25 Mar: From London, JM writes Roseborough in Paris on his US obligations (which include care for family dog, Mitou, at $15 per month and $6 per month for storage of car, while he and Silvia are in London and Anna is in New Jersey with the Swatlands). Other expenses he lists include money each month to Aline Monnet, Gaston's daughter and to Madame Boccacini and Comtesse Memmo [who are very old friends of Silvia]. In related note to Roseborough, JM lists his annual[business]income as: Draw from partnership: $8000; dividends: $27,500; Advance: $3000. [This total personal income of $38,500, aside from his British salary, would be the equivalent of about $500,000 in 2007]. FJM AMD 13/3/12; FF I, 1995

26 Mar: From New York, Murnane writes JM in Paris that he is in constant touch with mutual friend and lawyer Donald Swatland who reports Anna[Gianinni, JM's step daughter] is doing well, living in normal surroundings with youthful contacts which allow her individuality to prosper. "From all quarters I get testimony of your fine work and your eminence.... Your preoccupations [with war work] are viewed by me with pride and especially now that Roseborough will draw together the loose strings...I think you can settle

to your task with no thought about our own [partnership] affairs...." FJM AMD 10/5/34

Monnet is now almost completely separated from his business partnership role even though he and Murnane are still sorting out the details of the separation, including their original investments and what, if any, profits might still come from the work in China which Monnet conducted. The following Murnane report indicates that Monnet's initial capital in the partnership (which be borrowed from Dulles among others) was not matched by any funds from Murnane. Monnet's gesture in not accepting accrued interest from his partner indicates a generosity to a friend, an indifference to financial matters, or both. Still his persistence next month in seeking compensation for the partnership's work in China illustrates a businessman's discipline and, possibly, a need for income in a period when compensation for his war work was both limited and uncertain.

28 Mar: In New York Murnane continues report to JM in Paris on their business partnership: "At the outset you introduced some capital---I had none. Our operations did not produce enough net to cover our drawings. I therefore acquired a red balance." Now the accountants point out a provision in our partnership that partners should get 10% interest on their credit balance. What this means and should mean I do not know. What do you think.? [Later Roseborough replies for JM that the partnership articles on interest credited and debited should not apply and that JM wants any accruals from them to his benefit to be cancelled.] FJM AMD 10/5/35

-----: Communique from Supreme War Council, where Paul Reynaud had just succeeded Edouard Daladier as French prime minister, said UK and France declared intention "to maintain, after conclusion of peace, a community of action in all spheres for as long as necessary to effect reconstruction...of an international order...of peace in Europe." This was one of several ideas circulating about Anglo-French cooperation beyond immediate war needs. RM 65

22 Apr: British Foreign Secretary Lord Halifax presents proposal by the "uncompromising federalist" Lionel Curtis to small ad hoc UK government committee seeking joint Franco-British parliament and joint executive for defense and foreign policy with its own financial resources from both countries. This is one of several proposals for innovative and permanent British-French association beyond that of normal allies. Several weeks before the anticipated military break through by the Germans, JM and Arthur Salter jointly prepare their own draft which calls for more urgent action in the context of the immediate military situation. It includes need for US entrance into war "as a belligerent" and the continued role of France in the war no matter what action Germany takes. Finally the draft calls for a "dramatic declaration by both governments" that they should be "acting in all things as one... in speech and in formal assembly and ceremonial." RM 66-7; MB 184

25 Apr: JM writes CDFC board on MM's hard work for corporation and "unfortunate misinterpretation" of our 1934 agreement. Murnane is working on CDFC matters in NYC and Roseborough in Paris while Drummond, Denis and I are in war work. FJM AMD

26 Apr: JM in London where he lunches at Sanford's with Herbert Morrison, Oliver Harvey, Leon Blum and Sir Alfred Baker (legal adviser to Labour Party). OHT 224

10 May: JM get telephone call at dawn from Paris by Alexander Parodi, permanent Under-Secretary of French Ministry of Labor, announcing start of long awaited German offensive. Later, on way to his office, JM meets General Ismay, secretary of he Imperial Defence Council, who tells him the German drive is "exactly what we've been hoping for." JM later reflects that the French generals had the same illusion of trapping the German army just north of the Maginot defensive fortifications of France. JMM 17

-----: With sudden German attack, AFCC intensifies its work with JM traveling more often between London and Paris, enlarging the committee's staff and obtaining A Salter as his vice chair. NAUK CAB 85 cited in AS 213

-----: JM writes Winston Churchill, who has become British Prime Minister, that Nazis will have gain strategic victory if Britain and France should now start to think of waging war separately. JMM 20; Churchill has replaced Chamberlain who stays on in cabinet. By end of month Churchill appeals to Roosevelt for more help. WSC I 599

------: JM proposes Belgian, Dutch, Norwegian and Polish representatives join the AFCC which now reaches its peak of efficiency and scope. NAUK CAB 85 cited in AS 216-218

------: JM cables A Purvis from London on agreement of British and French ministries to make all steel purchases through AFCC office in NY. An AFCC mission is leaving next week for NY to make these arrangements. WCB

16 May: Roosevelt message to Congress asks for production of 50,000 aircraft a year; two weeks later he asks additional $1.2b. for accelerated arms production. In June $43m in surplus arms goes to Britain. EAH 363

17 May: A Purvis delivers handwritten appeal to Morgenthau after getting urgent cable from JM for additional supplies, supporting Churchill's similar request to Roosevelt who had already discussed it with the treasury secretary. HMD 263

19 May: Pleven returns from aircraft purchase mission in U.S. to meet with de Gaulle, JM and others on consequences of French military defeats. FJM OH; CB 65

19,20 May: In letters to French and British prime ministers, JM proposes coordination of Anglo-French food purchases in the US through the joint purchasing board in NY. Expanding on Churchill's recent call for all American aid short of war, JM asks Reynaud and Churchill to move beyond increased aircraft production and "make similar arrangements on the widest possible scale for the types of munitions and armaments...essential for continuation of the war." JMH II:258;DH 159; NAUK CAB 85 file 77 cited in AS 223-9

20 May: As AFCC chairman, JM writes Churchill and Reynaud, repeating arguments which "had convinced their predecessors, and which I was now hoping patiently to preach to them." In looking back at the letter, JM added: "The claims of a balanced budget or the superiority of national weaponry were no longer relevant."The letter noted that no only aircraft but "the most essential types of arms and ammunition" from the United States are needed "without delay." Securing agreement from the two leaders, JM cables Purvis on 24 May asking him to meet with Morgenthau to develop the "vast capacity" for producing others arms that had already been done for aircraft. JMM 137-8

27 May: JM supports steel purchases through his committee and the joint purchasing board in the US as part of increasing the efficiency of the AFCC. NAUK CAB 85 file 67 cited in AS 224.

28 May: MM Paris lawyer Arthur Roseborough writes Mazot (Monnet, Murnane agent in Hong Kong) that he is sorry that JM letter upset TA Soong who expected a personal approach from him instead of a corporate one. FJM AMD

The imminent crisis in the defense of France pushed Monnet for a brief period into a prominence exceptional for an appointed allied official essentially concerned with supply issues. By early June he was writing directly to Churchill in London and, through his partner in Washington, Arthur Purvis, in parallel communications with the highest American officials. He did not shy from this propulsion into the highest Allied political circles but he did not seek either attention or influence for their own sake. He remained remarkably focused on his work even when those labors became, in the month's climax, increasingly desperate and ultimately futile.

------ Desmond Morton writes note to Churchill: JM today said French political circles are losing confidence in Reynaud. NAUK Prime Minister files 3 188/4

LATE MAY: Allied forces fall back in France in face of overwhelming German armored advance.

3 Jun: JM and Purvis discuss making the AFCC and its US purchasing board an independent operation with central control for all purchases in US but project fails because of imminent military collapse of French army. NAUK CAB 85 file 59 cited in AS 226

4 Jun: JM sends note to Churchill on conversation previous night with Purvis on armament purchases. NAUK Prime Minister files 3/468 folio 178 (cited in MG-FH 462-3

-----: Allied evacuation from Dunkirk saves major part of British force in France and 26,000 French troops who are brought to Britain too. JMM 139

5 Jun: JM sends note to Churchill and Reynaud to expand the AFCC scope to include almost all raw materials, machine tools, weapons and ammunition which the US might provide. NAUK CAB 85 file 12 cited in AS 225; JMM 20

6 Jun: JM writes Churchill personal note proposing that UK and French air forces "are treated as one.... "[T]he issue of the war may depend upon an immediate decision to use our combined strength, both of aircraft and pilots, as one force." In accompanying official letter, same date, to Churchill, JM outlines his efforts "to secure the best utilization in the common interests of the resources of the two countries." He is intensifying the coordination of supplies for the British expeditionary force and adds that he is going to France at once to see Reynaud and Dautry and will convey any personal message for Reynaud. "Apart from this I have some urgent matters which can only be put to you personally...if you could see me for a quarter of an hour sometime today. On same day, Cabinet secretary Edward Bridges writes note to Mr Seal [WSC personal aide?] saying JM wanted to see WSC to convey letter on air power. Bridges supports request for personal meeting, adding JM background on WWI work and fact that his is one of the "dures" not one of the "douces" [within French government] at present time. NAUK Prime Minister files 3 188/4; JMM 20, 139

In an interesting reflection made over 30 years later, Monnet recalls asking without success for a personal meeting with Churchill sometime during these frenzied months. In explanation of this refusal, Monnet, in 1970, said: "He [Churchill] saw I was speaking of the future and he had to deal with the critical present." (AW)

8 Jun: JM sends "most immediate" cable to Purvis asking for 347 field guns with high explosive shells most urgently. NAUK CAB 85/13 (cited in MG-FH 484)

9 Jun: In London JM sees de Gaulle, who has just arrived, immediately before his meeting with Churchill which JM had arranged. JMM 25

-----: Combined Production and Resources Board, long recommended by JM, is officially established, headed by Lord Lyttelton who has succeeded Beaverbrook as Minister of Production. RM 129

10 Jun: Reynaud sends desperate plea to Roosevelt via Bullitt for public statement that US will give all possible aid to Allies "short of an expeditionary force." FDRL, Rosenman Papers, Container 41

13 Jun: JM and Salter finish draft paper on Anglo-French union. "The very first words stressed the need for rapid action. 'Within a few days the most vital decisions may have to be taken....Paris may fall at once and the present line prove untenable.' On the following day, when Monnet sat down to revise Salter's

draft, he had to write: 'Paris has fallen.'" JMM 21-22;RM 67.

"Meanwhile the idea of a declaration of union had been put forward by [JM] directly to Neville Chamberlain through Sir Horace Wilson." JM is also discussing with Purvis diversion of war supplies from French to British ports. MB 184

14 Jun: JM meets Horace Wilson, private secretary of Neville Chamberlain, who agrees to pursue union proposal with former prime minister as means of getting favorable attention of Churchill. JM and Pleven also meet with Vansittart and Churchill's aide, Desmond Morton, on project. JMM 22-23; MB 185; CB 72

The proposal for a complete union between Britain and France at this crucial moment is one of the stranger episodes in the Second World War. Monnet treats it as a genuine, if desperate, effort to inspire the French to continue the war and to mark the true interdependence of the Allies. Others, including probably Churchill and de Gaulle, saw the union plan as a quixotic but moving gesture. Historians usually agree that a plan to merge two ancient nations in a moment of extreme crisis was not to be subject to normal political analysis. One of the skeptics, historian David Reynolds, notes, however, that the union plan, although a "half-baked and last ditch bid to keep France in the war", also "reflected a strong tide of official opinion in 1939-1940 that an institutionalized Entente Cordiale was essential to win the war and secure the peace. Mindful of the alienation of the interwar years, Sir Orme Sargent of the Foreign Office had proposed on 28 February 1940 'such a system of close and permanent co-operation between France and Great Britain---political, military and economic---as will for all international purposes make of the two countries a single unit in post-war Europe,'" according to Reynolds.

An equally strange episode at the same time also involves Churchill and is also reported by Reynolds. Churchill apparently believed, and tried to persuade Reynaud, that the United States would declare war if France continued to fight. The British prime minister was a go-between trying to get President Roosevelt to make public a strong message of support for France and to persuade the French leader to continue the fight against Hitler. Monnet in his Memoirs does not comment on this effort which he probably did not know of at the time. Historian Reynolds terms the effort to tie France's continuation in the war to direct American participation in the conflict "a grave misconception on Churchill's part---his most serious error of judgment with regard to the United States in his whole career---yet it seemed fully justified" because of the confusing messages Churchill was receiving from the American side. D. Reynolds, In Command of History, (London, 2005), 168-9; 192-3.

In looking back on this episode over 30 years later, Monnet saw the Anglo-French Union proposal as the "first attempt for a supranational union of destinies and of sovereignties." (AW)

15 Jun: JM has dinner at his Mount Street apartment for de Gaulle who has just arrived again in London after a few days in France. JMM 24,25

-------Chamberlain brings Anglo-French union plan to cabinet meeting but without fully accepting it as proposed in a memo prepared by JM, Morton, Salter, Pleven and Robert Vansittart, Permanent Under Secretary at Foreign Office. Churchill is also reserved on the idea. Eventually the Cabinet approves in principle the union idea. Meanwhile, the French military situation deteriorates and discussion of a separate French armistice begins. MB 185-7; JMM 23, 26

-----:Col. Paul Jacquin, head of French aviation mission in US, cables Purvis: We are defeated. Do you want to take over our contracts? Purvis replies: Thank you. I could not dare have asked this of you. [Bloch-Laine subsequently turns over French contracts to British for one dollar]. JMH I; JMH II: 258; DH 146-52;

16 Jun: War Cabinet approves Anglo-French Union declaration which is transmitted by phone to Reynaud. JMM 24-7; MB 192

-------: JM meets de Gaulle in JM office on declaration of Anglo-French union and its transmittal to Reynaud in Bordeaux. Events overtake the union project and Reynaud is succeeded as prime minister by Petain. After lunch with Churchill, de Gaulle departs for Bordeaux but returns immediately [the next day] after fall of Reynaud government. MB 189-95; JMM 26-27,141; BH 55-6

------: JM, de Gaulle and Churchill discuss France's dire military condition; JM proposes transferring American orders for French weapons to British. He also makes futile plea to WSC for fighter aircraft to stop German attacks in France. WSC II 189

-------US acting Ambassador Anthony J D Biddle Jr talks with French Prime Minister Reynaud who laments failed Anglo French Union plan." It might, Reynaud said, have marked the beginning of a United States of Europe---the chance has now been lost." FRUS I 261-2

17 Jun: At JM's suggestion and with support of Churchill, Purvis signs agreement transferring about $600 m in French arms contracts in US to British responsibility. DH 146-52; WSC II 189

18 Jun: De Gaulle speaks on BBC in appeal to French people: "France is not alone! She has a vast Empire behind her. She can make common cause with the British Empire...[and she] can, like Britain, use to the full the immense industries of the United States." JMM 31

19 Jun: JM and Pleven fly to Bordeaux on plane provided by Churchill to see representatives of Petain government on union plan and to persuade those opposed to armistice to flee to North Africa. But his pleas, including the union proposal, fail. JMM 32-35,141; CB 75

------: "[in Bordeaux]...Jean Monnet (of the Anglo French Purchasing Board) walked in.... His plan was to offer the French Government all shipping facilities to evacuate French soldiers, equipment, individuals etc provided the French government went at once and set up fresh government overseas. [He was] unaware of situation today, viz, that the French government has gone some way to anticipate this.... Monnet seemed a mixture of gangster and conspirator and wants to get busy collecting men for a suitable government. I don't care for him and I don't trust him though in England they think him the cat's pyjamas." OHT 396

-----: De Gaulle cables Gen. Charles Nogues in North Africa, who had announced he was continuing the struggle, that de Gaulle was ready to serve under Nogues or do anything else his senior general requested. It was clear, however, to JM that de Gaulle intended to organize and run the London committee of free French which would represent the legitimate authority of the French people now under occupation. JMM 142-3

The above comment by British Ambassador Oliver Harvey suggests both class and bureaucratic disdain toward Monnet which was exhibited by some British officials over much of the Frenchman's life. Monnet was a self-made man with many of the characteristics of self-confidence, independence of spirit and disregard for authority that might accompany such a background. Harvey was a well-educated and tradition-minded diplomat who remained skeptical of amateur envoys like Monnet, especially when they had well-established political connections.

20 Jun: JM returns to London with a few officials who want to continue the fight from London but without success in getting French government to leave with them. The union proposal is abandoned. Leon Blum, former prime minister, and a Jew, was among those who refused the chance to leave with JM. Pleven, however, met his own wife and children on a Bordeaux street and they were evacuated as was Henri Bonnet, French diplomat and later a member of the French Committee on National Liberation (FCNL) and his wife. JMM 34-35,141; CB 75

22 Jun: Pleven writes a memo of his account of the Anglo-French union proposal. CB 66

23 Jun: JM writes de Gaulle advocating an independent French government in North Africa and opposing any organization set up in London that appears in France to be operating under British authority. JM supports a committee to unite all Frenchmen who wish to continue the struggle alongside Britain. AS 235; JMM 144-7; CB 82

-----: British government breaks relations with Petain government and recognizes de Gaulle's National Committee as sole legitimate French authority. JMM 143

24 Jun: After delivering strong message to French people on BBC the night before, de Gaulle replies to JM: "At a time like this, it would be absurd for us to move at cross purposes; we can each do much toward our common goal. Come and see me whenever you can; we shall agree." But in the end they do not

agree on JM's eventual decision to work in Washington and on what he saw as a personal and political ambition behind de Gaulle's decision to remain in London. JM wrote, "he respected my choice as I admired his determination." JMM 146-7; RI:GE 246; DEG-L, I 237-8

27 Jun: JM writes TV Soong asking firmly for a 25 per cent MM share of Burma Szuhuan railroad. FJM AMD

Writing to Soong for money in the midst of the collapse of France seems out of character for Monnet. But he may have been close to desperation over the possibility that he would soon be without work, without access to his property in Cognac, with sizeable debts and no foreseeable way to make a living except in undefined war work which had yet to be found.

Monnet must have experienced in these days some of the despair felt by Frenchmen everywhere at the nation's capitulation to Nazi Germany. He describes in his memoir that the couple who cooked for the Monnets and kept their apartment were too ashamed to go out on London streets after the armistice. JMM 142

2 Jul: JM writes letter of resignation to Churchill and Petain; to Churchill he adds a paragraph indicating willingness to work elsewhere for the war cause. JMM 147.

6 Jul: North American Supply Committee set up in London [as replacement for the Anglo-French Coordinating Committee] with JM's friend, Arthur Salter, as chairman and William Gorell-Barnes as secretary. MG:FH 666

Salter recalled, in an interview many years later, that he went to Churchill to rescue Monnet from the suspicious British bureaucracy which feared, with the fall of France, that the Frenchman might go back to France or someplace else and misuse the secret information he had acquired in his London position. Salter said that Churchill knew nothing of these fears, which Salter clearly belittled. Salter then suggested Monnet be sent to help the British supply effort "at the highest levels" in Washington. FJM OH

11 Jul: In House of Lords, Lord Barnby praises JM for work in AFCC. House of Lords Official Reports, 5th series 1939-40, 939

15 Jul: Against advice of JM, Pleven (joined by an assistant, Pierre Denis, both former aides to JM) decides to stay in London on de Gaulle's staff. RC 152. Pleven says JM preferred to divorce himself from the Free French movement under General de Gaulle because of the "pronounced antimilitarism of this old Charentais." CB 83; DEG-L I 240; RC 152

16 Jul: Churchill writes JM accepting resignation and asking him to go to Washington to continue his work with Purvis on obtaining American supplies. JMM 148.

France's tragic transformation from a fighting ally of Britain to a defeated

and partially occupied victim of the Nazi regime induced countless personal transformations, including Monnet's. He had been in London only about eight months when France fell and his future was unclear. He clearly, hoped, however, that his could continue the efforts started in London to use America's industrial strength to preserve Allied resistance and ultimately to defeat Germany. He briefly considered staying in London with General de Gaulle but he was skeptical of the general's personal ambitions. Instead, Monnet chose to use his American experience and friendships in the United States. Churchill readily agreed.

For Monnet's personal life, this decision meant leaving his London apartment and returning with Silvia to the United States to rejoin their daughter Anna. They would not see their Paris apartment on rue Fabert near the Invalides for more than four years. They left for New York where the Anglo-French Purchasing Commission was still located. Soon they moved to Washington, the center of the American political and economic effort to sustain Britain.

17 Jul: A. Greenwood, British minister, writes JM, at Churchill's request, on arrangements for new post with British Purchasing Commission in New York. "I think it will be convenient to postpone...precise terms of your appointment...until you have had personal consultation with Mr. Purvis...." JMH-I; NAUK FO 115; FJM AME 10/1/2

23 Jul: Morgenthau hosts meeting with Stimson, Purvis and others. Purvis gives background of his work, with JM, in early Allied orders which "...were not governed by their needs....[but] by the productive output of the industry as added to by the Allied money...; This was a privilege for us and ...not without value to you." HMD 285

24 Jul: JM replies to Greenwood: I greatly appreciate what you said in the House of Commons and in your letter to me....I am taking a few days to see I have ... sufficient knowledge of the anticipated requirements of the different departments of supply here....I expect to leave very shortly. Letter refers to AFPC work in New York City indicating move to Washington not yet anticipated. JMH-I; FJM AME 10/1/3

31 Jul: Hitler orders all-out air offensive against Britain, giving effort eight days to destroy British defenses; otherwise, he says, invasion of the island nation will be postponed until May 1941. WSC II 281-2

AUGUST: JM writes a memo to his British colleagues summarizing the joint committee work with this conclusion and, indirectly, underlining the importance of the American production and supply effort: "The enemy cannot establish a reserve of weapons beyond the range of [our] bombers. You can. You cannot win by force of arms without overwhelming superiority in the air and without machines of at least equal performance. This cannot be achieved by British production alone. It is therefore no exaggeration to say that not a day must be lost in establishing this [American] reserve, which may make all the difference between defeat and victory." JMM 148-9

6 Aug: A Salter writes British Ambassador Lord Lothian in Washington: "...Monnet is coming out [to United States]...at the invitation of the Prime Minister....I will only add that Monnet has not only been a close personal friend for over 25 years but a colleague with whom I have worked in closest association. I am confident that his services can be of the greatest value to the British Purchasing Commission." NAUK FO

11 Aug: JM friends Dean Acheson and George Rublee, in a letter to the NY Times, join two other prominent lawyers in defense of legality of Roosevelt's plan to transfer 50 destroyers to Britain.

12 Aug: T Brand writes JM who is about to depart for US, listing British weapon needs. FJM AME ll/5/5. In second note Brand lists personnel in British Purchasing offices. FJM AME 11/5/12

13 Aug: JM enters US by Pan American clipper; His departure from London coincides with surprising resilience of British to Hitler's intensive air war which fails during first phase from mid-July to mid-August where goal was to render London open to unrestricted bombing. WSC II, 282-3.

15 Aug-24 Sep: JM stays at Hotel Lowell NYC. In this period, FBI investigation starts at request of H Morgenthau. FBI 2-55

Monnet was well paid by British government standards in his London job as chair of the Anglo-French Coordinating Committee with a salary of about 200 pounds a month. In his move to the United States the awkward question arose of who was now to pay him in his subordinate and undefined role in Purvis' office and how much. The internal British discussion, probably unknown to Monnet in detail, was resolved with a salary the same as his London pay.

This was a good income in Washington in 1940 ---more than a member of Congress but somewhat less than a cabinet member---but it is not clear that Monnet ever took it. He told treasury secretary Morgenthau, and others, that he never took any pay from the British, to avoid any criticism after the war from Frenchmen sensitive to the appearance of French dependence after their military defeat. Perhaps Monnet used income from investments and some from the Murnane partnership to cover considerable expenses with a rented house in an expensive Washington neighborhood, a household staff and a growing family. (HMD 3 Jun 1942; NAUK AVIA 12/33; BP)

21 Aug:(Englewood, NJ). " Lunch at the Lamont's meeting Mme Tabouis--the Dorothy Thompson of France--Jean Monnet's great friend." ECM

SEPTEMBER: JM meets Roosevelt for second time. The President is anxious about the ability of the British to fight and survive alone. At the White House meeting, JM tries to dispel the pessimism that he suggests exists throughout the country and even with its leader. JMM 151

Monnet recalled, many years later, that he was impressed in Washington

by the American attention to liberty as it aided Britain. There was "not any spirit of domination; Arms were important but this inspiration was primary." (AW)

2 Sep: Roosevelt announces transfer of 50 overage destroyers to Britain in exchange for US base rights in Caribbean, Bermuda and Newfoundland. NYT. Earlier, JM recalls in his memoir, the President had asked for a billion dollars in defense expenditures and 50,000 military aircraft. In a month, the figure expanded to three billion. But in this period the President also had to contend with a sense of isolationism in the country which resisted Roosevelt's military preparations which included legislation to draft an army. JMM 151-2

6 Sep: ECM writes sympathetically of her daughter Anne Morrow Lindbergh's turmoil over strong public criticism of Charles Lindbergh for his isolationist views on war. Anne's new book Wave of the Future--a moral argument for isolationism--will come out in October. "She has suffered terribly for the unfair criticism of Charles...." The next week Elizabeth Morrow agrees to sign letter of William Allen White's Committee to Aid the Allies supporting sale of destroyers to England at request of her English son-in-law, Aubrey Morgan. ECM

10 Sep: Henry L Stimson [a prominent Republican recently appointed Secretary of War by Roosevelt as a gesture of bipartisanship in an election year] has long meeting with Purvis on British war purchases after which he notes: "When I came to Washington ...I found that relations with the British [supply] mission were in the hands of the Secretary of the Treasury---a very singular situation." The role of British procurement with the War Department was "very much complicated and chaotic" partly because the President felt he could not get on with my predecessor [Sec of War Woodring]."To my surprise I found that Arthur Salter, whom I know so well, is...the boss of Purvis and also that he has asked Walter Layton...another very close friend of mine, to come over here to act as an investigator." HLSD

------: T Brand sends JM personal note forwarding mail; two days later Brand writes again on Pleven's delayed trip to Washington due to US treasury restrictions on his assets; he also comments on JM view that Britain has to think in larger terms on planning for full war. NAUK AME 11/5/14,15

24 Sep-30 Sep: JM joins Silvia at Carlton Hotel, Washington DC, [completing family's move from New York]. FBI 1-73

30 Sep: Monnets move to Wardman Park Hotel. FBI 1-73

OCTOBER-NOVEMBER: ECM working for [Wendell] Wilkie [for President] Committee. Con [daughter] voted for FDR; Anne and Charles [Lindbergh] for Wilkie. ECM. Charles Lindbergh [returned from his self-exile in Europe after the kidnapping and murder of his son] assumed a leading role as a spokesman for isolationists. He told supporters: "Our dangers are internal. We need not fear invasion unless we bring it through our own quarrellings and meddling in affairs abroad." JMM 152 [quoting Robert Sherwood's book, Roosevelt and Hopkins, (New York, 1950) 153

15 Oct: JM and family move from hotel suite to 2415 Foxhall Road, apparently exchanging housing with Baron Maximilian Hugo Von Pagenhardt, a Washington area builder. FBI 2-34.

The comfortable (but not extravagant) rented house on Foxhall Road was, as JM said in his memoirs, on the edge of the city and adjacent to a greenway which led to Rock Creek Park, a principal recreation area of Washington. Monnet started a pattern here which continued for the rest of his life: choosing living quarters outside the inner city, creating a sharp break between office and home. He also started walking alone regularly in his suburban surroundings for an hour each morning so that 'the worries of yesterday which I took to bed disappeared.' AW

21 Oct: John Foster Dulles sends a revised proposal on Atlantic Union to Clarence Streit, founder of Union Now! movement, with note: Monnet was in New York today. I spoke to him of our talk. He will be back in Washington tomorrow and would...like a chance to talk with you." JFD

24 Oct: C Streit writes John Foster Dulles: "I had a long and very constructive talk with Jean Monnet yesterday." JFD

27 Oct: From Brazzaville, Congo, de Gaulle issues ordnances setting up Defence Council of the Empire in effort to start the reconquest of France from French Equatorial Africa. DEG-L (v. 1) 281

30 Oct: Roosevelt announced in Boston that Britain would get 26,000 aircraft it had requested and that the US would become "the greatest airpower in the world." JM saw this as sign isolationism was ending in US. JMM 156

31 Oct: T Brand writes JM complaining of Beaverbrook insistence on managing all details of US air procurement, ignoring the Salter-Purvis mechanism. JMH I

5 Nov: Roosevelt reelected to unprecedented third term. NYT

6 Nov: JM (Foxhall Rd) to Lamont (NYC) I am returning your draft speech "The Far Eastern Threat". It is very good. LA

14 Nov: John Foster Dulles writes C Streit, about meeting on 13 Nov with JM on how to form an Atlantic union. JM advised caution and patience, Dulles writes and suggests meeting soon in New York. "I think Monnet would come over [to] New York and I think his judgment and counsel are very useful." JFD

------: Dulles writes JM enclosing draft of Atlantic Union plan which he had also sent to C Streit. "Perhaps it does not go far enough but it illustrates an alternative approach. I exclude [here the details on] the invitation to form the Union." JFD

15 Nov: JM writes long letter to A Salter urging large scale thinking and planning by Britain, not counting the costs in money; "The defense of England [for the American people]...is the defense of America. They will...do whatever England requires them to do. They will not for the moment go to war---in time they may---I personally believe they will sometime next year....

The...consequence of this is the strong desire to...give Great Britain any material help needed. [Later]...as regards myself, Purvis and I were asked to submit to London a proposition ...about my status, position etc. We did not do so [because of other more urgent needs] but now it is apparent that if my effectiveness...is not to peter out...I must be 'labeled.'" JM also refers to a possible trip to London after Purvis returns. FJM AME 11/5/16; JMM 156-7

-----:JM writes memo to W Layton who is visiting Washington on British war procurement issues suggesting more vigorous British approach using a balance sheet analysis of British needs versus German strengths coupled with a frank account of dollar shortage. JMH-I; JMM 156

20 Nov: JM wires T Brand: Your personal and secret letter of 31 Oct safely received. In future put on all such letters 'To be opened by Monnet personally.' Earlier in week, JM wires Brand [who is still affiliated with Lazard Freres bankers in London] that business mail should come to him at 30 Broad Street (MM office]. FJM AME ll/5/19

Monnet's plea for privacy in his mail probably reflects some concern about his unusual status as a Frenchman in a British supply mission. Although not centered on personal status, he judged his effectiveness to depend both on being accepted fully as a team member and as a somewhat independent operator. He was also aware that some British and American observers doubted both the propriety and the usefulness of his role. He had a young English secretary assigned to him and he insisted she not open his mail. AC

27 Nov: JM serves as chairman of "Coordinating Committee" which is informal organ to bring US, British officials together on certain supply matters. JMH-I

30 Nov: JM writes memo on the arms available to the Axis power versus what Britain has with aid from the United States. It is essential, he writes, to state and to maintain a balance sheet on these armaments. JMM 161; FJM AME 11/15/24 cited in ER 262

DECEMBER: JM has office in room 931 of Willard Hotel, where British Purchasing Commission (BPC) leases two floors. BPC also has offices at 729 15 St NW in Washington and at 37 Wall Street and 43 Exchange Place, NYC. NAUK FO 115

2 Dec: Stimson describes "one of the most interesting lunch conferences I ever had" with Frankfurter and JM. Stimson recalls knowing JM "quite well" during 1929-33 years when Stimson was secretary of state under Hoover. JM

"gave me a most clear and penetrating analysis of the situation in France. He sees two major goals: 1) Prevent France from joining the New Europe of Hitler; 2) Keep North Africa from German control. A US declaration is needed for both goals. JM gives Stimson memo on these points. HLSD; FJM AME 18/4/2

-----JM writes F Frankfurter: I enclose the memorandum [on German pressures on Vichy] we discussed and I am sending a copy to Mr Stimson. FJM AME 18/4/2

Monnet had easy relations with Felix Frankfurter, a Supreme Court justice and Roosevelt confidant, and with Henry Stimson, a distinguished Republican who had already served as secretary of war and of state before being asked by Roosevelt to take over the war department again. These friendships would be unusual for any foreign resident in Washington in 1940 and especially for a Frenchman whose country had just capitulated to the Nazi Germany. It is a tribute to Monnet's ability to inspire trust and to his clear dedication to serve the Allied cause that Frankfurter and Stimson became channels for Monnet to extend his Washington network in his still undefined role at the British Purchasing Mission which he had, until a few months before, supervised from his London job.

Monnet knew Stimson in the 1929-33 period when he was secretary of state to President Hoover and he may have first met Frankfurter at the end of WWI when both were involved in the Paris Peace Conference.

4 Dec: Stimson gives Col. William Donovan copy of JM memo [presumably on France and North Africa] which he read with interest and said would be useful on Donovan's coming trip to Europe. HLSD. Two days later Donovan left for Europe. R. Dunlop, Donovan, America's Master Spy (New York, 1982) 232

8 Dec: Churchill, in "one of the most important [letters] I ever wrote," gives Roosevelt a detailed and urgent plea for transatlantic transport and for relief from the dire finances imposed by the costs of war. WSC II 494-501; JMM 158

Whether Churchill's letter was influenced by JM's 15 Nov letter to Salter is not known, but the two messages had similar themes: forget the traditional view of arms trade between two countries and, instead, see the war, and Britain's survival and victory, as a common cause which cannot be measured or limited by the dollar sign. America does not have to join militarily in the war effort (which will probably happen anyway, Monnet thought) but it must if it must fully support Britain.

12 Dec: Lord Lothian, UK ambassador in Washington, dies suddenly. NYT

14 Dec: JM writes Bullitt note inviting him, and his aide, Carmel Offie, to lunch tomorrow. FJM AME 20/4/32

16 Dec: Roosevelt, back from Caribbean vacation, tells press US must do all possible to help Britain defend itself. He describes future program to build up America's defenses and to lend or lease military goods beyond its own need to help those countries whose defense is vital to the United States. His goal is to eliminate the "dollar sign" in that defense. RM 97; JMM 159-60 (citing RE Sherwood, R&H 224-6)

18 Dec: JM sends F Frankfurter at Supreme Court a memo for Roosevelt with a cover note: I am enclosing first memo I promised; the second one, on North Africa armaments, will come tomorrow. FJM AME 18/4/2 . Memo enclosed is on the Nazi "New Order" in Europe and starts with Roosevelt's recent press statement indicating US security is tied to British fighting capacity. JM urges next speech by president include support for French resistance to Hitler's attempts to incorporate France into a "`United Europe' brought about by coercion, fear and terror." Roosevelt's statement that US would refuse to recognize such a "New Order" in Europe would galvanize Europe-wide resistance. JMM 168; FJM AME 11/5/26; MF 566-8

19 Dec: Frankfurter writes Roosevelt on enclosed JM memo, describing latter "... as a `free' Frenchman of proven sagacity, extraordinarily well informed about French currents of opinion.... He is a man in whose understanding and discretion I have complete confidence." FLF; MF 566-8

------: Lamont cables JM at Willard Hotel: When you will next be in NY? LA

20 Dec: JM sends Frankfurter memo on North African armaments. FJM AME 18/4/6

22 Dec: JM writes Frankfurter: I have just had a short but good interview with Admiral Leahy [who is US ambassador to Vichy France]. FJM AME 18/11/2

Besides being and intermediary with the Roosevelt Administration for Monnet, Frankfurter introduced the Frenchman to many key people in Washington including Phil Graham, one of Frankfurter's law clerks and later publisher of the Washington Post, and Milton Katz, an official in the War Production Board. Katz recalled talking with Monnet in his office he had in the Combined Production Board Office in the same building with Katz. Monnet had a tiny, inside office which Katz apologized for. Monnet replied:" My young friend ···I have been engaged in private business in Paris, London, New York and Shanghai. I served the French government in World War I and I serve it again in World War II.... I have learned that there is no international problem whatever that can compare in difficulty with the allocation of office space."

24 Dec: Former French Prime Minister Daladier writes Bullitt from prison supporting further US aid for Britain in the hopes of defeating the Nazis. He asks Bullitt to write him via the American Embassy in Vichy. Daladier compares his treatment by the Vichy government to that give Dreyfus and says the does not

know the outcome of his pending trial which will apparently be conducted under extra-legal procedures. WCB

27 Dec: JM writes long memo for Purvis on July-December 1940 background of capital financing of UK war production. Morgenthau helped when Purvis and Sir Walter Layton made proposals in Sept, Oct 1940; Sir Frederick Phillips visit in November continued talks with Morgenthau. FDR then supported same efforts and told press that US aid to Britain would be in weapons, not money and that subject to new [Lend Lease] legislation all UK armament order to be placed by US as American orders. Finally War Dept helped with interim financing to complete major orders. JMH-I

29 Dec: Roosevelt delivers "fireside chat" on US role in arming anti-Nazi forces using "arsenal of democracy" phrase which JM originated in conversation the previous week with Frankfurter. President proposes lending arms to Britain without payment. JMM 159-60; RES-R&H 226-7

30 Dec: JM sends note to Roosevelt "It was with deep emotion that I listened to your speech last night," adding that he is now working in Washington with Purvis. FJM AME 11/5/31

------: JM writes long memo for Purvis who is meeting today with Morgenthau. Gives assessment of coordination of British orders and costs indicating very limited resources Britain has left for payments to US arms makers. JMH-I

------:JM writes memo reviewing US aircraft production potential for 1941, citing French and British orders in spring and fall of 1939 as helping expand US production capacity. JMH-I

1941

EARLY JANUARY: JM writes President Roosevelt on reducing the gap between a "balance sheet" showing the material needs for the war and the actual production. "If this gap can be filled up, the war may be shortened by a year." JMM 163

3 Jan [4500 Broadbranch Road Wash DC] "...tonight Secretary Stimson and Mrs. Stimson and the Monnets were here.... After the S[ecretary] left we had a little informal visit w. Jean and Silvia. He speaks w[ith] high praise of Pres. Roosevelt and is deeply interested in the progress of war sympathy in this country. George [Rublee, host] too feels that Pres R. has done better thanW W[ilkie] could have done." ECM; HLSD

------: Morgenthau writes note to JM: "Your letter of Dec 31st has given me the greatest pleasure. I am grateful for your kind thought of writing to me at this time and also for what you have said about my work. Please accept...my thanks for all that you have done." FJM AME 11//5/32

Despite Roosevelt's brave words in his fireside address, he was still unsure about how to respond to Churchill's plea of one month earlier. He also lacked

a personal bond with the British leader whom he had only met once more than twenty years earlier. Roosevelt would have preferred a personal meeting but, as he told Harry Hopkins, his trusted aide, this was not the right time to arrange it. There was no American ambassador in London and no British ambassador in Washington. Hopkins suggested he go himself but the President demurred. But after several aides supported the Hopkins trip, Roosevelt agreed without even telling Hopkins before he announced it to the press. Monnet then played a role in preparing Hopkins for the challenge he was to face in London: Winston Churchill. More important, however, for Monnet, his meeting with Hopkins marked the start of a decisive friendship, as important as any he would have within the Roosevelt administration. RES-R&H 230-232; MATA 27, 46-8; JMM 80

5 Jan: President Roosevelt announces that Harry Hopkins, his special assistant, will go to London to meet Churchill. NYT 6 Jan

6 Jan: In address to Congress known for its "Four Freedoms" theme, Roosevelt asks for "lend-lease" program to aid Britain; eventually over $50 b is provided to Allies under the plan; Churchill sees this as direct answer to his 8 Dec plea but JM is disappointed that the address does not refer to France's status in the war. JMM 168-9; WSC II 502-3;506-8

7 Jan: Hopkins leaves for London, armed with the good news about the lend-lease proposal, and aided by a long talk with JM about the importance of Churchill whom Hopkins tends to underestimate. RES-R&H 232; JMM 165-6

-----: Bullitt gives speech at Chapel Hill, NC on international situation, coinciding with the effective date of his resignation from Roosevelt Administration. B&B 273-4

8 Jan: JM writes Bullitt, on BPC Washington letterhead: Listened to your very good speech last night; We'll discuss it when we lunch. WCB

10 Jan: "I would consider, as [does]...Jean Monnet (with whom I am working toward this end) that a true engagement by the United States (in the European conflict) would create a fait accompli, which certain leaders are secretly seeking, and the United States would become the ally of us all overnight."Letter from L Rajchman, writing from Washington, to a friend in Europe. BM II 154

Exactly what work Monnet and Rajchman undertook together in 1941 Washington is not clear. Perhaps they only met for mutual support and encouragement but Monnet had great respect for the Pole's idealism and dedication to world peace from their time together in the League of Nations. Rajchman is one of the few individuals praised in detail in JMM.

14 Jan: Churchill cables Roosevelt, thanking him for sending Hopkins who had arrived a few days earlier. The same day, Hopkins wrote the President from London that Churchill "is the government." JMM 166

15 Jan: T Brand writes JM: "You may be hurt and are certainly irritated by the way in which we have dealt with personal questions concerning yourself....Purvis and Morris Wilson [Purvis' deputy] had to do more that just be glad of your service. [Now] they really want you to stay and help them and have a real confidence in your judgment. Secondly, the U S administration, particularly one or two of them, had to accept you as one of us and at first they were critical of your inclusion." Also the reactions of certain departments here (Foreign Office for instance) to the US administration's views took time but is "absolutely OK" now. Also, "certain events caused you to express your feelings very strongly when you were here. This incident was, as you know, magnified by certain people but it has not been forgotten."

Letter ends with Brand urging JM to visit London now that his membership on new British Supply Council in Washington has been announced. [This trip never took place]. FJM AME 16/8/24

-------:JM named today to British Supply Council (BSC), new roof organization over all British purchasing agencies in US. FJM AME 10/2/5

Monnet's status in Washington was publicly clarified with his appointment to the British Supply Council but this did not alter his anomalous position. He was a citizen of a defeated country working at an undefined job among former allies in a neutral capital. Tommy Brand's letter of 15 January reflects some of the frustrations Monnet must have felt in his first months after he lost his London job. The letter's allusion to opposition to Monnet within the US administration was a portent of further antagonism toward him by Henry Morgenthau, the politically powerful treasury secretary and confidant of President Roosevelt.

19 Jan: JM writes memo on Britain's inability to defeat Axis in 1941 even if it gets the resources to prevent its own defeat. Only aid from the United States, as proposed by Roosevelt in lend-lease program, can create the production needed for victory. FJM AME 11/5/36 cited by ER 266

27 Jan: Anna Monnet, daughter of Silvia, writes the President that she saw his inaugural parade. She encloses ten dimes for the infantile paralysis campaign which Roosevelt's own illness inspired. MF 580

FEBRUARY: Lord Halifax, former British foreign minister, arrives in Washington as ambassador replacing Lord Lothian who died in December.

3 Feb: F Frankfurter writes Missy LeHand, Roosevelt's secretary: "Madame Monnet has a daughter about 9 years old who fell violently in love with the President on Inauguration Day. As is true of other ladies under similar circumstances, she poured out her heart and ...here's the result." Enclosed letter from Anna Monnet says "I was at the inaugural parade and heard everything over the radio in the morning. It was very nice. I liked it so much, didn't you? In this letter are ten dimes for infantile paralysis. It is very little but it is all I have and I hope they will help. Happy birthday, Mr. President." FLF; FDRL President's

Personal File

6 Feb: JM and Purvis meet with Lord Halifax, the new British ambassador, on how Lend-Lease bill, when enacted, will help restore some balance in British-Axis war materiel. RM 107

7 Feb: Roosevelt replies to JM daughter, Anna, with note of thanks. FDRL PPF; MF 580

8 Feb: JM writes memo assuming passage of Lend-Lease bill with a program of action directed to the highest levels of the US government. This transformation will create new industries, change old ones and require an organization charged with coordination of the entire US and UK production. FJM AME 11/5/40 cited in ER 266-7

17 Feb: Hopkins, back in Washington, dodges reporters queries about his time in Britain with Churchill. NYT 18 Feb. Soon after, he develops a more personal relation with JM at dinner en famille at Foxhall Road home. JMM 166-7

25 Feb: Roosevelt writes Morgenthau in anticipation of Lend Lease bill's passage to ask treasury secretary to help H Hopkins who will direct administration of foreign arms sales under new law. HMD 378

In March, Congress approves Lend Lease program, greatly aiding Allied access to US production and moving supply management from Morgenthau's treasury department to Stimson's war department. This transfer eases some strains in Monnet's life since his prickly relations with Morgenthau still shadow his British Supply Council work. Even after Morgenthau gives up his foreign supply role, he continues a close watch over Monnet through both a continuing FBI survey and internal treasury department investigations.

3 Mar: H Morgenthau drafts reply to Roosevelt accepting role on committee advising Lend Lease program, thus marking end to treasury secretary's central role in foreign arms sales. HMD 378

11 Mar: Congress approves Lend Lease Law. NYT 12 Mar

3 Apr: JM greets old friend A Salter who arrives in Washington for visit to British Supply Council and related US officials. NYT 4 Apr; JMH-I

25 Apr: JM attends lunch by British Supply Council at Willard Hotel with Clive Ballieu, head of BSC; Robert Brand, head of British Food Mission; treasury secretary Morgenthau, Arthur Salter and other visiting British officials. HMD

19 May: Lamont writes JM: Sorry we haven't met lately. Bob Brand is giving a talk to a small Council of Foreign Relations dinner on June 3. I wish you could come. JM replies four days later that he will try to attend. LA

21 May: "Late in the afternoon I called JM at the BPM [British Purchasing Mission]down to see me [Stimson] and McCloy....He is a very able man and a

believer in free France and a disbeliever in Vichy, shown by his attaching himself to the British Purchasing Mission. HLSD

26 May: During a "fireside chat" address, Roosevelt declares an "Unlimited National Emergency" providing basis for government to commit itself fully to war mobilization. NYT 27 May; JMM 169

28 May: JM and McCloy draft order asking government departments to compile a balance sheet of Anglo-American and German forces which will become basis for "victory program." JMM 169

3 Jun: JM attends Council of Foreign Relations dinner in NYC for Bob Brand, chairman, British mission in Washington. LA; JMH-I

21 Jun: Hitler invades Soviet Union which becomes ally of US and UK and thus a participant in the American war supply effort.

27 Jun: Pleven leaves on another mission to Washington at request of Gen. de Gaulle for whom Pleven serves as Director of Foreign and Economic Affairs at Free French headquarters in London. He likely meets JM who was starting his most frenzied work leading to the Victory Program. Pleven reports back on divisions between the old line French community in US and new refugees from occupied France with many of the second group more loyal than the first to Free France movement. Pleven stays in Washington until October when he sees Secretary of State Cordell Hull and his deputy Sumner Welles. NAUK FO 371 28321-5; CB 108

30 Jun: JM lunches with Herve Alphand where they discuss respective roles: JM as an Anglo-French official since war began and Alphand as a French official now ready to join de Gaulle in London. JM does not resent de Gaulle's attempt to "play politics" to ensure his postwar role in French government. HA 80

By 1941 the U.S. center of British war purchasing shifted from New York City to Washington where Monnet was already established. The British Supply Council (BSC), with Monnet now a member, was a roof organization and its chairman Arthur Purvis moved to Washington while keeping a New York office. The BSC represented all of the separate British supply organizations in the United States; Monnet, the only non-British member of the council, was also the only member who does not represent such an organization. This might have been an uncomfortable anomaly for others but Monnet seemed to find freedom in his unique BSC role. He spent little time in the Willard Hotel headquarters of the council, preferring to visit American officials in their offices. He made frequent, sometimes daily, visits to Frankfurter at his Supreme Court office. He saw McCloy often at the War Department and visited Bob Nathan and others at the War Production Board constantly.

He saw his role as a prod and sometimes an irritant to those not as obviously single-minded as himself in expanding America's war production. He

could be patient, or brusque, depending on the moment's need as he practiced and perfected his dual strengths: concentration and persuasion. As Frankfurter put it, "He had blinders on. For the things that he's interested in he doesn't dissipate his energies, or doesn't take time off, or doesn't listen to anything else. [In] Jean Monnet, the central quality that I call resolution---will--- was manifested in an extreme intensity." FFR 184

Bob Nathan, who worked as closely with Monnet as any American in this period, occasionally clashed with him on the means to their agreed goal of increased production. Nathan wrote: "Monnet was an impatient man because he knew better than most the grave jeopardy of Great Britain. He would not waste precious time with small talk or socializing....He had an unusual ability to spot effective operators and quickly discard those not in a position to help. He was persistent when he sensed an opportunity to recruit an effective operator. But he had no time or energy for ineffectual or phony persons." BH 206

1 Jul: JM writes T Brand on need to develop a plan of production which, by the end of 1942, will yield arms of all kinds exceeding those of Germany. FJM AME 14/1/3 cited in ER 270

2 Jul: JM prepares draft letter from War Secretary Stimson to General Marshall on need for a complete balance sheet of Allied and German war production. JMH-I

3 Jul: JM talks with General Burns, Lend-Lease executive officer, on need for a balance sheet to show US and UK arms production vs German arms. DH 325. JM tells Burns broad balance sheet useful even though British cannot give details for whole new fiscal year at this point. JMH I

9 Jul: Roosevelt asks War Secretary Stimson and Navy Secretary Knox to explore "at once the overall production...required to defeat our potential enemies.". Letter did not assume US entry in war, only its continuing role as arsenal for countries fighting the Axis. This move welcomed by army staff, Undersecretary of War Patterson, and JM, among others, as start of strategic planning which became Victory Program. GLS 126-9

2 Aug: JM represents Britain at first meeting of Anglo-American-Russian Committee which Roosevelt has just named with object "to get Russia as much aid as possible out of stocks on hand and out of production.... Monnet would have to clear most of his important points with London." Oscar Cox diary, FDRL; J. Lash, Roosevelt and Churchill, 1939-1941 (NY,1976) 377

7 Aug: Stacy May flies to London with US side of balance sheet which JM helped prepare and which will show US-UK strength compared to Axis. JMH-I (quoting Purvis cable Pursa 525); JMM 170

9-12 Aug: "Atlantic Charter" issued by Churchill and Roosevelt at their seaborne conference outside Argentia, Newfoundland. RM 114; JMM 172

19 Aug: JM writes paper on need to speed up US arms output; W. Batt repeats point at Victory Program conference next month. DH 334

20 Aug: Arthur Purvis, JM's boss as head of the British Supply Council, killed in plane crash in Scotland on his way back to US with preliminary copy of the crucial balance sheet showing British needs and production. JMM 172

21 Aug: T Brand writes JM describing air accident which killed Purvis, Beaverbrook's positive attitudes toward Purvis and discussions about his successor. JMH-I

------: JM writes Morgenthau on death of Arthur Purvis in plane crash the day before and says that he wants to call on him. HMD 433

23 Aug: JM telephones London to say Roosevelt accepts idea of Victory Program Conference on 15 September. DH 331-2

29 Aug: JM writes Carmel Offie, Bullitt's assistant, enclosing $224. for shipping effects of JM partner, George Murnane, from Paris. WCB

EARLY SEPTEMBER: JM writes memo on balance sheet that government economist Stacy May took to London in early August: This is document of major importance. Never before have Allies, even while at war, given each other such detailed information. Balance sheet shows that US, even with twice the resources, would, by Dec 1942, produce less than half arms of UK and Canada. Latter are devoting half of national income to war with US devoting about one fifth. "We [the Americans] have not yet earned right to call ourselves the arsenal of democracies...." JMH-I; JMM 170

4 Sep: JM sends T Brand a letter for Lord Beaverbrook. "I also add for your information a very secret memo which I made up after the President had written his instructions to the War Department [on the Victory Program]" You might show it to Layton and any intimate friends you choose." I suggest you destroy it because it should not be left in the files...." JMH-I

Monnet's admonition to Brand about destroying correspondence reflects a concern for security which sometimes seems excessive. He had earlier told Brand to send mail to him in Washington marked "To Be Opened Only by Addressee." Monnet had no staff other than a young French-speaking British secretary who was actually a student stranded in the United States with the start of the war. He locked up his files when he left the office and he never told her where he was going. (AC) He was leading an unusual life as a Frenchman operating in a British supply mission in wartime Washington and his concern for secrecy may have reflected his own insecurity and, as Brand hints below, uncharacteristic depression in Monnet.

12 Sep: T Brand writes JM from London: Noel Hall, whom I have just met, tells me the last time he saw you, [you] seemed depressed and pessimistic. I hope this has passed. I put this down to the end of the Washington summer which

is enough to make anyone gloomy. [I] hope that you are in your usual frame of mind by the time you get this letter. FJM AME 16/8/23

All of the reasons for Monnet's worries are not known but the stress of the Victory Program work may have been involved as well as his anomalous role at the British Supply Council. Silvia Monnet was in her final months of pregnancy which may have increased personal tensions for Monnet who, at age 53, was about to be a father, and not only a stepfather, for the first time. More immediately Morgenthau was continuing an investigation into Monnet, Murnane's prewar war work and into Monnet's tax status.

15 Sep: Victory Program Conference starts in London, now folding aid to Russia into US production goals. A. Harriman represents US, Beaverbrook, UK. DH 332

MID-SEPTEMBER: Stacy May returns from London with top secret balance sheet showing American, Canadian and British production and requirements. JMM 172; D. Nelson, Arsenal of Democracy (NY, 1946) Ch. 4

20 Sep: R Nathan sends JM memo replying to Ordnance Dept views on "Military Requirements and Material Production," the draft of the Victory Program. JMH-I

25 Sep: Victory Program presented in rough and incomplete form to Roosevelt by Stimson and Knox. President approves it. EL 124; IMW 141; GLS 128-9; JMM 172

26 Sep: JM writes State Department in support of visitor visa request for Pierre David-Weill "[whom] I have known...for many years....Since he became a partner in Lazard Freres Ltd in London, I have seen him frequently." JM identifies himself as "Frenchman in this country on a diplomatic visa serving the British government as a member of the British Supply Council in Washington." FJM AME 20/2/6

29 Sep: Stimson sends memo to McCloy reviewing draft Victory Program just given to Roosevelt: This data must be continuously revised and consolidated by May and Nathan under your supervision. JMH-I

1 Oct: Pleven, on extended mission for de Gaulle in U.S., is coolly received by Sumner Welles, US under secretary of state, who says U.S. wants to see the restoration of the "independence and integrity of France and its empire" but will not break with the Vichy regime. CB 108

3 Oct: JM notes that combined needs of US, UK and Russia exceed [our] capacities; priorities will have to be set: "...it will be necessary to decide on the highest grounds of strategy which requirements must be cut." DH 334; RM 118

9 Oct: JM sends Amb. Halifax two documents which war secretary Stimson had just given to Roosevelt on US war production. At about same time, JM prepares a detailed balance sheet comparing US and British-Canadian

production which is probably the basis of the Stimson documents. This balance sheet shows US lagging behind British-Canadian total arms production in 18 months ending 31 Dec 1942. Only in final quarter of period will US move ahead. Halifax replies: "a pretty depressing picture." JMH-I

29 Oct: T Brand writes JM that Victory Plan discussions will start in mid-November. "Congratulations on getting $1.4 b. in new funds for common types [of arms]...no one else would have got as much." FJM AME 16/8/23-26

NOVEMBER: Marianne Monnet born to Silvia in Washington. JMM 175

6 Nov: H. Freeman Matthews at American Embassy at Vichy writes Bullitt in Washington about JM's request "some months ago" to forward some documents to his family in Cognac for signature and return to him. Matthews tried through JM's secretary, Ms. Miguez, to do this but without success. WCB

14 Nov: F Frankfurter writes Lord Halifax, who has been British ambassador in Washington since early in the year: "You have asked me to put on paper the view taken here of Jean Monnet and his services. Because of the very high regard in which I have him... [I can say]"I have heard no higher praise of any official entrusted with British interests that what has been accorded Monnet by men charged with the highest responsibility. I have heard Harry Hopkins, Secretary Stimson, the two assistant secretaries of war, McCloy and Lovett, and leading men in the army, Lend Lease Administration and in OPM [Office of Production Management] speak of Monnet in ...highest esteem and admiration. He has been a creative and energizing force in...our defense program.... "He possesses an extraordinary clarity of mind, a power of concentration...pertinacity, experience with technical defense problems as well as large experience in the delicate task of currying successful collaboration between two governments.... Finally he possesses the rarest of talents: the power of self-abnegation...Everyone to whom I have spoken...has absolute confidence in his trustworthiness, discretion and single-minded devotion to the cause he is serving...." FLF

Halifax, the former foreign secretary, must have known Monnet in London, during the 1939-40 period when the Frenchman headed the Anglo-French Coordination Committee. Why Halifax would now inquire of Frankfurter about Monnet is not clear but it was almost certainly related to Henry Morgenthau's continual effort to discredit the Frenchman as later conversations of Halifax and Morgenthau suggest.

18 Nov: WC Bullitt named ambassador at large by Roosevelt as his personal representative in Africa and the Middle East after nearly 18 months interlude since the end of his ambassadorship in Paris. B&B 281

Monnet kept in touch with Bullitt during and after the ambassador's awkward departure from Paris and the equally awkward interlude before Bullitt's assignment to the Middle East and Africa but the old intimacy seems to be gone. Both men were engaged in tasks related to the war but their work never brought them together. This rupture coincided with a change in Bullitt's relationship with Roosevelt which had deteriorated for several reasons and never returned to the level of 1938-40 when both men worked frantically to help prepare France to defend itself.

4 Dec: Nathan's feasibility study of Victory Program presented to War Production chief Donald Nelson who gets it to Roosevelt. EL 124

-----: Outline of the secret Victory Program published in two isolationist newspapers, the Chicago Tribune and Washington Times-Herald. EL 124-5

7 Dec: Japanese attack on Pearl Harbor and other Pacific targets marks start of war for US. NYT 8 Dec; JMM 173

10 Dec: During preparations for Arcadia conference, JM advises Roosevelt that US General Staff munitions program could be increased by 50 per cent. JMM 173

11 Dec: Hitler asks Reichstag for declaration of war against United States basing his arguments partly at least on information about the Victory Program leaked to American newspapers. Germany must anticipate, he said, "the concentration of forces of enemy powers in accordance with the now known Roosevelt plans." EL 125

Hitler's decision to declare war on the United States must rank as one of his most disastrous moves. Roosevelt apparently had no plans to declare war on Germany after the Pearl Harbor attack by Japan. If his country had gone to war only against Japan, what would have happened to Monnet's role in Washington? His work there was based on the assumption of Churchill, Roosevelt and Monnet himself that the defeat of Germany was the principal goal of the Anglo-American supply operation. If America's attention were now to be directed only or principally to the Pacific War, both Britain, and Monnet's work, would have suffered. Hitler seemingly could have divided Britain from the United States if he had not declared war on America. Whether his outrage at the Victory Program truly explains his decision to declare war on the U.S. will remain one of history's greatest unanswered questions.

12 Dec: Letter from T Brand to JM:" Morale is good despite the bad news from the Far East [where Singapore had just fallen to the Japanese.]. . . .[Later] I give you the heartiest congratulations on the ...victory plan. I am glad to note that quite a number of the people concerned realize where the real credit is due.[i.e. to JM]" JMH-I; FJM AME 16/8/26

Monnet was not a trained economist and certainly not a technician capable of close monitoring of industrial production. He relied on others for such expertise but he effectively pressed Nathan and others to raise quotas for the critical war materials even when told that unplanned increases would actually confuse and delay production. His singular effectiveness was as a persuasive advocate of whatever was needed to win the war. But this talent seemed to

*limit his understanding of other aspects of production problems. His memoirs
naturally and in retrospect, gave his perspective while those who had to work
with him---never an easy task---may have had more qualified judgments. But on
Monnet's side is the judgment of the eminent economist John Maynard Keynes
who said that the Frenchman's persistence in increasing American aircraft
production goals by fifty percent, which Roosevelt ultimately accepted, was
probably responsible for reducing the war by one year. (MATA 42; JMM 161-3)*

15 Dec: JM writes W Batt of Raw Materials Division of Office of
Production Management (OPM) on changed outlook for Victory Program now
that US has entered war and enclosing memo on divided jurisdiction over raw
materials compared to strict controls operating for them in Britain. (JMH-I; FJM
AME 14/1/6 cited in ER 275-6); JM suggests that for each commodity in short
supply there should be "one central statement continuously kept up to day by
information supplied by each Government." These "basic running statements"
would cover all basic facts on the material; there should be "one single
organisation centralising all this information...." Batt should chair the inter-
departmental committee doing this "central work" JM said. Soon thereafter, FDR
took up the idea, supported by H. Hopkin's parallel memo, and the Combined
Raw Materials Board was established in place of the proposed Batt committee.
HW 267-9

17 Dec: Supreme Court Justice Frankfurter sends Roosevelt long four-part
memorandum based on draft by JM on "defects and inadequacies in the British
and French war effort" and steps needed now that US is in war to maximize
production and organization of allied efforts. Frankfurter also sends copy to
Harry Hopkins. RM 125-6

22 Dec: Churchill arrives for "Arcadia" conference with Roosevelt on
allied war needs and strategy. NYT 23 Dec

24 Dec: Admiral Muselier, acting under orders of de Gaulle, occupies
small French islands of St. Pierre and Miquelon near Canadian coast. State
Department is upset because move contradicted its assurances to Vichy
government but American public opinion is strongly on side of de Gaulle and
against the State Department. The episode steels the State Department hostility
toward de Gaulle. William L Langer, Our Vichy Gamble (NY, 1947) 212-224

26 Dec: War Secretary Stimson presents target figures on US-UK-
Canadian war production based on third revision of JM's September balance
sheet. But JM meanwhile had prepared a revision himself on 10 Dec which
argued for a 50 % increase over the Stimson figures. Beaverbrook, Churchill's
war production chief, agreed and led effort to raise the US figures. RM 120

LATE DECEMBER: Lord Beaverbrook, in Washington with Churchill, writes
Roosevelt on need to devote full US industry to munitions. WSC,III 610; JMM
173-4

JANUARY: US Treasury Department memo describes its inquiry of American Bosch Corp, chaired by George Murnane, JM's partner, because of firm's ties with German Bosch company. Murnane earns $15,000 annual salary from company which will probably be judged to be under German control and subject to US enemy property laws. HMD 495

2 Jan: Lamont asks JM if TV Soong is still in Washington. If so would JM ask Soong to call Lamont for a breakfast or luncheon meeting in NYC? LA.

6 Jan: Roosevelt gives first wartime State of Union address to Congress, announcing the final Victory Program and using Nathan's feasibility study in outlining war production goals but greatly increasing the targets as JM and Beaverbrook had suggested. EL 124; GLS 197-9; RM 122; JMM 174

12 Jan: Lamont asks JM if he will be in New York in next fortnight "...I want to ask [of] you some opinions and no one else but you can give me the points involved" LA

With America's entrance in the war neatly meshing with the announced Victory Program, Monnet's role changed. He was vindicated in his obsession during the past year on increasing production goals. But the Americans themselves were now the bearers of that obsession and Monnet's place was no longer clear nor primary.

He confirmed in these months another key friendship: Harry Hopkins. Monnet had advised Hopkins early in 1941 to concentrate on Churchill when Roosevelt's aide visited London. Hopkins seemed to resent this adulation surrounding Churchill but realized, after his trip, that Monnet was right: Churchill did hold Britain together in the crucial months between France's fall and Russia's entrance in the war.

Together with Morgenthau and Frankfurter, Hopkins was in the closest Roosevelt inner circle and all three were well-known to Monnet. But only Frankfurter and Hopkins were personal friends of Monnet, visiting in his comfortable, European-style house near downtown Washington. And only Hopkins---while his health allowed---was in a position in the American government to keep Monnet protected from adversaries and productive in his work.(MATA 46-56)

14 Jan: JM writes H Hopkins on latter's role supporting the President's decision on setting high production goals and naming Donald M Nelson as overall production manager. "No country at war has taken such fundamental decisions in such a decisive manner.... I know how much we all owe to you." HH-G

------:Roosevelt and Churchill [just as latter was returning to London] agree on Combined Raw Materials Board which JM had suggested in December as the "Batt Committee." But it takes six months more for the board to become fully effective. HW 269-70; JMM 175

15 Jan: H Hopkins replies to JM's note yesterday: "There are great and heroic days ahead. I think we have laid the ground work for final victory. Not the least important thing ...is that France shall be free. You too have played a great part in the past as you will in the future." HH-G

16 Jan: Roosevelt replaces Office of Production Management with War Production Board (WPB) which becomes principal focus of JM's work, IMW 54, 236-40

26 Jan: Combined Raw Materials Board, pushed by JM, is finally announced after Churchill gets War Cabinet and Commonwealth agreements. HW 269-70

10 Feb: Memo from aide Thurman Hill to H Morgenthau gives background of American Bosch corporation whose chairman is George Murnane, JM's business partner. "A primia facie case has been made by the Treasury that the company is still controlled or influenced ...by the German Bosch Co or the Reichsbank." HMD 495

 5 Mar: T Brand writes JM that Oliver Lyttleton will definitely be the one responsible for coordinating the combined U.S. and UK resources. JMH I

6 Mar: JM writes to T Brand enclosing detailed memo on a proposed Combined Production Requirements Board to break administrative barriers to better integration of British and American production. JMH-I

17 Mar: T Brand replies to recent JM letters on US organization for expanded war production, insisting that the British counterpart organization must contain military service representatives. JMH-I

22 Mar: JM writes R Nathan: I have changed your draft considerably. We can discuss the reasons by phone. FJM AME 20/l/282

24 Mar: JM writes D Drummond (in Surrey where he is working on supply matters for Russia) announcing Marianne's birth: Silvia is well, so is Anna. "Cognac is occupied and the German commander has chosen our house to live in which is a compliment to the house but a damn rotten thing for us---at least for my mother who has lived in the house all her life. " FJM AME 20/l/400

26 Mar: JM and Silvia dine at Stimsons with Knoxes and McCloys. HLSD

7 Apr: Planning Committee of War Production Board established with JM friend and confidant R Nathan as chair. Minutes, War Production Board (Washington, 1947)

22 Apr: H Morgenthau calls Grace Tully, Roosevelt's secretary, to alert the President that Mr.[Robert] Brandt (sic) who is in charge of food at the British Purchasing Mission has been proposed to take over the whole [British Supply Council] mission and that the President should oppose this. Morgenthau gives

background of Brand as "one of the principal partners of Lazard Freres....I think its terrible because we've kept the JP Morgans and the Lazard Freres out of this war purchasing ..." and putting Brand in this position would have them "on the inside of all of our military secrets." Two days later, Morgenthau makes same plea to Hopkins to oppose Brand's appointment to succeed Purvis. HMD 519, 520

1 May: Douglas MacArthur of American Embassy, Vichy writes Bullitt assistant Carmel Offie: I was able to send the JM documents to someone who will get them to Cognac. WCB

7 May: Morgenthau replies to Roosevelt on questions latter raised on American Bosch company and background of JM who shares Murnane's earnings as chair of company: Morgenthau has questioned JM, citing information that German Bosch retains control through Swedish intermediaries. JM doubted this but said he would ask Murnane. In second talk, JM reports Murnane view that no German strings are attached to Swedish ownership. "I was not satisfied that Monnet was telling all that he knew." After further review of JM role in 1939 in Bosch tactics in Amsterdam to obscure German interest in American Bosch shares, Morgenthau adds: "Monnet also told me that up until the latter part of 1938 he was a believer in rapprochement between France and Germany." HMD 525

This month marks another peak in Morgenthau's up-and-down obsession with Monnet and his international banking friends. But beyond the previous suggestions that Monnet and his business friends are enemies of the Roosevelt administration, here Morgenthau suggests that Monnet lacks political judgment or, even worse, was a "believer in rapprochement" which the treasury secretary clearly likens to a serious moral defect.

Perhaps in response to Morgenthau's efforts, Monnet drafts a curious letter to the State Department about his background and his Washington assignment. It is not clear this letter was ever sent.

14 May: JM drafts long letter to State Department giving his personal background from Nov 1939 when he headed AFCC until he was sent to Washington as British official. In part it says: "Mr. Monnet is a citizen of France bearing a French diplomatic passport. At the same time he is one of the most senior British officials in the US....he is responsible only to His Majesty (sic) government whose confidence he completely enjoys. In the difficult circumstances now prevailing it is thought that the unique situation in which Mr. Monnet stands should receive at least the recognition of the US and British governments." FJM AME 10/1/4

15 May: JM meets with W Layton, Stacy May, Nathan, T Brand and others during first Oliver Lyttleton visit to Washington. JMH-I

24 May: JM writes Hopkins asking that he arrange meeting of Jean

Bernard (cover name for Free French agent Etienne Hirsch) with Roosevelt. JM describes Bernard, who has apparently already seen Hopkins, as a leader of the resistance in France. RES

26 May: Under Secretary of State Sumner Welles discusses France with Raoul Aglion, representative of de Gaulle's London committee in the United States. Welles describes divisions he sees among the French in the United States and in England. He cites JM, Alexis Leger, Jacques Maritain, Antoine de Saint-Exupery and Andre Maurois among those who distance themselves from de Gaulle. Raoul Aglion, *De Gaulle and Roosevelt* (Paris, 1984) 72-4

3 Jun: Memo to Morgenthau by his senior staff (Foley and Pehle) on "Jean Monnet and George Murnane" giving background on Monnet, Murnane firm and its principals. Details on JM include: He earned $54,000 in 1940; His US assets in 1941 totaled $109,000 of which $99,000 was in MM. This partnership earned $78,000 net in 1940 and $110,000 in 1941. Some of the MM income goes through its Hong Kong company which earned $200,000 on Czech coal mines sold by a Jewish family, the Petscheks, to German interests in 1938. The Petscheks were thus able to get $6.5 m paid to them in the US. HMD 536

[JM's earnings of $54,000 would be the equivalent of over $600,000 in 2007]

This report to Morgenthau by his Treasury Department aides gives some insight into Monnet's personal life. His 1940 income of over fifty thousand dollars puts him in the top bracket of American incomes, much more than any one else in Washington government service including the President.

9 Jun: Combined Production and Resources Board and Combined Food Board created after visit by Oliver Lyttleton, UK Minister of Production. DH 379

15 Jun: JM joins Stacy May, Nathan, T. Brand, Walter Layton, and others for meeting during visit of UK supply minister Lyttleton on problems between U.S. and Britain. May, leading the meeting, says there are not sufficient materials to meet the 1942 production goals but by handling raw materials carefully and reducing new construction, the goals could be met. This will require reexamination of U.S. forecasts and priorities and closer integration of UK and U.S. production. JMH-1

17 Jun: Morgenthau writes memo on long luncheon meeting with British Ambassador Halifax and visiting minister Lyttleton. Morgenthau inquires who will replace Purvis [who died last August in plane crash] as head of British Supply Council and "What are you going to do about Monnet?" Morgenthau tells visitors that JM gets no salary from British because he has told people he did not want it said after the war that he had accepted money from British. Also, that "if I had anything to do with it I would not have him around." Morgenthau also says he warned Purvis about JM when latter arrived and "Purvis sort of shunned him for six months ...[but] could not find anything against him." HMD 540

The treasury secretary's continuing hostility toward Monnet, mixed with respect, is curious and explicable more by Morgenthau's background and political outlook than by anything Monnet does. They had met early in the Roosevelt Administration when Morgenthau headed the Farm Credit Administration and Monnet was starting work for T.V. Soong, the Chinese finance minister. Morgenthau, son of the US ambassador to Turkey during WWI, had a vivid and often exaggerated distrust of international bankers and their war profits. He viewed Monnet as part of this suspect group even though (or perhaps because) when they next met Monnet was seeking military aircraft for France.

Roosevelt endorsed the French rearmament and Morgenthau went along but always suspecting Monnet's motives. Unlike Monnet's ties to Frankfurter and Hopkins, with Morgenthau there was never any personal friendship or warmth.

19 Jun: Memo to Morgenthau from his staff (Foley and Pehle) on continuing investigation of Monnet, Murnane and Petschek case including interviews with Petschek family and Gert Weisman. [Petscheks were Czech Jews whose coal mines had been sold to the Germans just before the war with Monnet, Murnane as intermediary]. HMD 541

23 Jun: British ambassador Halifax calls on Morgenthau to follow up previous week's discussion of JM. Lyttleton has since interviewed JM which upsets Morgenthau because JM will know that Morgenthau is source of information the minister raised. HMD 542

--------: Morgenthau and Halifax talk by telephone after earlier meeting. Latter hopes that "there will be no gossip spread about Monnet," a comment which "irritated" Morgenthau. HMD 542

13 Jul: JM attends meeting of Combined Production Requirements Board and argues for earliest possible completion of 1943 requirements. JMH-I

15 Jul: JM gives stag dinner for Donald Nelson (head of War Production Board); his deputy, James Knowlson; General MacReady, British Military mission; T Brand and McCloy. "Business of evening" was discussion of materials and production of Britain and UN [US and other Allies] according to strategic plans i.e. "pooling resources." HLSD

16 Jul: Memo from E H Foley, Treasury general counsel to Morgenthau on "Jean Monnet and George Murnane.... I think, if you agree, an intensive fraud investigation should be made...by the intelligence unit." HMD 550

------: Edward Bridges, secretary of UK War Cabinet, writes Bullitt, who is visiting London, that JM has suggested the two get together. Bridges and Bullitt meet for lunch on 20 Jul at Claridge Hotel. WCB

19 Aug: British and Canadian troops stage ill-prepared and disastrous raid on Dieppe, France in which more than half of Canadians die or are captured. The lesson from the raid is that any full scale invasion on the continent would require greater planning and massive force. RM 136

28 Aug: JM invites R Nathan to informal dinner at home. FJM AME 20/4/120

31 Aug: JM writes Hopkins: Thanks for your nice note. My wife and I are also anxious to meet Mrs. Hopkins. Silvia and the children are in the Adirondacks where I will join them for a few days. We will return about Sept 15. HH

2 Sep: JM receives gas ration book for three months with justification: "Driver takes Mr. Monnet to and from office and to other American government offices; [Car] also used by Mrs. Monnet, two children, the nurse, cook, butler for all their affairs. The household has only this car and there are no busses or streetcars within reach." FJM AME 15/5/29

22 Sep: Louise Weiss, old friend of JM, writes him from Vichy with account of her recent visit to Cognac where she saw JM's mother and sister. FJM: Louise Weiss,(Lausanne, 1994) 375

23 Sep: JM writes Lt. George Murnane, son of his partner, who is stationed in nearby Virginia: Hope to see you soon. Come to Washington whenever convenient for an hour or stay overnight. FJM AME 20/l/277

29 Sep: JM writes Hopkins: My wife is now back in town and we are looking forward to meeting Mrs. Hopkins and you very soon. Could you dine with us one day early next week ---en famille? HH

Monnet's role of pushing US production became more selective and less vital in the war effort because many Americans were now doing the same work without the hesitation or doubt they may have shown him in the pre-war period.

His attention turned back to France. Monnet's free-wheeling role on the BSC left him time to plan his future. The possibility of a strong Allied military offensive against the Axis gradually focused on North Africa where French forces might play an important part.

This possibility drew Monnet into another role: Expert adviser on French attitudes and capabilities. By the end of the year, after French North Africa became a major military scene, Monnet felt confident enough to start writing memos on France aimed at Frankfurter and Hopkins, two of Roosevelt's principal, if unofficial, advisers on foreign affairs.

While hardly an expert on French political or military matters, Monnet had enough experience with de Gaulle in London in 1940 to be suspicious of the general. These sentiments were present even stronger in Roosevelt and his Secretary of State, Cordell Hull. Monnet's first attempts at French political analysis were strongly supportive of what he knew the President wanted to hear: Watch out for de Gaulle! Monnet was also seen by his British mission colleagues as a channel to Hopkins among others, a further indication of the Frenchman's skill in acquiring and using key friendships.

8 Nov: Allied forces land in Operation Torch at Casablanca, Morocco and Oran and Algiers, Algeria, led by Gen. Dwight D. Eisenhower. NYT 9 Nov;

JMM 178,180

16 Nov: H.T. Weeks of British Mission, Washington sends JM long note and attached draft of briefing memo for use by Hopkins concerning British army program. The memo helps prepare Hopkins for coming [second] visit of Oliver Lyttleton, Minister of Production which JM had requested because Combined Production and Resources Board was not functioning properly. JMH-I; JMM 176.

25 Nov: JM sends Bullitt, his old friend and former ambassador in Moscow and Paris, now an adviser in Navy Department, an invitation to dinner tomorrow at Monnet home. FJM AME 20/4/31

21 Nov: JM sends advance copy of his Army and Navy Journal article to Bullitt at 2447 Kalorama Rd NW, Washington. WCB

26 Nov: JM drafts memo for R Nathan to present to War Production Board (WPB) Chairman Nelson on respective roles of WPB and Joint Chiefs of Staff on scheduling procurement of weapons. Memo complains that real scheduling has not been done despite WPB request that the JCS submit 1943 requirements no later than 19 October which was not done. Memo concludes with announcement that the WPB vice chair, C E Wilson, will be responsible for scheduling production. JMH-I

7 Dec: JM article "France at War" published in Washington in special issue of "Army and Navy Journal" titled United States at War. He describes a "France cut in two" and where the people [like his mother and sister] are forced to live in their own homes together with occupying German soldiers. But soon France will see the liberation of North Africa by the American and British soldiers. That liberation of France overseas has brought the occupation of the whole of France into focus...France had to be lost, lost in her entirety, so that she could be saved.
Referring to three German invasions of France --- 1870,1914,1940 --- he writes: "the purpose was the same---domination, destruction of the principles of freedom on which Western civilization, European and American, has been built...."
"The eyes of the French are now turned toward North Africa awaiting the rise of a French army. They are awaiting the day when again the voice of France can speak of liberty, freedom and bring once more its contribution to the building of a safer Europe, of a better world." Army and Navy Journal, Dec 1942, 8.

10 Dec: JM sends Lamont copy of Army and Navy Journal with article he wrote on France at war. LA

There were two exceptions in wartime Washington to Monnet's preferred "insider" style of operation: This article written for a prominent American military journal and, 18 months later, a speech he gave in the Metropolitan Opera House in New York after his return from Algiers. In both instances, he was a spokesman for France but in 1942 it was a self-identified role while in 1944 he was a principal official representative of France in Washington. His problems with Morgenthau may have been on Monnet's mind when he accepted these (for him unusual) public appearances. Perhaps he hoped they might dampen down the treasury secretary's obsessive concern with Monnet and Murnane as devious international bankers.

17 Dec: JM thanks Lamont for his speech mentioning France, adding: I welcome the North African situation since it allows France to have an army around which all Frenchmen can unify. LA

23-24 Dec: JM writes long memo for Hopkins in several versions on North Africa including armaments problems but broader by including political assessments under title "North Africa; Summary of Proposed Course of Action." He outlines argument that French sovereignty must be safeguarded and no decisions taken during the war which compromise the French people's right to choose their own postwar government. France must participate in the war effort. JM sends copy to Frankfurter. Substance of memo is incorporated in President's 1 Jan letter to Churchill and in speech of 12 Feb to White House correspondents. FJM AME 18/4/12; RES-R; RES-R&H 680-l; MATA 52-3,68; AK 31; FLF-LC; JMM 181-83

27 Dec: JM writes Hopkins asking for urgent meeting on North Africa,updating 24 Dec memo and taking account of Admiral Darlan's assassination on Christmas eve in Algiers and his replacement by Gen. Giraud. JM decries the political vacuum in North Africa after Darlan's death. RES-R; MATA 52-3,68

29 Dec: Sec of State Hull complains to Stimson on JM's role as supporter of de Gaulle and facilitator of recent visit of Gen. Bethouart who is seeking recognition of de Gaulle as civil leader of occupied France and of French territories. "Monnet did this [Hull says] on claim that Murphy [former US ambassador to Vichy and now US political advisor to Eisenhower] had made such an agreement with de Gaulle on instructions from the President." Hull was much disturbed by this.

I [Stimson] told him we were treating M.M[onnet] purely as an agent here to purchase supplies...in all our talks. While we were in the conference, Welles [under secretary of state] came in with a message from the President denying that he had ever authorized Murphy to make such an arrangement." Cable sent to Murphy in North Africa seeking clarification. HLSD

This episode reflects a curious hostility within the State Department to Monnet. Yet Hull, despite his role as Secretary of State, was not a close adviser to Roosevelt so this hostility to Monnet only illustrated the fecklessness of Hull. But why Roosevelt, in a subsequent reply to Hull, seems to support the suspicions about Monnet is harder to explain. The President often manages (some say manipulates) his advisors so he may have merely wanted to move Hull along

*from his hostility to Monnet to another and more positive notion: If not Monnet,
then who should be sent to North Africa? Meanwhile, Monnet himself is either
unaware of these suspicions about him passing between the White House and
State Department or he ignores them. He writes memos to those like Hopkins
and Frankfurter who do trust him and who also are closer to the President that
Secretary Hull.*

1943

EARLY JANUARY: JM suggests to Hopkins that he go to Algiers where his
"most useful role would be at the heart of French affairs." JMM 183-4

*This suggestion follows the Christmas Day assassination of Admiral
Francois Darlan, claimant of "civil" authority in North Africa, and the
subsequent furor in American press about the anti-democratic French rule in
an area where the US armed forces were now based and supplying Free French
military units.*

4 Jan: Frankfurter describes dinner with Monnets, Ben Cohen, Milton
Katz and Nathan on civilian supplies in face of expanding war needs. FFD 143-4

10 Jan: JM in talk with Henri Alphand insists that Free French elements
must unite. HA 140

16 Jan: At Casablanca Conference, and apparently at Hopkins' suggestion,
FDR asks by cable for Hull's view on sending JM to N. Africa where [FDR says]
JM's lack of recent ties with the French political scene, the need for an outside
civilian figure and his own very favorable view of him seem to make him the
right person. Hull disagrees, replying JM is too close to de Gaulle and suggests
ex-French diplomats Roger Cambon or Alexis Leger. RES:R&H 679; FRUS
Casablanca Conference, 809

18 Jan: In response to objections by Secretary of State Hull to Monnet's
proposed trip to North Africa, and his suggestion of alternatives, FDR replies:
"Do you think [Alexis] Leger could be usefully used over here? I agree with what
you have said about Monnet. Also please let me know what you think of Roger
Cambon who is universally respected and through his father knows much about
North Africa." FRUS Casablanca Conference 816

*Secretary of State Hull may have been skeptical of Monnet's political
sympathies but this attitude seems based less on his superficial information on
Monnet and more on the State Department's fierce hostility toward de Gaulle and
its conviction it could influence the Petain government at Vichy to stay neutral
or even become anti-German. Hull had previously and vigorously resented de
Gaulle's grandiloquent gesture in December 1941 of occupying St. Pierre and
Miquelon islands off Canada. Now he saw Monnet, who though hardly an agent
of de Gaulle, was still linked to the general through their London days together
and through Pleven, proposed as an American intermediary in North Africa
where the intra-French political intrigue was reaching a high point. But Hopkins'*

strong support of Monnet would not yield to the State Department's opposition. Roosevelt resolved the problem by appearing to agree with Hull about Monnet's unsuitability but then letting Hopkins do what both President and advisor wanted: Send Monnet to North Africa to see how the intra-French squabbles could be ended and the French engaged in the war effort. As in many other cases, FDR had more confidence in his own judgment than in that of the Hull's State Department.

19 Jan: JM writes memo on his goal in proposed visit to Algiers: It is not to reconcile different personalities like Giraud and de Gaulle but rather to insure that the principles of democracy for which the Allies are fighting are maintained in any authority representing the French. AK 39

21 Jan: Frankfurter diary: Morning papers report Robert Sherwood, presidential aide, going to North Africa to help straighten out situation and to balance Murphy. I call him suggesting he meet with JM first. Sherwood and I dined then at Monnet's discussing whole North Africa situation and future of France. JM and I said Roosevelt and Churchill should express themselves "as trustees of a free France, that no party outside of France could claim to be [such trustees] and that we could not recognize the claim of anyone not called by the free will of France as a provisional government..." and that this policy should be announced right away. FFD 164-5

23 Jan: Gen. de Gaulle, newly arrived in Algiers at request of Churchill and Roosevelt, meets with Giraud and proposes merger of their organizations with the two men alternating as chairmen. Agreement fails, however, on committee's membership. After Churchill and Roosevelt depart, the two generals issue bland joint statement which JM reads in Washington newspaper. He is skeptical about the French generals' commitment to the democratic principles for which Allies are fighting. RM 153

25 Jan: Frankfurter diary: Dined at JM's with Col. Llewellyn, former minister of aircraft production, now resident minister of supply in US; Sir Robert Sinclair, chair of British Supply Board; Donald Nelson; C.E. Wilson, president of General Electric; Sir Arthur Salter; Francis Gibbs, naval architect and WC Bullitt. Subject: How to meet submarine menace. FFD 168-9

27 Jan: Monnets dine at Frankfurters with McCloy who is leaving soon for visit to North Africa. FFD 172

EARLY FEBRUARY: JM writes R Brand (both in Washington) asking financial advice before he leaves for Algiers. What is present value of his assets, including Blair, Lee-Higginson and National Department Stores [stock] positions? Are these subject to tax? Also asks about life insurance policies and their conversion. BP. [See 21,23 Feb for further discussion]

2 Feb: JM receives formal invitation from Gen. Giraud to visit Algiers. FJM AME 26/4/5 cited in ER 290.

JM had asked Hopkins to arrange for the mission to Algiers because, with the Victory Program well underway, his work could now center on French affairs. It had also become clear, during 1942, that the growing American military predominance in the war meant a diminished role for Monnet as a member of the British Supply Council.

Subsequently, JM had discussed with Jacques Lemaigre-Dubreuil, a Giraud aide visiting Washington, the possibility of a Monnet visit and from whom he had an encouraging response when Lemaigre-Dubreuil returned to Algiers. JMM 183; FJM AME 26/4/2,3 cited in ER 289-90

----- Stimson notes that Monnet came to say goodbye before leaving for North Africa "to straighten out Giraud on the purchase of material for the French army...." HLSD

3 Feb: Gen. M E Bethouart, chief, French military mission, Washington, writes Gen Marshall listing goods Giraud says are needed based on agreement at Casablanca between Giraud and FDR. Summary: France to get priority shipments to equip three armored and eight motorized infantry divisions and 500 pursuit, 300 bombers and 200 transport planes. GCM

5 Feb: Memo from Hopkins to FDR:" Monnet showed me a wire that he has from Giraud asking him to come to visit. I think it would be a very good idea. I am attaching a memorandum for you to send to Secretary Hull if you agree." HH FDRL

-----: Hopkins' draft memorandum for Roosevelt to send to Hull: Jean Monnet has a wire from Giraud asking him to visit at once; not a permanent assignment. I think it is a good idea. I wish you would have a talk with Monnet. I think perhaps it would be best that he go to look into questions of supplies for the French army. HH

-----: Frankfurter reports JM told of his talk with Hopkins to whom he told of cable from Giraud asking JM to come to North Africa. Hopkins said President had suggested this assignment when he talked in Casablanca with Giraud, naming 2-3 Frenchmen who could be useful but particularly suggested JM. Hopkins then told JM he should keep clear of French factions and go as part of task of rearming French troops. JM told Hopkins of his duty to keep Halifax informed; Hopkins said he would clear matters with Halifax. FFD 182-3

6 Feb: JM writes Hopkins in White House: I attach the draft on the subject [French political situation] you mentioned to me yesterday. Felix Frankfurter told me last night that Bob Sherwood and Mr. Rosenman had asked him to suggest something along the same lines---he wishes that you consider the attached draft as representing our common endeavor. I am looking forward to seeing you very soon to continue our talk. I hope you are taking care of yourself. FJM AME

7 Feb: Frankfurters dine with JM who is anxious to discuss implications of his North Africa trip and whether he should "throw in his lot completely"

with Giraud." Frankfurter suggests JM see trip as a request of UK and US governments. FFD 184-5

9 Feb: JM tells Frankfurter of his "most satisfactory" talk with Hull and that "Hull was entirely agreeable to have him go [to Algiers] on basis of temporary agent of both [UK,US] governments. "Next day Jean told of his talk with Hopkins and Halifax so that Giraud gets notice from two governments of terms of his mission." FFD 186

10 Feb: McCloy leaves Washington for Algiers visit. HLSD

--------: JM meets Roosevelt third time before leaving for Algiers. "Roosevelt Day by Day." FDRL; Roosevelt describes visit in cable to Eisenhower on 22 Feb. JM refers to the meeting in 8 Mar letter to Hopkins. HH

--------:JM describes to Frankfurter his recent talks with Hopkins and Halifax. FFD 182-3

12 Feb: Roosevelt addresses White House Correspondents dinner incorporating some of JM's ideas on French sovereignty which latter presented in 23-27 Dec 1942 and 6 Feb memos to Hopkins. Roosevelt says French sovereignty rests with the French people and it has been only temporarily suspended during the German occupation. When the enemy has been expelled, the French people will then be represented by a government of their choice. JM's memo had said "no French political authority can exist or be allowed to create itself outside France." RES R&H 680-l, 702; MATA 52-3, 68; S I Rosenman, Working with Roosevelt (NY, 1952) 378; JMM 183

14 Feb: Bullitt and JM discuss de Gaulle's "bad behavior" before and at Casablanca conference which JM describes to his old friend. WCB

This is the last recorded meeting of JM and Bullitt. The former US ambassador to Moscow and Paris has lost his close ties with Roosevelt for several reasons concerning Bullitt's personal style and FDR's loyalties. Although assigned briefly as assistant to Navy Secretary Frank Knox, Bullitt never found what he considered his right place in the war effort after the Paris excitement. He served as Roosevelt's special envoy to the Middle East and Africa and eventually volunteered to serve in the Free French army after being rejected for active service by the US military.

Monnet's unsentimental attitude toward friendships is well illustrated by Bullitt. The two men grew apart first because of different war time responsibilities. Bullitt was also alienated from Roosevelt whom Monnet regarded highly up the President's death in 1945. Bullitt also turned against Roosevelt's successor, Harry S Truman in the latter's 1948 reelection and eventually became a Republican.

But aside from their diverging wartime roles, the two men grew apart intellectually which seems surprising since Bullitt became, sometime during the war, a leading member of the American Committee for a Free and United Europe.

By 1948 he was vice president of the group under Senator William Fulbright. But this interest may have reflected as much Bullitt's increasing hostility toward the Soviets as sympathy for European integration.

For whatever reason, the man Bullitt described in 1934 as a close friend was out of Monnet's life before the war ended.

16 Feb: Frankfurters and Monnets dine together prior to JM departure for North Africa. FFD 186

17 Feb: Frankfurter talks with JM and Milton Katz on B Baruch as possible replacement for D Nelson in war production job. FLFD 186

20 Feb: JM and Silvia dine with Frankfurters, Feises and R Brand. FFD 188

21 Feb: JM talks by phone with R Brand on his financial situation before leaving for North Africa. JM had sent Brand a memo on subject earlier which asked advice on various investments and assets. His balance shows he still owes large sum to Lazard Freres (where Brand is a partner). JM still earns $1800 monthly from MM but has apparently refuses any pay from British government for Washington work. BP

22 Feb: FDR writes and cables Eisenhower on JM coming arrival in Algiers (JM carries the letter for personal delivery to Eisenhower): Three weeks ago, Giraud asked Monnet to come. I encouraged the visit [FDR says] because Monnet knows a great deal about the supply system and can tell Giraud about it. He can also help Murphy and Macmillan, as well as Giraud, understand how North Africa is viewed from here. I have discussed these matters fully with him. I know how busy you are but you can be sure that Monnet will cover the business with you is a brief manner as far as you personally are concerned. No announcement should be made by you of this visit. HH

----: Hopkins drafts letter to JM for Roosevelt which quotes Hopkins own draft letter same date on his North Africa assignment: "You will acquaint General Giraud with the situation here, review this matter with General Eisenhower and Gen. Giraud and generally be concerned ...with matters affecting military supplies for the rearmament of the French forces." Hopkins signs letter as chairman, Munitions Assignment Board. JMM 184; HH, FDRL

------: JM calls Frankfurter on departure tomorrow for North Africa: "He remarked laughingly `I am not a modest man but I would never have written such a letter [about] myself as the President has given me [for Eisenhower].'" FFD 195

------ JM pays farewell call on Stimson before departing for Algiers. HLSD

23 Feb: JM leaves Washington for Algiers on assignment from FDR and Hopkins to assess rearmament of French forces but hopefully to bring Generals Giraud and de Gaulle into cooperation. His circuitous route via Miami, British Guyana, Brazil, and west Africa is for security. JMM 183-5; AK 78

------:Morgenthau discusses report from staff that FDR is sending JM to Algiers to comply with Gen. Giraud's request. HM considers whether President really wants JM to go and consequences of his travel on tax investigation of JM. HM: "Could we make him put up a bond like we did with Marlene Dietrich?" Morgenthau doesn't "like this stuff [JM leaving the country] and indicates JM's 1941 tax liability was $1750 and that JM's secretary at Monnet, Murnane estimated his 1942 liability at $7500. HMD 179

------: R Brand memo on JM finances: His Suffolk shares worth about 5000 pounds; National Dept Stores shares worth about 8000 pounds. JM memo same day to R Brand: I owe Lazard Freres 94,800 pounds against which I have 86,000 pound collateral including life insurance [which is apparently payable to Lazard]. BP

26 Feb: Silvia goes with Mrs. Stimson and Mrs. McCloy to Chinese embassy reception for Madame Chiang Kai Shek. HLSD

27 Feb: JM arrives in Algiers. JMM 185

MARCH: "In Monnet's first talk with me, he frankly stated that he had come to Algiers not so much to serve Giraud as to seek...unity among all French factions....but months passed before we learned that Monnet's idea of unity challenged Roosevelt's conception." RDM 179.

Murphy's retrospective doubts about Monnet's motives contrast with Eisenhower's matter-of-fact assessment of the new arrival. Murphy was the State Department's political advisor to Eisenhower and reflected the skepticism of his boss---Secretary of State Hull---toward Monnet and especially toward de Gaulle. Eisenhower, with a military mission to perform, judged Monnet as someone who might help keep the political tension among the French at a minimum and therefore welcomed the arrival of the Frenchman who seemed well-backed by Washington.

3 Mar: Eisenhower writes Hopkins: "I think Jean Monnet, as both you and the President indicated, should be very helpful over here. He will certainly be given every opportunity. I am impressed by his record and his appearance. HH

8 Mar: JM writes Hopkins: I have been here one week but Eisenhower and Murphy have been cordial and helpful. I have devoted most time to Giraud whom I like and I respect his character and ability. He has little knowledge of the world and of global relations. I have tried to give him general principles and to dispel his suspicions of the U.S and Britain. I attach great importance to rearming the French army as does Giraud. We have agreed on eliminating all laws against Jews. Then I am preparing a general statement of principles Giraud will release next Sunday, dealing with French sovereignty with two conclusions: Vichy's laws are null and void and the North African administration is a trustee and not a political authority. HH

9 Mar: Lewis Strauss writes JM in Algiers that Louis Walker, son of

Elisha, now in US Navy is coming "where you are" and may be of help. JM replies 22 Apr that he does know how long he will be there and that his work does not involve US Navy and therefore Louis should continue with what he is doing. Strauss Papers, Monnet folder, HHPL

11 Mar: JM writes Hopkins letter marked "Secret": Giraud and I have had a number of intimate conversations on views expressed during last conferences in Washington on need for reaffirming through words and deeds French traditional principles of democracy and liberty. Also agreed on sovereignty retained by French people [which] can only be expressed after liberation. Meanwhile no French organization can act as French government but only as trustee for preserving and administering overseas territories. Britain and US will help raise and arm French forces for aiding liberation of France. He also agreed on immediate action canceling anti-Jewish decrees and to reinstall local elected councils. He will speak next Sunday and I am working on draft. "I am confident of success when the bitter test of decisions on men and final drafting comes although I may partially fail in the final enactment of this program." RES-R&H 721

Monnet's hint that he might not succeed in all he has undertaken in Algeria may have been remembered by Hopkins later when the Washington assessment of the Monnet mission is made but there is no recorded reflection on this by Hopkins himself now or later. What is important is that Monnet kept Hopkins---his principal link with the President---informed of his work and of his cautions. Murphy and others will, however, eventually criticize Monnet for his Algiers performance because they were misled by their own misunderstanding of what Monnet sought and achieved: French unity in the fight against Hitler, not a simple effort supporting Giraud. Further, it is likely that Monnet himself only slowly gained a clear view of what was possible with Giraud and with the importance of French unity with or without the general.

14 Mar: Giraud gives major address which JM, Macmillan, Murphy and others have drafted. Themes: Laws of the Third Republic reaffirmed; Vichy legislation is void; 1940 armistice is rejected; resistance to Germany continues. JMM 186-90. Giraud is interrupted 26 times by applause during the 21 minute speech which was given at a reunion of Alsace-Lorraine followers. NYT 15 Mar

------: H Macmillan: "The North Africa New Deal has begun. On Sunday we had Giraud's speech. The days immediately preceding it were days of the wildest rumors and the most fanciful intrigues. On the one side was M. Monnet....He gained great influence over Giraud and was able, from the point of view of a detached Frenchman, to give him a picture of his duty which was on the same lines as that we have been trying to paint...." HMI 43-5; AK 96-108; RES: R&H 721. Murphy cables Hull and Roosevelt twice about Giraud speech, concluding: "Monnet has done a grand job." FRUS II 71-4

-----:Giraud calls the occasion, which culminated six weeks of pressure by JM on the general and his chief of staff "the first democratic speech of my life." Gen. Giraud is clearly impressed with JM from their first meeting in Algiers: "Bright eyed, subtle spirited, prudent in speech, [Monnet] has his idea, he pursued it, he did not reveal it....From the start I sensed that this man of honor wanted a place in the French adventure and I was ready to give it to him." Giraud, Un Seul But, La Victoire (Paris) 118-121

-----: JM cables Hopkins on Giraud speech and sends him separate written account. FRUS II 73; RES:R&H 721

15 Mar: Eisenhower cables Gen. Marshall: "Since his arrival here, Monnet has accomplished much. He deals with local problems on the basis of principle and much good will eventually comes out of his work. Assuming that the US government approves of the pronouncements made by General Giraud on Sunday...each checked by Monnet, he believes that some expression of presidential approval would be most helpful to further progress." DDE 1036

-----: Hull makes public statement supporting Giraud speech according to suggestions of Murphy whom he cables confirming his action. FRUS II 74

-----: Generals Giraud and de Gaulle exchange messages that seem to indicate reconciliation. JMM 190-1

17 Mar: Kindersley [Lazard Freres chairman] writes R Brand from London on JM personal finances: We will renew all JM insurance policies for one year. He should sell National Dept Stores. BP

-----:Macmillan dines alone with JM. HM-I 46

-----:Halifax says Macmillan gives JM full credit for Giraud's speech and for repeal of the Vichy laws. FLF

19 Mar: In a positive Washington reaction to Giraud's speech, John McCloy, Assistant Secretary of War, cables JM of the "enthusiasm in the press and radio and a great change in public opinion." Quoted from JM papers, AK 109

22 Mar: JM cables Frankfurter through Murphy and State Department refuting Edouard de Rothchild's negative interpretation of Giraud decree on Jews in North Africa. JM agrees instead with Murphy's interpretation in earlier cable. JM asks Frankfurter to make this matter clear. FLF

23-24 Mar: JM in discussions on rumors of coup by monarchists against the Giraud administration. One rumor is that JM and Giraud's chief of staff, Col. Linares, were endangered by a kidnapping plot. AK 131-32

27 Mar-1 Apr: JM drafts memo for Giraud in reply to Gen. Catroux, de Gaulle aide, who just arrived in Algiers and who asked about Giraud's intentions. JM begins complicated balancing act between the two generals starting criticism of JM by some Americans. AK 133-4; JMM 192

1 Apr: Macmillan discusses with JM the principles underlying the

constitution of the third republic. HM I 54

-----: Planning Committee of War Production Board holds final meeting, ending power struggle between military and civilian leaders over production planning with military prevailing. IMW 510-511; D. Nelson, Arsenal of Democracy (NY, 1946) Ch.19

The final meeting of Nathan's WPB Planning Committee marked the end of a critical growth stage of military control of war production. The committee went out of existence in June, a sacrifice to the growing ascendency of the US armed forces over war production. The committee chair, Robert Nathan, JM's closest colleague in such matters, was out of a job. He soon gave up his military deferment and entered the army as a private. Thus the Monnet-Nathan team which had worked so closely on the Victory Program and through the first year of American involvement in the war came to an ignoble end. When the two meet again it will be near the end of the war when both start postwar planning.

2 Apr: JM forms small committee in Algiers in anticipation of arrival of major US convoy bearing arms for French North African units. Committee is to use information and timing of arms arrival to build support for Giraud's attempts toward a democratic cast of his regime and toward reconciliation with de Gaulle. RM 174

3 Apr: Pleven cables JM asking for a private meeting of the two old friends before de Gaulle, for whom Pleven now works, arrives in Algiers. JM replies that he hopes to come to London but on his way home after finishing his work in Algiers. He would, however, gladly come now to London if Pleven and de Gaulle think his efforts or advice are serving the cause of French unity. FJM AME 27/6/2,3, cited by ER 330

4 Apr: Macmillan dines alone with JM. HM-I 56

6 Apr: De Gaulle, in London, upset at Algiers talks, wants to negotiate directly with Giraud. Macmillan gently advises delay through Eisenhower to Churchill but de Gaulle communique accuses Allies of interfering with French union. HM-I 57-8

7 Apr: JM cables F Frankfurter in response to latter's telegram on the Cremieux Decree which had granted Algerian Jews full French citizenship but which had been annulled by the Vichy regime. JM assured Frankfurter he will work for the decree's restoration. FJM AME 37/5/32 cited by ER 397; JMM 190

-----:Giraud gives speech written by JM at opening of commission to revise legislation, including plea on reintegrating Jews into North African life. AK 126

8 Apr: Silvia Monnet dines at Stimsons. HLSD

13 Apr: First large shipment of American military material arrives in Algiers, speeded by JM's ties to Hopkins and McCloy. In next few months

supplies for four French infantry divisions arrive. "These efforts, which were vital to France's recovery and hence to her independence, were no less urgent and important than the establishment of power structures; and I was concerned with both." JMM 205-6

15 Apr: JM sends Walter Lippmann copy of his 1 Apr memo to Giraud, asking the American journalist's comments which come 20 Apr in general but positive form. AK 156

20 Apr: De Gaulle emissary, Gen. Catroux, brings back reply from London to Giraud's proposal of 1 Apr: Will Giraud give up military or civil authority? De Gaulle also proposes new form for a ruling general council in Algiers. JMM 191-5

26 Apr: Sherwood back from Africa "to say that it is a perfect Godsend to have JM there....Before he went to Africa, [Sherwood]... thought it was all hunky-dory....[He] evidently has come back a somewhat wiser and sadder man." FFD 229

27 Apr: Giraud to rewrite his memorandum to de Gaulle in a more friendly manner, aided by JM whose version "will be long and pedantic" [Macmillan suspects]. Purpose is to seek a quiet meeting in North Africa of the generals and then to co-chair a war cabinet. HM-I 72

28 Apr: New and final phase of negotiations begins between de Gaulle and Giraud forces which climaxes on 30 May with de Gaulle's arrival and, soon after, an agreement. AK Ch 8

-----: Dinner with Monnet; "the same talk as usual until ll pm and so to bed." HM-ll 74

30 Apr: Giraud and JM invite Alexis Leger, former secretary general of the French Foreign Ministry, now employed in the Library of Congress in Washington, to come to Algiers. Leger does not go but sends a long memorandum expressing concerns about the legitimacy of de Gaulle's authority and suggesting other ways for Giraud to seek a legitimate authority for his own position. FJM AME 29/4/l,2 cited by ER 331-333

In Algiers, Monnet gradually became immersed in intra-French politics for the first time since his League of Nations days. While he had been sent by Roosevelt and Hopkins to help Giraud, he gradually realized that this courageous French soldier was hopelessly lost in politics. Meanwhile a fierce political problem---the composition and direction of the French response to the country's defeat and occupation by the Germans---was dominating the unoccupied French territories and especially North Africa where French military assets were still assembled. Monnet led Giraud as far as he could in presenting himself as an enlightened general ready to take control of free French forces. But Giraud was no match for General Charles de Gaulle who, financed by the British government, gradually and effectively cast himself both as the spokesman and the military leader of all Frenchmen, wherever located. As de Gaulle's strength grew, so did his arrogance which appalled Monnet. De Gaulle's growing influence created problems for Monnet whose delicate task was balancing the two French generals so that France's war effort, backed by American arms, could aid the defeat of the Axis powers. In this task, Monnet had to jeopardize his most valuable asset: the support and trust of his American friends.

4 May: De Gaulle speech in London reveals details of his long-distance talks with Giraud, upsetting the negotiations and beginning a process of trying to displace Giraud. JM comments "We could not allow our two generals to go beyond the point of no return." He notes "Never was the unity of Frenchmen at war so gravely threatened as in those Spring days." JMM 196

5 May: De Gaulle's speech yesterday attacking Giraud is dismissed by Macmillan: "I told them [including JM] that in my country [when] one politician makes an offensive speech about another...this was almost recognized procedure preliminary to forming a coalition government. This chaff didn't go awfully well. It shocked Murphy (who didn't particularly want the union to come off anyway) but amused Monnet." HM I 80

But JM was himself uncharacteristically incensed at de Gaulle's 4 May speech, calling it `Hitlerian' in several letters, including the following one to Hopkins.

6 May: JM sends long letter to Hopkins mostly on Giraud-de Gaulle relations: Giraud has "constitutional" difficulty in making strong decisions. But progress with revision of Vichy laws and first shipment of armaments has given "great heart" to army and people here. We are working on unity problem. Gen. Catroux has, since arrival, helped process but some of de Gaulle emissaries have caused disturbances. While Giraud was awaiting replies to his letter and memo of 27 April, de Gaulle made London speech two days ago which disregards all negotiations. "It is...a straight bid for arbitrary power." The basic difference is de Gaulle wants a government now while Giraud wants a council with functions but not status of a government. De Gaulle wants arbitrary power, Giraud, democratic process. HH; ER 336-40

8 May: "3pm: Monnet. Talk, talk, talk." HM I 82

-----:Roosevelt drafts note for Churchill who is about to arrive in Washington: "In my judgment, there should be a reorganization of the French National Committee removing some of the people we know to be impossible such as Phillippe [Andre Philip?] and include in it some of the strong men like Monnet and others from Giraud's North African Administration...." FRUS, Conferences at Washington and Quebec, 1943 320-22

9 May: French army stages parade in Algiers to mark arrival of long-awaited US equipment, with JM on the reviewing stand. Later in day, Macmillan, his secretary, John Wyndham, and JM drive to Tipasa on the coast for nude

bathing and a quiet picnic lunch before spending the night at a small hotel in Cherchell. RDM 194; HM I 82

-----: JM writes Hopkins a summary of conclusions from a longer report sent earlier but which Hopkins may not yet have: Great progress has been made toward reestablishing democracy as guiding principle for free French today. Giraud fully accepts this as seen in his 14 Mar speech, his 1 Apr memo to de Gaulle and his 27 Apr letter to him (which Murphy has sent and which will be published Monday). We are also getting rid of the anti-democratic laws and decrees of the Vichy regime. All this happens whether or not de Gaulle and Giraud come together. Their disputes concern: measures to be taken before and after liberation of France. Before liberation, we must ensure collective responsibility with the two generals sharing authority but also sharing responsibilities with other committee members. It is essential to eliminate "the risks of dictatorial tendencies of some of our London friends." After liberation, Giraud wants a provisional government immediately, meaning that the committee or council we set up would end its role then. De Gaulle seems to want the committee to continue to act until general elections. If there is a break between the two viewpoints, we must reduce the consequences. The British who support de Gaulle must take a firm position. Murphy and Macmillan are both cooperative. HH

13 May: All Axis troops in Tunisia surrender; this second major British victory in North Africa (after El Alamein) ended Axis presence in Africa, marked highpoint of British military role in war, and convinced de Gaulle to accept Macmillan-Monnet terms. Alistair Horne, Macmillan, Vol I, 183

14 May: JM begins extended discussions with Giraud on reply to de Gaulle speech and 10 May letter. AK 179

------:Hopkins sends both Halifax and Hull two recent JM letters with the cover note to Hull stating: "They are very interesting and ...indicate that Monnet has done a first rate job." Halifax sends acknowledgement same day with note to Hopkins: I expect you will already have shown them to Winston [Churchill who is on his third wartime visit to Washington.] HH; WSC, vol IV 706-14

15 May: De Gaulle learns that resistance groups in France form a National Council with him as sole leader, strengthening his position. DeG II 121-2.

17 May: Giraud draft reply to de Gaulle is adjusted by JM and Macmillan, accepted by Giraud. Tone is conciliatory and text a clear statement of how an executive committee can be jointly formed and managed. HM I 84; Letter, providing for balance between Giraud and de Gaulle forces, is carried to London by Catroux and Macmillan on military plane provided by Eisenhower. De Gaulle generally accepts letter's provision but actually plans to undermine Giraud by traveling to Algiers and to "attack from within." JMM 196-7

------:George Murnane Jr, stationed in North Africa, writes JM that Silvia has given him several things for delivery to JM. FJM AME 20/1/279

------: Gen. Bethouart, head of the Free French mission in Washington, cables JM on meeting he just had with Sumner Welles, undersecretary of state, on the desire of influential American Jews to see the Cremiuex Decree restored. FJM AME 37/4/11 cited by ER 398

18 May: "Lunch with Catroux, Monnet, Princess Merod [and others]; a very ill-sorted party. At 5:30 I went off with John [his aide] and Monnet to Tipasa to our little quiet hotel." HM I 86

19 May: JM cables Hopkins via State Department on latest political situation. HH

20 May: "Left Algiers with Roger Makins, Murphy, Sam Reber (aide to Murphy), Monnet and some others [for] Tunis for ceremony with Eisenhower, Giraud, Alexander, Patton, Tedder, Doolittle etc" HM I 87

28 May: JM sends radio message to Hopkins via Gen. Marshall on letter exchange of Giraud and de Gaulle. JM optimistic and will accept role on committee which Giraud has offered. HH

------ Hull acknowledges Hopkins 14 May cover letter and JM correspondence with non-committal note. HH

------ JM drafts note suggesting governing committee be established as soon as possible but proposes deferring nominations of members, other than Catroux, de Gaulle and Giraud. AK 180; FJM AME 30/1/4

30 May: Frankfurter, after noting North African political developments including Giraud and de Gaulle coming together on council where JM also sits, adds:" It will require all of Jean Monnet's infinite patience and complete disinterestedness and extraordinary resourcefulness to evolve ...good will necessary to revive the forces in France ...[and for] her to take her place again as a great nation." FFD 248

-----:[Sunday] De Gaulle arrives in Algiers and is met by Giraud; by mid-week, after final skirmishes, French Committee on National Liberation (FCNL) is agreed by both sides. HM I 94-110 ------: De Gaulle has long meeting with JM who [later to Macmillan] describes the general alternating between "comparative calm and extreme excitability." De Gaulle says Anglo-Saxon domination is a threat to Europe which, if continued after the war, might force France toward Germany and Russia. "Monnet finds it difficult to make up his mind as to whether the general is a dangerous demagogue or mad or both." HM I 97

31 May: Meeting of Generals de Gaulle, Georges and Giraud and JM, R Massigli and A Phillip who were supposed to be first nominees to French Committee on National Liberation. (FNCL) Bitter arguments revolve around management of North Africa affairs with JM trying to mediate between de Gaulle and Giraud positions. Later, Macmillan criticizes JM failure to follow proper

procedure at meeting and insist on a resolution and vote. HM I 97; "... there were seven of us around the table; Some of those present undoubtedly saw this as the first Cabinet meeting of the new legitimate Government of France....But for me...we were merely entering a new phase in the slow and difficult unification of the French." JMM 197 [where JM apparently mistakenly indicates the meeting took place on 1 June.]

1 Jun: R Brand in Washington, after reviewing past work together, writes JM: "...I cannot say how I regret that our collaboration on the Supply Council has ceased....The old combination of Purvis, you, Arthur Salter and me has ceased to exist." Brand then recounts Washington situation on food board and other supply questions; he speculates on postwar political cooperation and asks JM's views. BP

-----: NYT reports JM position in Algiers, together with that of Gen. Georges, now ambiguous.

-----: Macmillan and Murphy meet with Giraud, then de Gaulle. Latter insists North African administration be run very much like a government with appropriate ministries. "Monnet was a good man [de Gaulle said] but more of an internationalist than a Frenchman and would be most useful on that [French] side." De Gaulle is critical of both American and British governments for not recognizing his authority: "I represent future France and it will be better for us all if you will support me." HM I 99-100; Further tension flared between Giraud and de Gaulle over role of "men of Vichy" still in Algiers resulting in latter's leaving meeting in exasperation. Two days of "intense agitation" follows with rumors of a coup. JMM 199

2 Jun: Bullitt reports meeting with Secretary of State Hull on North Africa policy of US government. Hull complains that he is not being informed of cables from Murphy and JM from Algiers. Bullitt, who is adviser to Navy Secretary, tells Hull that Murphy is being undercut by some people in his government, especially by the OWI [Office of War Information.] WCB

3 Jun: The French Committee of National Liberation (FCNL) is established. JM is one of Giraud's two nominees; various other personnel decisions are made by the new committee which shares power between de Gaulle and Giraud. AK 188; FRUS II 134-5; HM I 107-9; JMM 200

4 Jun: Frankfurter note to JM: " We are following events in North Africa with the same anxiety [as] from the sickroom of a loved one....my confidence is most deeply founded on the fact that you are there ...resolutely determined to subordinate everything to give a great people and a great civilization the opportunities for its rebirth." FLF

-----: De Gaulle, Giraud, Churchill, Eden speak at Algiers luncheon given by Admiral Cunningham marking launch of the FCNL. Churchill toasts "La Belle France, la France victorieuse." JM attends and is included in well publicized photo of participants who believe past difficulties are over. HM I 109; RDM 207; JMM 201

-------: Murphy reports on FCNL meeting and talk with JM who reports Giraud encouraged by Washington's message of support for him; JM also says that Giraud can command majority on FCNL if he proceeds with reorganization and modernization of French Army. JM upset that Giraud has not moved far in this direction. FRUS II 135-6

5 Jun: FCNL meets to add new members and to distribute portfolios to its members; JM given charge of armaments and supplies. Problem for Giraud was committee's decision to double its size to 14, with four of new seven chosen by de Gaulle. RDM 208; JMM 202

-----: De Gaulle and Giraud address France by radio. "De Gaulle's speech ...was pompous; Giraud's, although five minutes too long, was excellent: simple, moving and very much to the point. Must have been written by Jean Monnet." Edouard Daladier, Prison Journal (Paris, 1995) 207.

7 Jun: Murphy is called to Giraud's headquarters by alarmed aide who shows him several decrees, negotiated over several weeks with JM, which Giraud has just signed. The general, when confronted by Murphy with implications of these decrees, is astonished but resigned to "internal" French affairs which do not seem to interest him if he can keep the military command. But in several weeks he is to be relieved of that by de Gaulle. RDM 180-1; JMM 203

8 Jun: JM named Commissioner of Armaments, Supply and Reconstruction by the sharply divided FCNL. He is the only member who is accepted by both the de Gaulle and the Giraud factions. NYT; JMM 203

9 Jun: De Gaulle resigns as co-chairman and member of FCNL in letter to its members because of committee's ineffectiveness and pressure applied to it by Allies. Committee appoints JM and Andre Philip to find solution. AK 188; FRUS II 146-7; JMM 204 10 Jun: JM joins Macmillan and Giraud in discussions of de Gaulle's resignation which Giraud regards as personal victory. JM and Giraud argue about merit of latter accepting the resignation. JM insists question of de Gaulle should not distract from focus on problems of France. Later, at night, JM meets with Massigli and Philip on military organization paper for tomorrow's FCNL meeting. HM I 117-18

11 Jun: Murphy sends dispatch to State Dept on FCNL meeting today held without de Gaulle and which discussed his letter of resignation without acting on it. JM plan for compromise discussed includes role of Giraud as commander in chief of all forces while commissioner(s) for national defense will oversee reorganization of army. Giraud and Gen Georges cool but JM hopes to persuade them. Committee would then ask de Gaulle to do same. Eisenhower, Macmillan and I believe these talks essentially internal French affair unless we later judge them detrimental to Allied interests e.g. if de Gaulle gains entire control or our

military position jeopardized. I suggest we might insert our conditions (whatever they may be) into any formula. However if de Gaulle resignation prevails, Giraud may ultimately be weakened here and abroad on judgment he blocked reorganization. FCNL not yet strong enough to be sole authority with whom Allies can deal. But once new structure is firm, anyone resigning from it would clearly appear as spoiler. HH

JM wants de Gaulle resignation delayed until Giraud gets control of his military organization. Under JM plan Giraud will be commander in chief of all French Forces and de Gaulle, as Commissioner of National Defense, will plan military reorganization. Giraud resisting this plan. FRUS II 147-150; JMM 203

15 Jun: De Gaulle rescinds resignation; FCNL expansion from seven to 14 members seen by press as de Gaulle victory and defeat for Giraud. JM is widely recognized as facilitator of decent compromise. AK 189-90

16 Jun: Murphy cables Hull that Gen Giraud "this morning [said] that in his opinion Monnet has betrayed him." Murphy comments that despite daily talks with JM he never indicated that he had persuaded Giraud to increase FNCL to 14 members. "It is obvious to us that things have gone to Monnet's head and that he feels [like de Gaulle] that French rights and sovereignty must be more aggressively asserted...." FRUS II 152

17 Jun: Hull complains that JM "has proved to be a traitor" because Gen. Giraud has been isolated and de Gaulle will be in power which we have tried to prevent. Hull says President sent off "red hot telegram" to Churchill and Eisenhower on possibility de Gaulle will control French troops. Stimson agrees this could be a catastrophe if it comes to a fight between French and Allied troops. HLSD

-------:FDR cables Churchill: "I am fed up with de Gaulle...there is no possibility of working [with him]." "...I agree with you that the time has arrived when we must break with him." Please let me have your thoughts. FRUS II 155-6

Murphy and Hull's anger with Monnet was understandable if short-sighted; Roosevelt's impatience is still directed to de Gaulle as his cable shows. Gradually, Monnet seems to have concluded that de Gaulle, despite his autocratic style, finally had to prevail over the politically inept Giraud who never seemed fully to understand the maneuvers of de Gaulle. In his memoirs, Monnet concludes that "the legal [and political] niceties escaped" Giraud. De Gaulle "resolved to have done with his troublesome rival," which he accomplished several months later.

18 Jun: Churchill replies in general agreement with FDR on de Gaulle but prefers not to break up FCNL. Supports FDR directive to Eisenhower that Allied Supreme Commander must direct French army. FRUS II 159

------:Stimson asks Frankfurter if he thinks highly of JM. I reply we share high opinion of Monnet but Stimson said "there is a good deal of talk around [about] Monnet. He [Stimson] went on to say that poor old Cordell Hull, who is all jittery about the French situation and almost irrational about Monnet, said he had sold out to de Gaulle. I said that was all rubbish of the worst sort..." and that Monnet had to work with de Gaulle. Stimson agreed, adding it is very difficult to talk with Hull because he is so touchy and "irrational on this subject." FLFD 260

------: "Visitors include Monnet, to discuss and argue and deplore and hope---really for me to hold his hand...." HM I 127

------: R Brand writes Kindersley enclosing JM's 23 Feb memo on his finances; Brand suggests that Lazard Freres write down JM debts to 50,000 pounds, maintain his life insurance and then accept insurance and 13,000 in share value if JM dies, leaving cognac firm to his family. In handwritten postscript, Brand adds: "...for reasons you can understand, M. never asked for remuneration from HMG [His Majesty's Government]" BP

-----:Murphy cables State Department that Rene Massigli disputes Murphy's 16 June cable on JM role: "Like Monnet, he [Massigli] says that he was unaware that we were ignorant of the changes in the formation of the Committee made on June 7 and about which we learned on June 15. He admits that he should have informed us." He and Monnet should be considered, with five others, as independents opposing domination by either Giraud or de Gaulle. FRUS II 157-8.

19 Jun: Gen Eisenhower receives de Gaulle and Giraud at his villa and demands that latter remain commander-in-chief of French forces and the only one Allied command would deal with. JMM 205

Monnet was caught in a nearly impossible situation. He was entrusted by Hopkins and Roosevelt to make political sense of the French rivalries in North Africa, knowing that his American sponsors greatly distrusted de Gaulle. Monnet had arrived with the intention of helping de Gaulle's rival, Gen. Giraud, in this contest. Yet he soon realized that this was not a balanced competition. As Maurice Couve de Murville, a future French Prime Minister but now a key Giraud aide, described it: We were all conscious that Giraud did not have the political breadth...He was a good soldier. Monnet knew this like the others. It was a question of an unequal rivalry between the two generals." FJM OH, Couve de Murville.

21 Jun: JM refines compromise between de Gaulle and Giraud which gives military control to a Permanent Military Committee formed by the two generals and their chiefs of staff; Giraud commands troops in the north and west of Africa, de Gaulle, other forces. Together they chair the new committee. AK 199

22 Jun: Eisenhower cables FDR once and Gen. George Marshall twice on political developments in Algiers; To FDR, he reassures that control of French army in North Africa remains under Supreme Allied Commander's control; In

first cable to Marshall, Eisenhower reports de Gaulle's influence is declining and that FCNL should not be dissolved because then Giraud would be reinserted at top of political order with all hope of unification destroyed. This would jeopardize local security which Allied forces cannot divert strength to control. In second cable to Marshall, Eisenhower says FLCN has" effectively established" Giraud as head of French African army, thus preventing de Gaulle from such control. DDE 1204-5, Nos. 1068-1070.

----: JM gives press conference to announce agreement in response to Eisenhower written request to divide command roles of Giraud and de Gaulle between North Africa, and all other areas, respectively. Plan, to create a Permanent Military Committee, temporarily forestalls immediate split of generals. RM 214; JMM 205

23 Jun: Murphy cables Hull that compromise leaves Giraud commander of French forces in West and North Africa and de Gaulle in charge elsewhere. This is "satisfactory as temporary solution", Macmillan and I believe. But we "have no illusions over the continuing determination" of de Gaulle to dominate. He has been able to frighten FCNL members, including Monnet, to either accept his view or produce unstable compromises. The de Gaulle forces have taken advantage of Giraud's weaknesses. FRUS II 164-5.

24 Jun: Raymond Clapper dispatch from London: "...the chief hope [of finding a leader for France after Germany's defeat] lies not in prima donnas [like de Gaulle and Giraud] but in such practical and skilful negotiators as Jean Monnet who has the confidence of the British as well as of the Americans. When he was in Washington...Mr. Monnet won the confidence of Americans and had the respect and confidence of the White House to a degree that makes him for more useful than figures who are in the spotlight." NY World Telegram 17

25 Jun: Lamont sends Silvia Monnet copy of article of 24 June on JM in Algiers by Raymond Clapper in NY World Telegram. LA.

3 Jul: JM writes Hopkins via Silvia. [He may have intended this letter ultimately for Roosevelt]. He speaks frankly about the limitations of Gen. Giraud who is presently visiting Washington. JM also warns against some of the people in Giraud's entourage including Poniatowski, Averell Harriman's brother-in-law, and Beauffre, both of whom he describes as indiscreet.[R Sherwood later tells JM that Sherwood's book Roosevelt and Hopkins will not use this letter which JM apparently believed, even in 1948, would embarrass him]. A 7 Jul radio message from JM to Hopkins says that letter being sent via Silvia and asking for confirmation of its receipt. RES-R

6 Jul: Murphy writes Roosevelt: "Jean Monnet arrived with a definite objective---to see French unity. He succeeded. Some of his critics describe the result as a confirmation of disunity. Monnet respects the United States and Britain ...but he is definitely out to gain every advantage for the French....he is

loyal neither to Giraud nor de Gaulle but to France and to Monnet... His long term objective is to represent his country at the peace negotiations." RES-R

"Murphy drew the correct conclusion that a new epoch had begun, but also the unjustified inference that I had somehow tipped the scales. 'Monnet thus politely declared French independence,' he [Murphy] wrote. Myself, I never believed that French independence could be 'declared.' At that time, as always, I was convinced that it could only be brought about by the united efforts of the French. JMM 203-4 (citing RDM 227)

21 Jul: Note from Silvia Monnet to Hopkins :"I am taking advantage of your friendly offer and sending you a cable for Jean. It is a great relief indeed to feel that I am not anymore in the impossibility[sic] to communicate with him from time to time." HH; HH G

22 Jul: JM writes Hopkins that recognition of the FCNL by the Allies is imperative to limit the influence and power of de Gaulle. The committee should be seen by the U.S. as an interim device until the French people are liberated and can form their own government. FDRL, Hopkins Papers in Sherwood collection, cited by ER 373

Mid-summer 1943 marks the most hazardous part of the year for Monnet in consideration of his American relationships. Giraud and Hull both accuse Monnet of betrayal, the first with subdued resignation, the second in self-vindication. Others like Murphy, Eisenhower's political adviser, and probably President Roosevelt himself are angry and confused by the events which now clearly place de Gaulle in ascendance and Giraud in decline.

Monnet's difficult role in this transition is not respected by all observers either in Algiers or in Washington. At one extreme, people like Macmillan, who had worked with Monnet to have free France emerge as a fighting force now and a restored democracy after the war, saw the Frenchman as a partner in the awkward success which had simply recognized de Gaulle's role in leading free French forces. At the other, Hull, and occasionally Roosevelt himself, resented the events which left de Gaulle in charge and sought to blame someone for them. Monnet was an easy target. To his credit, Roosevelt never seemed to blame Monnet but some subordinates like Hull and Murphy certainly did. Others were confused or annoyed. This irritation at Monnet is clear but transitory.

By the time Monnet returned to Washington in October he was apparently as close to his American friends as ever before. His enemies, like Hull and Morgenthau, were likewise unaltered in their hostility toward him.

Despite the generally positive depictions of the Monnet "method" in dealing successfully with people, it is clear this method sometimes failed.

24 Jul: US ass't navy secretary James Forrestal writes JM in Algiers that five US senators, including Richard Russell, chairman of the armed services committee, are coming to Algiers bearing this letter of introduction; letter ends "Your friends here are watching your work with interest and confidence."

Forrestal papers, PU

28 Jul: JM writes memo on France's postwar need, concluding that pre-war laissez-faire economic policies no longer apply and that his country needs both help from US and a determined effort on its own. RM 221

29 Jul: "Monnet came in on a fishing expedition: What would happen if Giraud resigned? What would happen if the Committee were `to dissolve'? He caught nothing." HM-I 168

END OF JULY: JM accused by American diplomat of secretly backing the British in favoring de Gaulle over Giraud, thereby thwarting the goal of American policy in North Africa of preventing Gaullist dominance of Free French efforts. KP 162-5

5 Aug: JM outlines some ideas on Europe's future in incomplete note, stressing France's role at the heart of Europe. Europe must see itself as larger than its nation-states. Protectionism, the quest for national sovereignty and small inefficient national markets must end whether in a federation or some other kind of European "entity." JMM 222; DG 272

17 Aug: JM dines with Macmillan and US officials on supply matters. HM-I 182

------: Note from Silvia Monnet to Hopkins from PO Box 416, Narragansett, RI: I would be so grateful if you could send this cable to Jean. Did you have any news of him? HH

20 Aug: Single page of longer memo by JM on postwar Europe assumesa single European economic unity ("unite economique") after the war. When the occupation armies "depart no measures should be taken which restore the previous economic nationalism or which create anew the conflicts of interest between each country." Unfortunately, JM notes, these matters cannot be submitted to an international authority which does not yet exist.[Subsequent pages missing] FJM AME 32/2/11

Monnet's concern about a revival of economic nationalism in the postwar era reflects his experience in 1918-19 when the United States rejected the continuation of wartime economic coordination. He feared the same mindset when this war ended without, however, specifying whether his fears were again focused on the United States or more broadly on the Allies whom he assumed would be victorious.

26 Aug: FCNL recognized by US, UK and USSR but with varying degrees of formality. RM 215; JMM 211

15 Sep: JM shows FCNL balance sheet on armaments from US which shows Giraud's Casablanca agreements were being closely followed. JMM 209

20 Sep: JM asks FCNL to relieve him of responsibilities for armaments so

he can concentrate on civilian aid to France. JMM 209

25 Sep: Modus vivendi on lend lease and reciprocal aid negotiated at Algiers, by JM between FCNL and US government provides that military supplies for the French Committee will come under lend lease and civilian supplies will be paid for in dollars by the committee. FRUS III 748

In press release in Algiers, JM says "completion of this agreement is an additional symbol of the solidarity of the French and American peoples in this world conflict....I wish to pay homage to the wisdom of President Roosevelt, his administration and the American Congress.... When history assesses the contribution to victory the Lend Lease program will be considered one of the most important factors. I was myself in the United States in the critical days of the early spring 1941...and I often remember what new encouragement we all drew from the knowledge...that American industry would be whole heartedly devoted to the ideals for which we are now all fighting." FJM AML

2 Oct: De Gaulle persuades FCNL to vote for a single president to whom commander-in-chief of Free French armed forces would be subordinate. Eventually Giraud is stripped of all political power. DEG-L 494; JMM 207 [JM cites 1 Oct]

8 Oct: Mrs. Alfred A Knopf, on behalf of her family's publishing firm, writes JM at suggestion of journalist Charles Collingwood. She proposes JM write a book on "postwar France, the problems of France or whatever other suggestions you might yourself have." FJM AME 63/2/57

This approach by a prominent American publisher was the first recorded occasion when Monnet was asked to write a book about his work. Collingwood's suggestion indicates Monnet growing prominence at least among knowledgeable journalists. Although the Knopf effort ultimately proved fruitless, it is likely that here Monnet began to consider writing an account of European events and his role in them.

14 Oct: Churchill writes Duff Cooper, under consideration to replace Macmillan in Algiers, that de Gaulle has been an obstacle to US-UK in war effort and has tried to split them: "De Gaulle, I fear, has contracted a deep antipathy to both these countries. He is a man Fascist-minded, opportunist, unscrupulous, ambitious to the last degree, and his coming into power in the new France would lead to great schisms there and also to the considerable estrangement between France and the Western Democracies." Duff Cooper, by John Charmley, (London, 1986) 168-9

17 Oct: DeGaulle hosts animated lunch for JM, Rene Mayer, Herve Alphand and Andre Diethelm in Algiers. JM reviews relief programs France will need after liberation and muses on postwar Europe: France will find its security in an economic union which includes Germany, perhaps divided into several parts, but all units will be treated as equals. If not, Germany will reassert

itself into a vast power at the center of Europe. Instead there must be a great European industrial country composed of the Ruhr, the Saar, the Rhineland and Luxembourg for the benefit of all Europe. De Gaulle disagrees; France and Germany cannot be part of one union. "You will never be able to put France and Germany together in any one unit after this war." RI-GE 286; FD 127-8; HA 168

18 Oct: R Brand, in Washington, writes Ronald Campbell, UK embassy, Washington: JM's wife handed me a sealed envelope today of his papers to be kept in the embassy which I enclose. BP

20 Oct: Radio message by JM to Hopkins says that he will arrive in Washington next week. HH

21 Oct: Cremiueux Decree restored, granting French citizenship to Algerian Jews, which had been cancelled by Vichy and whose restoration had been sought by Washington as part of JM mission. Christian Science Monitor, 23 Oct

29 Oct: Lamont writes JM at Foxhall Road: They tell me you're back; you are one of the "makers and shakers of the world." LA

END OF OCTOBER: JM returns from Algiers to take up new duties in Washington, stopping en route to attend Atlantic City conference on United Nations relief and rehabilitation program (UNRRA). JMM 209

------: Macmillan assesses JM Algiers role: " Monnet's chief efforts were directed to two main purposes. First, that whatever `administration' or `Government' came into being, it should not be based upon personal rule, but on Cabinet responsibility. Secondly, he strongly maintained that after the liberation of metropolitan France some constitutional method of procedure should be used. There should be no imposition of a dictatorship....France owes much to Jean Monnet. His work at Algiers was absolutely vital to any solution. He was the lubricant, or even catalyst, between the two bitterly opposed factions....He never swerved from his concept of the close cooperation that should exist, during and after the war, between the New World and the Old." HM II 297-8

------ Murphy gives another view: " Having accomplished what Roosevelt did not want to see accomplished [de Gaulle displacing Giraud], Monnet returned to Washington ... with apparently undiminished influence in the Roosevelt administration." RDM 182

Others may have been assessing Monnet's Algiers' role but he was concentrating on other things. He headed France's delegation to the UNRRA conference but this was just a stop on his way to new work in Washington. The capital had not changed greatly: the city was still thriving with military and civilian leaders and their agencies still engrossed in the war.

Monnet was now to play a much different role from the one he left in February. Before, he was a minor, if vital, figure in the British supply effort. Now, he was a major official in the renewed but quite limited French war effort which was directed to the coming invasion and liberation of his home country. Before, he reported ultimately to the British ambassador in Washington; now he reported to General de Gaulle in London. Before he was never sure of exactly what his role was; now his task was clear: to maximize the role of France in the coming war effort and to prepare her way in postwar Europe.

2 Nov: JM writes Hopkins estimating relief supplies needed in France after 1944 invasion. Asks for appointment upon arrival in Washington. HH

-----R Marjolin, aide to JM, replies to Alfred A Knopf on letter of 8 Oct from his wife about a book by JM on postwar France. JM cannot consider proposal now but will if possibility arises. FJM AME 63/2/57

-----: JM to "Mr. Lamont": I will be back in Washington after a few weeks at the conference on relief and rehabilitation. I hope we can meet. LA.

3 Nov: "Jean Monnet of the French Committee on Liberation discussed with me at length the problem of reconstructing France after the Germans were expelled. What he wanted principally was money and he talked vaguely about a large loan to France to be repaid in fifty years with nominal interest. He was a brilliant advocate and spent an hour with me pleading his case." WDL 190 [Leahy, formerly US ambassador to Vichy France, is now White House chief of staff.]

5 Nov: Lamont to "Jean" at French Supply Council, 1523 New Hampshire Ave NW Wash DC: Thanks for your note; I happen to be on a small advisory committee at Atlantic City [UN conference on relief and rehabilitation-UNRRA] at Gov. Lehman's request. LA

6 Nov: Frankfurter gives dinner honoring JM on his return from N. Africa. Guests include Stimson, Rosenman [FDR aide and speechwriter], Stettinius [deputy sec of state], Acheson [asst sec of state] and McCloy. JM "gave a very clear and incisive statement that [France needed] an opportunity to develop her own methods of food distribution as soon as the Germans were out." HLSD

10 Nov: JM attends first session a UNRRA Council member representing FCNL at Atlantic City conference which lasts until 1 Dec. UNRRA vol I 24-5

11 Nov: R Brand writes Halifax: "Mrs Monnet has told me that Jean Monnet [returning from Algiers] has asked that his kindest regards be given to you and his appreciation for all that you do for him here." BP

MID-NOVEMBER: JM "offers his services to UNRRA providing he could be made Director-General. I told him that I feared this was not practicable as the Americans would undoubtedly have to make the major contribution to the cost of the organization and they would expect that an American would be appointed to head it." Money Talks: The Autobiography of Frederick Leith-Ross,(London,1968) 301-2

--------:JM is seeking appointment as head of European Commission of UNRRA.

BM 191 (quoting diary of Ludwik Rajchman)

The Leith-Ross and Rajchman comments seem reliable accounts based on direct contact with Monnet. They probably reflect his concern that working as de Gaulle's representative in Washington may not have the stability, scope and freedom he seeks. Also, he is already looking ahead to the end of the war and to what his place might be in that new world.

12 Nov: JM reported saying Gov. Lehman's election as head of UNRRA is "first act of the United Nations in organizing peace." NYT

14 Nov: Theodore Revillon writes JM from New York on regrets that JM could not attend Hunter College meeting [where he was invited to speak] because of the UNRRA meeting in Atlantic City. Three days later JM replies with "Cher Revillon" note. FJM AME 62/3/305, 306.[See also 20 Feb 1945]

15 Nov: JM leaves Atlantic City conference to take up Washington post. JMM 211

25 Nov: JM visits Stimson to seek some FCNL symbol on currency US troops will use in liberated France. Situation complicated because JM has apparently got Treasury approval. "I was ready and armed for him and though he argued hard for his currency he after awhile gave it up. Monnet admits that France is not exactly like Norway, Holland and Belgium where the exiled governments were recognized by us [which is not true of the FCNL]. HLSD

26 Nov: Mrs A Knopf writes JM again on book idea, following up her second cable to him of 10 Nov at Hotel Claridge, Atlantic City, FJM AME 63/2/59,60

29 Nov: Stimson notes that Roosevelt [writing from Teheran Conference] says military not civilians should control France after liberation because "his experience with the French Committee in North Africa has been so unfavorable." Now, FDR adds, Monnet who represents French Committee here [Washington], wants its recognition as French government.
Stimson adds: "I have carefully avoided...[doing anything] which would by indirection constitute such a recognition. Throughout fortunately my views have exactly coincided with those of Mr. Hull."
On another matter, JM discusses with Stimson the French currency question: "He is pressing us to use some likeness of the FCNL on the French currency. We don't want to nor does Hull or FDR." HLSD

1 Dec: First UNRRA Council session ends in Atlantic City, NJ. UNRRA 25

7 Dec: At his regular meeting with Hull, Stimson described his meeting with JM on design of currency Allied troops will use in France after liberation. "I told him Monnet had pressed very hard that we should allow the Committee of which he is a member to issue the currency marked `Republique Francaise Tresor

Centrale' and that I had refused, telling him that would amount to recognition of the sovereignty of the French Committee....He acquiesced...." HLSD

The currency question, seemingly a minor matter in the midst of war, assumed a major meaning for de Gaulle, and therefore, for Monnet in defining the French role in the Allied partnership. De Gaulle insisted that France be treated as a full partner in the liberation of its territory. Roosevelt, and some of his advisers, still resented de Gaulle's behavior and wanted to regard France, after the invasion, as occupied territory under military government until free elections were held. Churchill, in an awkward middle position, saw the merit of de Gaulle's view that he was provisional leader of France where liberated but the British leader did not want to offend Roosevelt whose dislike for de Gaulle he largely shared. Monnet, who in 1941 had advised Roosevelt to resist de Gaulle's grasp for power, now worked for the general and thus found himself caught between de Gaulle and the Roosevelt administration. (JMM 217-18)

21 Dec: France discussed by Stimson and McCloy: Latter is against "too rigid a position against the FCNL because that could mean losing help from the French when we invade....Hull sees red when he hears `French Committee.'" HLSD

------[Tues]Englewood, NJ: "Dean and Ann Jay were there and I had a little talk w/ Dean ab[out] Monnet and France." ECM

24 Dec: JM sends unsigned memo of conversation he had with Frankfurter and Hopkins on US views toward France. Memo is used on 1 Jan 1944 in letter from Roosevelt to Churchill. Goal of memo and letter is to create a "solid and durable foundation" to US policy in North Africa, preserve French unity during and after the war and put in place a government in liberated France which will participate in the reconstruction of Europe. The memo is in response to criticism of US North African policies but also to relate accurately the US position and its fidelity to the Atlantic Charter. AK 31

31 Dec: JM sends Eisenhower New Year's greetings with wishes for success in the "great enterprise" he would soon lead and the hope they will soon meet in Paris. Pre-presidential papers, Box 78, Eisenhower Presidential Library, cited in Pascaline Winand, "Eisenhower, Dulles, Monnet and the United of Europe," in MATA 108

1944

1 Jan: Murnane partnership dissolved and firm name changed to Murnane & Co, ending JM's business career. FJM AMD 13/3/28

The end of the partnership apparently signifies no falling out with Murnane but rather a realization by Monnet that his future was not in business. In its nine year life, the firm was never a great financial success but, more importantly, Monnet's interests clearly moved toward renewed public service in peacetime.

7 Jan: Memo by JM to Dean Acheson, Ass't Secretary of State, on operation of the 25 Sept 1943 lend-lease modus vivendi between FCNL and US government: FNCL has only $25m in its treasury while it owes US $50m. FRUS III 748

8 Jan: Morgenthau and McCloy visit Roosevelt on French currency question. FDR adamant that "Republique Francaise" not appear on provisional currency Allied forces to use after invasion. Later that day the treasury secretary and the assistant secretary of war meet with JM who insists "Republique" is crucial to differentiate new government from Vichy regime. Morgenthau says he will try again with FDR, adding "But we are all subordinates." T. Morgan, FDR (New York, 1985) 717-718 (quoting HMD.)

25 Jan: Memo by R Brand, two days after long talk with JM on personal finances, indicates: JM has ceased partnership with Murnane and will not resume it after war; JM owes $45,000 in US taxes, with his assets in MM $35,000 to $40,000; JM is closing Washington house with Silvia who is going to Narragansett, RI and Anna entering [boarding?] school; JM will get 1200 pounds a year from French National Committee [about half of what he earned in London as head of the AFCC and less than the 1800 pounds he annually drew from MM]; He cannot afford the $500 annual interest he owes [presumably to Lazard]. BP

-----: JM writes in apology to Mrs A Knopf for delay in replying to her cable and letter to Atlantic City on book idea. He "regrets greatly" he cannot comply. (Correspondence continues in January, February and, finally, August). FJM AME 63/2/61-64

27 Jan: Acheson replies to JM memo of 7 Jan: Involved US agencies want to help solve these problems. Lists several steps to help increase funds to FCNL and reduce its payments. FRUS III 749-50

12 Feb: JM writes Pierre Mendes-France in Algiers on recent Washington planning meetings on postwar monetary policies in Western Europe. The meetings, organized by Harry White, under secretary of the Treasury, concentrated on exchange rate policies and sought a balance between the extremes of excessive deflation and catastrophic inflation. PM 283, citing French National Archives Economiques et Financieres document.

------JM writes Acheson on use of lend lease credits for food and clothing for French prisoners of war and on other aspects of lend-lease program. FRUS III 751

22 Feb: State Department receives message and inquiry from its representative in Algiers to FCNL who reports JM has been sending committee members optimistic reports from Washington on prospects of US government recognition of FCNL as provisional French government. British representative Duff Cooper also hints Churchill shares this opinion on FCNL as provisional government but has not yet told FDR of his view. Can Washington clarify

position to JM and to US press to end this confusion? FRUS III 651-2

------: Rajchman writes a friend about the possibility of further collaboration with JM from whom Rajchman has heard his "audacious ideas about the future of France and of Europe." During the previous month, JM had also suggested that Rajchman might help plan the restoration of the French public health system. BM I 298

28 Feb: Stimson prevails with FDR who had wanted to send Eisenhower rigid plan on how to treat FCNL. McCloy had objected, saying FDR plan would humiliate de Gaulle. President finally accepts a Stimson draft. HLSD

11 Mar: JM addresses victory bond rally in NY Metropolitan Opera House (broadcast live on radio)."Germany must be transformed not only in organization but in military traditions...and its material strength....We must establish conditions for a peaceful German people to cooperate with other nations..." but France alone cannot do this. "...France alone cannot solve the problem of living next to a nation which three times has invaded France and twice brought US armies to Europe." JM identified as commissioner-at-large of FCNL. NYT 12 Mar 1944, "Frenchman Urges Changes in Reich"; FJM AME 62/2/40 (broadcast text)

This appearance and nationwide broadcast from the prestigious Metropolitan Opera House is unusual in Monnet's life: a prominent public event where he is speaks for France. Neither in World War I and its aftermath in the League of Nations, nor in post World War II France, did history record another Monnet appearance like this one. Perhaps wartime America, with de Gaulle far away, (and Morgenthau still so close at Monnet's heels) was the right time for him to try out his public speaking skills and to arm himself with a public prominence.

His New York appearance, at age 56, may have been important in reminding Monnet of his strengths and weaknesses. He was no public speaker, able or willing to rouse an audience. His method was to persuade men to work together for a common interest and to let others take the credit.

In his memoirs he said he concluded about this time that he was not destined to be a politician. He lacked, he said, the self-centered view which statesmen need to succeed and he did not like the constant turmoil of new problems each day and new but temporary solutions. His mind, he said, needed to concentrate on one problem and never on himself. JMM 229-31

15 Mar: JM and staff meet with Acheson and other State Department officials on a mutual aid agreement with FCNL for all territories under its jurisdiction which would replace the Sept 1943 modus vivendi. JM objects to many provisions.in the proposed agreement all of which concern restrictions on dollars to and from the FCNL. FRUS III 751-55

22 Mar: JM dines with William Leahy, Roosevelt's chief of staff, and Vice

Admiral Fenard. "[A}n exceedingly clever man, [Monnet] discussed the merits and purposes of the de Gaulle Committee on National Liberation of which he was the political representative in Washington. Monnet renewed his appeal for a loan to France of several million dollars at a nominal rate of interest. WDL 227-8

31 Mar: JM writes detailed letter to Morgenthau on printing a second series of French currencies for use by Allied forces and civilians. FJM AME 48/3/85

12 Apr: JM cancels talk he is scheduled to give at American Academy of Sciences in NY because, he tells his friend Thomas Lamont. "I have been sick and forced to stay at home. Hope to make the trip in the near future when we can meet." LA.

28 Apr: Morgenthau replies to JM letter on currency, giving cost of $696,150 plus shipping for the French notes ordered. Notes, Morgenthau says, will be kept by US Treasury until ordered released by "the appropriate authorities". FJM AME 48/3/lll

29 Apr: JM replies to Acheson with detailed comments on the State Department aide memoire [on lend lease] given him on 15 Mar meeting. In general, JM wants to use model of British lend-lease agreement for new French agreement and suggests specific means for easing FCNL financial problems. FRUS III 755-7

30 Apr: De Gaulle shows irritation with JM's efforts in Washington on lend-lease agreement talks and, generally, with continued resistance of Roosevelt administration toward granting FCNL full recognition. Letter to JM from Rene Massigli, writing for de Gaulle, expresses this impatience. In fact, others in the Washington mission, including [FCNL Ambassador to US] Henri Hoppenot, an old adversary of JM, joined in the criticism which some hoped would end in JMs permanent recall to Algiers. MR 120; ER 414-18

MAY: JM and Raymond Fosdick, an old American acquaintance from the early League of Nations days, try but miss meeting in Washington. Fosdick was one of the original deputy secretaries general of the League. He is now president of the Rockefeller Foundation in New York. FJM AME 63/2/313

3 May: JM replies to Morgenthau with note of thanks "for the cooperation that you and the Treasury have give us in this difficult matter" [of banknotes]. FJM AME 48/3/118

12 May: R Murphy cables State Department that de Gaulle indicated a desire to repair his bad relations with Washington and regrets having an incompetent ambassador [H Hoppenot] there. NARA 851 001/50, cited by ER 420

14 May: Asst War Dep't Secretary J McCloy tells WC Bullitt that Roosevelt distrusts McCloy's view on France because he [McCloy] is "too much

under the influence of Jean Monnet." Memo by Bullitt on long talk with McCloy. WCB [See also August 25 below]

16 May: US Assistant Secretary of State James Dunn tells JM US cannot deal with a "provisional [French] government" because doing so would create many difficult problems. IW II 28

19 May: Morgenthau complains to UK Ambassador Halifax about plans to name Thomas Brand, JM's friend from Lazard Freres, as UK treasury representative in Washington. Morgenthau reminds Halifax "I spoke once before to your government about sending Mr. Monnet over here as deputy to Purvis, and Mr. Churchill went right ahead and did it anyway." HMD 733

20 May: JM asks Asst Secretary of State Dunn for US government view if FCNL should change its name to Provisional Government of the French Republic [as is being discussed by Committee in Algiers]. Dunn discourages such action. FRUS III 689-90.

22 May: McCloy and JM, accompanied by A Tixier and P. Mendes-France, discuss how the FCNL should deal with Eisenhower in the coming liberation of France. NARA 851 00/5201 cited by ER 419-20

27 May: JM writes Maj Gen J H Hilldring, director, Civil Affairs Division of US War Department on shipping needed for France after liberation. JM sends copies to Dean Acheson, John McCloy and Leo Crowley, Administrator, Foreign Economic Administration. FJM AME 51/l/136

4 Jun: Isaiah Berlin reports from UK Embassy in Washington to London that Roosevelt recently gave interview to reliable journalist citing JM "plan for economic reconstruction of Europe entailing internationalization of `metallurgical heart of Europe' i.e. portions of Rhineland, Alsace Lorraine, Luxembourg, Belgium etc, which Monnet proposed to discuss with Harry Hopkins when latter returned [from hospital]". I. Berlin, Washington Dispatches 1941-1945 (Chicago, 1981) 365

5 Jun: Morgenthau replies to JM regarding 27 May letter from P. Mendes-France on financial measures to be taken after Allied troops land in France. FCNL views have been conveyed to Allied military forces, Morgenthau says. FJM AME 48//3/162

6 Jun: Allied forces land in Normandy, France in Operation Overlord from ships based in England in history's largest amphibious operation, led by Gen. Eisenhower.

10 Jun: In the midst of dispute between French and Allied authorities on currency for use in liberated France, Morgenthau threatens to "throw Monnet out of Washington no matter what the State and War departments want" if de Gaulle causes trouble during the invasion and liberation now underway. HMD 742

11 Jun: JM writes Morgenthau that Mendes-France, now in Algiers, left enclosed letter on currency rate of exchange for delivery now. FJM AME 48/3/169

12 Jun: Massigli, in charge of foreign affairs for FCNL, Algiers, complains to Robert Murphy, US political adviser there, that JM and Admiral Fenard were "always interfering with what are normally Hoppenot's functions" [in Washington where latter is FCNL official representative.] FRUS III 710-711.

------:In cable to FDR, Churchill reviews currency problem in France: "The question whether the position [taken by the US] was agreed with British Treasury and whether Messrs. Monnet and Mendes-France fully understood does not admit of a plain yes or no.... Monnet argued very strongly in favor of a French national currency but when he found that the President seemed quite unmovable on the point he reluctantly acquiesced in the preparation of [US] military francs on condition that a separate issue of French national currency should be printed at the same time and used to redeem the military currency very promptly. [We] thought the Americans would produce the separate issue of French national currency promptly....In fact the Americans have so far as we know not yet begun to produce the French national currency....Mendes-France was only appointed as Financial Commissioner after the time when the matter was on active discussion with Monnet. Mendes-France protested actively when he was recently in Washington." NAUK Prime Minister files 3 177/2

13 Jun: FDR cables reply to Churchill's cable on status of currency to be used in French liberated areas. Roosevelt insists he never had accepted JM's, or, later, de Gaulle's insistence on a rapid substitution of a FCNL currency for the initial [military] franc currency as a condition for issuing such military script as Churchill's message implies. "We intend to continue to use the supplementary franc currency as has been fully understood by Messieurs Monnet and Mendes-France of the French Comite." FDR added: "It seems clear that a prima donna [de Gaulle] does not change his spots." NAUK PREM 3/177/2; R&C 530-1; HMD-JB, III 171-3

14 Jun: De Gaulle arrives in Bayeux for brief first visit to France since 1940. DEG-L 528-30

22 Jun: JM, Undersecretary of State Edward Stettinius Jr, John McCloy and Admiral Leahy spend evening on Secretary of Navy Forrestal's yacht. Forrestal and Leahy are "brutally frank with Monnet on de Gaulle and French situation...emphasizing that if American public knew the truth" about de Gaulle and his committee there would be a breach between US and France. "Monnet made a rather feeble attempt to defend the French situation but his argument lacked force and carried little conviction." Diaries of Edward R Stettinius Jr (NY, 1975) 90-1

27 Jun: FDR cables Churchill: We should not proceed on assumption

that US and UK are responsible for redemption of the military francs because no agreement has been reached with the FCNL. Any successful government in France will have to accept the validity of the military francs issued by Eisenhower who is the only authority in France to issue money. If FCNL wants, we will conclude agreement with it like I have concluded with Belgium, Netherlands and Norway: We provide dollars for their currencies used for our troops pay and they pay us for supplies for the local population. NAUK PREM 3 177/2

30 Jun: R Brand writes Silvia at Narragansett, Rhode Island [where she is moving after she and JM give up expensive Foxhall Road rented house in Washington]. BP

3 Jul: According to Murphy, JM, who has just arrived back in Algiers, told de Gaulle's top aide there, Louis Joxe, that Roosevelt said "Je cederai rien" [I will concede nothing] concerning de Gaulle's coming Washington visit and the issues dividing the two leaders. FRUS III 719-20

6 Jul: JM in Algiers dines with Macmillan. HM-I 482; JM had left Washington because de Gaulle did not want him present during the general's visit there. JMM 220

Monnet's ordered return to Algiers came apparently because de Gaulle did not want to appear dependent on him in Washington when the general arrived there. It was a humiliating example for Monnet of de Gaulle's determination to dominate, a characteristic Monnet despised in both men and nations. His brief return also prompted some in his Washington FCNL office to hope Monnet would not return. His response to this hostility shows a side of Monnet's personality often overlooked: persistence and determination against opposition he does not respect.(JMM 220; MR 120)

6-10 Jul; De Gaulle visits United States, sees FDR three times. Afterwards, he visits Canada before arriving in Algiers for Bastille Day. DEG-L I 537-47

7 Jul: In Algiers, JM and Macmillan discuss Germany and Europe after the war: "In his view the whole future of Europe depends upon the solution to the German problem and the effective reduction...of the German war potential. [A] full United States of Europe is still beyond realization but a strong League [of Nations] possibly combined with inter-State trade and monetary arrangements could be made effective ...[in] Western Europe. In this England must take the lead and France must support her." HM III 188

19 Jul: JM lunches in Algiers with Dorothy and Harold Macmillan, Rene Mayer and Adrien Tixier, FCNL Commissioner for Labor, and wife. HM I 486

20 Jul: State Department offers France new aid agreement during General de Gaulle visit to Washington. This continues discussions led by JM in January-

April and continued by him after de Gaulle departs. FRUS III 757-63

------JM writes Pleven from Algiers that he will continue with the tasks of providing for food and other material needs of France. He expects he will be able to hand over this work to others by August or September at the latest. Then he wants to concentrate on some broader matters and on European questions.FJM AME 46/3/13, cited by ER 426-7.

JM's old friend and former US ambassador in Moscow and Paris, William Bullitt, is in Algiers coincidentally during JM visit; Bullitt is now special assistant to US Navy Secretary. FRUS III 727

LATE JULY: Long interview of JM by John Davenport appears in Fortune magazine outlining his views on postwar Europe, Germany and giving summary of early life in France and North America. JM wants to see "Germany shocked and stripped of part of her industrial potential" but also, through yielding of some national sovereignty, a more unified Europe to prevent that race of nationalism which, he says, "is the curse of the modern world." He suggests the "possibility the great Rhine coal and iron fields [be] run by a European authority for the benefit of all participating nations...." Fortune, August 1944 121-25; 214,216

2 Aug: Mrs A Knopf writes JM again, probably after seeing Fortune article, on idea of book on postwar France and asks to meet him at Mayflower Hotel in Washington on 7 Aug. FJM AME 63/2/64

The Fortune magazine article (and his broadcast speech at the Metropolitan Opera House on March ll) both reflected and raised Monnet's profile in that segment of American public opinion concerned with international events and, specifically, with postwar Europe. The renewed approach to him by publisher Alfred Knopf reflects this interest. Although Monnet's prominence rose to a peak in the 1950s after the Schuman Plan was announced, he then again rejected the insistent proposals of another American publisher, Doubleday, (in 1953-54) that he write about his work. It was only in the late 1960s when he was in his eighties that he sought help in assembling his papers and recollections for the long delayed writing of his memoirs.(Doubleday file, Library of Congress manuscript division; interviews with Francois Fontaine, Monnet's collaborator on his Memoirs).

18 Aug: De Gaulle leaves for France after nearly one month in Algiers. DEG-L 562. Shortly after, JM returns to Washington. JMM [Neither book indicates whether the two had substantive discussions in Algiers but it seems likely they met, perhaps often, in this Algiers interlude.] JMM 220

23 Aug: Morgenthau and Stimson discuss JM idea for international control of the Saar [and Ruhr]. HMD 765

25 Aug: Stimson, at lunch with Roosevelt, discusses Germany's disarmament; "I feared ...a division of Germany which would prevent her from being industrialized....I...suggested the possibility of internationalizing the Ruhr

and the Saar as suggested by Jean Monnet whose name I did not mention." HLSD [Stimson probably did not mention JM because he knew the President was suspicious of the Frenchman's influence on Stimson's deputy, John McCloy who was recently told by Roosevelt that he (McCloy) "was not to be trusted in French matters because he was too much under the influence of Jean Monnet." Memo by WC Bullitt, 14 May 1944 after long talk with McCloy. WCB]

4 Sep: Sir Alexander Cadagon accompanies UK Ambassador Halifax to meeting with Harry Hopkins on future of Germany. Hopkins wants to "eliminate" Ruhr "(as against [Jean] Monnet's scheme of internationalization). Attractive but I don't know how practical it is." The Diaries of Sir Alexander Cadagon, ed by David Dilks, (New York, 1972) 659-660

-----:In a dinner at his home, Morgenthau outlines his plan for postwar Germany to Stimson, McCloy and Harry White of Treasury staff after earlier session in Treasury Department with larger staff group, same subject. HMD 768.

5 Sep: JM accepts proposal by Leo Crowley, head of Foreign Economic Administration, to facilitate aid to liberated France with easing of dollar restrictions on payments. JJD 176

6 Sep: Morgenthau and Stimson outline present respective and conflicting views on how to treat defeated Germany in White House meeting with Roosevelt, Hopkins and Hull. Stimson praises JM's idea on internationalizing the Ruhr which seems "moderate and reasonable". HLSD; HMD-JB,262-3.

7 Sep: Stimson lunches with JM and McCloy; "I asked him to go over his proposition for internationalizing the Saar-Ruhr under trustees" to enhance the reconstruction of Europe. JM stresses he speaks only for himself, not for French colleagues. HLSD

-------:JM phones White House requesting personal visit with President because he is returning to France soon. Hopkins also phones supporting this request. FDRL PPF

9 Sep: JM sees FDR before returning to France. They discuss using lend-lease to help rebuild French industry after war. FDRL, PPF; FRUS III 760

-----: JM writes McCloy (also on 12, 15 Sep) on shipping and supply needs of France. FJM AME 52/2/35,46,55

-----: JM dropped from provisional government cabinet of FCNL by de Gaulle but retains title of Commissioner on special assignment. JMM 224

For months Monnet had been concerned with France's needs from the moment liberation began. He had returned to Washington from Algiers in 1943 with the title commissioner for supplies and reconstruction. When that title was removed he became commissioner on special assignment. Titles did not seem to bother him nor did de Gaulle's suspicion that Monnet was too close to the Americans. Monnet concentrated with his own special intensity on continuing

American economic support during and after France's liberation which was now underway and without yet showing much concern for political maneuvers in France.

11 Sep: Secretary of State Hull writes FDR on aspect of French lend-lease raised by JM in recent visit with President: Need of France for aid to get its industries going again. Hull says 20 Jul agreement seems to prohibit this but "I do not recommend such a flat rejection nor do I believe you intended it. I recommend long-term items be supplied France on case-by-case basis." FRUS III 760-1

-----: JM talks with Frankfurter by phone; latter says Morgenthau plan for Germany will fail when FDR sees its flaws. HLSD

11-16 Sep: Second Quebec Conference on final war strategy and postwar Europe. Morgenthau attends and convinces Roosevelt and Churchill on dismemberment of industrial Germany and its replacement by a "pastoral" economy.(This position repudiated quietly by the two leaders one month later). EAH 386

14 Sep: Stimson and McCloy distressed at press account of Morgenthau's summons to attend Quebec meetings despite chairmanship of Hull (who did not attend) of cabinet committee on Germany. HLSD

16 Sep: Hopkins asks US army to arrange plane for JM to Paris on 19 Sep, returning following week [although actual return was in November]. HH

18 Sep: JM writes FDR in follow up to his 9 Sep visit, encloses "interesting letter" he recently received from friend of Silvia who reports visit by someone to a small French village recently liberated. In a home the visitor sees a 1941 calendar on war marking date of Lend Lease Act. The Frenchman kept the calendar displayed because he knew on that date that the war would be won. FDRL PPF.

19 Sep: R Brand memo on talk with JM by phone: France has $2 billion in gold and $1 billion more in French interests (in Swiss banks) in US banks. BP

------: JM writes Hopkins just before departing for his first visit to Paris since 1940: asks that Marjolin, his Washington assistant, be contacted if Hopkins wants to send messages. HH

20 Sep: McCloy memo describes meeting with Morgenthau, Hull, Stimson and others on Quebec results; Morgenthau gave Roosevelt note on ending lend-lease to France to counter Hopkins effort to continue this aid "which he had been discussing with Monnet". HLSD

3 Oct: Hull asks FDR for authority to continue talks with French on final aid agreement which Hull had proposed to negotiate in 11 Sept memo. French are pressing for action. FRUS III 761-2

11 Oct: JM, in Paris, writes to French minister of health enclosing notes from three pharmacists and doctors in Cognac on products they need. "Surely the problem is not only in Cognac but is an indication of an urgent national problem...." FJM AME 27/2/32

13 Oct: JM writes Hopkins from Paris on Bristol Hotel stationary just after meeting with Supreme Court Justice James Byrnes who carries letter back: My three weeks here have taught me so much! I have been working on readjustment of import program I mentioned to you and will have it finished by next week. I expect to be in Washington in 10 days. HH

23 Oct: FCNL recognized by US as Provisional Government of France. JMM 220

NOVEMBER: Silvia Monnet, who has moved to Wakefield, Rhode Island with the children, exchanges cables with JM who is in France and, later, London. He misses family and wants to see them in Washington when he returns soon. Since his stay in Washington will be for unknown period, he suggests keeping Wakefield house which apparently was rented to reduce the family's living costs over the more expensive Washington home. FJM AME 63/2/213-6

7 Nov: Roosevelt reelected to fourth term; shortly afterwards, he accepts resignation of ailing Secretary of State Cordell Hull and replaces him with JM acquaintance, Edward Stettinius Jr, Undersecretary of State. FDR:FF 567-9

10 Nov: JM outlines French imports needs for 1945 in memo requested by de Gaulle. US would be main provider for foreseeable future, including supplying 50% of food imports. IW 36, citing AN F60, 921 memo by JM

11 Nov: French Ministry of Finance confirms contract with Robert Nathan for consulting work at $500 per month with JM, chairman of the Committee on Imports, retroactive to 1 September. FJM AME 63/2/236

This renewal of ties with Nathan must have pleased both men after an interlude of over two years. From their earliest meetings in late 1940 Monnet grew to trust the straightforward and astute man he described as "a shaggy-looking force of Nature." (JMM 172) Nathan has already begun work as a economic specialist in overseas economies as the prospect for peace grew clearer. He was to spend several months in close collaboration with Monnet's work on reviving the postwar French economy.

25 Nov: JM writes Hopkins from Bristol Hotel, Paris: "Just a word about the man the French government proposes to appoint ambassador in Washington. His name is Georges Bonnet....I don't know whether you have met Bonnet. He's a friend of mine. I have known him for 25 years. Felix [Frankfurter], Oscar [Cox] know him also. In my opinion he is the best possible appointment...." RES G

26 Nov: JM meets in France with Allied colleagues on Import Committee which he chairs. He has chaired meetings of committee on 13,16,18 and 20 Nov

but now turns chair over to Pierre Mendes-France since JM is returning (via London) to Washington where he will head French Supply Mission. NAUK CAB

21 Dec: Acheson tells Stettinius, new Secretary of State, that JM has returned to Washington and that a draft French lend-lease agreement has been approved by State Department in form consistent with 15 and 20 Jul memoranda which was also agreed by war and treasury departments. Monnet now back with authority to negotiate urgently this new agreement. Acheson asks Stettinius to call treasury secretary Morgenthau and foreign aid administrator Leo Crowley stating that State Department has drafted new agreement based on president's July memo. FRUS III 762-3

Monnet's return to Washington marks a very different turn in his work compared to one year earlier when he came back from Algiers. Then he was seeking recognition for the FCNL and a definition of its role in the war. Now he returns from Paris and intensive negotiations with the American and British governments on France's active role in the war, the liberation of the country and its need for greater lend-lease support. Before he was seen as an agent of de Gaulle; now he is accepted as France's spokesman on lend-lease immediate needs and after the war ends. But in both returns, Monnet meets resistance due to continuing resentment toward de Gaulle and to the competing interests of the British and other lend-lease recipients.

23 Dec: JM, Acheson and Will Clayton (Asst Secretary of State for Economic Affairs) meet at State Department on French lend-lease and supply questions, including the future of lend lease. Clayton memo, 29 Dec to Secretary of State, Clayton office files, HSTL

27 Dec: JM acknowledges letter of T Revillon who writes JM from New York on his "great emotion" at France's liberation and his regret at not seeing JM in Washington on recent visit. FJM AME 63/2/309

28 Dec: Lamont writes JM: Heard of your return; I know you are busy but hope you can come to lunch or dinner. "Let me get some of your wisdom in all confidence. You are aware that Morgan et Cie [Paris] kept their doors open through the occupation and despite Gestapo threats carried on without doing a stroke of business with any German interests." LA

26 Dec: Will Clayton meets again on supply problems with JM who promises memoranda on the problems. Clayton memo, 29 Dec, Clayton office files, HSTL

28 Dec: JM tells Clayton that supply problems for January resolved and he is now working on February and beyond. Clayton notes that White House is handling supply problems for France. As for lend lease, JM is seeking a redefinition of France's status since it "is now in the war, furnishing several divisions at the Fighting Front...[and] her productive facilities are available

for war purposes...." JM intimated France would like better lend lease terms if sympathetic US response is likely. Clayton memo, 29 Dec, Clayton office files, HSTL

31 Dec: JM celebrates New Year's Eve with Rajchman and new French ambassador Henri Bonnet. Soon afterwards, JM warns Rajchman that Poland may fall under Soviet influence and suggests he keep ties with TV Soong concerning China. JM is also concerned about the United Nations Conference in San Francisco which may lead to a "new League of Nations." Rajchman diaries, cited in BM II 189

1945

2 Jan: JM writes Secretary of State Stettinius that "in spite of what has been done [by Allied efforts], the economic life of France is steadily approaching extinction." FJM AME 53/3/1; HH quoted in JJD 167.

-----: NYT reports that JM discussed with State Department the report from the Anglo-French-US Committee in Paris on French needs in January-June period in order for it to play a full role in the war. NYT 3 Jan

-----:JM writes identical letters to visiting UK Minister of State Richard Law and Secretary of State Stettinius, with attached memo, on French needs in imports and shipping with strong statement of active French role in fighting Hitler alongside UK and US. NAUK AVIA 38/1204

2,9 Jan: JM writes US Treasury on needs of France for supplies and for priority in getting shipping for them. HMD, Miscellaneous Papers

8 Jan: [On recent visit in Paris] JM asked France to import US machinery and raw materials to provide pre-fabricated temporary housing for French workers. NYT

8 Jan: JM writes Stettinius requesting allocation of shipping for France; sends copy to Hopkins. HH.

-----JM writes State Department asking for a single program for all imports into France and complete French responsibility for handling it. State agrees only conditionally because of US military preference for handling some imports itself. HSTL, Acheson files: France.

10 Jan: JM, McCloy, Stimson and wives have dinner at Stimson's. "Monnet has asked for a meeting with me and this was the way we can get it by having them here for dinner." HLSD

11 Jan: White House meeting of Acheson, Clayton, Hopkins, Law, McCloy, Brand etc: McCloy says JM wants equal status for France with UK on imports. Acheson says JM wants a reserved seat but must settle for ticket without a number. "He is sure to get a seat but could not tell in what part of the house," Acheson added. McCloy agrees, according to British memo of conversation.

NAUK AVIA 38/1204

-------: Richard Law, UK Minister of State, on Washington visit, meets JM on French import program. JM wants approval of a single French import program for Jan-June and an allocation of shipping for same period or at least for first quarter of year. NAUK AVIA 38/1204

13 Jan: US Treasury officials write JM at French Supply Council in response to his recent letters on supplies for France: Sympathetic but non-committal replies and without personal references. HMD, Miscellaneous Papers

15 Jan: JM to negotiate lend-lease deal for France after Washington meetings with R Law and US officials. Shipping is major problem for French imports. NYT

--------: Halifax reports to London that Will Clayton wrote JM today agreeing with latter's 8 Jan letter on need for single French war import program. NAUK AVIA 38/1204

16 Jan: NYT reports on State Department press conference: JM is head of special economic mission in Washington on supplies for France which will receive an increased shipping allowance. JM issues own press statement later on work: "...since my return two weeks ago I have been discussing with Mr Stettinius ... and Mr. Clayton...the urgent needs of France....[T]he full participation of France in the war will hasten the day of victory." NYT 17 Jan; FJM AME 53/3/12

19 Jan: Cabinet meeting discusses lend lease and shipping needs for France after "recent errands" of JM and Richard Law, UK representative. "I warned of a similar situation [for France to that of UK shipping] and that Monnet was dissatisfied with the number of ships [allotted to France] and it would be challenged by him." HLSD

22 Jan: Livingston Merchant of State Department suggests W. Clayton endorse JM approach to French imports and reject alternate military approach but confer first with Under Secretary of War Patterson. HSTL, Acheson files: France

--------:JM writes Secretary of State Stettinius on French war import program; he writes McCloy on same matter, adding he is departing soon for Paris. NAUK AVIA 38/1204

30 Jan: JM achieves consolidation of import and relief programs for France with key American support. JJD 172

-------A D Marris, of UK Embassy, Washington: Saw JM this morning; he hopes to leave for Paris in 2-3 days, pending Lend Lease talks. He wrote McCloy on 22 January on ending several import programs for France by 1 March and replacing them with a single French-run program. NAUK AVIA 38/1204

------: W. Clayton, FEA head, calls Morgenthau on conversation just completed with JM who is upset about article [in today's Washington Post] about a single French import program and related shipping questions. Morgenthau then talks with McCloy (War Department), Oscar Cox, lend lease legal aide, and his own staff on matter, complaining that he does not know details of negotiations. Morgenthau calls meeting same morning in his office with Clayton, Cox, McCloy and his own staff to be informed on negotiations and to discuss handling press. HMD 814

1 Feb: JM refutes published reports of difficulties in US-French talks on imports and shipping. "Certainly the present shipping allocations for our imports are below our needs. We are confident that the French needs ...will now receive full consideration and a fair share of available shipping. NYT 1 Feb, 7

8 Feb: State Department tells NYT that the proposed lend-lease agreement and a reciprocal aid plan for France are completed and have been presented to JM who is taking the documents to Paris for study. Plan will give about $1 b in long term credits. During negotiations US felt France should supply cash or credits for part of its needs. If the agreement is approved and signed by 1 Jul, the US can continue shipments to France until 1948. NYT 9 Feb,9

20 Feb: Letter exchange begins with Theodore Revillon, 57 East 88th Street who notes that JM was not able to give the Hunter College talk in November 1943 because he was at the Atlantic City conference; he praises JM for his work on behalf of France. JM replies warmly ("Cher Revillon") [his old colleague from Allied Maritime Executive of WW I]. FJM AME

24 Feb: French cabinet approves new lend-lease agreement negotiated over past year by JM who will return to Washington next week for signing ceremony. Agreement covers $2.5 b of which $900 m is immediate 30 year credit and rest is lend lease which will be converted at war's end to further 30 year credit. NYT 24 Feb; Subsequently, JMs work was hurt when this aid was sharply cut by US in act of "faithlessness" by Leo Crowley, aid administrator, according to British economist John Maynard Keynes. Keynes, Collected Works, Vol XXIV 360

28 Feb: In Washington France and US sign new lend-lease agreements negotiated by JM. FRUS III 763,795

1 Mar: French lend lease program signed [yesterday] in Washington by JM and French ambassador Bonnet and acting Secretary of State Joseph Grew. For the first time the program contains postwar reconstruction aid. Maximum aid will be $2.575 b. JM: The aid "will give French life a new start." NYT 1 Mar,1

2 Mar: JM thanks Roosevelt for recent lend-lease agreement in note sent to White House secretary Grace Tully asking her to give it to the President. FDRL, PPF 7365

13 Mar: US and France sign "Mutual Aid" agreements in which French

provide work and services in exchange for over two billion dollars in consumer goods. Agreements last until July 1946. JMM 225-6

22 Mar: Morgenthau recounts in memo to FDR which he wrote last night and in talks with HM staff his views on Germany after war ends. He complains that on 10 March a [War or State Dept] memo undermined completely the Morgenthau position on Germany. "We got the President to recall 10 March [memo] and he wholly accepted the one which was done here last night...."

Morgenthau wants "industrial disarmament, demilitarization, reparations and relief of liberated areas.... Germany should not have a higher level of living standards than any neighboring UN country nor should it be able to develop its war potential. All Nazi party members who were more than nominal participants in its activities to be removed from office. War criminals to be brought to trial and punished." HMD 831

25 Mar: JM writes Roosevelt expressing appreciation for new lend-lease agreements between France and United States. FDRL PPF

12 Apr: President Roosevelt dies suddenly at Warm Springs, GA. JM hears news during meeting in State Department office of Will Clayton and aide Emilio Collado. JM and Clayton were "deeply concerned and deeply depressed and Monnet said: `My country has lost a great friend.'" E. Collado oral history, HSTL

15 Apr: Roosevelt burial at Hyde Park, NY which JM attends. HMD 839

Roosevelt's death was a personal blow to Monnet who had first met the president in 1938 when his commitment to aiding the allies united against Hitler greatly impressed the French visitor. He was never to develop close ties to Roosevelt's successor, Harry Truman, and it was 1952 before Monnet could resume close ties to the highest levels at the White House and the State Department with the Eisenhower administration.

21 Apr: Morgenthau recounts conversation with JM who had talked with Bernard Baruch. Latter had talked with President Truman on postwar policy on Germany. The new president, Baruch says, wants to be very tough on Germans and would "cut his heart out" if Will Clayton was softening views on Germany after FDR death.

JM also asks Morgenthau to see Rene Pleven who arrives in Washington on Sunday. "Monnet also gave me an invitation to visit Paris in May to talk with the French. He thought it would be very good for their morale to carry on the Roosevelt line of thought." HMD 839

23 Apr: JM issues statement in Washington praising Franklin Roosevelt and the lend lease program he sponsored. The statement also describes the US government's support for the national import program of new supplies for the French people.

Gen. Eisenhower announces agreement that as of 1 May US will give

French government task of providing all civilian goods except coal and oil. Agreement was negotiated by JM who said in Washington today that the UK and US have done their best with these supplies. JM praises American lend lease saying "The name of Franklin D Roosevelt will always be associated in the minds of Frenchmen with the liberation of our country. And it symbolises for us the world wide cooperative spirit which is the best augery of the future of all of us. NYT, Apr 24, Apr 11

APRIL: Clementine Churchill tells Lord Moran, Winston Churchill's doctor: "He said to me yesterday: 'If I were ten years younger, I might be the first President of the United States of Europe.' " Churchill: Taken from the Diaries of Lord Moran: The Struggle for Survival 1940-1965, (Boston, 1966), 265

MAY: JM exchanges letters with State Department on additional aid beyond that allotted in 28 Feb lend lease agreement. HSTL, Lend Lease files

4 May: JM visits Stimson to request locomotives under Lend Lease and to expedite orders for both war use and in rehabilitation. HLSD

8 May: V-E (Victory in Europe) Day celebrates signing of unconditional surrender the preceding day by German Field Marshall Jodl. The agreement was ratified in Berlin the following day. EAH 378

14 May: Long letter from R Brand, in Washington, to economist John Maynard Keynes, London, on the end of Lend Lease cites JM's recent experience in negotiating an amount [of Lend Lease aid] with the US government only to have it sharply reduced before it even went to Congress. We must avoid this outcome for Britain. Keynes, *Collected Works*, Vol XXIV 331-5

31 May: Morgenthau writes condolence letter to Robert Brand on death of his son of which the treasury secretary heard from JM. HMD

MID-JUNE: JM induces French government to invite Morgenthau to open war bond exhibit in Paris in early July but President Truman hesitates in approving trip which never occurs. HMD-JB 461

24 Jun: JM visits Morgenthau at home. Afterward, the treasury secretary noted that he told JM: "A lot of things have been going on and I don't know whether my people know about it or not. I want a meeting ...showing the flow of goods from this country to other countries and how they are being paid for." HMD 858

27 Jun: James Byrnes replaces Edward Stettinius as US Secretary of State.

3 Jul: JM writes letter to his departing French-Canadian secretary Yvette Poirier who is succeeded by L. Boissoneault. FJM AME 63/2/231; 63/1/9

AUGUST: JM sees de Gaulle for first time in six months during latter's visit to Washington. They discuss rebuilding of France which de Gaulle sees as a restoration of it greatness; JM stresses need to modernize the country and improve its productivity. He accepts de Gaulle job offer with responsibility for the transformation. NYT 25 Aug; JMM 228

This conversation with de Gaulle decisively influenced Monnet life. With the end of the war in Europe his thoughts had turned to his role in the postwar world. He had always been active at the start of major events in his life. He had started with French supply problems soon after World War I began in August 1914. He was with the League of Nations from its start. He had sought airplanes for France in 1938 more than a year before another world war started. He was, as a long time friend, Jacques Van Helmont, noted, a man for beginnings. (BH 218)

He had decided in early 1944 to end his investment banking partnership. Now he wanted a place in the massive rebuilding of France and Europe. De Gaulle offered him a role which he eagerly accepted. If he had doubts of his ability to rebuild a country he hardly knew, he hid them. He had never before worked in France or with Frenchmen except in wartime or regarding international banking. Now at age 57, he had to master a new brief and learn to know his compatriots as never before. Monnet must have reflected on the magnanimity of de Gaulle's offer, coming as it did from a man with reservations about Monnet's loyalties and who certainly knew of Monnet's reservations about his leadership.

15 Aug: VJ (Victory in Japan) Day ends World War II after Japanese surrender follows US atomic bombing of Hiroshima and Nagasaki.

22 Aug: Truman gives White House dinner for Gen. de Gaulle. NYT 23 Aug

27 Aug: JM notes conversation with Will Clayton: "The real difference between Mr. Clayton and me is that he wishes and is intent upon having negotiations with us bring about commercial arrangements for reduction of tariffs etc between the United States and France on the basis of the present situation and of the present loans.... I think such commercial arrangements can only be a consequence of what arrangements may be made to meet the general needs of France enabling her to change her internal conditions completely." FJM AMF

EARLY SEPTEMBER: JM takes over chairmanship of French Supply Council in Washington; hires G. Ball as general counsel. JMM 226-8; GB 69,72-6

-------JM and Acheson correspond on introduction of American feature films into France. NARA RG 59, Box C-584, 851.24 cited in S. Pisani, The CIA and the Marshall Plan (Lawrence, KS, 1991) 102-3

This is an awkward phase in Monnet's move from being a Washington-based official of the French government dealing with lend-lease and supply matters to his coming role as head of the French Plan for economic reconstruction. He has to deal with bureaucratic problems at his Washington mission, a task for which he is neither inclined nor skilled. Although he soon turns the supply questions over to a trusted aide, Leon Kaplan, Monnet still moves between the two capitals even handling minor problems for an important friend like briarwood exports to the United States. In December he apparently still believes he can remain formal head of the French economic mission in Washington while starting the planning mission. He does not reckon with the sudden resignation of de Gaulle as head of the French government nor the jeopardy in which that change puts his new job.

21 Sep: JM arrives in Paris for talks on financing purchases in US which must now be paid in cash without lend lease aid. He suggests that some of the French gold reserves must be used for these purchases. NYT 22 Sep

29 Sep: Asst Sec of State Will Clayton cables JM in Paris, in follow up to 25 Sep letter to him, on briarwood imports from French North African territories, a matter JM had already discussed personally in Washington with Sol Bloom, chairman of House Foreign Affairs Committee. Bloom, a pipe smoker, had asked JM, upon his return to France, to free French restrictions on briarwood exports to the US where pipe manufacturers (including some in Bloom's New York district) were desperate for the high quality North African wood. The following week, on 5 Oct an American embassy officer in Paris writes R Marjolin, JM's aide, to follow up their earlier luncheon on same subject. FJM AMF 3/5/50,51 (See also 7 Mar 1946)

8 Oct: J McCloy visits JM and family at Houjarray, a restored farmhouse in the Ile de Paris, near the Rambouillet forest. The house, which JM has just acquired, is still somewhat primitive in its equipment for the coming cold weather but the family seems happy there. McCloy diary, Amherst College, cited by ER 454

17 Oct: In Paris JM says in press conference that the Big Five (Britain, China, France, Russia, USA) ignore the French view that the Ruhr and Rhineland must be separated from Germany as essential to European industry and world peace. NYT 18 Oct

24 Oct: JM meets in Paris with Supply Committee of Foreign Economics Relations Direction of the Ministry of Economics and reviews American aid at the end of 1945 after termination of Lend Lease. France has just received a new American commitment of $550 m for goods requisitioned but not yet contracted. We must use, JM says, the American methods of planning and statistics which gave them such an incredible productivity in the war.

To ensure that our program is well coordinated we have asked, JM says, Mr. Silverman to fill this role. He is formerly a professor of planning and statistics at MIT who also served four years in the War Department as Chief of Planning of Aircraft Production. Thanks to him we have put in place the program for the end of 1945 which you just received. He is now organizing a method of using economic data to give us immediate and accurate measurement of each stage of our Program. Precise planning is becoming essential for France. Mr.

Silverman will also help train young Frenchmen to learn these new methods. When they return they can pass on their knowledge to our national services.

JM also tells committee that American foreign economic policy has changed drastically when one compares its actions at the end of World War I and now. In 1918 the US suspended credits to its allies who were then unable to obtain private credit. Further, the Americans raised their tariffs and settled into an isolation from the rest of the world. "That isolation, I am convinced, was one of the principal causes of the war in 1939." AN, Carton 19273, Ministere de l'Economie, Direction des Relations Economiques Exterieures, 27th meeting of Commission des Approvisionnements, reprinted in Institut Politique Renouvin, Paris, IPR Travaux et Recherches, No 2, fall 1988; JMM 227 (on Silverman which is misspelled Silbermann).

Abraham G Silverman was hired by the French in Washington in mid-1945, after his War Department service, and worked about one year, according to a French colleague, Rostislaw Donn, who recalled Silverman gathering statistical evidence and arguments justifying American credits for French after Lend Lease ended. It is not clear that Monnet ever met Silverman whose credentials were more modest than described and who was one American among a large staff of the French Supply Council. Further evidence that Monnet relied on information from others concerning Silverman is his assertion in his memoirs that the economist was seconded or detached from MIT. In fact, Silverman taught at MIT in 1924-31 while a doctoral student at Harvard from which he graduated in 1930. He had not been at MIT for 14 years when hired by the French Supply Council. In 1944 he was an analyst for the Army Air Corps' Assistant Chief of Staff for Material, Maintenance and Distribution. Between MIT-Harvard and the Army Air Corps job, Silverman had a number of jobs as an government economist in Washington, starting in 1933.

Donn, whose task in Washington was to study why American industrial prosperity was so much greater than France's, concentrated on US labor productivity and eventually met James M Silberman, a Department of Labor productivity specialist. When Silberman was sent to Britain and France to aid labor productivity under the Marshall Plan, Donn arranged for him to meet Monnet who was greatly impressed and used Silberman to help revitalize the French work on productivity. Monnet and Silberman worked together until Monnet left the Plan in 1950.

In writing his memoirs 30 years later, Monnet apparently combined inadvertently his recollection of these two American economists with similar names. (Interviews with Donn, Silberman, 2002-3. See also 29 Oct 1948)

In a strange turn of history, Abraham G Silverman was identified in 1948 by two witnesses (confessed spies themselves) as a member of a Soviet spy network which operated in Washington before and during World War II. He was never tried or convicted. He refused to testify on these charges in congressional hearings. (NYT, Washington Post, 13 Aug 1948) Donn never heard of these charges until 2002 and there is no evidence that Monnet knew of the accusations against the man of whom he spoke highly in 1945 and whom he mentions favorably in his memoirs.(See below, 12 Aug 1948)

LATE FALL: JM renews discussion of consultant fees with Robert Nathan for work on economy of newly liberated France. Nathan, who was leaving post as deputy director, Office of War Mobilization and Reconversion, was about to resume his economic consulting firm in Washington. RRN I; FJM OH, Robert Nathan by Len Tennyson on 18 Nov 1981

NOVEMBER: JM makes what becomes a permanent move to Paris, leaving Leon Kaplan in Washington to complete negotiations on $550 m. loan from US Export-Import Bank. Sets up offices in Bristol Hotel and prepares memo to de Gaulle on modernization of France and also engages George Ball, former Lend Lease lawyer, to advise on devising an economic renewal plan for France. JMM 227-8

8 Nov: JM, in Paris, meets with Foreign Minister Bidault, Herve Alphand, director of ministry's economic services, and US ambassador Caffery on bilateral commercial policies. FRUS IV 768

25 Nov: JM, in London, called back to Paris instead of continuing on to Washington. FRUS IV 773

4 Dec: JM finishes preliminary plan on a rapid rebuilding of France which he gives to de Gaulle the following day, emphasizing France's need to modernize as it rebuilds. adding that without modernizing, France will not find its place in today's world. He also warns of danger of inflation. Calling for rapid action, the memo described the methods and a timetable for work under the Plan. DEG III 634-39, reprinted in PM 114

13 Dec: JM gives detailed memorandum to de Gaulle on modernization. JM-N; HR:RC.

14 Dec: After weeks of negotiation, begun while de Gaulle was in Washington in August, JM secures 10 year loan of $550m at low interest from US Export Import Bank. JMM 228; RM 223

21 Dec: In Paris JM named by French cabinet Commissioner of National Council to plan country's modernization. NYT 22 Dec

23 Dec: In Paris JM tells NYT correspondent Dana Adams Schmidt he would remain titular head of French Economic Mission [in Washington] even while assuming job as High Commissioner for Planning, Modernization and Equipment under General de Gaulle. JM emphasizes that new plan would go forward without regard to US credits being negotiated. He notes that French loans from US are needed for country's rebuilding and modernization while British loans from US are needed to live. NYT 24 Dec

With the war over and his return to France, Monnet wrote that he assessed his life at age 57. In his memoirs he described his reflections on his past work in which he was constantly involved in public affairs. But unlike politicians who faced endless choices in infinitely complex situations, his life had involved key points where he concentrated on a single aim. He saw that it was not his nature to be a politician but rather to focus on influencing them at crucial decision points. A key to his success was letting the politicians take credit for his ideas. (JMM 230-1)

Earlier, he had reflected [in 1971] on some hesitation he had at the end of the war about a possible entry into French politics. He discussed this with Silvia. "I saw that presentation and competition for power was primary over setting the policies. I saw that I was committed to France and Europe. It was hard to get political power but not as hard to reach the people in power." (AW)

Age 58 to 62 (1946-1950)

JANUARY: JM and R Marjolin, his deputy, begin work on the Plan with these goals: Regain the 1938 levels of national production by the end of 1948; reach the level of 1929 by 1949 and exceed, by 25%, the 1929 levels by 1950. MR 167

1 Jan: G Ball postpones opening of his Washington DC law firm to continue consulting work for the Plan. GB 76

3 Jan: French government publishes decree establishing the Commissariat du Plan [under JM] and requiring a Plan for economic modernization within six months. PM 118

9 Jan: R Brand writes JM at Plan office in Paris: [Now] you will be the "organizer of peace, rather than an organizer of victory, the first being ...far more difficult than the second." BP

14 Jan: JM and his planning staff meet at American Embassy, Paris on commercial policy where he tells embassy officers Livingston Merchant and Ivan White that France requires large scale US credits which will allow it to become "just as important as Great Britain in the world-wide scheme of things" and allow it to play the global role in free trade which Washington wants. IW 89-90; FRUS V 399

20 Jan: De Gaulle resigns as head of French government [in dispute over role of political parties]. JM thus loses a key supporter. HR:RC; JMM 231,244

26 Jan: Felix Gouin succeeds De Gaulle as prime minister.

7 Feb: JM prepares letter of resignation from Plan which is never sent. Addressed to Prime Minister Felix Gouin, the letter refers to Gouin's desire to place JM (and the entire Plan) under the Ministry of National Economy. JM insists that he will only work directly under the prime minister. FJM AMF 1/3/129

Monnet's detailed involvement, in the following entry, in the search for North African briarwood for American pipe smokers is amusing but indicative of his willingness to spend time and energy to service important American friends. Sol Bloom, chairman of the House Foreign Affairs Committee met Monnet during his days in Washington after his return from Algiers and knew that Bloom would be important in passing any legislation affecting the postwar recovery of France and Europe.

7 Mar: Congressman Sol Bloom cables JM at Bristol Hotel, Paris on briarwood exports from North Africa to US: When [House Foreign Affairs Committee aide, Boyd] Crawford saw you in Paris recently he was told briarwood would be shipped soon. Now we are told that order was rescinded. (Boyd Crawford had traveled from London to Paris in early January to see US embassy and JM on briarwood problem at request of Bloom who was at UN

General Assembly meeting in London. Bloom's New York constituency included briar pipe manufacturing). In draft reply to Bloom JM indicates he uncovered and is resolving problems delaying briarwood exports. FJM AMF 3/5/61,62; Crawford interview 25 Sep 1989

16 Mar: First session of the Conseil du Plan. JM proposes ambitious Plan goals: to reach 1938 productivity by 1948; increased by 25% a year later, and to raise that by another 25% by 1950. HR:RC; JMM 248

17 Mar: Former French Prime Minister Leon Blum, now ambassador extraordinary, heads delegation which includes JM heading to Washington for major economic talks, FRUS V 418; JMM 249

19 Mar: After planning council meeting, JM flies to Washington to join Blum in economic discussions in aftermath of end of Lend Lease program and to arrange follow-on to last November's $650m. loan which he had arranged. JMM 249

10 Apr: JM meets in State Department during Blum negotiations. Aid to France is major topic. FRUS V 426

21 Apr-2 May: R. Nathan visits Paris at JM request [but in his absence] to assist in developing Plan approach to French reconstruction. Nathan writes first three of series of memos this year at JM's request on the French plans for reconstruction. RRN-D; FJM AMF 5/3

24 Apr: Nathan visits Houjarray for first time to lunch with Silvia. [JM is still in Washington with Blum delegation.] RRN-D

25 Apr: Nathan begins memos for Plan on "General Organization of statistical compilation and analysis in the American government" and "Comments on national income estimates for France." FJM AMF 5/3/2

27 Apr: Creation of Institut National de la Statistique et des etudes Economiques (INSEE) intended to gave solid statistical and forecasting basis for Plan. HR:RC

29 Apr: Nathan writes memo: "Suggestions for consideration in manpower area." FJM AMF 5/3/4

-----Dean Acheson writes memo to Secretary of State Marshall explaining the financial scope of talks JM is leading in Washington for France under Leon Blum: The new money for France would be $650 in loans but could be "dressed up" to seem two billion to appear like the sum promised Britain. IW I 91-2 citing NARA 851.54/4-946

30 Apr: JM cables Paris on his talks explaining the Plan to American officials who find it viable: They saw "no reason why the French people cannot achieve the goals fixed in the plan." IW I 91 citing FJM AMF 4/8/137; JM's defense of the Plan and of the Blum-Byrnes talks seems optimistic since the Plan

was not fully developed at this point and Blum himself considered going back to Paris for "consultation" because he was disappointed in the results of the talks. IW-I 91 citing PM 128-33 and JMM 253-4

8 May: Frankfurter replies to letter from JM who asked, on behalf of Leon Blum, head of French delegation in Washington, for a memo on US Supreme Court's power to invalidate a law. FF

12 May: JM cables Robert Sherwood, former aide to Roosevelt and Harry Hopkins, who is writing a Hopkins biography, from Washington: Was delighted to see you yesterday. Enjoyed our talk very much and evening with Mrs. Harriman [who had given dinner at her apartment for Sherwood, his wife and JM whom she had wanted to meet, according to an undated Sherwood letter to JM]. RES

15 May: JM sees Acting Secretary of State Acheson and asks that the Secretary of State James Byrnes, in Paris for Council of Foreign Ministers meeting, be notified of urgent French need for German coal to sustain recovery and use meetings with French Foreign Minister Bidault and UK Foreign Minister Bevin to discuss problem. German coal not discussed at CFM but was to be taken up at 10 Jul meeting. FRUS V 779-80

23 May: JM drafts report to French government on Blum-Byrnes accords just agreed: "The [Monnet] plan has made possible the accords; the accords will permit the execution of the plan." IW I 91 citing FJM AMF 4/5/2

24 May: JM dines with Robert Sherwood on latter's biography of Harry Hopkins. JM recounts first meeting with Hopkins in January 1941 at Felix Frankfurter's home and his initial doubts that Hopkins was right person to visit Churchill as FDR emissary. After Hopkins' successful visit to England, however, JM worked closely with him on arms production. "The minds of Monnet and H.L.H. entirely different---the former orderly, precise, logical, French---the latter darting, intuitive, penetrating." RES

28 May: Blum mission ends with his return to Paris and announcement of large loan and settlement of all lend-lease accounts. Agreement, signed for France by Blum, French Ambassador Henri Bonnet, and JM, calls for $1.4 b in credits, of which $650m was in Export-Import Bank credits for capital goods and raw materials, $300 m for purchase of US war surplus in France, $420 m for lend lease inventories and $25 m to buy surplus Liberty merchant ships. FRUS V 463-4; HSTL, PSF France; GB 69-77; JMM 254

6 Jun: R. Marjolin reports to JM on progress made on the Plan during his absence in Washington. Marjolin also warns of hostility by Benoit Franchon, Communist Party leader, who sees dangers of delivering control of French commerce to the Americans. There are also divisions within the cabinet over JM's plan on restricting imports. PM 148

25 Jun: Georges Bidault succeeds Gouin as prime minister. JMM 256

30 Jun: JM meets with chairmen of the Plan's major committees to report on results of the Blum visit to Washington. PM 148,166.

In the midst of a very active life divided between his American and French circles of influence, with frequent travel, Monnet is also getting to know his native country. He tells an acquaintance in 1946 "I have never lived as much in my country as in the past two years and I am beginning to understand her." JD 159 (Although often a visitor, he had not lived and worked in France since the 1920's.)

1 Jul: George Ball ends temporary consultations with JM for the Plan and rejoins his Washington law firm which immediately takes on work for JM and the Plan. FJM OH, Ball; GB 69-77

2 Jul: Nathan writes JM about his aborted flight to Paris which was cancelled at last minute in New York by JM cable. Encloses three memos and asks for firm date to reschedule visit. FJM AMF 5/3/54

----: JM writes Nathan, apologizing for abrupt cancellation of trip [at New York airport]:"...we were not ready" for visit and asks instead for Nathan visit at end of month. FJM AMF 5/3/53

10 Jul:[Allied] Council of Foreign Ministers meets in Paris to discuss increasing German coal exports which JM had earlier urged to insure continued French recovery. FRUS II 878,885-7,901-2,928,938

1 Aug: French Assembly approves Blum-Byrnes agreements. JMM 251

2 Aug-2 Sep: R Nathan visits Paris at JM request for second consultation on French reconstruction Plan; Writes long series of memos on approach of the Commissariat du Plan which JM heads. RRN-D; FJM AMF 5/3

During this visit Nathan met a young French economist, Pierre Uri, who was working at the Institut de Science Economique Applique (ISEA) and recommended him to Monnet for a job with the Plan. Nathan told JM: "You made me come five thousand kilometers but you have a guy two hundred meters from here who can tell you about these things as well as I can." Uri was later to play an important role in the Schuman Plan design and deliberations and in Monnet's later work. P. Uri, Penser Pour l'Action,(Paris, 1991) 46-7; RRN-I

4 Aug: JM gives lunch at Houjarray for Nathan, Will Clayton(US Assistant Secretary of State), and the Leon Blums. RRN-D

6 Aug: JM signs contract with R. Nathan for $15,000 requiring an extended visit to Paris for his "constructive critiques" of the entire work of the Commissariat du Plan. PM 136.

-----: Nathan memo to JM "Comments on Table of Production Objectives." FJM AMF 5/3/6 [This is the first of over thirty memos and commentaries Nathan wrote from 6-27 August while in Paris in consultation for the Plan. FJM AMF 5/3/6 through 5/3/34]

13 Aug: Nathan memo to JM on "Strategy and Presentation" advocates summary presentation of Plan with details later. FJM AMF 5/3/15

16 Aug: Nathan memo to JM on "Broad Philosophy and General Objectives" of Plan, a key memo among the many Nathan did for the Plan. FJM AMF 5/3/17

19 Aug: Nathan memo to Plan staff "Comments on Coal and Electricity Consumption". FJM AMF 5/3/22

26 Aug: Nathan submits long memo to JM and his Plan team covering consumption, production, international finance and investment. Modernisation ou Decadence: Contribution a l'Histoire du Plan Monnet et de la Planification en France, B Cazzes and P. Mioche, eds, (Aix en Provence, 1990), 325

Nathan, who first knew Monnet in the midst of war production preparations in 1941, has now worked with him in two month-long visits to Paris. He has clearly reflected on the man who brought him on this exciting diversion from his new economic consulting firm in Washington. In a personal letter, never intended for publication, he captured the Monnet method of work.

27 Aug: Nathan writes long letter to family on his impressions of JM gained in a long visit to Paris: "He has almost invariably attracted outstanding assistants and has had their full respect and loyalty. Yet he is very demanding and wears them out. At times he seems relentlessly inconsiderate of a person's welfare and then again he is warm and thoughtful....[H]e sees only the objectives and won't be delayed or diverted.

"Monnet has an amazing combination of capacities that just are very rare in the same person. He has a fine mind that grasps and retains and relates ideas....[H]e understands a fairly complex conception very quickly....He sees all the relationships and implications almost automatically. This is the result of ...his almost unparalleled capacity of figuring how to move and sell and get backing and put things over. At that he is a genius.

"He is full of new ideas stemming from the problem in hand...like a series of radiations from a central theme with new big themes at the end of each radiation, repeated over and over again and all again related to each other. So he ends up a job with thoroughness and with coordination." RRN-D

29 Aug: Final Nathan memos "Final Miscellaneous Observations" and "Social and Equitable Implications of the Plan", latter marked "To M. Jean Monnet. No other distribution." FJM AMF 5/3/33-4

3 Sep: Nathan returns to Washington from consultations with JM on Plan. RRN-D

6 Sep: US Secretary of State James Byrnes tells Stuttgart audience that

Ruhr should remain German but under some kind of international control that would not subject it "to political domination or manipulation by outside powers." Dep't of State Bulletin, 15 Sep, 501

19 Sep: Winston Churchill speaks at Zurich City Hall on Europe's future: What is this sovereign remedy [which can transform Europe]? It is to recreate the European family....We must build a kind of United States of Europe....The first step...must be a partnership between France and Germany. Churchill: Taken from the Diaries of Lord Moran, The Struggle for Survival 1940-1965 (Boston, 1966)

2 Oct: Nathan writes JM enclosing report on fiscal policy to fight inflation. FJM AMF 5/3/62

13 Oct: Referendum on the constitution of the Fourth Republic. HR: RC

26 Oct: Nathan writes JM on US economic situation and the possibility of doing some work in Poland for Ludwig Rajchman, JMs old friend. Encloses a picture of Nathan children and of R Marjolin and wife. FJM AMF 5/3/64

28 Oct: Back in Washington, Nathan writes JM with brief comments on American and French domestic situations and asking what work Nathan Associates should expect to do for the Plan in 1947. FJM AMF 5//3/64

23 Nov: JM writes to members of the Council of the Plan on dangers of inflation, echoing similar concerns Nathan made in his reports earlier in the year. PM 140

27 Nov: Final 200 page report on goals and methods of French modernization completed by the Plan staff under JM and discussed at second session of Plan Council. "Modernization is not a state of affairs but a state of mind," JM wrote in its introduction. "Frenchmen today," he continued, "are no different from those who were born when France was a great power. But in those days we were ahead of our time. It depends on us whether we pull ahead again...The only alternative to modernization is decadence." JMM 259-260; HR: RC

18 Dec: Leon Blum forms new government, succeeding Bidault whose government fell 28 Nov. JMM 260

26 Dec: JM sends holiday greetings to Nathan. FJM AMF

1947

7 Jan: Third session, Conseil du Plan. HR:RC

-----: Nathan writes JM in Paris on Washington situation; refers to seeing [Pierre?] Denis regularly as well as French ambassador Henri Bonnet. Nathan praises recent report of Plan but worries about inflation which must, he says, "be attacked vigorously" or "the whole Plan will continue to rest on shaky ground." FJM AMF 5/3/65

16 Jan: French government decree announces launch of first five-year Monnet Plan. HR:RC Blum's government resigns the same day in unrelated move. He is succeeded by Paul Ramadier who is less sympathetic to the Plan. RM 236

17 Jan: John Foster Dulles, JM's friend from interwar business deals and now a Republican foreign policy adviser, advocates binding Germany to an economically integrated Europe for which the Ruhr is the key resource. In speech before the National Publishers Association, Dulles suggests the New York Port Authority and the Tennessee Valley Authority as models for a Ruhr authority to put it beyond German national control. DP, cited in HS 76

This Dulles speech is one of many precursors for what finally became the Schuman Plan. Without detracting from the eventual initiative of Monnet and Schuman, it is clear that many other key people, like Dulles, Adenauer, Will Clayton (US assistant secretary of state) and Georges Bidault, French prime minister, focused on the Ruhr and its resources in remaking Europe. (For more on these earlier ideas, see William Diebold's chapter, "An Old Dream," in The Schuman Plan (NY, 1959) pp 21-46.)

23 Jan: JM arrives in London at invitation of UK government for economic consultations. NYT 24 Jan

30 Jan: W Clayton, US assistant secretary of state for economic affairs, writes Dean Acheson, undersecretary of state, that the time is not yet ripe for pushing Europe to form a special body to coordinate its reconstruction. JM is cited as opposing such a plan (which former US official Chester Bowles had proposed) since "he apparently shares the general French view that France can and must go it alone economically...to achieve security vis-a-vis Germany." NARA FW 840.50 MEA/1-1847

FEBRUARY: First report of the Monnet Plan covering November 1946-January 1947 begins with remark: "Modernization is not a matter of things but of spirit."

12 Mar: President Truman, in response to British withdrawal of aid to Greece and Turkey, announces eponymous "doctrine" of assisting European countries which face Communist advance. JM later calls this "decisiveness that was to mark his actions as President." JMM 265

20 Mar: Walter Lippmann, JM friend and prominent columnist, advocates Europe-wide aid program, rather than grants to individual countries by the US. RM 239

28 April: JM in London for Anglo-French economic talks. NYT 29 Apr

8 May: Dean Acheson, undersecretary of State, endorses in Mississippi speech a Europe-wide recovery program which "remains a fundamental objective of our foreign policy." RM 240

12 May: US ambassador Caffery in Paris cables State Department on need

to revise Monnet Plan for greater realism in several areas especially agriculture. FRUS III 712-3

------: JM sends long memo to Finance Minister Schuman on need to establish a Caisse Autonome [independent financing authority] to implement the Monnet Plan. MSC 23-31. Effort failed but JM continues to seek separate financial authority for more than two years, always confounded by the opposition of the traditional ministries. FD 173-5; In same memo, JM cites needs of French military security as a justification for the Plan's emphasis on heavy industry. IW-I 93

22 May: Nathan letter to JM describes his coming trip to Poland and says he may stop in Paris on his way to see JM. FJM AMF 5/3/67

5 Jun: Secretary of State George Marshall, in commencement address at Harvard, proposes European countries initiate a plan for rebuilding Europe which US would support. NYT 6 Jun

12 Jun: Marshall in cable to US ambassador Caffery says scope and nature of aid plan he proposed is not yet clear; cites Monnet Plan as possible model for all of Europe. FRUS III 249-51

------: Marshall holds press conference discussing his eponymous plan; he cites Churchill's speech in Zurich nine months earlier (See above, 19 Sept 1946) advocating a United States of Europe as influencing his (Marshall's) belief that the Europeans could work together with American support. (NYT 13 June 1947) Churchill later writes Leon Blum, French Socialist leader and JM's friend: "I feel greatly honoured to have been the link in setting in train the Marshall Plan upon which all our Governments are united and all our hopes depend." 7 Apr 1948 letter, Churchill Papers 2/18. Both the Marshall press conference and Churchill's letter cited in Martin Gilbert, Churchill and America, (NY, 2005), 380-1

14 Jun: Ernest Bevin, UK foreign secretary, wants to meet French ministers next week on Marshall's idea. Bevin will ask that JM, now in Basil, also attend. FRUS III 253

15 Jun: JM tells President Auriol of his success in obtaining credits for the Plan. VA 276

16 Jun: Ernest Bevin tells US embassy aide that he favors "a British-French Monnet plan for Europe as the first step" in responding to Marshall's Harvard speech on European reconstruction. NARA 840.00/6-1647; FRUS III 254-5

17 Jun: French government announces it will accept Marshall Plan aid. HR:RC

28 Jun: JM discusses both broad goals and specific needs of country in long talk with President Auriol. The President afterwards notes that JM shows intelligence and astuteness in his judgments about the need for the French people

to work together as never before. A complete rebuilding of French society is needed, JM says. They discuss the military budget, taxes, food production etc. JM believes the French people must rise to challenge to rebuild after suffering the occupation. VA 308-10

1 Jul: JM writes Finance Minister R Schuman on need to prevent a break with the Soviet Union over the Marshall Plan, turning that program from economic aid to a political weapon. IW 99 citing FJM AMF 14/1/1

This sentiment, and JM's willingness to work with communist unions and ministers in the French government, led to suspicions by the American embassy's labor officer that JM was pro-communist. JM reports this accusation to visiting US Labor Department official James M Silberman (who was aiding US labor productivity programs about this time) and asks him to pass along to American embassy officials the injustice in these charges. Silberman reports this conversation to W Tomlinson, the embassy's treasury attache and a close friend of JM who is distressed that JM was worried about the labor attache's view and asks Silberman to reassure JM that no one else in the embassy takes the accusation seriously. (Interview with Silberman, 2002.)

Monnet's involvement with the communist ministers in the early postwar French governments, and with the communist unions, indicate both the dimensions of the Plan's responsibilities and his own pragmatic approach to his work. He was non-political; he wanted to achieve certain goals and was prepared to deal with those who could help. He did not ask, nor question, ultimate justifications for their work, or his. The task involved now was to rebuild the French productive structure and key ministers and important labor union leaders, even when these were communists, could make a contribution or hinder progress, depending on how they were handled.

That Monnet was accused by an American embassy official of being sympathetic to communism must have been as baffling to him as Henry Morgenthau's suspicion at the start of World War II that he was a tool of investment bankers or, even worse, sympathetic to Nazi interests. Ultimately he had no ideology beyond a hatred of extreme nationalism and a great respect for the western democracies for whom he worked in two tragic world wars. His conclusion from these earlier experiences seem to form a rather simple Monnet political philosophy: the need to cooperate toward building a peaceful and democratic world.

2 Jul: After Soviets refuse to participate, British and French governments issue joint call for 22 nation conference in Paris in response to Marshall Plan proposal. EAH 389

9-10 Jul: Will Clayton, US assistant secretary of state, and US Ambassador Caffery meet JM and Henri Alphand of French foreign ministry on US view of European economic situation and Marshall speech. JM shows proposed questionaire for each participating country in coming Paris conference on recovery. FRUS II 1001; FRUS III 315-18

12 Jul: Opening of Paris conference on Marshall Plan. FRUS III 331; Oliver Franks of UK is interim chairman of the Committee on Economic Cooperation created by the conference and JM is nominally vice chairman. GB 77; Franks relies on JM to get quick answers from French government and for informal advice on food, agriculture, and political connections. Alex Danchev, Oliver Franks, Founding Father (Oxford, 1993) 66-7

18 Jul: JM writes Foreign Minister Bidault suggesting Committee on European Economic Cooperation (CEEC) set up five-man committee with small staff to coordinate European response to Marshall's speech. Bidault responds suggesting JM head group but he refuses, to avoid blurring Plan responsibilities. DF 168

22 Jul: JM sends memo on the Conference on European Cooperation underway in Paris to Foreign Minister Bidault warning that Marshall Plan means that recovery of France and Europe is tied to future of Germany: "I do not believe the Soviets want to end their cooperation with Europe nor that the USA wants to create a Western block (sic) to provide itself with the Ruhr as an industrial-military force." Yet, he notes, these are current interpretations from the conference. He then reflects on differences between western attitudes and those of USSR; the war was an example of how these two sides understand cooperation very differently. The rupture at the conference reflects the different attitudes among the western powers on how to deal with both Germany and with Russia. France can play a key role.

Concerning the Ruhr, he writes, "the French consider [it] essential to their security and the peace of Europe. [They] can only have confidence [in US aid} if the development of German resources is coupled with safeguards...that they will not ...be used again by the Germans to make war.... The internationalization of the Ruhr is an essential element in European peace." FJM AMF 14/1/4; DF 184

In the 16-nation conference on Marshall Plan aid, Monnet and others are groping for an immediate solution to the problems of the German Ruhr region's coal and steel production. They also seek the longer term political goal of integrating Germany with its neighbors to prevent renewed German domination. As the following meetings and notes indicate, the thinking is still unclear as how this long-term goal can mesh with short term problems like the Ruhr. Monnet seems adamant that Germany must not again have the Ruhr under its exclusive control.

24 Jul: JM writes long memo to Georges Bidault, French foreign minister, on "Marshall Credits," reviewing steps to insure that French policy, in responding to the Marshall Plan, place highest priority on the Ruhr in a European context under which Germany prosperity is tied to Europe's. The two conditions for the Marshall Plan to succeed are a resolution of the problem of Germany satisfactory for France and insuring the maximum use of American credits for French

prosperity. FJM AMF 14/1/6 reprinted in CE 55-64

27 Jul: JM notes, in memo on coming Big Three foreign ministers meeting, that whatever happens to Germany, internationalizing the Ruhr is essential for the peace of Europe. The Ruhr must remain an `actif europeen' and not the mainstay of a remilitarized Germany. "The Ruhr must be the point in Germany where the occupation is indefinite and its exploitation must be directed internationally...." FJM AMF 14/1/4; IW I 99

29 Jul: W.Clayton, US ass't secretary of state, dines in Paris with JM who says France is the key to the Marshall Plan's success. France and the US must agree on Germany and France must get its monetary and financial house in order, JM says. Clayton notes: "Ruhr should not be internationalized or detached from Germany" but that there should be an "international authority of which Germany would be part, clothed with power of allocating [Ruhr] production as between domestic and foreign." FRUS II 1011-12

30 Jul: JM gives President Auriol copy of the memo he wrote to Prime Minister Bidault on French policy re Germany and US. "...certain German resources, like Ruhr coal, are necessary for the immediate recovery of Europe--and the recovery of Germany itself is a necessity for a prosperous Europe. Seventy million Germans should fill the role of producers and customers in a prosperous Europe....It is clear that no European program meets reality in the eyes of the Americans if it does not include Germany..." VA annex VII

4 Aug: JM has lunch with President Auriol and Leon Blum. With Auriol, JM discusses the Marshall Plan conference underway in Paris. The three then discuss the study committees, where Marjolin represents JM, looking at European payment mechanisms, electricity networks etc. Finally they discuss role of USSR in rebuilding Europe and possibility of rupture between east and west over the issue. VA 381-4

6 Aug: Clayton, French Foreign Minister Bidault and JM lunch in Paris; Bidault proposes a Ruhr board to allocate area's production. Before the peace treaty, the US, UK, Benelux countries and France would assign this production; after the treaty, Germany would become a board member. France has abandoned, Bidault said, any plan to detach the Ruhr from Germany or internationalize it. FRUS II 1022-23

7 Aug: JM sees President Auriol on progress of Committee of Sixteen (European countries planning response of US Marshall Plan). VA 388-9

10 Aug: G Ball gets phone call from JM and two days later arrives in Paris for urgent consultations on European committee's response to Marshall Plan. Ball expresses concern over size ($28b) and scope of draft committee report. GB 77-8

Monnet was often able to bring friends from earlier phases of his life into subsequent ones. He had known George Ball and Robert Nathan during World War II in Washington and greatly respected their dedication and energy. Earlier

he had used Dwight Morrow from his World War I days in London in his interwar business career as he had used Lord Kindersley from his Canada days selling cognac in those same London days.

He was able to soften these transitions---prompted apparently by a low threshold of boredom which caused him to change jobs every 3-4 years--- by these bridging friendships. These retained personal ties, however, were not prompted by any psychological dependence on Monnet's part; instead he used, even manipulated, his friendships, not for his personal gain, but for some public good.

12 Aug: French and American representatives start talks on respective positions on industry agreement regarding Germany. US and UK are already in general accord on subject which is urgent because the expanding German econcomy needs adjustments under current Western occupation. France wants strict limits, supported by other western countries, on Ruhr production to prevent renewed German militarism which has always depended on Ruhr production. US-UK position is that rebuilding of Europe, including Germany, under Marshall Plan will require full use of German economic resources, including industry. US public and Congress also need assurance that US aid is prudently used which means maximum use of German resources which are also involved in Germany's neighbors' economies. FRUS II 1028-31, 1047-60

14 Aug: US Asst Secretary of State W Clayton, American Ambassador J Caffery, French Foreign Minister G Bidault, JM and others end talks on Ruhr which Bidault insists must never again be used militarily against France and on proposed international board to control Ruhr production. American side will try to "whittle down" French demands to a minimum before coming London talks on German industrial production. FRUS II 1029-33, 1050-55

22 Aug: John Foster Dulles, in New York, writes JM in Paris: "I am wondering if you are coming over here....I think we might usefully talk together....I greatly hope something can be done toward achieving a greater degree of economic unity in Europe which I assume involves not only dealing with customs barriers, but with unconvertible currencies. The task is a hard one but one which all of your friends here feel you are uniquely qualified to lead to a successful conclusion." DP

Whether and how Monnet responded to Dulles' note is not clear. But the two had long and close personal ties and great mutual respect. Dulles kept active in international affairs while maintaining his partnership in a top New York law firm. During the war he led a church group supporting a world organization for peace and urged President Roosevelt to convert the United Nations from a wartime alliance to such a postwar union. After the war, he advised the State Department on the Japanese peace treaty and was an active laymen in the Federal Council of Churches. Recently he had become a leading foreign affairs adviser to Gov. Dewey of New York in the coming presidential election and the presumptive Secretary of State in a Republican administration.

From their friendship which began at the Versailles peace conference, Monnet and Dulles moved together on separate but compatible paths toward the agreed goals of peace and cooperation among men and nations. Their paths would, in a few years, converge in close and fruitful cooperation.

22-27 Aug: London tripartite talks on German industrial levels. Communique refers to possibility of international control of Ruhr. France also achieves goal of postponing major Ruhr policy changes at least until Big Three foreign ministers meeting in London in November or possibly in peace treaty. Split of US State and War Departments on German industry also postponed. FRUS II 1047-1066

27 Aug: JM tells President Auriol that US must know that Europe will collapse without American aid. They discuss need to organize French aid effort through committees which analyze needs and direct aid. VA 411

30 Aug: JM tells President Auriol "The year 1948 will be the hardest one for France but we will save ourselves if America does not let Europe collapse." VA 417

3 Sep: G Ball flies to Washington from Paris with draft text of Conference of Sixteen [nations] report to confer secretly with State Department allies. They share Ball's reservations. GB 78

5 Sep: JM tells President Auriol that the Conference of the Sixteen talks are going better. Europe needs six to eight billion dollars and France two billion of this sum for next year. Everything depends on France's stabilization. To convince the Americans of our need, we must do some difficult things: The Plan must draw up its program, the unions must support its execution and all branches of society must show their cooperation. VA 438

8 Sep: Ball flies back to Paris with informal US response to draft Committee of Sixteen report. GB 78

George Ball became another American intimate of Monnet; together with Dulles, Jack McCloy, US High Commissioner in Germany, and, later, journalist James Reston, these were among his closest lifelong friends, in the view of Francois Fontaine, the collaborator on the Monnet memoirs. Ball exemplified what Monnet wrote there: "...nothing important is done in the United States without lawyers...In the United States a great lawyer is a great citizen." Of Ball himself, Monnet wrote: "Powerfully built, he exuded strength and level-headedness, like many Americans of his type, whose massive appearance matches their striking command of both physical and intellectual resources. His wisdom, his boldness in taking decisions and his loyalty to his friends gave him great moral authority.... (JMM 227)

Ball later, reflecting on his friend's defining characteristics, wrote that "his apparent imperturbability...to the admiration of his friends and the

exasperation of his opponents" marked Monnet "as an incorrigible optimist."
Ball also witnessed Monnet's impatience; more than once he heard, through the
static on the trans-Atlantic phone lines, Monnet's hoarse words "Catch the night
plane for Paris!" (GB 76,98; D.DiLeo in MATA 141-169)

22 Sep: Sixteen European countries end conference responding to
Marshall Plan proposal of US Secretary of State. JM involved in drafting final
report on four year program including emergency aid for coming winter and
ambitious goals for long term reconstruction. NYT 24 Sep; FRUS III 438

28 Sep: G Ball in London hears in phone call from JM in Paris of his
distress that he [JM] had casually told visiting Congressman Christian Herter,
studying foreign aid needs, of a rumor that French peasants had at least $2 billion
hidden under their mattresses. Herter mentioned this belief in a press conference.
JM persuades Ball to get Herter to make clarifying remark but rumor persists.
GB 78-9

2 Oct: JM named by prime minister Paul Ramadier as chairman of
"special `balance sheet' commission" which will measure French inflation
problem for 1948. Other members include representatives of labor, farmers,
employers. NYT 3 Oct

5 Oct: Referendum in the Saar shows 91.5% for autonomy with less than
ten per cent for union with France. Coal from the region was to be removed from
the German production pool and attributed instead to France from April 1949.
PG 532

21 Oct: President Auriol receives JM who brings a letter from Leon Blum
which says that the issue of Palestine will be brought before the Council of
Ministers tomorrow. VA 480

31 Oct: First Six Month report on Monnet Plan says results are substantial
"even though obscured by the day-to-day struggles and anxieties of the French
people and the effects of the current monetary instability." Press Release, French
Embassy (Washington DC), 5 Feb 48

18 Nov: JM meets with President Auriol on the reform committee which
seeks to balance economic and fiscal factors in considering salaries and prices.
VA 549

19 Nov: JM discusses wage and other union demands with President
Auriol. VA 562

24 Nov: Robert Schuman forms government, succeeding Paul Ramadier.
RM 245

30 Nov [Sunday]: President Auriol telephones JM at Houjarray to discuss
the proposals of Daniel Mayer on prices and salaries. VA 597

6 Dec: JM proposes a "levy" or tax on higher incomes to Minister of

Finance Rene Mayer to cover partly an inflationary gap in country's budget. FJM AMF 1/13/245

19 Dec: President Truman implements Marshall Plan by submitting special legislative message to Congress on European Recovery Program (ERP). NYT; JMM 268

1948

SOMETIME THIS YEAR: JM meets Theodore H White who interviews him on the Plan, the first of many encounters between Monnet and one of his generation's most prominent American writers. They developed a close relationship founded on mutual respect and on JM's broad trust of American journalists. White, author of a dozen books on China, Europe and US presidential elections, called JM "a secular saint" and the "shrewdest of the postwar statesmen." But White also said JM was "warm hearted but cold blooded" and had "the irritating habit of abruptly presenting a critically important question [and then] snap `Don't explain. Just answer yes or no. We both know your reasoning either way. I just want to see how you add things up.'" TW 369, 425, 436-7

1 Jan: Regional customs agreement joins Belgium, Netherlands and Luxembourg in Benelux union. The agreement had been made in London in 1944 by the governments-in-exile of the three countries. RP I

2 Jan: Finance Minister Georges Bidault, at JM urging, insists on using French counterpart funds generated from US aid for the Monnet Plan. IW I 100

16 Jan: Prime Minister Schuman persuades Assembly to pass series of financial measures to insure the Monnet Plan has separate financing. JMM 263

20 Jan: In meeting with French President Auriol to discuss Marshall Plan, JM says France should not fear US conditions on aid; there will be a bilateral agreement but France must commit itself to a four year program for increasing production of key goods like steel, coal and cement. VA 44

12 Feb: US Ambassador in London Lewis Douglas suggests State Dept consider widening Ruhr Authority to include other European areas, possibly because of his conversations with JM. FRUS II 98-9 cited by P Winand in MATA 110-111

13 Feb: JM writes Frankfurter: "I had not, during all my life, excepting my younger years, stayed as long in France as I did for the last two years....I have formed now... of the character and temperament of my own countrymen, a judgment and opinion which certainly differ from those I had in the past." Asks Frankfurter to ask Robert Sherwood to send JM those papers of the Harry Hopkins memoir involving JM in the 1941-42 armament program. FF

This letter from Monnet, coupled with similar comments (below and in 1946) to a French acquaintance, may indicate only his casual reflections on how

little he knew about life in France in 1945 when, at age 57, he returned to his
native country to work there after a nearly 20 year absence. But his comment
to Frankfurter about his understanding of the "character and temperament" of
his own people suggests a deeper reflection about national character in which
Monnet does not often indulge. Even in his Memoirs, written almost 30 years
later, he does not venture into this subject beyond some compliments about
American dynamism and self-confidence and about the dire consequences of
European nationalism.

16 Feb: JM gives US Ambassador Caffery "strictly confidential" comments on French supply situation and its relation to $150 million US Export-Import Bank credit. FRUS III 626-8

24 Feb: R Sherwood writes JM, following up phone call, on latter's concern about what material from Algiers in 1943 Sherwood was planning to use in his forthcoming book on Roosevelt and Hopkins. RES

1 Mar: "Yesterday Jean Monnet ended by declaring: `I have never lived so much in my country as in the past two years and I am beginning to understand her.'" Jacques Dumaine, Quai d'Orsay, (London, 1958) 159.

11 Mar: JM, who has just returned from London trip where he explained Monnet Plan to Sir Stafford Cripps, UK Chancellor of the Exchequer, and discusses situation in UK with President Auriol: A British-French federation would strengthen both countries internally, allow their "full independence vis-a-vis the Soviet Union and the United States, and settle at once all problems between the two countries." A pessimistic JM thinks war is on its way, Auriol notes. JM also asks Auriol not to tell UK ambassador Oliver Harvey of this conversation since he will report everything to London. VA 144; JM had also renewed his acquaintance with Sir Edwin Plowden at these meetings. He had known Plowden during the war when the Briton was deeply engaged in aircraft production matters. Because of these meetings with Cripps and others, Plowden was named head of the Cabinet office of central planning [a counterpart to the French Plan.]JMM 278

Plowden later noted that Anglo-American relations had priority for UK [over Anglo-French ties] which had a different perspective from the French because American aid had allowed Britain to emerge victorious from the war. FJM AML 313/109 cited by HU 152

15 Mar: Committee on European Economic Cooperation (CEEC) meets in Paris to establish permanent body. JM uses advice from George Ball to propose a strong executive. When this fails, JM loses interest in resulting Organization on European Economic Cooperation (OEEC). He tells Ball "...[T]he OEEC's nothing; it's only a watered-down British approach to Europe---talk, consultation, action only by unanimity. That's no way to make Europe." GB 80-1; FRUS III 395; JMM 271

17 Mar: Britain, France, Benelux countries sign Brussels Pact setting up Western European Union (WEU), forerunner of NATO. MATA 81; RM 247

20 Mar: JM begins month-long visit to Washington---his first in two years--- to negotiate a wheat agreement to raise French bread ration from 200 to 250 grams per day. IW I 100; NYT 21 Mar

30 Mar: R Sherwood writes JM, enclosing copies of 11 Mar and 3 Jul 1943 messages from JM to Hopkins. He will quote from the first without identifying JM as author, and will not use the 3 Jul letter at all. RES; RES:R&H 721

APRIL: JM spends much of the month in Washington to obtain additional US wheat to help France until its own harvest arrives in the fall. But he also uses the time to refresh his acquaintances with "men who cannot afford to make mistakes---bankers, industrialists, lawyers, newspapermen." JMM 271

16 Apr: CEEC conference ends with western foreign ministers meeting which sets up permanent OEEC with JM aide Robert Marjolin as secretary general. FRUS III 423; GB 81. JM is skeptical, partly because unanimity is required for key decisions. He tells Robert Schuman that a true federation of western Europe is needed. RSC 37; JMM 267-72

Monnet gradually realized that the OEEC, useful as it might be, was not the answer to Europe's fractured condition, nor was aid from the Marshall Plan. Looking from Washington, he gropes again to find a new approach to Europe's political problems. In London in 1940 he grasped at an Anglo-French union to keep his country in the fight. In the midst of the war, in Algiers, he wrote a memo on how postwar Europe might organize. In 1944 he had discussed with journalist John Davenport and with US war secretary Stimson a plan to demilitarize the Ruhr in an international zone. Yet ideas about uniting Europe went back centuries; in the interwar years statesmen like Aristide Briand and Winston Churchill had speculated about how a subdued Europe could reorganize itself better. But Monnet's vision, even when chimerical as in London or incomplete, as in Algiers, was centered on small steps, not wide speculations.

Here, in writing Schuman from Washington, he commits himself to start thinking again, now in broader terms and in the midst of the Cold War. The example of the United States for a new Europe is on his mind he tells the French prime minister. Two years later the two men would produce an urgent, compact and bold answer using that example.

18 Apr: JM writes Prime Minister Schuman from Washington: "...[A]chieving the [Monnet] Plan is now possible because of the Marshall [Plan] credits."In same letter, JM says he refused Spaak's suggestion that JM head the OEEC executive committee.

He then reflects on the strength and dynamism of the United States and its willingness, however reluctant, to go to war even while doing everything it can to prevent a new conflict. " America is on the move....I cannot but be struck by the relationship that threatens to develop between this great and dynamic nation and the countries of Europe.... [T]o tackle the present situation...and to match the American efforts, the countries of Western Europe must turn their national efforts into a truly European effort."

When he returns he will, aside from his Plan efforts, devote himself to contribute to making a "real Federation of the West." FJM AMF 22/1/5 reprinted in MSC 37-38;EC 68-70; JMM 272-3

----- Monnet also writes the French Foreign Minister, Georges Bidault, from Washington with a somewhat different emphasis. While praising the "dynamism" of the US he suggests France is a pawn or stake ("l'enjeu") in the Cold War because of its dependence on the United States and that it must transform itself from this role to one of "independence and collaboration." Intergovernmental organs like OEEC will not suffice. Then Monnet's thoughts reconnect with his letter to Schuman telling Bidault also that the answer is a "federation of the West" but now to prevent war. Putting the thoughts of these two letters together, Monnet believes that the goal of independent collaboration with the United States can come best when France leads in constructing a "real Federation of the West." IW I 100 citing AN Papiers Bidault, 457 AP 21; IW II 165; FJM AMF 22/1/6 reprinted in EC 66-7; JMM 272

19 Apr: JM in Washington concludes talks on wheat allocations without getting increase of per capita bread allowance from 200 to 250 grams per day which US aides call impossible, citing difficulties in even maintaining the lower level. JM musters, without success, additional argument that French non-communist unions need support on bread allowance to counter communist unions goal of a 20% increase in industrial wages. FRUS III 631-2 (See 20 May)

23 Apr: WC Bullitt, JM's friend and former US ambassador to Moscow and Paris, is named vice president (President is Senator Wm Fulbright) of newly reorganized American Committee for a United Europe. NYT 24 Apr. But further changes under Allen Dulles, an influential committee members, drops both Bullitt and Fulbright as members, and adds new ones. 24 Nov 1949 letter [on historical background of organization] from Count Richard Coudenhove-Kalergi, President of Pan-European Movement, to Gen William Donovan, Chairman of the American Committee for a United Europe. WCB

30 Apr, 5 May: JM sees President Auriol briefly on results of Washington visit. VA

7-10 May: Congress of Europe held in the Hague brings 750 leading European politicians together.(JM was not among them having just returned from month in Washington negotiating a wheat deal with the US government). They agree on goal of European political and economic union, a European Assembly and a Court of Human Rights. One year later, the Council of Europe initialed the resulting Council of Europe statute. RM 262-3; JMM 273

10 May: JM sends Prime Minister Schuman proposed draft of speech to be given by the prime minister in Bordeaux on arrival of first ship with Marshall Plan aid for France. Speech cites last year's disastrous wheat harvest and consequent shortfall of 40% of nation's bread needs. US aid covered three quarters of shortfall. This US aid given free and without French counterpart payments. MSC 40-2

13 May: Milton Katz, an old JM acquaintance from the war years in Washington, writes JM asking help in finding an apartment for the next year when he becomes general counsel to the European mission to the Economic Cooperation Administration (ECA) under Averell Harriman. HSTL, Katz Papers

20 May: In "urgent, most immediate" telegram to Paris, State Department asks that JM be informed that US government is preparing extra wheat shipments to France in early July which will enable increase in daily bread allowance to 250 grams in June. Announcement should be made public to maximum extent possible in France, telegram advises. FRUS III 634-5 (See 19 Apr)

Monnet's plea in Washington just one month earlier for more wheat seems here to bear belated fruit. His emphasis in April on the political utility of more wheat as a counter to the French communist unions indicates that Washington listens (if hesitantly) to his advice on French politics.

1 Jun: London Conference, which started in February, ends with agreement on the creation of the Federal Republic of Germany from the three western allied zones of occupation. France fails to get further restrictions on German industrial development and has to be content with the International Ruhr Authority which puts the industrial area under western control but does not detach it from Germany as France wanted. PG 532

9 Jun: JM writes Hopkin's biographer, Robert Sherwood, from Paris on latter's draft chapter on Algiers: My efforts during this time "concentrated on bringing about the creation of the French National Committee---thus creating one democratic French expression for those Frenchmen who wanted to fight in the war and recreate the republic after liberation. Would it be possible when you mention `the progress that was being made in that direction' to set in its true light the essential part I played in it during my stay in Algiers?" RES

10 Jun: Creation of the Monnet Plan's Commission on Investments announced. HR:RC

25 Jun: Soviet blockade of West Berlin is answered by Allied air lift. RM 248

28 Jun: Franco-American agreement on Marshall Plan aid signed. FRUS II 715-16; NARA, ECA SRE France, Report #18 on Interim Aid, July 1948 cited in FD 172

7 Jul: JM see President Auriol briefly. VA

28 Jul: Robert Schuman replaces Georges Bidault as French Foreign Minister in the new government of Andre Marie, bringing into office a man strongly favoring French-German reconciliation. RM 247-8

12 Aug: Elizabeth Bentley, confessed Soviet spy, testifies before congressional committee [and later on 30 Aug and again in 1950, 1952 and 1953] that a fellow agent was George Silverman. The latter, employed in 1945 by the French Mission in Washington and cited by JM in his memoirs as a expert hired "to introduce our pioneer French planners to the new [economic measuring] techniques." When Silverman later gave limited testimony in his defense he did not cite his French mission work nor did JM apparently ever indicate that he knew Silverman personally nor that he realized that the American economist he cited in 1945 was ever involved in the spy scandals which dominated Washington political circles in the 1948-53 period. In fact, JMM seems to have confused George Silverman with James Silberman, another American economist whom JM did know well in 1948 when the latter advised the Plan on labor matters. NYT 13, 31 Aug 1948; 31 Aug, 1 Sep 1950; 24 Oct 1952; 24 Aug, 18,22 Nov and 17 Dec 1953; JMM 227; interview with Silberman, 2002

27 Aug: US State Department press statement, quoting preamble to the Economic Cooperation Act, says US "government strongly favors the progressively closer integration of the free nations of Western Europe...by the European themselves...." NARA 840.50/10-1848

28 Aug: President Auriol gets note from JM on France's serious financial state. VA

1-4 Sep: Bullitt attends Interlaken, Switzerland conference of the European Parliamentary Union as vice president of US Committee for a Free and United Europe. WCB

29 Sep: Thomas Finletter, head of ECA United Kingdom, writes long memo which ECA head Averell Harriman has approved, expressing concern ECA is pursuing goal of political not merely economic cooperation among Europeans. Memo also sees danger of isolationism in some expressions of European unity. NARA 840.00/ll-2048

30 Sep: Journalist Walter Lippmann writes JM that "it is important that French thought be put on the inevitable fact that a [US] military retirement from ...Germany...is over a time the only alternative to war." Lippmann speculates that US military involvement in Europe need not end entirely and that France could be reassured by some continued stationing of US forces at Germany's periphery. WL 524

6 Oct: President Auriol receives JM who is very pessimistic; he does not want to appear before Parliament to ask for tax increases. VA

29 Oct: JM appears before the Plan subcommittee on productivity with James M Silberman, a US Department of Labor expert who is on a Marshall Plan

mission to the UK and France. Silberman had met R Donn, a French embassy official in Washington, who was studying American productivity methods and it was Donn who brought together Monnet and Silberman before they made their plea for renewing the French productivity program which had faltered several years earlier. JM later set up a Group de Travail on productivity which was active for several years despite resistance from both industry and some labor groups. He later called Silberman "the most intelligent man I ever met." RK (Richard Kuisel) 337 citing AN 80AJ75 CG; Interview with Donn, May 2003

Silberman impressed Monnet and became involved in the Plan's labor productivity work as part of the Marshall Plan. But they first met in Paris in 1948 (and not, as the American historian Richard Kuisel, suggests, during the war). Silberman visited many French factories to study productivity problems and helped arrange visits by French specialists to US factories over the next four years. He was awarded the Legion of Honor by France for this work. (Interviews with Donn and Silberman, 2002-5)

18 Nov: JF Dulles addresses American Club of Paris on American attitudes toward European unity. "Americans are generally willing to join in one great effort to help end the disunity of Western Europe and to substitute for its weakness the strength of unity. That is what many Americans think they are doing as they contribute to the European Recovery program and as they contemplate joining in some Atlantic Pact for collective defense." European Movement and the Council of Europe (London, 1949) 162-3

30 Nov: In speech in the French Assembly socialist Andre Philip, former finance minister, urges government to accept international authority over Ruhr to divide its exports among European countries; he calls this plan, which could include the Saar and the Lorraine regions as well---for an international authority over European heavy industries, a "public cartel." NYT 1 Dec 1948; PG 535

1 Dec: President Auriol reports sharp attacks on JM during Council of Ministers meeting on US and UK demands that France raise taxes. JM is accused of supplying information to and supporting US. VA

8 Dec: JM visit Auriol, expresses his discouragement with budget and says he may resign. VA

21 Dec: Auriol reports JM still very pessimistic; the President then calls the prime minister and describes JM's feelings; Auriol notes JM does not have the authority or the responsibility [of the respective ministers]. VA

1949

This year saw Monnet's attention divided between his Plan responsibilities and the growing crisis in French-German affairs. The latter was marked by Germany's burgeoning growth following its currency reform the previous year and a growing fear in France that German industrial strength would outpace that of France. With his Plan responsibilities, Monnet keeps in close touch with

American adviser James Silberman who sought to focus the Commissariat au Plan on improving French productivity.

10 Jan: Journalist Walter Lippmann writes JM on appointment of Dean Acheson as Secretary of State and the reorganization of the State Department. Lippmann worries about the new Western European Union becoming "an agreement to maintain old style imperialism in Asia" and asks JM to express the anti-imperial tradition of the United States which would resent jeopardizing the "moral foundations" of the WEU. WL 525

29 Jan: Creation of the Council of Europe. HR:RC

7 Feb: George Kennan, head of State Department's policy unit, drafts proposal that Germany cannot be dealt with in isolation and that it must be integrated into a "general European union." But "form and pace" of this movement are for Europeans themselves to decide. Memo submitted to Steering Group on Germany, NARA

17 Feb: JM and aide E Hirsch have private lunch with Edwin Plowden as initial step in what French, and JM, hope will lead to extensive Anglo-French economic cooperation. JM hopes that Plowden, who became head of Central Economic Planning Staff (CEPS) and thus JM's counterpart, might work with French Plan on integrating two countries' planning. Plowden is cautious. EP 71-2

2 Mar: Frankfurter writes to JM that he talked with Sherwood as JM requested. "Come now, stop delaying your trip. Marion joins me in sending affectionate regards...." FF

-----: JM meets President Auriol on draft law JM prepared on Anglo-French economic cooperation. VA 137

EARLY MARCH: JM invited to lunch by French Finance Minister Maurice Petsche with his British counterpart, Sir Stafford Cripps to consider respective plans the two ministers had submitted to OEEC on ways to improve intra-European trade and to reduce need for dollars. "You won't reach agreement unless you make it your ultimate aim to merge the British and French economies," JM told the two men. JMM 277-8

3-7 Mar: JM meets in London several times with Plowden and others to encourage UK to take lead on resolving vacuum between western European communism and US capitalism by proposing joint French-UK plan on Germany. UK Foreign Office is wary but Plowden's boss, Stafford Cripps, encourages further talks. NAUK FO 371 77933; EP 73

10 Mar: JM tells President Auriol of his optimism on his plan establishing full economic coordination for the government. VA 229

26 Mar: Franco-Italian customs union, later enlarged by Benelux countries, forms Fritalux which seeks economic coordination but lacks central decision authority. JMM 281

29 Mar: WS Churchill addresses lunch at Ritz Carlton Hotel in New York of the American Committee on United Europe (ACUE), now chaired by JM acquaintance from WWII years, William Donovan. MG-ND; M. Beloff, The United States and the Uniting of Europe (Washington, 1963) 72.

In addition to seeking American support for European integration, ACUE later funnels funds to the European Movement, a counterpart organization already in existence in Europe. According to Tom Braden, first ACUE executive director, the organization got official US funds through the Central Intelligence Agency (CIA) for its support of the European Movement. Other members of the ACUE in 1950 include Stacy May, JM's colleague from the Victory Program days; Allen Dulles, brother of John Foster Dulles and later head of CIA; and Gen. Lucius Clay, US military commander. Interview with Braden, 25 Aug 1992

8 Apr: West Germany receives authority to resume its political life under the Washington Agreements of the occupying powers. This prepares for the election later in the year of Chancellor K Adenauer and President T Heuss. PG 532

20 Apr: Edwin Plowden, of Britain's cabinet planning office, comes to Paris with advisers and to JM's home in Houjarray for four day consultation. Hopes for specific economic cooperation between the two countries eventually prove impossible. JMM 278-80

25 Apr: At Westminster Conference of the European Movement, Andre Philip, chair of the basic industries committee, proposes a "European Public Institution" to set policies for basic industries of coal, steel, electricity and transportation. PG 527-528

28 Apr: Western Allies establish International Ruhr Authority but Germany refuses to take part until its equality is accepted. NYT 29 Apr; JMM 283; PG 535

21 Apr: JM hosts three day meeting with Plowden and his advisers Robert Hall and Alan Hitchman at Houjarray to follow up earlier meetings in London at which JM explained Commissariat au Plan and which helped influence British in planning operation of Plowden's office. JM hopes that Houjarray meetings might lead to deeper Anglo-French cooperation beyond short-term trade questions even toward federation but he concluded later in year that Britain was not prepared for anything beyond, in Plowden's words, "ordinary commercial exchanges." JMM 279-81; EP 74-5 (citing Richard Mayne, The Recovery of Europe); Robert Hall Diaries (London, 1980) 56-7; JMM 280-81

The meetings with Plowden confirmed for Monnet the impossibility of counting on Britain to help unite Europe. A year earlier he had told Stafford Cripps and his French counterpart, French Finance Minister Maurice Petsche, that "You won't reach agreement [on harmonizing their respective plans for OEEC cooperation] unless you make it your ultimate aim to merge the British and French economies." Now the talks with Plowden one year later confirm that Britain has no intention of delegating sovereignty. "We'd won the war" Plowden later told Monnet, "and we weren't ready to form special links with the continent." [See ERB 377-385 for reflections on these events in interviews with Hirsch and Uri.]

From now on Monnet would center on the French-German relation and where it could lead. This concentration coincided with Schuman's need to initiate a solution to the German problem by next year. American insistence, in the person of Dean Acheson, motivated the course taken cautiously by the French foreign minister over the next eight months.

SUMMER: Council of Europe assembly considers several ambitious goals including "creation of a European political authority with limited functions but real powers." But together with a later plan for a public steel authority these ideas failed when the council's Committee of Minister, representing national sovereignty, buried them. JMM 281-2

20 Jul: JM writes Frankfurter asking that he see Jean Forgeot, secretary general of the Presidence of the Republic, who is in the U.S. privately. He adds, "Anna has passed her baccalaureat which pleases her mother very much" FLF

23 Aug: At first session of Consultative Assembly of the Council of Europe several delegates, including the Frenchmen Edouard Bonnefous and Andre Philip, propose internationalizing European coal and steel industries but most delegates will not go that far. PG 528

15 Sep: Acheson, Bevin and Schuman and aides meet in New York at UN session and later in Washington and agree that Schuman must propose some solution to German problem by next May's meeting of the three foreign ministers in London. Acheson and Bevin tell Schuman: "We fully concur in entrusting our French colleague [Schuman] with formulating our common policy on Germany." JMM 299; FJM OH, Bernard Clappier

-----Discussions continue in Washington where the three foreign policy chiefs review the policy of dismantling German factories related to war production. After considering German request to end practice, Acheson notes: I said that we are faced with a miserable choice but that we had to make a choice....We are likely to yield eventually under German pressure [and US public opinion which also opposes dismantling] and not because of our own policy decisions....Perhaps the situation is hopeless. Maybe Germany can't be a useful quiet member of the European community....In the long run, if there is to be an answer, there must be a solution of French-German troubles under French leadership." Acheson Memo of Conversation, FRUS III 599-603

-----During long discussion between Acheson, Schuman and their aides, the French participants are told that Congress must be convinced that Europe is progressing toward unity and this need reflects US public opinion as a whole.

FRUS IV 654

16 Sep: Konrad Adenauer elected Chancellor of the Federal Republic of Germany just before the three-power Occupation Statute comes into force under which West Germany regains some of its sovereignty but not in foreign policy, armaments, reparations or decartelization. Adenauer makes clear his goal of seeking membership in both Council of Europe and NATO for Germany. RM 267-8

8 Oct: JM tells President Auriol it is absolutely necessary to prevent any wage increases which would causes price and then profit increases and produce a new and devastating devaluation. VA 365

11 Oct: JM discusses danger of German cartels with George Bingham, head of US economic aid program in France. Only US, JM says, can restrain Germany. FRUS IV 444

The problem of Germany arose gradually from different strands of concern by Britain, France and the US but with dramatic effects in France in 1948-49. The German economic recovery, following its currency reforms, meant for the French a renewed danger of German economic dominance and its political consequences. Dean Acheson focuses on France and its key role in resolving the problem of Germany.

19 Oct: Secretary of State Acheson sends long cable to American ambassadors of west Europe about to meet in Paris with his views on European integration. "A dominant consideration...is problem of Western Germany" which is showing signs "it is taking a familiar and dangerous nationalist turn." To prevent this, Germany must be "harnessed to the security and welfare of Western Europe as a whole.... The key to progress towards integration is in French hands....France and France alone can take the decisive leadership in integrating Western Germany into Western Europe ....We will certainly not acquiesce in any British attempts to obstruct integration.... By progress toward integration...I mean [the Europeans deciding] on a timetable for the creation of supra-national institutions [which] must be created by the countries who are to participate in them....[T]hey will fall short of the needs of the time if they did not involve some merger of sovereignty. NARA, 840.00/10; FRUS IV 469-72

22 Oct: At end of two day meeting in Paris with US ambassadors of west Europe, Asst Secretary of State Perkins replies to Acheson's 19 Oct cable and questions his view that France alone can effect Western European integration. "[W]ithout the active participation of the UK, western European integration will have little if any value." On this Perkins finds "complete unanimity of opinion" with US ambassadors Bruce [France], Douglas [UK], Dunn Italy], Harriman [special envoy for Europe], Kirk [USSR] and McCloy [Germany]. "British are holding back...and in some cases are actively endeavoring to restrain the continental powers in even the limited extent to which they are prepared to go."

Perkins said ambassadors opposed to "some new sweeping plan involving at this time extensive surrender of sovereignty" and prefer step-by-step measures within OEEC, Western Union or NATO.

British should be pressed, ambassadors believe, to live up to their commitments "to further and not obstruct European cooperation." NARA 840.00/10-2249; FRUS IV 342-44 (cable); 472-96 (summary of conference)

24 Oct: In continuing dialogue with US west European ambassadors, Acheson reminds them of 13 Jan 48 memo by UK Foreign Minister Bevin to US Secretary of State Marshall which stressed need for some form of western European union backed by "Americas and Dominions," that Britain "could no longer stand outside Europe and insist that its problems were separate from those of its European neighbors ... that policy outlined [above] would require lead from UK since Western Europe would look to it for political and moral guidance...."NARA 840.50

In another cable same day to same recipients, Acheson clarifies that he knows France alone cannot lead to solution of German problem; UK must help but France and others may be willing to go farther than UK in integration (including W Germany). NARA 840.00/10-2249

26 Oct: US ambassador Douglas in London cables Acheson on discussion that morning with UK foreign minister Bevin on needed British support for economic integration of Europe. Douglas cites strong congressional support he heard on last Washington visit for this integration. Bevin has doubts about Paul Henri Spaak, Belgian Socialist, as head of OEEC. Finally, Douglas reports, Bevin said Washington perhaps did not understand UK could not accept European integration that would impair other responsibilities. "She was, he said, a world power and not merely a European power." NARA 840.00/10-2649; FRUS IV 435

-------; UK foreign minister Bevin sends Acheson personal message on his country's attitude on economic integration with western European countries: UK realizes proposals on integration may now be presented. UK is a power with world wide responsibilities, as well as those under Atlantic Alliance and Brussels treaty. Also we want to avoid any objective incompatible with Anglo-American-Canadian economic talks last September.

In reply (28 Oct) Acheson says "frankly...I am troubled...by...what appears to me to imply the negative attitude of giving sympathetic consideration to proposals that might be put forward by others." Acheson hopes for a "more positive role but recognizes UK might not be able to "mesh its economy as fully into that of the continent as we believe it essential that the continentals do among themselves. But unity on the continent needs the US and US "not only to exert leadership but to participate as fully as the situation of each makes possible." NARA 840.00/10-2849

30 Oct: Before departing for Europe, Acheson writes two personal letters to Schuman. He reviews earlier discussions this year on French role in facing

problem of Germany. Because Germany now has a legitimate government, new problems arise involving, among others, German domestic policies, the High Commission's role and the rise of East Germany in the former Soviet occupation zone. The occupying powers bear a great responsibility in facing these problems but especially France. "Now is the time for French initiative and leadership of the type required to integrate the German Federal Republic promptly and decisively into Western Europe." After reviewing Germany's international role and its domestic problems, Acheson concludes: "We here in America, with all the will in the world to help and support, cannot give the lead. That, if we are to succeed in this joint endeavor, must come from France." Both letters photographically reproduced, with French translations, in Be/SC 40-55; FRUS III 621-25

31 Oct: ERP administrator Paul Hoffman makes major policy speech at OEEC meeting in Paris calling for European economic integration. NYT 1 Nov; MC 68-9

Hoffman's speech and Acheson's September conversations with Schuman and October letters and cables represented a major push for a more active American policy toward European integration, against the cautious approach of the State Department which warned that a strong UK role was essential (yet not forthcoming in the Attlee government). From the start of the Marshall Plan, the Americans insisted that the Europeans cooperate with each other in devising the recovery program. But now Hoffman saw a clarification of a trend underway since 1947: Europe must integrate its economies into one.

This development came partly in response to congressional pressure for some form of European unification and partly because Secretary of State Acheson himself realized that Britain could not be forced into anything beyond intergovernmental cooperation with Europe. His insistence in his 19 October cable that France alone could take the lead in the integration of Germany into Europe---against the unanimous advice of his European ambassadors who insisted Europe could only be integrated with the UK---meant, in fact, a willingness now by the top American diplomat to see European integration proceed even without Britain. With this policy shift, Washington was now ready for, in fact, insistent upon, a French initiative.

NOVEMBER: Schuman tells National Assembly "If I find myself occupying this position [as French foreign minister] it is not because I have sought it but doubtless because someone from France's eastern frontier was needed to try to achieve peaceful co-existence between two countries which have so often been at each other's throats." [Konrad Adenauer, from the corresponding border area of west Germany, was to become Schuman's counterpart and collaborator]. JMM 285

5 Nov: US State Department's European Bureau issues major briefing paper on European integration for Acheson's coming meetings with British and French foreign ministers: France is central to Germany's integration and must be

encouraged, with UK and US support, to take the lead. Hoffman's speech of 31 October supports this general approach although the ECA (Hoffman's agency) inclines to more radical and rapid approach than State Department, paper says. NARA 840.00/11-549

7 Nov: Recommendations from US ambassadors in western Europe meetings in late October are given to Undersecretary of State Webb who passes them on to President Truman. The meeting was called to give views to Secretary of State Acheson before foreign ministers meeting. The ambassadors repeat their view that an UK active role is essential for integration. NARA 840.00/11-749; FRUS IV 472-96

9 Nov: Acheson attends NATO foreign ministers meeting in Paris which discusses German problem. FRUS III, Ch IV, Part B 632ff

24 Nov: Petersberg Agreement begins international recognition of Germany which, in turn, allows Adenauer to accept International Ruhr Authority. JMM 283

17 Dec: American Ambassador Robert Murphy (Brussels) cables State Department that JM recently dined with Paul Henri Spaak, Belgian foreign minister, and told him he supports Spaak for head of Organization for European Economic Cooperation (OEEC). FRUS IV 462-3

19 Dec: Continuing the Council of Europe's consideration of new ways for Europe to organize its basic industries, the council assembly's Economic Committee adopts motion seeking creation of "European companies" which, whether public or private, could operate under the council's authority in several European countries free from customs or other taxes. PG 528-9

The same committee, chaired by Paul Reynaud, also proposes creation of a "public organization on steel" to study the industry's problems through a public-private mechanism. PG 530

1950

JANUARY: A growing crisis in overproduction of European steel focuses on need for pan-European cooperation on this industry. PG 529; H. Rieben, Des ententes des maitres de forges au plan Schuman (Lausanne, 1954) 318 ff

13 Jan: French Foreign Minister Schuman visits Bonn and, after a frosty reception induced by the French determination to annex the Saar, outlines three problems blocking Franco-German understanding: the Ruhr, the Saar and German rearmament. He determines to resolve the German question. PG 533-534; JMM 284; GE 547-8

19 Jan: Adenauer suggests to McCloy that internationalizing the Saar production may solve the problem of that border area. PG 536

24 Jan: US State Department conducts major policy review on European integration and UK role with G. Kennan, head of policy planning, C. Bohlen,

minister at US embassy Paris, and most of policy planning staff. Group reaffirms view of previous October meeting of US ambassadors in Europe that European integration can only proceed with British support. FRUS III 617-22

26 Jan: JM briefs US journalists in Paris on Plan; reviews problems faced in 1946 and gives figures for 1949 showing sharp rise in investments and financing, concluding with view that France, by 1952 when current Plan ends, will be independent of exceptional foreign aid. FJM AML

31 Jan: American Embassy London sends long memorandum noting "British have never accepted the concept of political integration [of Europe] involving any transfer of sovereignty"; UK regards United States of Europe as utopian concept; Even political unification meaning collaboration among sovereign states can come only gradually. The Council of Europe might play some useful but undeterminable role in this development but Britain is not now or in foreseeable future likely to lead in developing that role. UK role is limited by its Commonwealth and US relations; coming general election will not change these positions which are based on "deep seated qualities of the British character." NARA 740.00/2-250 London Embassy attachment by William C Trimble to Dispatch 503 of 2 Feb; (Summarized in FRUS III 768-70)

1 Feb: JM meets Plowden in Paris, renewing talks on Germany. JM notes that Finebel (a plan for economic cooperation between France, Italy, Belgium and Luxembourg) was becoming less attractive for France despite continuing American pressure for free trade through such regional groupings. Britain and France, JM tells Plowden, must work together on common economic and political goals to prevent a hostile Germany from arising. DF 188-189 citing NAUK Treasury 232/149

9 Feb: US Embassy London continues assessment of British attitude toward European economic integration: UK wants more open world trade and, in short term, better trade first among soft-currency countries of Western Europe. But "British clearly do not favor the complete economic unification of Western Europe. Assuming their participation in it, they fear the political integration which they think would necessarily have to accompany it and the consequent weakening of the sterling area. Assuming their exclusion, they are afraid of Western European economic autarchy dominated by Germany." UK fears weakening of its U.S. and Dominions relations were it to be "merely one of several economically integrated Western European powers." NARA 840.00/950; FRUS III 768-70

13 Feb: President Truman directs Acheson to discuss with National Security Council staff a review of European integration. Asst Secretary of State Perkins advises Acheson such a review would be useful and State Department should have role but leaves open how and by whom such review should be done. FRUS III 629-30

3 Mar: Provisional accords between France and the Saar defining the

region's autonomy and its economic attachment to France provoke strong negative reaction in Germany. PG 532

4 Mar: JM describes initial stages of a Plan study of American productivity methods in letter to Prime Minister Bidault. RK 337 citing AN F60 bis 517

9 Mar: Chancellor Adenauer tells Kingsbury Smith of International News Service that he would seek a complete union of France and Germany as the nucleus of a united Europe. He wants England, Italy, Belgium, Luxembourg and the Netherlands included, not just a Franco-German bloc.... This would give a "very sick Europe a new life." JM is sympathetic but skeptical of the timing.

Overall, the French response is cool. A leading French newspaper says "Adenauer wants to build Europe around Germany and for Germany." KA 244-8; JMM 285; PG 536

Monnet may not have supported Adenauer's striking approach but the German problem was on the Frenchman's mind as well. He confided in Bernard Clappier, Schuman's chief of staff: Monnet "had the same preoccupation as Robert Schuman concerning Germany....At the start of 1950 his ideas about what to do about Germany began to form. By the beginning of March he started to read me notes he had written on the subject. He did not let me see the texts themselves but this did not prevent me from discussing the ideas with Schuman." But the French foreign minister needed a written version to consider and the pressing occasion was the coming foreign ministers meeting in London. (Bernard Clappier, FJM OH)

Eventually the Schuman Plan became the answer to both the immediate problem of a French response to the Anglo-American challenge on Germany and to the wider questions: of the "war" industries of coal and steel which both divided and united France and Germany; of reconciliation between the two counties five years after WWII ended; of the pursuit of Europe's integration and its economic prosperity and of the need for a true international initiative for peace. (PG 538)

16 Mar: De Gaulle responds positively to Adenauer's remarks of 9 Mar, noting his long acquaintance with the German chancellor and referring to the "spirit of Charlemagne" which his remarks display. PG 537

23 Mar: Adenauer tells American journalist Kingsbury Smith that uniting the French and German economies would be at least a start. KA 244-8; PG 536. Adenauer, as early as 1923 during the French occupation of the Ruhr, had proposed a union of French and German heavy industries, according to Paul Weymar, Konrad Adenauer (Paris, 1956) 224, 260, cited by PG 536 n.

26 Mar: Schuman, appearing before his political party's [MRP] central committee, seems to respond cautiously but positively to Adenauer's interview three days earlier by affirming generally the goal of a European community and

improving Franco-German relations. He agreed to study in detail the unification proposals. PG 544-545

Monnet ended a two week hiking vacation in the Swiss Alps just before his meeting with his friend David Bruce described below. His mountain interlude, this year in the Huez range near Roseland, was an annual event whenever possible. He needed, he wrote, regular walking. When he starts out, "I take with me all the previous day's thoughts and worries. But when I have walked for half an hour or an hour, they begin to fade away.... I let my thoughts find their own level. I never force myself to thing about a given subject---subjects come to me naturally because I always follow the same time of thought, or rather, I follow only one at a time."

This time Monnet's thoughts centered on an "anxiety that weighed on Europe five years after the war: the fear that if we did nothing we should soon face war again....What could be done to link France and Germany and implant a common interest between them before it was too late? When I returned to Paris at the beginning of April, I still had no perfect answer: but I did have so full an account of the reasons for acting, and so clear an idea of the direction in which to move, that ...the time for uncertainty was over." (JMM 288-9)

30 Mar: JM lunches with David Bruce, US ambassador in Paris. He "was in an engaging philosophical mood. He has an astonishingly quick and comprehensive vision." DBD

31 Mar: Ministerial committee of the Council of Europe invites both West Germany and the Saar to become associate members, thus recognizing indirectly the autonomy of the Saar. The action continues the tension between France and Germany, and prolongs the fear that the latter is still not firmly attached to the West. PG 532-533

April 1950 is a crucial month for Monnet, for Schuman and for Europe. Monnet leads the action; he has a vision, as David Bruce's diary shows, to help France find its way out of an impasse with its Western Allies over Germany's future. In this month, Chancellor Adenauer renewed his hints that Germany is ready to become an integrated part of Europe as long as it is treated equally. The United States had already pressed France months before to take an initiative on Germany; when the Western Foreign Ministers meet in London, Schuman will have to respond.

During April Monnet and his staff are still groping for the right formula to allow France to lead the London discussions. Several false starts arise to distract him. Prime Minister Bidault presented a plan for an Atlantic Council. Adenauer continues his efforts through the American press to induce equality of treatment for Germany although he does not want that equality to include a German army. Monnet himself is distracted by the cold war pressures marked by the ominous Russian boldness in blockading Berlin. He writes a long memo on these concerns. (JMM 289-294)

The experiences of the First World War were also on Monnet's mind, he later noted. "In 1950 many thought the peace must be different from that after WWI. [But] many still wanted superiority or domination over Germany. (AW)

2 Apr: In a United Press Service interview, Adenauer expanded his comments on a Franco-German union to include the UK with a common parliament. But he made clear two weeks later than his basic condition for German entry into any European federation would be its treatment as a full equal. PG 536

4 Apr: JM thanks J F Dulles for advance copy of his book War or Peace which will soon be published. He adds a footnote after reading Dulles may be named to a foreign policy role in Washington: "I do hope that if this really happens you will not hesitate." DP, Box 54 cited by P Winand in MATA 103-39

10 Apr: During this week JM meets first with Bernard Clappier, Schuman's chef de cabinet, and then with Paul Reuter, law professor from Aix la Chapelle.

In a long conversation on 11 April, Clappier tells JM that Schuman is looking for an initiative he can propose at the meeting 10 May in London with Acheson and Bevin. Clappier relates that Acheson and Bevin charged Schuman with responsibility for finding a common policy on Germany last September when the three met in New York.

JM replies he has some ideas. But through a misunderstanding with Clappier the two do not yet proceed with more detailed discussions. JMM 294-5,298-99

12 Apr: JM meets law professor Paul Reuter for first time. They discuss Adenauer's proposals, a European parliament and the Monnet Plan applied to a wider area. Reuter responds with "intelligence and enthusiasm" to JM's ideas on France, Germany and Europe and agrees to outline a regional approach. NCN 137-39; CE 105; JMM 294-5, 299; FJM OH, Clappier; See also interesting reflections on these events by Etienne Hirsch and Pierre Uri, two key Monnet aides, in ERB 377-385 and by Clappier ERB 371.

14 Apr: JM asks Frankfurter to see Jean Serban-Schreiber who is coming to U.S. as first Smith-Mundt program visitor. FFD

The first draft of the Coal and Steel Community plan on this April weekend will change many times over the next three weeks but the essentials were fixed over these two days at the Monnet home at Houjarray. One paragraph which was eventually deleted by Monnet and his team indicates clearly the nature of their work: "This proposal has an essential political objective: to make a breach in the ramparts of national sovereignty which will be narrow enough to secure consent but deep enough to open the way toward the unity that is essential to peace."

Although these words were not in the final version, "they summarized its overall aim." The deletion was made not because the words were not true, but to avoid unnecessary provocation. (JMM 296)

15-16 Apr (weekend): JM meets with his aide Etienne Hirsch and Reuter in Paris and Houjarray on the outline of a coal and steel community: World peace is the goal and Europe must play its vital part. A federal Europe built on a French-German union is the political goal. The means are a coal-steel pool with common institutions. JMM 295; NCN 140-53

16 Apr: US Secretary of State Dean Acheson, in his memoirs, ties Prime Minister Bidault's proposed Atlantic High Council for Peace, made in a speech today in Lyons, to the later Schuman proposal for a coal and steel community. The Schuman Plan was JM's reaction to this `rather grandiose' idea [of Bidault]. DA 383

Even Monnet's friends sometimes misunderstood what he was doing as this comment from Dean Acheson suggests. This peculiar gap in Acheson's account of the Schuman Plan also seems to ignore the September 1949 charge he and British Foreign Secretary Bevin gave to Schuman to propose a solution to the German problem. The Schuman Plan was the French response framed by Monnet whose role in its creation was not determined by a Bidault speech but by a life-long interest in subverting nationalism and by an immediate need for a French initiative on Germany.

17 Apr: Paul Reuter delivers his first draft of the Schuman declaration to JM's office at rue de Martignac. JM asks Pierre Uri, Plan economist, to draft another version of what became Schuman Plan announcement. FJM AMG 1/2/1, 1/2/2 reprinted in NCN 157-61 and CE 114-121; JMM 297

19 Apr: JM writes note of introduction to J F Dulles for young friend, Jean Servan Schreiber, who has received first State Department study grant under Smith-Mundt legislation. DP, Box 54 cited by P Winand in MATA 103-3

20 Apr: JM reviews coal and steel proposal with B Clappier, Schuman's chief of staff. DF 200 citing G Elgey, La Republique des Illusions, Paris, 1965, 445

21 Apr: JM invites Bruce to lunch. "[I] had a long conversation with him on strengthening the Atlantic Treaty Organization and of extending its activities to the political and economic fields." DBD

26 Apr: Fourth draft of Schuman declaration (after undated third version) FJM AMG 1/2/3, 1/2/4 reprinted in CE 122-29

The numerous drafts of the Schuman declaration showed Monnet's writing style, or more precisely, his editing style since others did the drafting. He insisted on draft after draft of every important statement or letter. He saw this as a form of persuasion, as a means of ending suspicion. He embraced "the power of simple ideas expressed plainly and unvaryingly, over and over again. That at least disarms suspicion, which is the main source of misunderstandings." (JMM 330-1). Others commented, sometimes with frustration, often with bemused understanding of Monnet's insistence on going over and over a draft, simplifying and clarifying it, even if, sometimes, it ended up very close to the original. (George Ball, OH, FJM, 15; Robert Bowie, OH, FJM, 10)

27 Apr: Fifth draft of Schuman declaration. FJM AMG 1/2/5 reprinted in CE 131-35

28 Apr: US Ambassador David Bruce: "JM called to discuss Bidault's proposal for a High Atlantic Council of Peace and his own idea of a Franco-German economic union.... I went by Jean Monnet's office to read some paper he had on the revolutionary matter [the coal and steel community on which JM delivered a version to Prime Minister Bidault's office this same day] we had discussed this morning. " DBD

Bruce is apparently the first person, French or foreign, outside Monnet's and Schuman's offices, to see a draft of the Schuman Plan.

-----:Sixth and seventh drafts of Schuman declaration. FJM AMG 1/2/6, 1/2/7 reprinted in CE 137-40

------: JM, thinking that Schuman was not interested because Clappier had not responded, sends copy of plan for the coal and steel community to Pierre-Louis Falaise, senior aide to French Prime Minister Georges Bidault, with request to meet on the matter the next day.

Later this day, Bernard Clappier, aide to Foreign Minister Robert Schuman, calls JM with positive response to earlier discussion of JM's idea on what Schuman might propose at coming meeting of foreign ministers in London. JM gives Clappier same draft earlier given to Falaise and Clappier gives it to Schuman just as he departs for weekend in Lorraine. JMM 298-9; FJM OH, Clappier

30 Apr-3 May: JM writes long memo on the background of what becomes the Schuman Plan. He discusses the "perilous" situation created by the cold war which may lead easily to an actual war. It is necessary to change dramatically the assumptions of this dangerous situation, he wrote. "This requires a profound act...which changes the situation....One must change the assumptions and transform them....No matter where one turns, one sees impasses in the present situation: the inevitability of war, the problem of Germany, continuing the rebuilding of France, the organization of Europe, and the place of France in Europe and in the world....France must take the initiative before the London Conference [scheduled for mid-May]....Europe will not be born right now except by France. Destiny has chosen France for this role. If she takes this initiative, fear will be eliminated and hope restored for the creation of a force for peace." PG; FJM AMG 1/1/6, 1/2/9, 4/1/2 and reprinted in NCN 163-171 and CE 79-97 (Extracts in JMM 289-294).

By the end of April, the course of European history is altered by two men, Monnet and Schuman, one who works behind the scenes, the other a courageous politician. Monnet, the insider with a vision, has an amazing persistence and an

ability to reach and influence those in power. Yet Monnet would be the first to protest any exaggerated account of his performance. Now over 60 years of age, he saw himself as a willing instrument of events---including the political forces which Schuman represented---which had influenced his life in the first half of the century and which, he believes, now must be redirected if Europe is to survive.

1 May (Monday): Schuman returns from weekend at home in Metz where he reviewed JM draft plan. "I've read the proposal. I'll use it." Even before he took the draft to Lorraine for the weekend, he had told B Clappier, his chief aide, that of the two aspects of the plan, political and technical, he, Schuman, could handle the political but he asked Clappier if there were "technical problems." Clappier answered, "Absolutely not." JMM 299; FJM OH, Clappier (Reprinted in UMV 53-71)

------ JM drafts (and redrafts on 3 May) a memorandum to Schuman on the urgency of French action as a result of the Cold War and the problem of Germany. FJM AMG 1/1/3, 1/1/5

He also writes an eight page "Note of Reflection" on the Cold War and France's role in the world. After reviewing the Cold War's implications for Europe, he reviews the traditional problem of efficient German steel production and its consequent threat to French heavy industry. The answer, he says, is to move beyond these old structures and to find a new form of organization in Europe which, he believes, America will strongly support. His thoughts parallel those of American Secretary of State Acheson in urging France to move beyond the past and seize the present opportunity to redefine its role in history by finding a new relationship with Germany. Reproduced in draft form in Be/Sc 153-160

3 May: Prime Minister Bidault expresses unhappiness to JM over not knowing of coal and steel proposal which he just heard of from Schuman, in general terms, at a cabinet meeting. JM explains that Bidault's office had received a copy of the plan the previous Friday. JMM 299-300

4 May: JM's journalist friend Harold Callender reports from Paris that Schuman, at French cabinet meeting, announced he will "propose a new step toward the unification of Europe's basic industries in ...consortium embracing British coal, Ruhr steel and Lorraine iron..." in coming foreign ministers' talks in London. "In putting forth their industrial consortium proposal, the French will count mainly on the United States since the British have shied away from any `economic integration' with the Continent." NYT

-----: JM and his aides complete eighth draft of Schuman declaration. FJM AMG 1/2/8 reprinted in CE 145-48

6 May [Saturday]: D Bruce reports: "...I had a long talk with Jean Monnet about the coal and steel pool." DBD.

This is apparently the first extended discussion with anyone outside the intimate JM circle of what became the Schuman Plan. The Monnet outreach

came with the same close American friend, David Bruce, who had already read a
draft of the new plan.

-------: Ninth draft of Schuman proposal is judged final version by JM.
JMM 296; reprinted in NCN 177-81 and CE 149-52

7 May [Sunday]: French Foreign Minister Schuman and aide B Clappier
come to US ambassador D Bruce's house to outline for Secretary of State
Acheson a plan to pool French and German coal and steel resources under
a common authority. Acheson, on his way to London for foreign ministers
meetings with Britain and France, is sworn to secrecy by Schuman who has yet
to discuss details of plan with French cabinet or at all with the Germans or the
British. Acheson's initial response is cautious, hoping this is not a cartel plan, but
gradually seeing its imaginative thrust. DA 384; DBD

-----:Schuman writes Adenauer quoting key paragraphs of final draft of
his declaration scheduled to be given 9 May. Reprinted in NCN 182-84 and CE
159-61

8 May [Monday]: JM talks in Paris with John McCloy, US High
Commissioner in Germany, on Schuman Plan announcement coming next day.
McCloy gives Secretary of State Acheson more details supplementing 7 May
meeting where plan was "quite casually mentioned" and "in such general terms
prior to the announcement that I [Acheson] was unable by his [Schuman's]
reticence to gauge the full significance of the proposal." FRUS IV 694-5

-----: Schuman sends a friend, Robert Mischlich, to Bonn with two letters
to Adenauer on the coal and steel plan. The emissary is received by the German
chancellor the next day. After giving oral assurances to Mischlich (who phones
them to Paris), Adenauer replies with full support and thanks in both personal
and official letters to Schuman. Reprinted in NCN 186-88 and CE 162-64; MR
62-3; JMM 302

9 May [Tuesday]: Acheson meets Bevin in London but without being able
to reveal his knowledge of coming news from Paris and Bonn. When Bevin finds,
with the arrival of French ambassador, that Schuman is to make announcement
of his "plan" that afternoon, and that Acheson knew of the Schuman proposal,
his anger is directed both at Acheson, for not revealing the plan himself, and at
Schuman for not consulting with Britain. DA 384-85

-----: After a brief and general discussion with the cabinet on his plan,
Schuman announces to the press a "bold, constructive act" to create a European
Coal and Steel Community; Germany has indicated acceptance; plan will be open
to other west European countries including UK. JMM 303-4; KA 256-7; NCN
177; CE 175-80

-----:Adenauer has press conference two hours after Schuman's; The
German chancellor gives wide review of German role in Europe, accepts Council

of Europe's invitation to join, and announces support for French initiative on a coal and steel community. NYT 10 May; CE 185-93

-----:E Bevin, UK foreign secretary, advises his Paris embassy that R Massigli, French ambassador in London, presented him with urgent message from R Schuman concerning French plan for a European coal and steel authority which French cabinet just approved and which will be presented to press later today. Massigli later gives Bevin text of communique Schuman would present to press. AFD 3

Monnet and Schuman, as originators of the coal and steel plan, knew better than all how fragile an idea had been launched. Schuman, at his press conference just before leaving for the London foreign ministers meeting, was at one point vague about the plan's consequences. One reporter asked: "`In other words, its a leap in the dark?' `That's right,' said Schuman soberly, `a leap in the dark.'"

Monnet himself reflected that the agreement of Adenauer and Schuman was only the start. "I was impatient for only one thing---institutions to give shape to an agreement based on goodwill. Nothing is possible without men; nothing is lasting without institutions." (JMM 304-5)

[For a vivid personal account of the 1-9 May 1950 period, Bernard Clappier's recollections are unsurpassable. The chief aide to Robert Schuman recalled an "adventure" many years later. UMV 53-71; He also gave an interesting interview with a Danish writer on the 1950 events. ERB 371-2]

According to Pierre Uri, one of Monnet's key aides, Schuman later referred to his own role in the plan that bore his name with the words: "I was the adoptive father." France Forum (magazine) Nov 1963, "Hommage a Robert Schuman" 25; the same issue contains tributes to Schuman of Monnet, Hirsch, Uri and many others.

10 May [Wednesday]: Western foreign ministers conference opens in London in shadow of the Schuman Plan announcement. DA 393-400; Acheson cables State Department with more enthusiasm and more details on Schuman Plan, adding to his brief initial report earlier after briefings by Schuman, Monnet and McCloy. FRUS III 691-5; DA 384-85

US government reaction to Schuman declaration is mixed: State Department is suspicious that this is another cartel plan; Marshall Plan officials in Washington support idea as consistent with US goals in rebuilding Europe; American Embassy in Paris is divided with economic section skeptical and Ambassador Bruce and his US Treasury aide, William Tomlinson, supportive because they knew JM is behind the initiative. FJM OH, Stanley Cleveland

--------Schuman Plan announcement yesterday "caused a great stir everywhere. It is a bold proposition and...the most constructive thing done by the French government since liberation." DBD

--------At meeting of Prime Minister Attlee, Foreign Secretary Bevin, Chancellor of Exchequer Cripps and others, the British cabinet discusses the Schuman proposal. "There was general agreement that the French government had behaved extremely badly in springing this proposal [Schuman Plan] on the world at this juncture without any attempt of consultation with HM government or the US government." [Yet Bevin had fiercely attacked Acheson on his arrival in London from Paris for not advising the UK government that he had been briefed by Schuman, however summarily, about the plan.] Until more is known, it is "essential to adopt a very cautious and non-committal attitude." Memo of conversation in NAUK FO 800/517;

11 May: Meeting of Schuman, Acheson, Bevin in London: Schuman says France cannot "negotiate with Germany separately as the Occupation Statute made all three governments responsible. For this reason ...there was no question of a decision having been taken. It was merely a proposal.... Above all, this was no fait accompli." Bevin says, regarding Germany, that any discussion would be dealt with by the High Commissioners. Schuman agrees. NAUK Treasury 229/749; Later, Prime Minister Attlee makes positive but non-committal statement in Commons on French proposal. AFD 5

--------: Hall-Patch, UK representative at OEEC, writes Roger Makins in Foreign Office: Roger Stevens (Observer newspaper) saw JM last night who said "that not only were the ideas behind the [Schuman] project very largely his own but that he drafted the press communique himself....I [Hall-Patch] was able to see Monnet myself this afternoon. He was, for him, excessively coy....There was a hint of 'Well you had your chance' in his attitude and a sly reference or two to the talks with Plowden last year which we were not very keen about at the time and which came to nothing." NAUK Treasury 229/749

To maintain the momentum behind Schuman's announcement was now Monnet's major concern. He faced immediate resistance not only from the British Labour government but also from the Benelux countries which wanted Britain included from the start. France's ambassador in London, Rene Massigli, was among those diplomats with doubts about the Monnet insistence that a partial grant of sovereignty to the proposed High Authority was essential to the project's success. Monnet's obstinancy on this point, even if it meant proceeding without Britain, was central, he believed, to the political nucleus of the Schuman Plan.

--------Plowden tells Cripps:"...it would be right for this country to welcome in principle the proposed [High] authority but to wait to see how it progresses before committing ourselves to enter or not." NAUK Treasury 229/749

12 May: Bruce sends background cable from London with details on JM role in Schuman Plan. FRUS III 697-701

14 May: JM arrives in London with aides Hirsch and Uri to meet with British officials to explain Schuman proposal. AFD 6; JMM 306

15 May: JM meets Stafford Cripps, Chancellor of Exchequer, Roger Makins and E Plowden in London on Schuman Plan. Cripps seems ready

to accept UK participation even if political federation came later. Plowden astonished and warns JM that Cripps views had not been discussed in cabinet. Bevin and Attlee are informed of discussions. EP 87-8

McCloy and Harriman represent US in London talks which follow up the foreign ministers' session; their presence indicates Washington thought the question of British participation in the coal and steel pool was both important and still open within the UK government. JM's trip resulted from Bevin's assessment that the assurances he had from French Foreign Ministers Schuman were not satisfactory. (NYT 16 May)

16 May: JM meets Makins, Plowden and latter's deputy Alan Hitchman for breakfast at Hyde Park Hotel in London to continue discussion of Schuman's initiative. JM makes clear Schuman Plan involves surrender of sovereignty in key areas and that France will proceed with Germany without regard to other countries.

No documents exist yet beyond press communique, JM says, but drafting of the treaty is underway. The Benelux countries in principle favor the plan. The French government recognizes that the High Authority constitutes "the surrender of national sovereignty over a wide strategic and economic field and that they were prepared to do this in the interest of furthering European unity. UK summary of meeting in NAUK Treasury 229/749

-----:Interim report of UK inter-departmental Committee of Officials on Proposed Coal and Steel Authority ends: "M. Monnet took view that if HMG were to take a full part in the discussions [between France and Germany without committing itself] it would hinder negotiations...because the British representatives would in effect have a veto power upon any proposals that they did not consider HMG could accept. M. Monnet therefore suggested that UK should agree to accept the Schuman proposal as it stands as a basis for the negotiations." NAUK CAB 134/293

-----:UK Cabinet's Economic Policy Committee hears Chancellor Cripps account of his meeting with JM. Committee agrees to examine Schuman Plan without any commitment either way and with understanding that proposal does not involve federation. EP 87-88

17 May: H Macmillan gives speech in London expressing alarm at UK's hesitation in responding to Schuman declaration. "M. Schuman's proposal are an act of courage and imaginative statesmanship. They may produce a turning-point in the long and tragic story of Franco-German relations. If [the plan] fails, it will mean a serious deterioration and will be more than a set-back. It will be a disaster." HM III 189

Macmillan's enthusiasm for the Schuman Plan, and his criticism of the Labour Government's hesitation in supporting it, is short-lived. By August he has proposed a counter-plan which would make the coal and steel community an inter-governmental subcommittee of the Council of Europe. By then he also doubts other smaller European countries will join the proposed community.(See below August 6-10)

18 May: President Truman makes broad but positive statement on Schuman Plan ("an act of constructive statesmanship") NYT 19 May; DA 388

19 May: Robert Hall memo (to Plowden) on talk with Uri yesterday: "Uri said JM is `only authority on the plan....We still do not know where we are. It may be of course the case that JM himself does not know which of two concepts he wants to adopt: that of complete planning of [coal and steel] production or that of complete free trade'.... No government (Uri said) could possibly be committed to agree in advance to things they had not seen...."

"We could ask Monnet the plain question: Is the essential function of the new Authority to ensure equal prices and free movement or ...to give instructions to all producing units as to what they are able to do?" NAUK Treasury 229/749

------: JM returns to Paris from London. AFD 6. Among others JM saw in London was Arthur Salter, an old friend from WWI and LN days. Salter later told an interviewer "Monnet can't write, he can't read, he can't speak, but he always persuades." AW.

But on this occasion, JM's efforts failed to persuade the British government to accept his view of the Schuman Plan. Typically, he ignored the setback and resumed the effort to maintain momentum for the plan elsewhere especially in Germany and America, two vital centers of support.

------:Plowden and JM talk by phone: JM says Schuman will talk with Bidault and then deal further with Bevin in diplomatic channels. Plowden recommends speed and early action to produce the details of the Schuman proposals. NAUK Treasury 229/749

22 May: JM is leaving tonight for Germany, Bruce notes. "He is not discouraged by his recent visit to England although he thinks there is no possibility of the UK joining France and Europe...at this time. The proposal continues to have enthusiastic support from American newspapers. The thing is to press it vigorously and not permit it to lose momentum." DBD

-----: Macmillan and others write letter to Times in support of Schuman Plan provoking violent editorial attack from Lord Beaverbrook's Daily Express. HM III 189

23 May: JM meets Allied High Commissioners for Germany in Bonn-Petersberg on the Schuman Plan and briefs McCloy, Armand Berard, French deputy high commissioner and Gordon MacReady, economic adviser to UK high commissioner Brian Robertson. FRUS III,705-9; FJM AMG 2/3/8 reprinted in CE 213-224; JMM 309

In late afternoon, JM, Clappier and Berard meet Chancellor Adenauer and Herbert Blankenhorn of Foreign Ministry on Schuman Plan. FRUS IV 709; FJM AMG 2/3/11 reprinted in NCN 197-203 and CE 242-48; JMM 308-11

-----: Chancellor Adenauer meets JM in Bonn, calling him "The great force [Hauptmotor] behind the whole [Schuman] Plan." KA 263-4

Adenauer writes Schuman a personal letter, on his support for the coal and steel plan and on his talk with JM. He assures the French foreign minister that Germany will name a negotiator with the same spirit of commitment and cooperation as JM. CE 254

-----: Dulles praises Schuman Plan in letter to JM: "The proposal brings a new spirit into a western world which has so far not been able to imagine anything better than [the] dreary road...to war." He suggests JM clarify that a united Europe did not mean one hostile or indifferent to the U.S. DP, Box 54 cited by P Winand in MATA 103-39

-----: UK Committee of Officials on Proposed Coal and Steel Authority recommends proceeding with discussions with French on Schuman Plan. Cabinet accepts recommendation and authorizes note to French government. EP 88-89

24 May: Schuman sends message to Belgium, Italy, Luxembourg and Netherlands confirming their readiness to join France and Germany in opening the coal and steel community talks. CE 225-27

-----:UK government sets up inter-departmental working group on Schuman Plan. NAUK Treasury 229/749

25 May: French government sends memo to UK government with draft communique which Germany had already accepted and which Italy and Benelux countries were also receiving. It proposed a Schuman Plan conference on the basis of the 9 May statement with the final agreement to be presented to respective parliaments. This message crosses one from British asking for Anglo-French-German talks on the French proposal of 9 May. JMM 312; AFD 6-8; CE 228-29

-----: Plowden and JM talk by phone: JM says he is encouraged by visit to Adenauer who thinks ordinary Germans feel West has taken constructive initiative. JM says French government has sent detailed response to UK questions on Schuman Plan.

Later same day JM writes long letter (in French) to Plowden: You raised three points: What kind of High Authority with what kind of guarantees against arbitrary power is intended; How will High Authority relate to labor and full employment matters; What modes of intervention will the High Authority have with government and business. JM comments: We cannot have a High Authority of government representatives or delegates. We must find a small number of competent men to manage problems. These are, JM adds, my preliminary ideas. NAUK Treasury 229/749

27 May: British send response to previous note from Paris: If France insists on prior commitment to pool coal and steel and set up sovereign authority in advance of talks, UK regrets it cannot participate. JMM 312; AFD 8

------: JM meets US ambassador David Bruce in Paris; France will issue text of agreement with Germany, Italy and the Benelux countries next week. The UK desire to participate to "see how the scheme will operate in detail" is rejected as destructive of whole approach and understanding of Italy and Benelux participants. FRUS IV 709-11

------: JM attends dinner party at Paris home of radio correspondent David Schoenbrun where he talks with David Lilienthal and Averell Harriman. The latter comments that the Schuman Plan is a great thing because for the first time the French have taken the initiative. But other guests, Eve Curie [writer and lecturer] and Professor Perrin, have many questions about the Plan. DL Vol III ll

29 May: JM phones Plowden and invites him to Houjarray for secret talks to resolve UK-French discussions on whether British can participate in Schuman Plan talks. Plowden refers JM invitation to superiors but does not think more talks with JM will solve impasse. EP 90; JM says that Schuman Plan matters are now in hands of lawyers which means serious risk of failure. NAUK Treasury 229/749

30 May: JM, Clappier, Hirsch and Uri draft note to UK government to "deal with Britain anxieties" about the role of the High Authority over member governments under the Schuman Plan. The note nonetheless reaffirmed the "partial fusion of sovereignty" which JM believed was central to the Schuman proposal. JMM 313; AFD 9-10

31 May: Bevin sends note to French government finally rejecting the "prior commitment" of the draft communique which France proposed but proposing a further compromise giving Britain a special role in the coming negotiations. Schuman had seemed earlier to be ready to accept this compromise which Rene Massigli, the French Ambassador in London, who was consistently anxious to keep the British involved, immediately supported. But JM rejects it flatly. AFD 11-12; On Massigli, ER 545-550

------: In a confidential memo by JM, Hirsh and Uri to their own government, they insist that Britain, in seeking a special role in any Schuman Plan conference, would undermine the talks since Germany and then the other participants would demand the same. In a another note at the same time, they add that accepting the British conditions would doom the conference and France would be blamed. JMM 313; GE 55

1 Jun: Schuman presents British ambassador in Paris with "virtual ultimatum" asking for a yes or no by 7pm the next day on whether Britain would participate in Schuman Plan conference. MC lll; AFD 12

2 Jun: US State Department sends instructions to embassies in UK and six Schuman Plan countries that there should be "no further public statements [on Schuman Plan] except to reaffirm our general position.... The US is not a party to negotiations and is to have no official association or observers." DA 38

-----: French ultimatum to British on supranational High Authority expires without UK response; Attlee later tells French ambassador it was impossible for UK to sign "blank cheque." EP 90-2; JMM 313-14; British send note asking for a ministerial meeting; if this is not possible, the British accept that agreement with France seems presently impossible and asks to be kept informed of negotiations with other countries. AFD 13

3 Jun: French government publishes joint communique of six governments who will participate in Schuman Plan talks. EP 92; JMM 314; AFD 13-14

-----:British and French governments issue communiques expressing respective views of breakdown of their talks. AFD 14-15; British embassy in Paris suggests Schuman Plan, based on past examples of over-enthusiastic "fanfares," may fail. JMM 314

-----: JM takes American executive D Lilienthal to Houjarray for overnight visit. They discuss British refusal to participate in Schuman Plan conference because attendance required a prior commitment to the plan's principles. JM says that British will come along---they always do---after things get going. If in 1936 France had marched against the Rhine, the British would have followed suit and Hitler would have been stopped then, JM said. "I asked: How will the French people, who have suffered so much from the Germans, take to this? Madame Monnet quoted her young gardener---whom I met. `Something must be done to change things; we must try to forget the way we feel, forget the past, try to do better in the future.'" JM added that no one knew how the Germans would behave. "There is no leadership among them, he said, in response to my question.... Madame Monnet added something about how the French look for something `that is our own, that we have worked out, and not something we just get from the Americans' and she meant far more than just the money side, I am sure."
"The Ruhr of the tractors, not the Ruhr of war-making---this kind of phrase ran through much that Monnet said. One cannot make war without coal and steel. If they are owned by a common pool of French and Germans" they cannot be used against one another; "both must use them `for tractors.'" DL v III 13-14

7 Jun: Schuman has press conference on coal and steel plan: Each state that signs treaty commits in advance to decisions of the High Authority with some right of appeal to a tribunal. NAUK Treasury 229/749

8 Jun: American embassy London reports on JM talks with Edwin Plowden, chief planning officer, British Treasury: Plowden says JM, with whom he recently had six hour talk, was "unable to illuminate how the [Schuman] plan would work." Plowden expressed opinion JM himself highly uncertain on basic details of operation. Plowden suggested possibility of "third force" [i.e. neutralism] thinking in French motivation for Schuman Plan; this impression "came from talks with Monnet." FRUS III 724-6

The dramatic month from early May to early June 1950 thrust Monnet into a prominence which the 62 year old Frenchman had never before experienced. Although this public attention gradually diminished, he was to remain a force in every subsequent move of Europe to unite and a counter to every maneuver resisting this union. A generous assessment (below) of the Monnet role came, not surprisingly, from a friendly American journalist.

11 Jun: NYT writer H Callender profiles JM's "inconspicuous and unspectacular role" in Schuman Plan talks. He is an "outstanding integrator" and "is almost automatically placed in the small company of the men rated as peculiarly fitted to grasp the character and scope of the economic and social tasks that preoccupy Western leaders....He is capable of vast, almost passionate concentration ....He is cocksure but he is often right.... He combines Anglo-Saxon respect for the facts and imaginative ability of the French or Latin mind." NYT

Callender's characterization of Monnet as 'cocksure' catches his important self-confidence but it must be balanced by the Frenchman's own view of his method of operation. Monnet knew he had to establish trust at the conference. He had considerable experience working with other nationalities and had learned that trust was the key to his successes. "To establish trust is more straightforward that is often thought: straightforwardness, indeed, is the secret of how it is done. If some delegates had arrived full of suspicion, they gradually found that we had nothing to hide. We demonstrated to them, day after day, that all our intentions were set out in the Declaration of May 9...." (JMM 329)

12 Jun: French interministerial council hears JM presentation on High Authority, its independence and its responsibility to a parliamentary body. "Thus," he said, "we shall lay the concrete foundations of a Federation of Europe." The council asks him to proceed. JMM 321; S&P 13

13 Jun: Prime Minister Attlee speaks in House of Commons on Schuman proposal, noting problem for UK of French government's requirement that parties commit in advance to the Schuman plan principles without knowing how they would work out in practice. JMM 307

------British Labour Party publishes European Unity, a policy statement of its National Executive Committee written by Hugh Dalton and others. It states that "The European peoples do not want a supra-national authority to impose agreements. They need an international machinery to carry out agreements which are reached without compulsion." Although not written in direct response to UK's talks with France on Schuman Plan, the document is seen by JM as confirmation of party's "wholly intransigent attitude". JMM 314

15 Jun: D. Lilienthal talks with Edwin Plowden, chief UK government planner, on the Schuman Plan: "He [Plowden] had talked to Monnet at length about it. [I] Agreed with him [JM] it couldn't have been launched at all if it had to be discussed in advance with the British....Monnet is obsessed with idea

that [the High] `Authority' should be without restraint....Impossible for British conditions---or American either, [Plowden] surmised. The Plan is wrong [Plowden said] because it seeks to solve a political question ---the unity of Europe---by economic means. I disagreed; I said I thought Monnet's approach was right."

[Later] at dinner with Plowden, MP R Butler and G Crowther, editor of "Economist", Lilienthal quotes Crowther saying of Schuman Plan: "`Monnet said in this very room that [the Schuman Plan] proposal has as its purpose setting up of a neutralized group in Europe---if France need not fear Germany, she need have no other fears, i.e. Russia; that they were tired of the cold war, which was something we here said Russia was engaged in, but which is now something America is pursuing.' He [Crowther] found it ironic that the Monnet proposal, essentially a neutralizing idea, is praised to the skies in America; British position, which definitely and flatly rejects neutral status, is criticized [there]!" DL v III 15-16

------: President Auriol notes Guy Mollet's trip to London seeking to alter British government view against the Schuman Plan recently expressed in Labour Party pamphlet. JM accompanies Mollet but Auriol thinks "Monnet is rather Anglophobic. He is not qualified for this kind of mission. I am afraid he will not advance the talks." V Auriol, Mon Septennat (Paris, 1970) 268; Mollet traveled as part of delegation of European socialist parties conferring with Labour government on Schuman Plan. NYT 19 Jun

The French President's view that Monnet is "Anglophobic" is puzzling. Monnet knew the British well and like and respected many Britons. But he also knew their limits when it came to radical ideas like the Schuman Plan. Auriol's remark may reflect simply Monnet's realization that the British would not go along now with the High Authority idea. Or the remark may suggest that Monnet had, during one of his frequent meetings with Auriol, lost patience in describing the British position against joining the Schuman Plan. When Auriol further suggests, however, that Monnet is not "qualified" for the task of converting the British, the President seems out of touch. Monnet had spent much time already trying to convince the British, starting with his meetings months before with Edwin Plowden and continuing even now with the Mollet mission. In between he had spent many hours in London since the May 9 Schuman declaration dealing both directly with top British leaders and less directly with Plowden and others to get the British to participate. But now Monnet had concluded that France and Germany (with American support) had to go ahead without Britain. This was what he conveyed to Auriol perhaps with a bit of impatience which the President may have misunderstood.

16 Jun: Lilienthal has lunch with several Conservative MPs and Thomas Brand in discussion of Schuman Plan. "`Schuman said to me,' said David Eccles, `Why all this fuss about coal and steel? I might well have started with cabbages.' Astounding admission. Plan was not economic at all.... Monnet apparently has a reputation as an original and provocative force in European politics. Brand noted:

`Monnet is naughty, you know---always has been.'" DL v III 19-20

------: Chancellor Adenauer, in letter to JM, supports latter's view that speed is important in agreeing on details of Schuman Plan treaty after Walter Hallstein is named as German negotiator. JMM 320; NCN 241

20 Jun: Schuman, at opening of conference of six nations [France, Germany, Italy, Benelux] on the coal and steel plan, explains secrecy of original announcement on May 9: "Experience has shown that the most hopeful initiatives die away before seeing the light if they linger too long amidst preliminary consultation." NAUK FO 371/85851 quoted by Roger Bullen, ed. in Ideas into Politics (Sydney, 1984), 193;

"We believe that we cannot afford to fail, to give up without reaching a conclusion. But never before have States undertaken or envisaged the joint delegation of part of their national sovereignty to an independent supranational body," Schuman said. On procedure, he added, "We shall work as a team and not as a negotiating conference with rigid, pedantic rules." JMM 322; S&P 14

------: In secret report by UK Committee of Officials on the proposed coal and steel authority, final section on "Constitution of the Authority" concludes: A detailed constitution for the Authority will have to be elaborated at a later stage. We consider that the Authority itself should...consist of independent people that should be responsible to an inter-governmental body consisting of government representatives only and that it should start by having only advisory functions though ...later on...functions of a mandatory character might be entrusted to it...." Preface to report notes that committee has taken Schuman statements and the JM glosses on them as basis to make concrete schemes acceptable to HMG and other governments involved. "We are all very conscious...that if a scheme satisfactory in its economic effects would be evolved, it would bring not only economic advantages but also great political benefits in...French-German relations." NAUK CAB 134/293

This neutral comment by a high-level British group reviewing the Schuman Plan masks a fundamental and long-lasting difference between the Continent and the United Kingdom: Britain seemed to recognize the importance of the Schuman Plan but could not find a way to participate itself (for now). Monnet, in his memoirs and probably at the time as well, saw that the practical nature of the British political system would eventually embrace a uniting Europe. But for now, the illusion of separateness (and superiority?), based on victory in WWII and on the defeat or occupation of the Schuman Plan participants in that war, made the British reject the Plan. Monnet personally believed that Britain would eventually, with its parliamentary traditions, make a great contribution to the European political structure. (AW; MC Ch.4)

21 Jun: At international conference to start coal and steel community talks, JM makes the opening statement: "We are here to undertake a common task---not to negotiate for our own national advantage but to seek it in the

advantage of all." He discusses the French text for two hours without distributing it to encourage ideas from other delegations. "All difficulties and all suggestions will be pooled, so that the draft, although originally French, will become a joint work."

Also on first day of talks JM underlines the independence of the High Authority. "It should...have its own revenue, drawn from a levy on coal and steel production and not depend on government subsidies. JMM 323-4; FJM AMG 3/2/3. He also discusses but does not distribute a draft text of 40 articles which stresses the supranationality of the High Authority. S&P 14

Monnet's challenge to delegates, including himself, not to seek national goals was remarkable for an international conference but a theme he recognized early in his life. At the start of the League of Nations he wrote a long memo in which he said men and nations tend to see problems from their immediate viewpoints. But if they can be presented with "the problem as a whole" then "all parties' points of view will be modified." Timing is important here: People and nations must agree first to cooperate before even setting out their respective goals in their own minds. Not showing other delegations at the Schuman Plan Conference his own text was a corollary of this same idea: Keeping our minds open to new ideas by avoiding fixed approaches, even one's own. [JMM 76-76 and pp 39-40]

22 Jun: In new procedure, heads of delegation at Schuman conference, with only one or two advisers, meet to deal with institutional questions. JM arranges some sessions at his Rue de Martignac office with French delegates where informality and intimacy prevail. "Over the months," JM comments, "I came to know them; but what mattered now was to bring them rapidly to look at the problem from the same point of view and tackle it as a common task...." JMM 324

24 Jun: First week of Schuman Plan talks conclude with focus on institutional questions and national industries. S&P 15-16; French government communique cites JM press conference on first week's work. FJM AMG 25/1/28

For the first time in his life, Monnet played a central, sustained and public role in the daily events which dominate the front pages of European and American newspapers. Without displacing or imitating the political leaders involved, he was, as head of the French delegation and the inspiration behind the Schuman plan, clearly directing the articulation of the proposal.

25 Jun: JM works at Houjarray with George Ball and others on Schuman Plan negotiations when they hear of North Korean invasion of South Korea. JM says: This could be something catastrophic for our plans or it could be very useful. Shortly after, when Korean war increases pressure from US for German rearmament, France responds with Pleven Plan for a European Defense Community which JM works out with Pleven who will soon become prime minister. JMM 336; GB 90-91

27 Jun: Second week of Schuman Plan talks shadowed by Korean war outbreak. Talks now center on role of High Authority and national governments influence on it. JM faces resistance from Benelux countries on question. S&P 15-17. JM and Hallstein, head of German delegation, unite on strong High Authority role, supported in rare intervention by Schuman. JMM 332

28 Jun: Ambassador Bruce reports from Paris that JM no longer has any hope of UK participation in Schuman Plan conference, adding JM also believes "... France now has to go to the end but at least the British clearly understand that, if the Schuman proposal reaches a successful conclusion, then a mutually satisfactory relationship can certainly be worked out with the British." etc FRUS III 738-9

1 Jul: Second week of Schuman Plan talks ends with a sharpened focus on the Benelux countries and limits on the High Authority. Some delegates favor a specific role for a Committee of Ministers and for the Common Assembly. S&P 15-17

11 Jul: Rene Pleven replaces Georges Bidault as French Prime Minister; JMM 339

12 Jul: JM calls in Schuman to address the negotiators; the French foreign minister stresses the independence of the High Authority. Gradually during the following week a solution appears on exactly how limited delegation of sovereignty to High Authority would work. Out of discussions comes agreement on role of Council of Ministers as intermediary between Coal and Steel Community and national governments. JMM 331-2; S&P 17-18

20 Jul: Dutch delegation agrees on idea of supranational High Authority. The Council of Ministers will not be above the High Authority but, with the Court of Justice and the Common Assembly, part of the same structure. But JM later presents memorandum on subject which seems to drop some key points of other delegations. S&P 17-18

22 Jul: Acheson sends memo to all other NATO countries requesting nature and extent of their increased defense spending in light of Korean invasion. FRUS III 138-41; Two days later he asks all UN member countries for maximum direct participation in Korean operation. FRUS III 457-8

23 Jul: McCloy speech notes it is "very difficult to deny the Germans the right and the means to defend their own soil." NYT 24 Jul

25 Jul: Schuman announces that agreement had been reached on all major points at the Paris conference on the coal and steel plan. DA 388

31 Jul: Bruce reports conversations with JM and others on preparations for Schuman's coming meeting in the Hague and Strasbourg with Brussels Pact foreign ministers and Council of Europe Consultative Assembly, respectively. Schuman will elaborate institutional details of coal and steel community which are being worked out. State Department should await Strasbourg session before

making public statement of support for Schuman Plan talks. FRUS III 742-44

1 Aug: Andre Meyer, investment banker residing in New York, tells D Lillienthal that he visited recently with JM in Paris and suggested to him a way to finance the coal and steel community. Meyer had been dubious about the Schuman Plan but now says "It will go through, I have no doubt of it and it will work." DL v III 29

5 Aug: JM drafts memo for French government response to Acheson's 22 Jul request on increased defense spending, stating that rearmament must be collective measure, not simply sum of individual responses. It should involve supranational means of control, a common defense fund and fair burden sharing based on national incomes and equality of burdens. Washington is skeptical of this approach which suggests collectivizing Indochina war burden of France and US assumption of Europe's defense responsibilities. I Wall in BH 106 and FJM AMI 4/2/3; For US reaction to French plan, FRUS III 152

-----: As Schuman conference approaches summer recess, memorandum consolidates the institutional structure agreed upon: High Authority, a Common Assembly, the Council of Ministers and the Court of Justice. Efforts to weaken the High Authority or reassert national powers over it are overcome. JMM 333

The Korean war and the consequent demand by the US for tangible support from its NATO allies threatened to disrupt the apparently easy success of the Schuman Plan as the first step toward dramatic European cooperation. Suddenly, military concerns seemed more important than coal and steel or even than European unity. American historian Irwin Wall comments that: "The continuity in Monnet's response to the latest American challenge was striking: the search for supranational solutions, the breadth of vision extending beyond Europe to the Atlantic Community and the world, the quest for American support, and the attempt to harmonize American, European and French national interests. These considerations had worked brilliantly through the triptych of the Monnet, Marshall and Schuman Plans." But, as Wall continues, this newest problem---a common defense which involved both military and political cooperation---caused Europe to stumble. (IW I 106)

Only after the defeat of the European Defense Community in the French National Assembly in 1954 could the path toward European unity resume. But then it would grow under the shadow of a European concern that the initial American interest in European political integration was being replaced by Washington's desire for a strong military alliance in Europe. NATO, not the European Community, would become the centerpiece of American policy in Europe.

6 Aug: Harold Macmillan, foreign policy spokesman for UK opposition Conservative Party, prepares to present a counter-plan to the "Monnet proposals" [i.e. the Schuman Plan] in Strasbourg at Council of Europe assembly. His plan, called the Macmillan-Eccles proposals, would make the proposed Coal and Steel

Community a substructure of the ministerial committee of the Council of Europe i.e. under inter-governmental control. Macmillan hopes Churchill will endorse the counter-proposal. HM III 205-8l HM IV 4

8 Aug: Macmillan discusses his plan at Strasbourg press conference but without mention of possible Churchill support. HM IV 5

8 Aug: JM responds with letter to Macmillan which also circulates in Strasbourg strongly opposing Macmillan plan. JM calls Schuman proposals "revolutionary or they are nothing" in their goal of "building of a new Europe through ... a supranational regime" which necessarily involves "the abnegation of sovereignty in a limited but decisive field...." JMM 315-16. Macmillan calls JM letter "long, argumentative but friendly." HM IV 8.

Macmillan also considers his plan a "compromise" between the Monnet-Schuman side and those in various countries, including UK, who want a more restrained approach to European cooperation. HM III 201

-----: R Schuman address Strasbourg session on his proposals but does not mention Macmillan-Eccles counter-plan. Macmillan wonders if this is a "snub" as some suggest but he believes that when Holland and Belgium, among other governments, get Schuman details "they will shrink from some aspects" and when "French parliament and people realize that it means going in without Britain they may shrink from handing over their rather weak...industry to German control." HM IV 8

Macmillan serves well as a symbol of British ambivalence toward a closer European union. Britain had already rejected initial membership in the coal and steel community when Macmillan appeared in Strasbourg. His counter- proposal there and his view that the Schuman Plan represented a bad combination of mysticism and superplanning (see below after "Late August") indicates much more modest goals for Britain's European role. Monnet believed, and related in his Memoirs, that Britain would eventually go along when it saw that the European Community was a success. He seems to have been only partially correct. Britain eventually joined the European Economic Community in 1973 after a humiliating initial rejection by de Gaulle of Macmillan's earlier application. But there remains a strong current in British political life that the UK must supply a firm and constant restraint on the unrealistic idealism of continental backers of the Monnet-Schuman idea. (For a more comprehensive view of British reservations about joining Europe, see MC)

-----: Schuman Plan conference adjourns to 1 September to allow delegations opportunity to report to respective governments on progress. Grant of sovereignty to High Authority is still intact with a proposed Council of Ministers to represent national governments. On the same day, Schuman, in his speech at the Council of Europe meeting in Strasbourg, explains the work of the coal and steel treaty conference and defends the independence of the High Authority which will be "neither a committee of ministers, nor a cartel, nor the instrument of an industrial combine, nor a production syndicate, nor a simple management board." It would have to be, he said, an autonomous institution which the treaty must define with specific powers. S&P 19

11 Aug: Churchill addresses Council of Europe assembly in Strasbourg on European army idea but avoids Schuman Plan and Macmillan counter-proposals. His resolution on the European army passes 89-5 with 27 abstentions. HM IV 9

14 Aug: JM sends Schuman memo on relations between Schuman Plan institutions and those of the Council of Europe. In accompanying letter, JM notes the great confusion in Strasbourg where the Council is in session and where Britain "is waging a clever campaign to defeat our plan." MSC 48-53; FJM AMG 23/3/15

15 Aug: JM writes memo on Western defense needs. FJM AMI 4/2/10,11

------: In letter to Schuman, JM warns of British attempts to "sabotage" the coal and steel plan with its maneuvers at the Council of Europe's assembly in Strasbourg. JM fears last-ditch efforts by some continental Europeans to seek a compromise with British intransigence on the Schuman Plan. MSC 48-9; JMM 334-5

19 Aug: Macmillan considers "how to steer the Schuman Plan debate to an agreeable finish when [the resolution] comes out of committee." French have put down a resolution we cannot accept. HM IV 11

LATE AUGUST: JM writes his former colleague Rene Pleven, now French Prime Minister, a long letter from his annual vacation on the Ile de Re in Charente. JM is worried about the emphasis on a victory in the cold war, especially with the French concentration on a military win in Indochina which he believes is distracting the country from its role in western defense in Europe. As a result France is increasingly dependent on the United States. France needs new ideas on defense and America would listen to a positive and practical plan. JMM 339-40

The start of the Korean War in June 1950 had diverted some of the attention on the Coal and Steel Community to military matters after the United States sought an active role by its European allies in the UN-supported resistance to the North Korean invasion of South Korea. The idea of a European army drew even sharper divisions of public and political opinion than had the coal and steel plan. Monnet's letter to Pleven can be seen as prelude to the Pleven plan for a European Defense Community. It took four years before the French Assembly rejected participation in the EDC but already the divisions shown in the abstentions from the Churchill resolution in Strasbourg indicated this split.

By November 1951, the British Conservative Party itself reversed course on a European defense force when Foreign Secretary Anthony Eden says the UK would definitely not join although in the 1950 debate (above) led by Churchill the party supported a European Army. Macmillan, commenting on that reversal 15 months later, asked "But how can Britain be represented in the devitalized and denationalized army which Pleven and Monnet plan to make.... Schuman and Monnet have made the same error with the army as with Iron and Steel (sic). It is curious but, I fear, inevitable, since one is a mystic and the other a super planner." He then speculates if both the European army and the Schuman Plan are lost, the UK might take the lead and "create a Europe which will work." HM IV 120

SEPTEMBER: European Payments Union (EPU) goes into effect,

9 Sep: McCloy tells American press that US government wants "a fully armed German force of ten divisions integrated into a west European army." NYT 10 Sep

-----: JM discusses with Schuman, before latter's departure, the coming Washington conference of Big Three foreign ministers. He cites danger of putting aside the goals of the Schuman Plan, especially the historic reconciliation of France and Germany, because of the urgent need for military cooperation among the Europeans and with the Americans. He fears that Germany might sense a way to get equality, its principal goal in the Schuman Plan, more easily in a European army which the Americans want so badly. JM urges Schuman to keep in mind the two main goals for France in the Washington talks: Reaffirmation of the Schuman Plan as the start of common market which will help both France and Germany both economically and politically, and the position of France as a leader in the great initiative taken on 9 May. FJM AMI 4/4/1; MSC 53-55

12 Sep: Ambassador Bruce reports that JM dismisses defense questions (which American embassy has repeatedly raised) in the Schuman Plan negotiations as not a real issue and which has not been seriously discussed in the conference. FRUS IV 748

------: Schuman leaves for Western foreign ministers meeting in New York with Korean war the principal topic. JM visits Schuman in Paris before his departure and warns "You won't prevent German rearmament coming up early in your talks.... Nothing should be decided in New York outside the context of the Schuman Plan which has defined a new French policy toward Germany....For if the Germans get what the Schuman Plan offers them, but without the Plan itself, we shall run the risk of their turning their backs on us." JMM 341

In the autumn of 1950, German rearmament became the dominant issue in American-European relations. It consequently cast a deep shadow over the Schuman Plan talks. Monnet feared that Germany might seek full equality through quick action by the foreign ministers discussing its rearmament rather than through the patient construction of the coal and steel community. While Monnet supported the French government position that Germany should not have its own army again he gradually came to the view that a European army could contain German units. How to reach this compromise without undermining the Schuman Plan became Monnet's goal when the negotiations resumed. The plan to create a European army would be made in the corridors and intermissions of the Schuman Plan conference.(JMM 344-5)

14 Sep: JM cables Schuman [in New York] on detecting a change in the German attitudes toward rearmament now evident in the Schuman Plan negotiations. The Germans are aware of their vital role in the security of the West and they want to use that fact to gain leverage in the talks on a customs barrier of the Six against outside countries. JM fears that the European single market would become a German market and that if German rearmament and the Schuman Plan talks proceed separately, the latter talks will fail and Germany will return to its traditional temptations. He adds that he has informed Bruce of these and all other matters in the negotiations. FJM AMI 4/4/2 reprinted in MSC 56

15 Sep: Western foreign ministers meet in New York. NYT, 16 Sep

16 Sep: JM writes Schuman [in New York] on the effect of the Korean war on German rearmament and on the Schuman negotiations. He notes that France, Britain and the US face three choices on Germany: Do nothing (but is this possible ?); Or, treat Germany as a national issue but thereby make a European constitution and the Schuman Plan impossible; Or, integrate Germany into an expanded Schuman Plan.

JM's accompanying memorandum accepts that German participation is essential to the defense of the West. But how Germany participates will either restore national rivalries or allow its reconstruction and integration into Europe. In the first instance, Germany would be tempted to be the nation to balance itself between Eastern and Western Europe. There are signs that Germany itself is divided on this question and that those seeking a national solution are growing in strength. Only by reaffirming the Atlantic Community of the US, Britain and continental Western Europe can this problem be solved. France can take the initiative to enlarge the Schuman Plan to cover defense and to include Germany in this expanded structure. FJM AMI 4/4/3 reprinted in MSC 58-9; JMM 342-3

28 Sep: JM discusses Germany with Ludwig Erhard, the German economics minister who says he is worried, as is Adenauer, that the spirit of the Schuman Plan is not being followed either in the Plan's negotiation where French protectionism is evident or in the occupation authorities who proclaim an anti-cartel policy in Germany without even consulting our government. JM sends a note to Schuman on the meeting, saying he sympathizes with much of Erhard's complaint. JM hopes the situation will improve when the Schuman Plan talks end successfully. FJM AMG 6/6/3 reprinted in MSC 60-1

29 Sep: JM has lunch in Paris on Schuman Plan with Clarence Randall, expert and spokesman on American steel, who gives JM copy of his Atlantic Monthly article "A Steel Man Looks at the Schuman Plan." "They [JM and his colleagues] did not regard coal and steel as important in themselves. Those industries merely afforded the best medium for the prime objective...to break down national barriers." That adds to Randall's "apprehension....[that] he[JM] isn't too much concerned about...coal and steel provided he advances...a United

States of Europe. JM's "second thought was deep dismay that in New York [at the foreign ministerial talks] there was sentiment for permitting Germany to have...its own army. He said dramatically `If that happens, we are all lost.' He wants it to be a European army, or the Schuman Plan repeated in defense." C Randall papers, Box 1, PU

5 Oct: J Webb, acting US Secretary of State, cables all major US embassies in western Europe on proposed "high level" (but not State Department) paper on European "union" in context of "aggressive Sov[iet] tactics and rising East-West tension." Paper [possibly by National Security Council staff] would cite European morale and "responsible leadership" [of France, Germany, Belgium, Italy and Netherlands] favoring integration and losing faith in national governments. Responses from US ambassadors take exception to some or all of paper's proposed conclusions. FRUS III 629-30; 674-5 (See also 13 Feb 1950)

7 Oct: JM has Clarence Randall (and son Tom) to office lunch at rue de Martignac; JM maintains industry must be "self-policed by actual and vigorous competition." Industry must serve the people, JM said, and private arrangements that limit this function must be prohibited or the public will protect themselves against this violation by steps, including nationalization. Randall says that US government should give JM "clear and authoritative statement" of support. "Monnet has one of the most facile minds I have ever met, and one of the most honest...." C Randall papers, Box 1, PU

11 Oct: Maurice Lagrange, Paris lawyer, receives call from friend who says JM wants to see Lagrange the next day. JM asks him to work on Coal and Steel Treaty then being negotiated. Lagrange initially refuses, then agrees to work on Court of Justice provisions. "Paul Reuter, whom I succeeded, used the High Authority idea from the American TVA (Tennessee Valley Authority). " FJM OH

Monnet now writes Prime Minister Pleven on the need for a French initiative on German rearmament as six months earlier he had appealed to Schuman to seize the idea of a coal and steel community to solve a similar impasse on Germany.

14 Oct: JM writes Pleven to stand firm against American policy for a German army but to propose instead a European solution on defense as the Schuman Plan was proceeding toward economic integration of basic industries. He insists that the defense plan must come only after the Schuman Plan is approved. JMM 345-6

-----: JM drafts long letter to Schuman on the links between the Schuman Plan negotiations and other European problems, especially Germany's growing role. Whether the letter is ever sent is not clear; perhaps JM decided a personal meeting with the prime minister and his foreign minister was better. MSC 61-3

16 Oct: JM confers with Pleven and Schuman on the German rearmament crisis and its effect on Western defense. France had just lost a major battle in Indochina which would provoke a major parliamentary debate and perhaps a crisis for the French government. France needed to restore its prestige in Europe, JM said, in proposing a government statement on a European army in the same spirit as the Schuman Plan. JMM 346-7

24 Oct: French Prime Minister Pleven proposes European army with a European defense minister responsible to common institutions but with a vagueness necessary to cover "the contradictions and equivocations which were in time to eat it away." JMM 347-8

9 Nov: JM's first draft of final Schuman Plan treaty meets opposition from Benelux countries and Germany, with both objections centering on role of High Authority. S&P 20-1

13 Nov: Jules Aubrun, head of the French steel makers group, complains to Pleven in letter, with a copy to JM, that his members' view are being ignored in the Schuman Plan talks. MSC 64-7

17 Nov: JM replies to Aubrun, with a copy to Schuman, dismissing his complaints as without substance and noting how carefully the French delegation to the Schuman Plan talks has worked to keep French industry informed. MSC 64, 67-9

30 Nov: JM sends long memorandum to Schuman on status of negotiations on the Schuman Plan treaty. MSC 70-73

3 Dec: JM refers in note to the foreign minister to useful talks he, Schuman, Clappier [Schuman's aide] and W Hallstein [head of German delegation] just completed and on Hallstein's immediate return to Bonn for consultations. JM invites Schuman to lunch or dinner. MSC 73-4

4 Dec: JM sends Schuman several detailed memoranda on the treaty, its goals, a transitional annex, proposed commercial policy and the treaty's effects on the French coal and steel industries. MSC 74-89

5 Dec: Dutch delegation raises question of Saar in Schuman Plan talks but German delegation asks that issue be withdrawn since it could wreck the negotiations. The consequent vague status of the territory remains: France represents Saar which is an autonomous area economically but not a true sovereign state in the sense of the proposed coal and steel community. JM advises Schuman of the Dutch moves. S&P 20-1; MSC 89

13 Dec: JM prepares note to Schuman on objections to the Schuman Plan treaty by the French steel industry FJM AMG 18/2/11 cited in MSC 94 n.3

14 Dec: Schuman Plan negotiations nearing end; JM has assured Germans that German steel would have "equal status" and that the Ruhr Authority would "disappear without difficulty." FRUS III 765-6; Saar and the International

Ruhr Authority again threaten briefly to interrupt conference but are put aside. Other important issues, including some like defense and Germany's continued occupation which were outside the conference, continue to occupy delegations until early in 1951. S&P 21-23; JMM 348-9,353

Although the Paris Treaty on the coal and steel community would not be signed until April of the next year when the final details were agreed upon, 1950 ends with great success and satisfaction for Monnet. A "bold and constructive" idea for peace and reconciliation had been placed into treaty form by six countries all of whom had recently suffered defeat, humiliation and occupation during the world's worst war. Even the problems and distractions of the Cold War in Europe, the Korean and Indochinese wars in Asia and the residual suspicions among the treaty partners had been put aside as Monnet had asked until the Schuman Plan treaty was finished.

15 Dec: JM issues statement on the work completed by the coal and steel community conference. FJM AMG 10/4/3

17 Dec: JM explains coal and steel conference work to French interministerial committee. FJM AMG 22/3

22 Dec: JM writes Schuman on decartelization and decentralization in Germany which must be addressed before the final treaty signing. MSC 90-1; S&P 22-3; JMM 351-2

In June, Monnet had anticipated a quick agreement on setting up the High Authority. This was ultimately not possible, he later wrote, because "nationalist and conservatives everywhere were hostile to the plan.... But in the end we made a virtue of our disappointment. We used the long, painstaking negotiations to draw up an entirely novel Treaty...." In concluding this account in his memoirs, he added: 'We should waste no time in regretting what never happened, but profit instead from the unexpected circumstance that fate put in our way." JMM 321

28 Dec: JM writes Schuman on the results of a 15 Dec meeting of the French ministerial committee on the Schuman Plan talks and sends him copies of letters from several ministers containing their concerns on the final treaty including the issue of the Saar. MSC 91-3

The year, and this period of Monnet's life, end with him at the close of a brief and atypical period of public attention. He was now to settle, in his mid-sixties, into the busy but somewhat anti-climatic work of managing the coal and steel community. His work fell into a routine which soon bored him, as a man made for beginnings. But Europe seemed to find its postwar footing even though no one---except perhaps Monnet---knew the long-term significance of the coal and steel community. At least French-German tensions had eased, the West seems united against the perceived Russian truculence and the United States is committed, at least for now, to helping Europe unite.

EPILOGUE

Jean Monnet was never preoccupied with self-reflection. In the remarkably few letters he wrote, he seldom discussed himself. But toward the end of his Memoirs, prodded perhaps by his collaborator, Francois Fontaine, he reflected on his long life and what kind of person he was. (He is approaching ninety years of age when he finished the memoirs):

> A friend, Monnet recalled, once told him that there were two kinds of people, those who wanted to be someone and those who wanted to do something. Dwight Morrow, the friend, put Monnet in the second group and the Frenchman agreed: "Life is prodigal of opportunities to act but one has to be prepared, by long reflection, to recognize them and exploit them when they occur. Life is made up of nothing but events: what matters is to use them for a given purpose. Mine was collective action." (JMM 519-20)

But this anodyne reflection may obscure an important Monnet characteristic: he learned how to find the precise point where to use his talents. Edward Heath, British prime minister, saw Monnet's genius as always knowing where to find the "point of decision" in any endeavor. Sometimes that point, Heath said, was not at the top but somewhere down the line. (AW)

The collective action in this chronology has been the roots of European integration, the most successful story of international cooperation of the twentieth century, or even in all human history. Would it have happened without Jean Monnet?

The answer to that question, I believe, is No. Something else might have happened in 1950 or 1951 to resolve the Franco-German tension. Europe might have come together otherwise than in the EU institutions which started so tentatively with coal and steel in 1950. Other heroes of European integration would have stepped forward perhaps. But the history we know and which this chronology portrays would not have happened without Jean Monnet and his circle of friends, and collaborators and the peculiar method he devised to get people to do the right thing at the right time for the benefit of the enterprise.

Another important aspect of his life was his view of nationalism. Monnet was born into a world at the zenith of the nation-state. Yet from his birthplace in Cognac to his early work experiences in London and Canada, his travels in the Middle East and Asia and his public and private careers in international enterprises, his life pressed continually against the limits of national identities. His life culminated in his efforts to unite Europe after World War II but everything he had done before that war led him to distrust and resent national ideals. His education from his European enterprises began, therefore, at birth and continued with each aspect of his first sixty years until, in 1950, his work culminated in the making of a new Europe.

Monnet closed his life story with a final, somewhat puzzling thought on Europe, provocative especially for those who saw his goals limited to economic union or to Europe: "Like our provinces in the past, our nations today must learn to live together under common rules and institutions freely arrived at. The sovereign nations of the past can no longer solve the problems of the present; they cannot ensure their own progress or control their own future. And the [European] Community is only a stage on the way to the organized world of tomorrow." (JMM 519-24)

In conversation with Katherine Graham, publisher of the Washington Post, Monnet once said he had only one idea in his life without ever saying explicitly what that idea was. Francois Fontaine, who knew Monnet as well as anyone, thought the idea was simply human cooperation. However we might try to express Monnet's single idea what impresses is how single-minded he could be in pursuing it. Early in WWI, he showed a remarkable ability to work across national lines but also to inspire confidence wherever and with whomever he worked. French, British and American colleagues in that war came under this peculiar Monnet influence.

But what did this vague phrase---human cooperation-- mean? Negatively, it meant an end to narrow tribalism and nationalism. The strongest emotional references Monnet made in his memoirs were to personal and national efforts at domination. But what did he mean by suggesting the European Community was only a stage? What did it mean in organizing the "world of tomorrow"? Did it mean that the form and institutions of the European Union should be applied worldwide? What about regional organizations, NATO or the United Nations?

Dealing with such questions in these terms was alien to Monnet. He would probably point instead to European integration. Was war between his France and Germany now impossible? Were more than a dozen countries in the EU now living in peace, harmony and cooperation? Was there ever again a chance of civil war erupting in Europe? Was the ancient continent of superb accomplishments and of incredible violence now changed forever? Let us continue, he might say.

Jean Monnet would rest with the facts of the European transformation and leave the abstractions to others. He was, after all, he believed, a simple man from the Charente making his way in world.

ABBREVIATIONS, SOURCES AND ACKNOWLEDGEMENTS

ACKNOWLEDGEMENTS: A book of this length and detail, gathered over many years of research and study, accumulates enormous debts to colleagues, archivists, librarians and friends of both the author and of Jean Monnet himself. The sources listed only begin to acknowledge this debt. Of Monnet's colleagues, Francois Fontaine and Jacques Van Helmont, were most helpful in countless and extended interviews. Francois Duchene and Richard Mayne, both of whom worked for Monnet and wrote about his work, supplied helpful insights and incidents; Mayne also generously supplied an unpublished and unauthorized biography written from public documents while he was still working for Monnet. Henri Rieben and his talented staff at the Fondation Jean Monnet a l'Europe in Lausanne supplied endless documents and contributed countless hours to discuss, clarify and fill my requests. I am similarly indebted to the archives and libraries listed below for their help.

In the final stages of writing, I called again on colleagues and friends to read sections of the text and to answer specific questions. I want to note the help of Theo Junker and Karlheinz Neunreither, friends from our common endeavors to bring the US Congress and the European Parliament into fruitful association; they read sections and offered useful comments. Bob Schaetzel and Edward Strauss, founders of the Jean Monnet Council, supported this work although neither lived to see its completion. Carine Germond and Holger Schroeder, and Hungdah Su helped in discussions which offered European and Asian perspectives in recent years. Finally the many colleagues and friends with whom I discussed Monnet's life and work over the past thirty years may not recall those conversations and discussions. I remember them, have used their insights, and regret only that I cannot list all of them here.

AA: Alan Artibise, Winnipeg: An Illustrated History, Toronto, 1977

AC: Interviews with Alison Carroll, JM's Washington secretary at BSC, 1994

ACCSM: Interviews with Albert Connelly, partner of Cravath, Swaine, Moore, and JM's attorney in 1935-6 for child custody case, 1993-4

AFCC: Anglo French Coordinating Committee chaired by JM in London, 1939-40

AFD: Anglo French Discussions Regarding French Proposals for the Western European Coal, Iron and Steel Industries, May-June 1950, London (HMSO), l950

AFPC: Anglo French Purchasing Commission, New York [1939-40]

AH: Academica Historica, Taiwan [contains some of the pre-1948 files of the Government of China]

AJS I: Arthur J Salter, Memoirs of a Public Servant, London, 1961; AJS II: Allied Shipping Control, Oxford, 1921

AK I: Andre Kaspi, Le temps des americains 1917-1918, Paris, 1976; AK II: ----- La Mission Jean Monnet a Algers (Mars-Octobre 1943) Paris, 1971

AML I: Anne Morrow Lindbergh, Diaries and Letters, Bring Me a Unicorn (1922-28); II: Hour of Gold, Hour of Lead (1928-32); III: Locked Rooms, Open

Doors (1933-35) IV: The Flower and the Nettle (1936-38); V: War Within and Without (1939-44), Boston, New York,

AN: Archives nationales, Paris

ANY: Arthur N Young, China's Nation Building Effort, Stanford, CA, 1971

AS: Unpublished doctoral dissertation of Alan Schadler "The Anglo French Coordinating Committee 1939-1940," 1975, Lehigh University, Bethlehem, PA which relied on access to JM personal files now in FJM

AW: Interviews by Alan Watson for BBC program on JM, 1971 in FJM AML 313/112

B&B: W Brownell and R Billings, So Close to Greatness,[biography of William C. Bullitt] NY, 1987

Be/Sc: Robert Schuman, ed. Henry Beyer, Lausanne, 1986

BH: Jean Monnet: The Path to European Unity, D. Brinkley and C. Hackett eds, New York, 1991

BIS: Bank for International Settlements, Basle

BM I: Marta Balinska, Une vie pour l'humanitaire:Ludwik Rajchman, 1881-1965 Paris, 1995; II: ------- English translation, For the Good of Humanity, London, 1998

BP: Robert and Thomas Brand Papers, Oxford University

BPC: British Purchasing Commission, New York and Washington DC [1940-41]

BSC: British Supply Council, Washington DC 1941-45

CA: Interviews with Colette Autigeon, JM's niece, 1992-95

CAL: Wartime Journal of Charles A Lindbergh, New York, 1970

CB: Christian Bougeard, Rene Pleven: Un Francais Liberal en Politique, Rennes, France, 1994

CDFC: China Development Finance Corporation which JM helped establish in 1934.

CE: Un changement d'esperance, Henri Rieben, ed, FJM Lausanne, 2000

CSRD:Chang Kia-Ngau, China's Struggle for Railroad Development , New York, 1943

CWR: China Weekly Review

DA: Dean Acheson, Present at the Creation, New York, 1969

DBD: Diary of David Bruce, Virginia Historical Association, Richmond, VA

DDE: Papers of Dwight D. Eisenhower, Vol II, The War Years, Baltimore, 1970

DDF: Documents Diplomatiques Francaises, French Ministry of Foreign Affairs, 1932-1939, (series, volume and document cited)

DEG: Charles De Gaulle, Memoires 3 vol., Paris, 1954-59

DEG-L: Jean Lacouture, De Gaulle: The Rebel 1890-1944, New York, 1990

DF: Francois Duchene, Jean Monnet: The First Statesman of Interdependence, NY, 1994

DG: Des Guerres Europeennes a l'Union de L'Europe,. Henri Rieben, ed, FJM, Lausanne, 1987

DH: Duncan Hall, North American Supply, London, 1955

DHM: David Hunter Miller, My Diary at the Peace Conference, New York, 1924

DL: The Journals of David E Lilienthal, New York, 1966

DWM: Dwight W Morrow papers, Amherst College

EAH: Encyclopedia of American History, Richard B. Morris, ed, New York, 1953

EB I:Eric Bussiere, Paribas, Europe and the World, Antwerp, 1992; EB II:------ Horace Finaly, Paris, 1996

EC: Etienne Clementel, La France et La Cooperation Economique Interallie, Paris, 1931

ECA: Economic Cooperation Administration: US agency for implementing Marshall Plan assistance

ECM: Elizabeth C Morrow Papers, Smith College, Northampton, MA

ECMD: Elizabeth C Morrow Diary, Smith College, Northampton, MA

EL: Eric Larrabee, The Commander in Chief, New York, 1987

EM: Emile Moreau, Souvenirs d'un Gouverneur de la Banque de France, Paris, 1954; EM-GF, same, English translation, The Gold Franc, Boulder, Co, 1991;

EMH: Papers of Edward M. House. Yale University

EP: Edwin Plowden, An Industrialist in the Treasury, London, 1989

ER: Eric Roussel, Jean Monnet, Paris, 1996

ERB: Erling Bjol, La France Devant L'Europe, Copenhagen, 1966

ERP: European Recovery Program (the Marshall Plan)

ERS: Edward R Stettinius papers, Alderman Library, University of Virginia;

F: Fortune Magazine, "Mr. Giannini, Branch Banker and Mr. Walker, of Blair and Co,", Jan 1931,

FB: Felice Bonadio, A P Giannini, Banker of America, Berkeley, CA, 1994

FBI: U.S. Federal Bureau of Investigation file on JM (August 1940-August 1943) (obtained under Freedom of Information Act)

FCNL: French Committee on National Liberation

FD: John Brigante, The Feasibility Dispute, Committee on Public Administration Cases, Washington, 1950

FDR: Franklin D Roosevelt

FDRL: Roosevelt Presidential Library, Hyde Park, NY

FDR:FF: Frank Friedel, Franklin D Roosevelt: A Rendezvous with Destiny, Boston, 1990

FEA: Foreign Economic Assistance program

FF I: Interviews with Francois Fontaine, 1990-95; FF II: Francois Fontaine, Plus Lois Avec Jean Monnet, FJM Lausanne, 1983, translated as "Forward with Jean Monnet" in BH

FFD: From the Felix Frankfurter Diaries, by Joseph P Lash, Boston, 1975

FFR: Felix Frankfurter Reminisces: An Intimate Portrait as Recorded in Talks with Dr. Harlan B. Phillips, New York, 1960

FJM: Fondation Jean Monnet Pour l'Europe, Lausanne; David Strathall Papers: ADS ; Jean Monnet Papers: AMA: 1888-1914; AMB: 1914 -1918; AMC: 1914-1923; AMD: 1923-1939; AME: 1939-45; AMF: 1945-50; AMG 1950-52; AML: Speeches, interviews, articles; OH: Oral histories

FLF: Felix Frankfurter Papers, Library of Congress

FPW: Francis P Walters, A History of the League of Nations, London, 1952;

FRBNY: Federal Reserve Bank of New York

FRUS: Foreign Relations of the United States (annual US State Department serial)

GA: Gordon Auchincloss papers, Yale University;

GB: George Ball, The Past Has Another Pattern, New York, 1982

GE: Georgette Elgey, Histoire de la 4eme Republique, Paris, 1993

GLS: Global Logistics and Strategy: 1940-1943, Section One, Vol 4, Part IV of US Army in World War II, US Army, Washington, 1968

GMD: Diary of Georges Monnet in possession of author

HA: Herve Alphand, L'Etonnement d'etre, Paris, 1978

HBC: Hudson's Bay Company files, Manitoba Provincial Archives, Winnipeg Canada· I: Prewar; II:French government business (WWI); III: Postwar; IV JM loan file; V: Compagnie de la Baie; (unless otherwise indicated)

HD: Thomas W Lamont, Henry P Davison: Wall Street and the Security Markets, New York, 1933

HH: Papers of Harry Hopkins, FDRL

HH-G: Papers of Harry Hopkins, Georgetown University Library

HHPL: Herbert Hoover Presidential Library, West Branch, IO

HLSD: Henry L Stimson Diary, Yale University

HM I Harold Macmillan, War Diaries: The Mediterranean 1943-1945, London, 1984; HM II: ----- The Blast of War, Memoirs, London, 1967; HM III:----- The Tides of Fortune, NY, 1969; HM IV: The Macmillan Diaries: The Cabinet Years 1950-1957, Peter Catterall, ed, London, 2003

HMD: Diary of Henry Morgenthau (number indicates volume), FDRL

HMD-JB From the Morgenthau Diary, ed. by John Morton Blum, Boston, 1967

HMSO: His Majesty's Stationary Office, London

HN: Harold Nicolson, Dwight Morrow, New York, 1935

HR-RC: Henry Rousso,"Reperes chonologiques". De Monnet a Masse:Enjeux politiques et objectifs economiques dans le cadre des quatre premiers Plan 1946-1965, Paris, 1986

HS: Holger Schroeder, Jean Monnet und die amerikanische Unterstuetzung fuer die europaeische Integration 1950-1957, Frankfurt/M, 1994

HSTL: Truman Presidential Library, Independence, MO

HU I: Hungdah Su, Jean Monnet Face a la Politique Europeenne du General de Gaulle de 1958 a' 1969, Villeneuve de l'Ascq , France; HU II:------- "The Father of Europe in China: Jean Monnet and the creation of the CDFC 1933-1936," Journal of European Integration History, 2007, v. 13, n. 1

HW: D. Hall and C. Wrigley, Studies in Overseas Supply, London, 1956

IMW: Industrial Mobilization for War: History of the War Production Board and Predecessor Agencies, 1940-1945, Washington, 1947

IW I: Irwin Wall, "Jean Monnet, the United States and the French Economic Plan" in BH;IW II: --------The United States and the Making of Postwar France

1945-1954, Cambridge UK, 1991

JBD I: Jean Baptiste Duroselle: "Jean Monnet a Londres 1916-1919", essay prepared for JM in the writing of his memoirs and relying largely on cited AN documents, FJM; JBD II ----- "Strategic and Economic Relations" in Troubled Neighbors, Neville Watts, ed, London, 1971

JD: Jacques Dumaine, Quai D'Orsay, London, 1958

JFD: John Foster Dulles Papers, Seeley Mudd Library, Princeton University;

JGM: Jean Gabriel Monnet, Monnet's father

JJD: James J Dougherty, The Politics of Wartime Aid, Westport, CT, 1978

JM: Jean Monnet, 1888-1979

JMH I: Interviews with and notes by John McVickar Haight given to author. The notes, made by Haight while preparing his book, are based on Monnet's personal files now in FJM; JMH II: -------- American Aid to France 1938-1940, NY, 1970; JMH III: --------"Les negotiations relatives aux achats d'avions Americans par la France pendant la periode qui precede immediatement la guerre," Revue d'histoire de la deuxieme guerre mondiate, no. 58, Apr 1965 1-34

JMM: Jean Monnet, Memoirs, Garden City, New York, 1978

JM N: JM interview with Sven Nordengren in Economic and Social Targets in Postwar France, Lund, Sweden, 1972

JMPF: JM personnel file, UN Geneva

JPM: J P Morgan, investment bankers

KA: Konrad Adenauer, Memoirs 1945-1953 London, 1965

KB: Kathleen Burk, Britain, America and the Sinews of War, 1914-1918, London, 1985

KGH: Karl Gustav Hildebrand, Expansion, Crisis, Reconstruction [of the Swedish Match Co], Stockholm, 1985

KP: Kenneth Pindar, Adventures in Diplomacy, New York, 1945, 1966

LA: Thomas W Lamont Papers, Baker Library, Harvard University

LC: Lester V Chandler, Benjamin Strong, Washington, 1958

LN G: League of Nations archives, Geneva

LN NY: League of Nations archives, New York

LNR: The League of Nations 1920-1946, A Retrospective of the First Organization for the Establishment of World Peace, New York, 1996

MAE: Ministry of Foreign Affairs, Paris

MAEJ: Ministry of Foreign Affairs, Tokyo

MATA: Monnet and the Americans, Clifford Hackett, Washington DC, 1995

MB: Max Beloff, "The Anglo French Union Project of June 1940" in Intellectual in Politics, London, 1970

MBJ: Marquis and Bessie James, Biography of a Bank, New York, 1954

MC: Michael Charlton, The Price of Victory , London, 1983

MF: Roosevelt and Frankfurter: Their Correspondence 1928-1945, Max Freedman, ed, Boston, 1967

MG FH: Martin Gilbert, Finest Hour, Vol III, Life of Winston S Churchill London, 1988

MG ND, ------- Never Despair, Vol VIII, Life of Winston S Churchill, London, 1988

MIS: Robert Mischlich, Une Mission Secrete a Bonn, FJM, Lausanne, 1986

MM: Monnet, Murnane limited partnership

MLY: F. Mlynarski, Wspomnienia [Memoirs], Warsaw, 1971

MM HK: Monnet, Murnane Hong Kong

MR: Robert Marjolin, Le Travail d'une vie, Memoires 1911-1986, Paris, 1986

MSC: Jean Monnet-Robert Schuman Correspondence 1947-1953, FJM, Lausanne, 1986

MY: Yuichiro Miyashita, Jean Monnet et l'Extreme Orient (1932-1940):un financier au sein de la diplomatie des Puissances, unpublished Memoire du DEA, Institute d'Etudes Politiques, Paris 2004

NARA: National Archives and Records Administration, Washington, DC, (Record Group 59, State Department unless otherwise noted)

NAUK: National Archive of the United Kingdom (formerly PRO q.v.)

NCN: La naissance d'un continent nouveau, FJM, Lausanne,1990

ND: Norman Davis Papers, Library of Congress, Washington DC

NP I: Nicole Pietri, unpublished dissertation on the League of Nations and Austria, Paris, 1981; NP II: ----- La Societe des Nations et La Reconstruction of l'Autriche, Geneva, 1970

NTJ: Nelson T Johnson papers, Library of Congress, Washington DC

NYT: New York Times

OB; Orville Bullitt, For the President: Personal and Secret, Boston, 1972

OH: Oral history

OHT I: Oliver Harvey, The Diplomatic Diaries 1937-40, London, 1970; II -------- The War Diaries 1940-1945, London,1978

Pease: Neal Pease, Poland, the United States and the Stabilization of Europe, 1919-33, NY, 1986

PEI: Prince Edward Island [Canada] archives

PB: Archives of Paribas Bank, Paris

PG: Pierre Gerbet, "La Genese du Plan Schuman," in Revue Francaise de science politique, Jan-Mars 1956 and revised version, same title, Lausanne, 1962

PM: Philippe Mioche, Le Plan Monnet; Genese et Elaboration 1941-47, Paris, 1987

PN: Peter Newman, Merchant Princes (history of the Hudson's Bay Co), Toronto, 1991

PRO: Public Record Office, London (now called The National Archive): CAB: Cabinet Office files; FO: Foreign Office files, I: series 371 (China, 1933-35); II: series 115 (1940-45); III: series 113 (1946-50); PREM: Prime Minister Office files; (unless otherwise indicated)

PU: Princeton University

RA: Riksarkivet, Stockholm, Sweden, Kreuger & Toll Correspondence files, Vols. 341, 369 (unless otherwise noted).

RBF: Raymond B. Fosdick, Letters on the League of Nations, Princeton, 1966

R&C: Roosevelt and Churchill: The Secret Wartime Correspondence, F Loewenheim, H Langley, M Jonas eds, New York, 1975

RES: Robert E Sherwood Papers, Houghton Library, Harvard University

RES G: Robert E Sherwood Papers, Georgetown University

RES R: Robert E Sherwood Papers, FDRL

RES R&H: Robert E Sherwood, Roosevelt and Hopkins, New York, 1948

RDM: Robert D Murphy, Diplomat Among Warriors, New York, 1964

RHM: Richard H Meyer, Banker's Diplomacy: Monetary Stabilization in the Twenties, New York, 1970

RI GE: Des Guerres Europeennes a'Union de l"Europe, Henri Rieben, ed, FJM, Lausanne, 1987

RK: Richard Kuisel, "The Marshall Plan in Action" in Le Plan Marshall, Paris, 1992

RM: Unpublished biography of Jean Monnet by Richard Mayne

RP I: Raymond Poidevin, ed., Origins of European Integration, March 1948-May 1950, Brussels, 1986; II: Robert Schuman, Homme d'Etat, Paris, 1986

RRN D: Diaries of Robert Nathan in his personal files.

RRN I: Robert Nathan interviews 1990-94

SE: Stephen Endicott, Diplomacy and Enterprise: British China Policy 1933-1937 Vancouver, BC, Canada, 1975

SH: Stanley Hornbeck Papers, Stanford University

S&P: Dirk Spierenburg and Raymond Poidevin, History of the High Authority of the European Coal and Steel Community, London, 1994

TA BA: Transamerica Corporation archives, Bank of America, San Francisco

TCF: The Cravath Firm, New York, 1948

TJM: Temoignages a la memoire de Jean Monnet, FJM, Lausanne, 1989

TP: Interview with Therese Payot, JM's niece, 1994

TW: Theodore H White, In Search of History, A Personal Adventure, NY, 1981

UMV: Une Memoire Vivante, FJM, Lausanne, 1986

UNRRA: George Woodbridge, A History of United Nations Refugee and Relief Administration, New York, 1950

V: Ivar Kreuger correspondence files, Swedish Match Company archives, Vadstena, Sweden

VA: Vincent Auriol, Journal du Septennat (Diaries, 1947-54, one volume each year), Paris, 1970-78

WDL: William D. Leahy, I Was There, New York, 1979

WL: Public Philosopher: Selected Letters of Walter Lippmann J M Blum, ed, New York, 1985

W&S: Wine and Spirits Museum, Stockholm

WC: Wayne S Cole, Charles A Lindbergh and the Battle Against American Intervention in World War II, New York, 1974

WSC: Winston S Churchill, The Second World War, 6 v, paperback ed, Boston, 1950

ZL: Z. Landau, Plan Stabbililzacyjny 1927-30, Warsaw, 1963

(Sources not otherwise referenced are indicated by [s]. Where appropriate time periods are indicated as follows: WWI, IW (Interwar), WWII and PW (Postwar), EI (European integration),

About the author:

Clifford Hackett began his formal education at St Louis University with a degree in philosophy and continued at Yale University with an MA in history. He served in Europe in both the US Army and the Foreign Service for ten years. He has worked for many years on international issues, especially European integration, in both Houses of Congress and as a consultant and writer.

He is an independent historian who published Cautious Revolutiton: The European Community Arrives (Praeger, 1990, 1995 rev, ed) and edited Jean Monnet: The Path to European Unity (with Douglas Brinkley), (St. Martin's, 1991) and Monnet and the Americans (The Jean Monnet Council, 1995). He lives in Berkeley Springs, WV and Washington DC.

The pages for this book were composed in Microsoft word, assisted by the author's daughters, Claire Adams and Nancy Hackett, and set in 10 point Times New Roman, printed on 120 gsm Ivory Woodfree paper and bound by China Color Printing Ltd, Taipei, Taiwan, ROC under the direction of Jennifer Lin.